Sport in the Global Society

General Editor: J. A. Mangan

RUGBY'S GREAT SPLIT

CASS SERIES: SPORT IN THE GLOBAL SOCIETY
General Editor: J. A. Mangan
ISSN 1368-9789

The interest in sports studies around the world is growing and will continue to do so. This unique series combines aspects of the expanding study of *sport in the global society*, providing comprehensiveness and comparison under one editorial umbrella. It is particularly timely, with studies in the political, cultural, social, economic, geographical and aesthetic elements of sport proliferating in institutions of higher education.

Eric Hobsbawm once called sport one of the most significant practices of the late nineteenth century. Its significance is even more marked in the late twentieth century and will continue to grow in importance into the next millennium as the world develops into a 'global village' sharing the English language, technology and sport.

Other Titles in the Series

Footbinding, Feminism and Freedom
The Liberation of Women's Bodies in Modern China
Fan Hong

The Games Ethic and Imperialism
Aspects of the Diffusion of an Ideal
J. A. Mangan

The Race Game
Sport and Politics in South Africa
Douglas Booth

RUGBY'S GREAT SPLIT

Class, Culture and the Origins
of Rugby League Football

TONY COLLINS

FRANK CASS
LONDON • PORTLAND, OR

First published in 1998 in Great Britain by
FRANK CASS PUBLISHERS
Newbury House, 900 Eastern Avenue
London, IG2 7HH

and in the United States of America by
FRANK CASS PUBLISHERS
c/o ISBS, 5804 N.E. Hassalo Street
Portland, Oregon 97213-3644

Website http://www.frankcass.com

British Library Cataloguing in Publication Data

Collins, Tony
   Rugby's great split : class, culture and the origins of
Rugby League football. – (Cass series : sport in the global
society)
   1. Rugby football – Great Britain – History – 19th century
   2. Rugby football – Social aspects – Great Britain
   I. Title
   306.4'83

ISBN 0-7146-4867-1 (cloth)
ISBN 0-7146-4424-2 (paper)
ISSN 1368-9789

Library of Congress Cataloging-in-Publication Data

Collins, Tony, 1960–
   Rugby's great split : class, culture, and the origins of Rugby
League football / Tony Collins.
     p. cm. – (Cass series–sport in the global society)
   Includes bibliographical references (p.   ) and index.
   ISBN 0-7146-4867-1 (cloth). – ISBN 0-7146-4424-2 (paper)
   1. Rugby League football–Social aspects–England–History.
2. Rugby Union football–Social aspects–England–History.
3. Working class–England–Recreation–History.   I. Title.
II. Series.
GV945.9.G7C65   1998
796.333'8'0941–dc21   97–43920
                                                         CIP

Typeset by Vitaset, Paddock Wood, Kent
Printed in Great Britain by
Bookcraft (Bath) Ltd, Midsomer Norton, Somerset

Table of Contents

List of Illustrations

Series Editor's Foreword

For rugby union read 'tories'; for rugby league read 'whigs'; for Thomas Babington Macaulay read Tony Collins! The analogy in terms of the history of (Northern) English sport is not all that far-fetched. 'Whig history', as Hugh Trevor Roper tells us in the Introduction to his *Lord Macaulay: The History of England* in the Penguin English Library (1979), is essentially English and a historical interpretation of events imposed on the English past for reasons of legitimacy and justification. Furthermore, 'Whig history' is English insular history: *Rugby's Great Split* is an English insular historical drama.

As for Tony Collins, consciously or unconsciously, he imitates Macaulay, much in the same way, as Trevor Roper informs us, Macaulay imitated Scott in 'his use of description, of local colour or popular tradition or ephemeral literature'. It would be rather nice, of course, if Collins had Macaulay's publishing success!

One great attraction of *Rugby's Great Split*, apart from the pellucidity of the writing, is the clarity, force and persuasiveness of Collins' argument that 'Rugby itself was used to define class'. Sport not only reflects culture: it shapes it. A further attraction of the book is Collins' appreciation of the significance of ritual, symbol and myth in modern social affairs – interestingly, a point first made strongly, and subsequently widely applauded, in a recent analysis of sport in those cultural bastions of middle- and upper middle-class England – the public schools. It is good to witness ritual, symbol and myth closely examined, with equal pertinence and pertinacity, in a wider cultural setting.

Collins is to be applauded for injecting a necessary reality into the reconstruction of the history of modern soccer with his 'heretical' observation that the assumption that the folk football of pre-industrial England was the direct precursor of modern soccer, is quite simply an absurdity. It is certainly time that it was recognised that sport and the British had a rather more complicated relationship than is sometimes asserted in sports history circles, and also time that the change and continuity associated with the evolution of the great games of British society were more carefully considered.

ix

'Whig history' does not have a lot to say directly on masculinity. It was hardly the issue it is now in past centuries, but with the canny social historian's capacity to feed the appetite of his contemporary audience, Collins makes it one of his recurring themes. And, a little to my amusement, since there is just the slightest hint of providing startling originality in his reflections on the issue, he argues that in the late nineteenth-century sport definitions of masculinity and violence were defined by class: 'Acts perceived as manly and character forming by the middle classes were interpreted differently when carried out by members of the working classes.' How true. As I remarked as long ago as 1981 in *Athleticism in the Victorian and Edwardian Public School* of the hugely popular annual Eton versus Harrow match at Lord's (no less) at the turn of the century: 'the younger supporters would clash regularly in front of the pavilion at the end of the match in a free-for-all that in a modern football ground would attract the opprobrium of a scandalised public. In those more robust times this exhibition of upper class virility was tolerated as a manly gesture of loyalty.' That muscular Corinthian tradition took a long time to die!

Rugby's Great Split is a valuable addition to the ever-increasing volume of works of quality in the history of sport. Virgil most certainly did not have Collins in mind when he penned his famous epithet: 'Lucky is he who has been able to understand the cause of things', but he might well have done.

J. A. Mangan
January, 1998

Introduction

Why are there two forms of rugby? This has been asked at one time or another by anyone with even a passing interest in sport, and given the profound changes which both rugby league and rugby union are currently undergoing, the question now has an importance which transcends mere historical curiosity.

This work aims to provide the answer. It looks at the development of rugby in the social context of late Victorian and Edwardian England and tries to demonstrate how the changing nature of that society shaped the sport and led to the creation of rugby league. At its heart is an exploration of how a game which was initially exclusively restricted to public school boys was transformed into a sport which became exclusively identified with the working classes of northern England.

Although it is to be hoped such a study is of value in itself, it also has a broader purpose. Despite the intentions or illusions of its participants, whether on or off the playing field, sporting culture reflects the society in which it is rooted and can offer us a window through which to study that society. This has been noted especially in the context of nationalism, race and gender but it is also true within the framework of class. As we shall see, rugby's growth and split brought to the fore all of these factors, but class was the fulcrum around which rugby turned. This work also aims to provide insights into how attitudes towards class were expressed in ostensibly non-political, recreational situations. The fact that discourse on class took place in a sporting context meant that views were often expressed without the need for social or political diplomacy. In exploring this aspect of class, I have deliberately allowed the participants to speak for themselves. Regardless of current academic debates as to the reality of class, it is clear that the term did have meaning for those who were engaged in the debates on the future of rugby at the time.

However the debates on class which took place in rugby were not about class alone. Rugby itself was given broader, and widely differing, meanings by members of different classes. Rugby league and rugby union were used

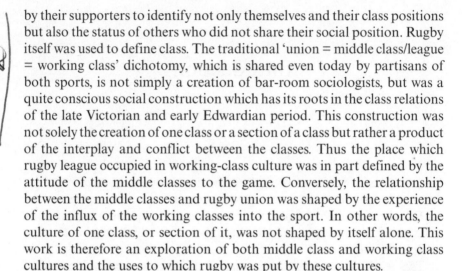

by their supporters to identify not only themselves and their class positions but also the status of others who did not share their social position. Rugby itself was used to define class. The traditional 'union = middle class/league = working class' dichotomy, which is shared even today by partisans of both sports, is not simply a creation of bar-room sociologists, but was a quite conscious social construction which has its roots in the class relations of the late Victorian and early Edwardian period. This construction was not solely the creation of one class or a section of a class but rather a product of the interplay and conflict between the classes. Thus the place which rugby league occupied in working-class culture was in part defined by the attitude of the middle classes to the game. Conversely, the relationship between the middle classes and rugby union was shaped by the experience of the influx of the working classes into the sport. In other words, the culture of one class, or section of it, was not shaped by itself alone. This work is therefore an exploration of both middle class and working class cultures and the uses to which rugby was put by these cultures.

Much of this work builds on themes in late nineteenth century British social history which have been explored by historians such as Eric Hobsbawm, Gareth Stedman-Jones and Eileen and Stephen Yeo; in particular, the question of the development of modern working-class culture. I share Hobsbawm's view that the late Victorian and Edwardian periods were crucial in defining working-class culture and leisure patterns, yet, as others have pointed out, there were many continuities from earlier times in this culture and many influences impacting on it from outside the working class. Stedman-Jones has argued that working-class culture in London during this period was being depoliticised by the influence of the music hall, yet in their edited collection *Popular Culture and Class Conflict*, the Yeos have claimed that recreational activities were sites of conflict as important as those in the workplace. In the case of rugby in the north of England however, it does not seem that involvement in rugby was an inhibitor of social or political disaffection. The 1890s, the moment of rugby's greatest popularity in the north, was a period of widespread and often violent class conflict in Lancashire and Yorkshire. Conversely, there is no evidence that working-class rugby players or spectators viewed the sport itself as an arena of class struggle to rank alongside the mill or the mine, although there is evidence that middle-class rugby supporters viewed the game as a microcosm of a wider struggle.

The 'turn to language' in investigations of class and class-consciousness during the 1870–1914 period has shifted the focus away from structural analysis of class to one in which words and symbols and their uses are central to understanding the process of the creation of class identity. While this may open the door in an idealistic way to discursive analysis isolated from material conditions, it can also open up new possibilities for social and cultural historians. Patrick Joyce's work on northern factory culture and the importance of language in the study of working-class culture is crucial to understanding the various components of working-class culture and their interaction on each other. For a social historian of sport, an area of culture which is communicated and preserved largely through oral tradition, folk memory and ephemeral press reports, Joyce's work provides a tool which can take our understanding of sport beyond mere recounting of data and towards an understanding of the role of sport in the creation of class culture and, at a deeper level, why it was important to those who participated on the field or on the terraces.

The best work on the social history of sport has drawn on these themes. Tony Mason's work on soccer and Wray Vamplew's analysis of the development of professional sport have established the social history of sport as a legitimate area of study. Gareth Williams has illuminated the links between rugby union and the growth of Welsh national consciousness. Richard Holt's work has followed more directly the work of historians such as Joyce and his *Sport and the British*[1] is perhaps the only major work so far to attempt to situate the history of British sport in the broader context of the development of society. Nevertheless, there is much work still to be done in the field of sports history, especially if the discipline is to break free from the celebratory/statistical strands of work which have dominated 'amateur' sports history and are still occasionally to be found in works claiming academic credibility.

As will be seen, this book is written largely in a narrative, rather than thematic, format, unlike similar work on other sports of this period, as for example Tony Mason's *Association Football and English Society 1863–1914* and Keith Sandiford's *Cricket and the Victorians*.[2] There are a number of reasons for this, the most obvious being that the chronology of rugby's rapid development leading to the 1895 split and subsequent evolution into two distinct sports lends itself perfectly to the narrative format. Without wishing to exaggerate, there is drama in the story. However, there are also methodological reasons for this approach. History is created by men and women pursuing their perceived interests in circumstances which are beyond their choosing. The danger of working in a thematic framework is that change, discontinuity and individual actions are ignored or underplayed in an attempt to uncover 'long waves' of historical development or to elaborate theoretical constructs. Periods separated by relatively short spans of time can be profoundly different, especially as perceived by the participants, a fact which is especially true of late Victorian sport. Rugby league in particular has a history which is defined by sharp twists and turns of fortune fashioned by the changing times in which it found itself.[3]

This should not be interpreted as a rallying cry for the primacy of empiricism over theoretical investigation, nor for history as a discipline over that of sociology. Rather it is an acknowledgement that without a firm grounding in the detail of historical events, any attempt at theoretical elaboration must remain at the level of speculation. Indeed, the weight of empirical data presents, in my view, compelling evidence for the primacy of the driving force of class relationships in the development of modern, mass-spectator sports and for the crucial importance of the uses made of sport, both formally and informally, by wider social forces.

One example of the tendency to subsume the conflicts, contingencies and disjunctures which mark the social development of sport is the way in which most historians of the various codes of football have telescoped the current balance of power between the rival footballs back into the past. The most absurd example of this is the widely held assumption that the folk football of pre-industrial society was the direct precursor of modern soccer. On a less egregious level, Tony Mason's outstanding history of soccer in its formative period gives little indication that, as we shall see, the north of England was dominated by rugby until the mid-1880s or that soccer's prominence was only established after a struggle for supremacy with rugby. Although not wishing to engage in speculation of the 'what if' variety, I do hope to demonstrate that the relative weights of the football codes were not inevitable but were contingent on both objective and subjective factors.

In passing, it should be noted that this emphasis on change and continuity has an impact on language. I have used the word 'football' in the sense in which it was used at the time: both as a generic term for all forms of football – folk, association, rugby union and Northern Union – and as signifying the dominant code in rugby-playing areas. Football as a nationally used synonym for association football appears to have been a post-World War One phenomenon. As a child, I found it mystifying to hear my grandfather refer to rugby league as 'football'. Now I know why he did so. No doubt to the chagrin of devotees of the round ball code, I refer to association football as soccer, which is not an American term as many claim but the word commonly used for the sport in rugby areas during this time, although I have shied away from its alternative spelling of 'socker'.

The narrative structure is therefore based largely on chronological order. Chapter one begins with the folk antecedents of modern football and seeks to demonstrate the deep roots of these early forms of football. In a sense, this is a pre-emptive strike against the belief that rugby football was the exclusive property of the public school educated middle classes, a view which is examined in the latter part of the chapter, which looks at the uses to which football was put by the public schools. The chapter moves on to discuss the spread of rugby from the public schools to the north of England and links the rapid growth of the sport to the sense of civic pride which prevailed among the industrial towns of the North and Midlands. Finally, the chapter ends at the moment at which rugby began to gain a following among the working classes in the late 1870s.

This new found popularity, and the disquiet it provoked among rugby's leaders both north and south, is the theme of chapter two. It analyses the means by which working-class men and women became involved in the sport and looks at the nature and activities of the rugby crowds of the period. Its key focus is on the ways in which working-class cultural practices became part of the fabric of the sport and the counterdevelopment of the ideology of amateurism as a method of suppressing this, culminating in the Rugby Football Union's introduction of its first set of regulations intended to stamp out incipient professionalism.

Chapter three examines the 'golden age' of northern rugby union in the late 1880s and early 1890s. By now the game in Yorkshire and in many areas of Lancashire was supported by all classes but with the working classes making up the majority of players and spectators. The chapter highlights how the demands of working-class players and the growing commercialism of the sport in the north undermined amateurism and made its implementation, despite the vigorous efforts of its partisans, impossible.

The breakdown in the consensus among rugby's leaders about how to deal with mass working-class participation and the events leading to the 1895 split are the focus of chapter four. This looks at the debates which took place about the role of working-class players, about amateurism and professionalism, and also about broken-time payments and unfettered professionalism. Much of the latter half of this chapter is taken up with tracking the events and political manoeuvring which took place in the two years following the RFU's 1893 annual general meeting, as it became clear that there was no longer room for compromise between the supporters of pristine amateurism and those of broken-time.

The aftermath of the split is dealt with in chapter five. As well as looking at the initial successes of the Northern Union and the devastation of northern rugby union football, it attempts to explore the reasons for the marginalisation of the NU, placing it in the context of a multiplicity of national and class-based forces. After examining the role of players in the game and the NU's reluctant steps to open professionalism, the chapter details the helplessness of the sport in the face of the tidal wave of soccer in the early 1900s.

The final chapter looks at the development of the NU as a separate sport, as it moved away from being merely a professional version of rugby union. It details the rule changes which created a new sport, its expansion to other countries and the growth of the game's distinct ideology. It examines the class composition of the sport's leadership and looks at the way in which it became identified almost exclusively with the working classes and how working-class cultural norms came to predominate, both on the field and in the crowds which watched the game.

Within this structure certain themes are explored on a recurring basis. The organisation of the material in this way helps to render understandable the changing nature of rugby and the society which shaped it. For example, at various points the relationship between rugby and masculinity is looked at in the context of public school rugby and the game under rugby union rules and Northern Union rules. I will argue that, first and foremost, definitions of masculinity and violence were defined by class. Acts perceived as manly and character-forming by the middle classes were interpreted differently when carried out by members of the working classes: thus hacking was viewed as courageous between former public school boys, yet outrageous when perpetrated by miners. Conversely, the predominantly working-class supporters of the NU found tripping and kicking unacceptable. The growth of imperial nationalism towards the end of the nineteenth century had a crucial impact on notions of masculinity: not only did it tie rugby closer to the perceived need to prepare for war, but it also had the effect of both excluding NU rugby from the pantheon of acceptable manly pursuits and of halting the significant support for the game given by women in the 1880s.

Similarly, the North/South divide is examined throughout the work. Again flowing from an understanding of the primacy of class relations to the development of the game, I will suggest that the importance of regionalism to rugby's 1895 split has been exaggerated, although the post-1895 period is a different matter. Certainly up to the late 1880s there was almost total unanimity between North and South on the need to oppose professionalism and, indeed, for many the proposal to introduce broken-time payments was an attempt to safeguard this unity. It was only in the early years of the twentieth century, as the Northern Union began to develop its own ideology, that 'Northernness' became an important factor in northern rugby.

Although class is viewed as the dynamo which ultimately drove rugby to schism, the role of civic pride among both the working and middle classes and commercialism is also examined in the changing contexts of the period. It was the growth of clubs seeking to represent their towns which opened the door for working-class involvement in rugby and it was the twin engines of civic glory and mass working-class involvement which provided the basis for the rapid growth of commercialism in rugby in Lancashire and Yorkshire in the 1880s. The clash between commercialism and amateurism is central to the first half of the book, as the exigencies of commercialism and the civic pride which it could bring became the wedge which split the RFU leadership's previous consensus over how to deal with the working-class influx.

The activities and motivations of players and crowds under the RFU and NU regimes are also highlighted separately throughout the work. The practices and cultural norms which working-class players and spectators brought to the game were crucial in undermining both middle-class control of rugby and the belief of some middle-class rugby administrators that the classes could be accommodated on the rugby field. Such practices were not fixed however and the development of the NU was accompanied by subtle changes in the behaviour of players and spectators, especially in the way the game was played and in the behaviour of spectators towards rival supporters.

The sources for this work came primarily from newspapers of the time, in particular *Athletic News* and the *Yorkshire Post*. This reliance on newspapers has its weaknesses: even in the late nineteenth century the sporting press had its own agendas and reporting was probably as selective and superficial as it is today. Any historian must be highly suspicious of such material. Nevertheless, both of these newspapers had a reputation for accuracy and from 1877 the *Yorkshire Post* carried detailed reports, and sometimes verbatim minutes, of meetings of the leading bodies of not only the Yorkshire rugby union, but also of the Lancashire, Welsh and English rugby unions, as well as the Football Association and Football League. In this, it was far more comprehensive than *Athletic News*, which was less inclined to involve itself in the politics of rugby or soccer. I have also made extensive use of the literary weeklies which flourished in Yorkshire in the 1880s and 1890s, which, as well as often producing dialect material, carried detailed reports of football and its culture. Curiously, the equivalent Lancashire journals of the time carried little football coverage, possibly reflecting the fact that rugby never occupied as central a place in the culture of the county as it did in Yorkshire. This lack of minutiae about the day-to-day activities of Lancashire clubs in the 1880s has forced me at times to place an unintentional focus on Yorkshire clubs during this early period.

By and large, I have deliberately avoided using such works as club histories. While there are honourable exceptions, a number of which are listed in the bibliography, it seems to me that many of these works are poorly researched and, especially when they are written about rugby union clubs, serve little purpose other than to assure supporters that their club can claim some form of dubious apostolic succession from the mists of time. In contrast, and no less flawed, most rugby league club histories assume a big bang theory, whereby the pre-split period was an unknowable primordial soup out of which clubs sprang fully formed in August 1895.

Sadly for the historian, and posterity, very few club records from the period have survived. The few which have are generally to be found in local libraries and archives. As many have pointed out in relation to other sports, the administrators of clubs and sporting bodies unfortunately seem to have little sense of the importance of preserving their history. I have made use of the minute books of leading committees at the headquarters of the Rugby Football League and the Rugby Football Union which, while useful, are usually little more than a written record of decisions made. The usefulness of the Rugby League's records is also undermined by the fact that they hold no minutes of the first four years of its existence – a crucial period in its development. The reliance on newspapers was consequently both enforced and by choice.

Finally, I have avoided direct controversy with other authors unless absolutely necessary, although I have referenced their works where appropriate. This is for two reasons, first of which is an urgent need to establish the historical record. Too much work on sport has been produced which relies on secondary sources and half-digested myth. In the case of rugby, Frank Marshall's admirable but flawed *Football – the Rugby Union Game*, first published in 1892, has too often been used uncritically.[4] Where prominent works are factually incorrect, I have pointed this out in footnotes. Secondly, I hope that, where its analysis and conclusions differ from others, this work speaks for itself. Certainly, the rise of professionalism, the reasons for the 1895 split and the composition by class of those involved in Northern Union is viewed from a different perspective from previous researchers.[5] Nevertheless, there is a sense in which I am indebted to all previous scholars and researchers of the social history of sport. Without their example, the task of exploring how and why men and women found twenty-six players in pursuit of an oval ball so fascinating would have been so much more difficult.

Although the writing of this work has been a singular exercise, it would not have been possible without the help of many people. I would particularly like to thank John Baxendale, Cathy France, Robert Gate, Trevor Delaney, John Jenkins and Piers Morgan for their support above and beyond the call of duty. For help, assistance and suggestions, my thanks also go to Tim Auty, Terry Bambrook, Bernard Booth, Walter Chamberlain and Heather Menzie, J. G. Davies of Leeds Grammar School, John Drake,

Dave Fox, Mike and Lesley Gardner, Trevor Gibbons, Elaine Hall, Chris Harte, Richard Holt, Rex King at the Rugby Football Union, Michael Latham, Tony Lewis, J. A. Mangan, Tom Mather, John Mitchell of St Peter's School at York, Colin Price and the team at Leeds Local History Library, Alex Service, Karl Spracklen and the Rugby Football League's Neil Tunnicliffe, not forgetting the staffs of the libraries at Barrow, Batley, Bolton, Bradford, Brighouse, Burnley, Castleford, Dewsbury, Huddersfield, Hull, Keighley, Manchester, Oldham, Preston, Rochdale, Salford, Wakefield, Warrington, Widnes and Wigan, the British Library at London and Wetherby, Colindale Newspaper Library, the Public Record Office at Kew, and the city archives at Hull, Leeds, Wakefield and York.

NOTES

1. Richard Holt, *Sport and the British*, Oxford, 1989.
2. Tony Mason, *Association Football and English Society 1863–1915*, Brighton, 1980. Keith Sandiford, *Cricket and the Victorians*, Aldershot, 1994.
3. While not necessarily agreeing with their overall approach, I accept that Eileen and Stephen Yeo make a powerful case for the importance of understanding change in the cultural context in their essay 'Ways of Seeing' in E. and S. Yeo (eds), *Popular Culture and Class Conflict 1590–1914*, Brighton, 1981.
4. Revd Frank Marshall, *Football – the Rugby Union Game*, London, 1892.
5. For example, see Eric Dunning and Kenneth Sheard, *Barbarians, Gentlemen and Players*, New York, 1979 or Gareth Williams, 'Rugby Union' in Tony Mason (ed), *Sport in Britain: A Social History*, Cambridge, 1989.

1

From Folk Football to Civic Pride: Origins to 1879

Rugby league football, like all modern forms of football, has its roots in the folk football of pre-industrial society. Many of the areas which became strongholds of the game had long histories of folk football going back far into the past. Hull, Huddersfield, Manchester, Rochdale, Whitehaven, Workington, York and many other towns in Lancashire, Yorkshire and the North West can all record football games from at least the seventeenth century.[1]

These early forms of football were intimately connected with the fairs, festivals and holidays of a predominantly rural nation. Shrove Tuesday, in particular, was the favoured day for many football matches across Britain. Christmas Day, New Year's Day and the Easter holidays too were popular dates for football. Other than two sides and the propulsion of a ball to a goal, the playing rules of the game could differ enormously from area to area. In some regions, the ball was driven primarily by foot. In others, the ball was carried or thrown. Quite often a mixture of the two was allowed, but, against those who would imagine folk football was a direct precursor to soccer, Montague Shearman's *Athletics and Football*, published in 1887, noted that 'there is no trace in the original form of [football] to suggest that nothing but kicking is allowed.'[2]

Folk football was primarily a game for large numbers played over wide distances, often involving the majority of the male population. In Derby, the game often involved around a thousand men, while the Sedgefield game involved 400 men per side. The goals were three miles apart for the Ashbourne game, while Whitehaven's goals were set at the docks and a wall outside the town. These organised games were also generally occasions for social mixing between the classes. The level of organisation required in many matches was considerable, often involving the closing of roads, prizes, arrangement of fields, suspension of regular business and newspaper advertisements, necessitating the patronage of local squires or landowners, but whatever its rules or wherever it was played, that folk football was extremely violent and disorderly, even in its most organised form, there can

1

be no doubt. Fighting, bloodshed and broken bones are words rarely absent from reports of football matches, and death was not an uncommon occurrence. It is fair to say that Joseph Lawson's description of the Pudsey street game of the 1820s and 1830s could apply to almost any area in which the game was played:

> Down-towners playing up-towners; in wet weather, bad roads and played through the village; breaking windows, striking bystanders, the ball driven into houses; and such 'shinning', as they called kicking each other's legs. It was quite common to see these up- and down-towners kicking each other's shins when the ball was a hundred yards away. Of course, many received serious injuries.[3]

By the early 1800s, the growth of industrial capitalism had begun to undermine the traditional social basis for folk football. The anti-Sabbatarian Horatio Smith, writing in 1831, described the way in which the urbanisation of London had driven out the possibilities for popular recreation:

> Every vacant and green spot has been converted into a street; field after field has been absorbed by the builder; all scenes of popular resort have been smothered with piles of brick; football and cricket grounds, bowling greens, and the enclosures of open places set apart for archery and other pastimes have been successfully parcelled out in squares, lanes or alleys.[4]

However it was not simply lack of green spaces which removed opportunities for play. Football had developed in a rural, feudalistic setting. The way in which it was played – the involvement of large numbers of people playing and watching, taking place over large areas and for long hours – ran counter to the discipline, order and organisation necessary for urban capitalism. As a critic of the Derby football game complained in 1832, 'It is not a trifling consideration that a suspension of business for nearly two days should be created for the inhabitants for the mere gratification of a sport at once so useless and barbarous.'[5] In 1835 the Highways Act banned the playing of football on public highways, imposing a maximum penalty of forty shillings. Religious objections to the playing of the game grew too, especially from nonconformist denominations who saw in football only licentiousness, debauchery and violence. Just as importantly, the old relationships between the classes no longer existed. The 1830s and 1840s saw the rise of the Chartists, attempts at armed insurrection in England and Wales and widespread fear of revolution crossing the channel, reducing to a negligible level the opportunities for social mixing across class lines. The gathering of large numbers of working-class people, for whatever purpose, was viewed with some suspicion by the authorities. Threats to public order were often cited as the reasons for the banning of football as, gradually, most of the remaining outposts of the traditional game succumbed to the exigencies of capitalism.[6]

Despite the vast differences in modes of play and methods of organisation between preindustrial football and its late Victorian forms, it is important to stress that many continuities and survivals from these earlier times became bound up in the culture of modern football. For example, there is little doubt that it was associated in the public mind with the common people. In 1720, *Stow's Survey* spoke of football as something with which 'the lower classes divert themselves', along with 'throwing at cocks and lying at alehouses', among others.[7] Joseph Strutt's 1801 survey of British sports describes football as 'formerly much in vogue among the common people of England.'[8] Occasionally football was used as a pretext for the gathering of large crowds to protest against a variety of injustices. A protest against enclosure at White Roding, Essex, in 1724 was initiated under the guise of a football match, while at Kettering in 1740 a match was organised as a pretext for the attempted pulling down of a local mill.[9] The importance of the game to some sections of the nascent working class can be seen in an 1845 comment of a working man in Derby responding to attempts to ban the annual game, 'It is all disappointment, no sports and no football. This is the way they always treat poor folks.'[10]

The decline and suppression of folk football was not without opposition nor was it totally successful. In Derby, for example, a protracted struggle took place in the 1840s against the local authority's outlawing of the Shrove Tuesday game, including the reading of the Riot Act and the calling out of troops in 1846.[11] Indeed, despite Strutt's belief in 1801 that 'of late years [football] seems to have fallen into disrepute, and is but little practised', a number of games survived until well into the mid-nineteenth century.[12] These survivals continued primarily in villages and rural communities where suspension of work could be more readily assimilated. This was especially true in areas where pre-industrial forms of capitalism such as outworking predominated, and where, more often than not, the patronage of a local landowner could be relied upon to provide the authority to ensure folk football's continuation; for example, the Duke of Northumberland rescued the Shrove Tuesday game at Alnwick in Northumberland in 1827 by providing a field for the game to be played upon and presenting the ball before the match.[13]

It is also clear that survivals of unorganised football, in the form of kickabouts in the streets or fields, continued to be played throughout the period of folk football's decline. Certainly, football was still played in the 1840s in villages near Huddersfield and Leeds.[14] In 1842 the Royal Commission on Children in Mines and Manufactories found that football was played widely, but informally, in the West Riding coal fields. It is also clear that in the mid-nineteenth century knowledge of football survived among the working classes in parallel with the development and growing influence of public school-derived football. For example, in Sutton, a village just to the east of Hull, a form of folk football was played up until at least 1871, and was the introduction to the game for at least one Hull FC player of the 1880s. Such evidence highlights the degree to which continuities and survivals of preindustrial practices coexisted alongside urban, industrial culture. It may well be that this residual consciousness of older forms of football was one of the reasons for the alacrity with which organised rugby and association football were taken up by the working classes in the latter part of the century.[15]

Yet as organised football faded almost to insignificance in urban society, it was beginning to acquire the utmost significance in the life of British public schools. By the time the Royal Commission on Public Schools had published its report in 1864, muscular Christianity's cult of games in the public schools had reached full maturity – and football occupied a central position in its pantheon of character-building sports. Nowhere was this more true than at Rugby school. Football had begun to be played by the boys of the school around 1800 and it is probable, although no definite proof exists, that the game they played was inspired by the annual New Year's Eve game played by the people of the town of Rugby in the 1700s.[16] Initially, the boys played the game with little or no interest from the school authorities but headmaster Thomas Arnold's reshaping of the school ethos in the 1830s led his successors to ascribe to football a central position in the school curriculum. Organised by the praeposters, the school's senior boys, football gradually came to occupy a key position not just as a winter recreation but also in the boys' hierarchical 'fagging' system.[17] While its origins at the school may be unclear, there is little doubt as to a key reason for football's popularity among the boys who played it or the partisans of muscular Christianity who championed it – its violent appeal to masculinity.

As Philip Mason has noted 'the [public school] process aimed above all at *hardening*. The public schools were meant to produce a ruling class, and there was a wide-spread view that great empires of the past had fallen because the ruling classes had grown luxurious and effeminate.'[18] As if in

4

[handwritten note: only upper classes (9) private school]

...y school game was marked by an
...ng' at each other's shins. Known
...of folk football from which the
...of the issues which divided the
...of 'dribbling' forms of football,
...of the Football Association in
...the Rugby game cannot be
...ool days in the 1860s at rugby-
...Rugby Football Union (RFU)
...oys practised hacking in their
...ly with an extra sole piece at the
...ed against the bars of the fire, or
...cked 'with the utmost violence'.
...played in bare legs, deliberately
...for Otley, Garnett told a team-
...u don't take that off, I will see if
...ague 'deemed it prudent to take
...nd E. H. Dykes, an archetypal
...urham School during the same
...llowed to any extent. "Hack him
...ing with the ball, and it was the
...ff their feet. A scrummage was
...He claimed that the hardest hack
...Calcutta, although he took the
...es by 'solemnly hammering my

As these examples from Blackheath and Durham demonstrate, by the 1850s the Rugby school game had quickly acquired adherents in other schools. Spurred by the popularity of Arnold's teachings (despite the fact that he personally showed no interest in football) and the proselytising zeal of old Rugbeians who became teachers, public schools across the country, especially the newer schools such as Clifton, Haileybury, Wellington, Marlborough and Cheltenham, took up the game. Public consciousness of the Rugby game was raised significantly in 1857 with the publication of old boy Thomas Hughes' *Tom Brown's Schooldays*, which sold 11,000 copies in its first year. While the game's initial popularity may have in part been due to its association with Arnold's reputation and Hughes' book, it was the distinctiveness of its rules which cemented its popularity among its players.

In 1845, a levee, or general meeting, of the sixth form published the rules for Rugby school football, highlighting the essential difference between their game and those of the other leading public schools: running with the ball. While other schools did not totally forbid handling the ball, only Rugby allowed a player to catch the ball and run with it. How this point of difference arose has become possibly the most famous example of myth-making in British sport. Ostensibly, as recorded in a plaque at Rugby school erected in 1900, one William Webb Ellis 'with a fine disregard for the rules of football as played in his time, first took the ball in his arms and ran with it, thus originating the distinctive feature of the Rugby game' sometime in late 1823. Unfortunately, no facts can be adduced to support this proclamation. The Rugby game originally had not allowed carrying the ball but by the early 1830s it had become an accepted feature of the game. There is no way of knowing who first ran with the ball at Rugby, but whoever did the deed was only continuing the age old traditions of folk football. If anyone could claim the mantle of originator of the carrying game at the school, it would be Jem Mackie, a pupil who became well known for his exploits as a ball-carrier in the late 1830s. Soon after, in 1842, carrying was formally legalised by a levee.

Ellis's name was first advanced in 1877, and again in 1880, by Matthew Bloxam, an old boy keen to prove that the Rugby game was unique to itself and was not a variant of older folk football. Other than in Bloxam's writings, Ellis's name is not mentioned in connection with the Rugby game in any work on the subject published before 1895. Even the 1895 inquiry of the Old Rugbeian Society into the origins of the game, which endorsed Bloxam's theory and led to the erection of the commemorative plaque, could not find a single witness who either saw Ellis's act or could provide even hearsay evidence of it. Although it has been suggested that the Rugbeians had a need for a heroic, Carlylean figure with whom to credit the origins of the game, the acceptance of Bloxam's myth and the invention of the Webb Ellis tradition served a broader function for both the school and the Rugby Union authorities at that time.[21] The school itself had ceased to play other schools at the game in 1876 after a series of losses, claiming that their opponents were playing non-school boys, only reviving inter-school games two decades later. The Webb Ellis myth allowed the school to do something it had been unable to do on the playing field: reassert its leading position in public school football over its more successful imitators. More importantly for the broader perception of the sport, the myth served to anchor the Rugby game as separate from the older traditions of plebeian folk football, creating a distinct middle-class lineage for the sport at a time when the middle classes in general were seeking to create exclusive recreational havens for themselves outside the prevailing mass sporting culture.[22] This explains why the myth was taken up with such alacrity and why previous claims to historical lineage – such as by the Reverend Frank Marshall in his 1892 history, *Football – the Rugby Union Game*, that rugby was 'the most ancient of British sports ... the legitimate refinement of the rough and crude games which in their main features are undoubtedly the source from which the Rugby game and the Rugby game alone are the true issue' – were so quickly dropped.[23] The legend also helped to delegitimise the 1895 split of the Northern Union by seemingly proving that rugby football was indeed the property of the middle classes, while by implying that Ellis was playing a form of soccer when he picked up the ball, it unwittingly lent support to the claims of association football that it provided the continuation of the folk football of the masses.

These developments lay in the future however. As pupils and masters left Rugby and the schools which had adopted the Arnoldian spirit, many took with them a continuing enthusiasm for the philosophy of 'mens sana in corpore sano'[24] and for the game they had learnt as boys. The sport had become, as one old Rugbeian put it in 1863, 'an enthralling, engrossing passion that seems to madden all who come beneath its influence as the Thrysi of Bacchus frenzied the Maendes of old.'[25] It was this enthusiasm which was to lay the basis for the formation of the football clubs which were to bloom in the 1860s and 1870s.

A GAME FOR GENTLEMEN THROUGHOUT THE LAND

It therefore did not take long for the spread of Rugby School football to reach Yorkshire and Lancashire, but this did not happen in a vacuum. The expansion of the middle classes in the mid-nineteenth century and the subsequent development of leisure time led to a corresponding demand for recreational activities from those engaged in white collar work. In this 'new leisure world',[26] there was a growing interest in physical activity, especially from former public school boys upon whom the importance of healthy minds and healthy bodies had been impressed from an early age. Physical recreation was, wrote a correspondent to the *Leeds Mercury* in early 1864, 'a subject which is becoming more and more recognised as one of the greatest importance to one class in particular ... namely, the young men who are all day engaged in the dispiriting and enervating employment of the shop, the office, and the warehouse, in our busy manufacturing and commercial towns.'[27]

The formation of the Rifle Volunteer movement in 1859 as a precautionary measure against the threat of a French invasion played an important role in both meeting and extending this demand. After the initial fear of invasion had passed, the Volunteers quickly enlarged their scope of activities to take in athletics, gymnastics and other sports. Their training grounds and fields were to provide the first playing pitches for Hull, Huddersfield and many other football clubs of the period.[28] Across England, organised athletic clubs were being founded, the formation of the Amateur Athletic Club in 1866 marking the start of attempts to regulate the sport.[29] Gymnasia had also been introduced into a number of northern towns by this time too, such as one opened in Huddersfield in 1850. The success of these ventures – Huddersfield Athletic Club recruited over 150 members within a month of its foundation in 1864 and Leeds Football Club attracted over one hundred in six weeks in the same year – was proof of the fertile ground into which the seeds of football were being planted.[30]

The first recorded non-school football match under Rugby School rules in the region took place in December 1857 at Edge Hill cricket ground in Liverpool, when old Rugbeian F. A. Mather and Richard Sykes, the current football captain of Rugby School, organised a 'Rugby versus the World' game. Around fifty players took part, most being Rugbeians, many being sons of Liverpool's merchant class and all being drawn from the upper echelons of society. This so encouraged Mather and his fellow-participants that it appears a Liverpool football club was formed some time after the match.[31] Sykes, who was actually a native of Manchester, was also one of the central movers in the foundation of Manchester FC in 1860, being its first captain. Like the key figures in the Liverpool club, Manchester's founders had learnt the game at public school, particularly at Rugby itself and at rugby football-playing Cheltenham College.[32] Hull Football Club was founded in a similar fashion in 1865 when a group of Rugby School boys returning home for holidays, led by the scion of one of Hull's leading shipowning families, W. H. H. Hutchinson, decided to form a football club.[33]

The widespread diffusion of Arnold's supposed ideals among public schools also meant that by the 1860s Rugby School was not the only school playing its version of football. Leeds Grammar School had formed a football club to play the game as early as 1851 and St Peter's School in York had published its football rules, modelled on Rugby rules, in 1856.[34] Pupils and former pupils of these schools were instrumental in founding the original Leeds club in 1864, the York club in 1868 and Leeds St John's in 1870, which was to become the Leeds club in 1890. Hull's founders also included pupils of St Peter's and Cheltenham College. The first Broughton football club in Manchester was founded as a team of Broughton College schoolboys in 1869 and, a year later, boys from Victoria Park and Chorlton High schools began the Manchester Free Wanderers club.[35] Also, as with the old Rugbeians, boys sent away to rugby-playing schools returned to the region with a desire to start their own clubs: Harry Garnett, the unreconstructed enthusiast of hacking, was educated at Blackheath Proprietary School in London (his younger brothers all went to Rugby) and brought back to Yorkshire an enthusiasm for the game he had played at school, as did former pupils of Mill Hill School and Christ College, Finchley in London and Durham School.[36]

As can be seen from this roll-call of public school alumni, the social character of these early clubs was uniformly middle class, albeit encompassing a wide spectrum of occupations and professions. Liverpool's leading lights were cotton merchants and articled clerks and Manchester's founders came from similar backgrounds. Robert Christison, the instigator of the York club, was a solicitor, while Huddersfield's Harry Beardsell was a wool merchant. In comparison to the sons of shipping magnates and clergymen who led Hull FC or the heirs to textile manufacturers who formed the Bradford club, the Leeds club was founded by members of the less exalted sections of this class. Henry Jenkinson, who placed the advertisement in the Leeds Mercury calling for the formation of a football club, was a clerk with the North East Railway company, although he later became a moderately successful author of walking guides, and of those who responded to his advertisement, one was a partner in a cap manufacturers, one a carting agent and another a bank employee. Barrow FC's team for their first match in December 1875 included seven old boys from Lancaster Grammar School, a solicitor, a clergyman, an accountant, a customs officer and a future Justice of the Peace.[37]

The narrowness of the social strata upon which these clubs were based can also be seen from the family relationships of many of the clubs' players and officials (although at this time they were usually one and the same). Christison was one of three brothers who founded York FC. At Hull three separate sets of brothers played for the club, three members of the Huth family played for Huddersfield, three Cariss brothers graduated from Leeds Grammar School to the Leeds club and four sets of brothers were involved in the founding of the Harrogate club.[38] Where the ties of family or school were lacking, the social connections of business could be substituted. On being questioned as to the respectability of his fledging Bradford club, textile dye works heir Oates Ingham replied, 'Well, you know me, and do business with my firm.'[39] More practically, the subscription money to join one of these football clubs was usually sufficient to restrict membership to the middle classes – Manchester charged ten shillings and sixpence, Rochdale ten shillings and Liverpool five shillings, rising to ten in 1875. Even the two shillings and sixpence charged by Bradford,

Huddersfield and Hull would probably have been beyond the reach of the wider population.[40] Rational recreation, the attempt by sections of the middle classes to take their idea of culture and recreation to the working classes, was most definitely not part of the ethos of any of these early clubs.

Indeed, the clubs formed in the 1850s and 1860s existed solely for the enjoyment of their members alone. Few, if any, spectators watched them play and the clubs paid little attention to those that did – not one of the 21 provincial football clubs is listed as charging an admission fee to their ground in the *Football Annual* of 1868. Play was organised according to the needs of members: the Leeds club practised every morning at 6.30am and in the evening at 7.30pm, attracting up to 60 players for the early session and 150 at night, with a fine of 6d for latecomers being 'strictly enforced for a time.'[41] Up to the mid-1870s, players would usually play the game in their ordinary clothes; Leeds's J. G. Hudson even played his entire career wearing spectacles, breaking them only once. It was only around 1870 that some clubs began to insist on players wearing a uniform, Hull's 1870 rule book specifying 'a striped scarlet and white jersey, a scarlet and white cap (if any), with white flannels.'[42] Even as late as 1874 Halifax played their first ever game, at Leeds Athletic, in everyday clothes.[43] Because interclub games were initially infrequent, although less so between school teams, clubs were more likely to play games between different categories of members. Liverpool played Rugby and Cheltenham versus the Rest, Bradford played Captain's side versus Secretary's side, the Leeds club in 1870 held a match between Dixon's Blues and Turner's Reds, and many clubs played A–M versus N–Z or some other alphabetical combination. St Helens in the early 1870s even played Fair versus Dark.

This preponderance of footballers playing Rugby School rules in the major cities of Lancashire and Yorkshire effectively meant that anyone wishing to play football in the region usually had to choose rugby, thus confining soccer, up to the 1880s at least, to pockets in eastern Lancashire and around Sheffield in south Yorkshire. The high social status of clubs led by old Rugbeians also meant that a significant social cachet was beginning to become attached to the playing of the game, giving newcomers to club football another incentive to play under Rugby rules. The dominance of the rugby code can be seen in the subsequent sporting activities of old boys of Bramham College near Leeds. Founded by the Liberal, nonconformist Dr Haigh in 1843 and based on a firm belief in muscular Christianity, it played a version of association rules and, indeed, became one of the first teams in Yorkshire to join the Football Association.[44] However, its old boys earned a place in the football history of the area for being the founders of rugby football clubs: Oates Ingham and Alfred Firth founding the Bradford club in 1863, R. J. Wade being instrumental in Hull FC and Harry Beardsell being a key mover in Huddersfield Athletic Club's formation of a football section.

Despite a common enthusiasm for the Rugby version of football, there existed wide variations in the rules, clubs each having their own greater or lesser peculiarities. This was not confined to the Northern clubs; there were similarly wide variations in the rules of the London-based clubs.[45] For example, there was little agreement on the number of players per side. At the extreme end of the spectrum were Leeds, who according to one of their founders 'did not trouble too much about [rules]' despite writing to Rugby School's headmaster, Dr Temple, seeking a game with the school.[46] More particularly, hacking, despite its popularity amongst some footballers, was frowned upon by many. Rochdale, Sale and Preston Grasshoppers were by no means unusual in playing non-hacking Rugby rules; even Hull, founded by Rugbeians, allowed tripping but not hacking. In contrast, York maintained the zeal for hacking, on one occasion playing the shinguard-wearing York Training College and, upon failing to convince them to discard their protection, proceeded 'to make them look a good deal worse for wear' by the time they removed the shinguards after the game.[47] Despite being founded by non-hacking association-playing Bramham old boys, Bradford also played full Rugby rules, including hacking. The original rules of St Peter's School in York allowed hacking too, although this was outlawed in 1873. The St Peter's rule book was also the source for one of the more bizarre statutes to appear in a club rule book – Hull FC's rule 20, stating that 'no player may stand on the goal bar to prevent [the ball] going over.'[48]

Yet as the number of clubs and players grew, so too did the desire to play new opponents. This necessarily led to compromises in rules and even the playing of other football codes: 'We played any mortal code possible with other clubs away from home so long as we could get a game of some sort', remarked Hull's William Hutchinson.[49] As late as 1873 Bradford still set aside two Saturdays a season on their fixture list for 'association practice.'[50] The most common arrangement in such situations was that which pertained amongst the public schools of the area, whereby the rules of the home club would be played. This presented little problem for games between clubs such as Leeds and Manchester, who first played each other in 1865, where there was common agreement as to the form of the game if not the precise rules. However, greater difficulties were experienced by clubs when they sought to organise matches with sides outside the rugby-playing areas.

The most popular source of non-rugby opponents was Sheffield, a stronghold of football but of the dribbling variety, as defined by the rules of the Sheffield Association, which had been formed in 1857, six years before the Football Association (FA).[51] The FA itself had initially investigated the possibility of forging a unified football code but this had been scuppered by supporters of dribbling rules who pushed through the adoption of the 1863 Cambridge University rule book; motions to adopt running with the ball and hacking by supporters of Rugby rules were decisively voted down by members of the FA. Nevertheless, the difference between rugby and the dribbling forms of football did not appear to be so wide as to make rapprochement impossible. Neither the Cambridge rules nor the FA rules forbade touching the ball with the hands, only running with it. The Sheffield code also allowed use of the hand to hit or push the ball, and both the FA and the Sheffield rules even allowed a player to make a 'fair catch' of the ball in general play, entitling him to have a free kick unchallenged by members of the opposing side. However, hacking, holding, pushing and tripping were explicitly forbidden by both sets of rules.[52]

In reality however, the disparity between the two forms of football and players' familiarity with their own code meant that the usual result was a victory for whichever side was playing at home under their own rules, giving an unwelcome predictability to such matches. In 1864 Leeds played Sheffield, winning at home and losing at Sheffield. Four years later Manchester easily defeated Sheffield by a goal and eight touchdowns to nil on home territory but lost two goals to nil in south Yorkshire. Similar difficulties afflicted Hull FC, whose football hinterland extended south of the Humber into association-playing Lincolnshire. Their first away game took place under association rules at Lincoln in 1866. Hull White Star, the club with which Hull FC would eventually merge, suffered in the same way, playing rugby rules at home, association when playing at Brigg and Market Rasen, and, more acceptably, a twelve-a-side variation of rugby at Gainsborough.[53] Gradually however, as the rules of the two games became more codified and as the players acquired skills developed specifically for their form of football, the desire and occasion for such hybrid matches declined.

By 1870, public interest in football was beginning to develop beyond the narrow circle of those who had played the game at school. Press reports of matches began to appear in local newspapers and, in particular, major matches, such as those between clubs representing towns, began to attract significant numbers of spectators. Like the players, the spectators at this time came almost exclusively from the middle classes. A match between Liberals and Conservatives organised by the Huddersfield club in 1869, with the teams being chosen by prominent local Liberal Edward Brooke and Tory C. E. Freeman was 'attended by nearly all the well-known ladies and gentlemen of the town, while the residents generally evinced an extraordinary enthusiasm for the encounter'.[54] That same year, 3,500 people had attended a match between Huddersfield and Leeds Grammar School. Given such numbers, it is probably safe to assume that some of these spectators came from the working classes, yet such interest was still very limited – and in some areas the working classes showed no interest at all in organised football. Jack Shaw, an early member of the York club, described how at the start of the 1870s:

> All the sport in which the working men of York seemed interested was rabbit coursing. Hundreds of them used to assemble on the Knavesmire on a Saturday afternoon to indulge in this so-called sport and when they saw the football players they made jeering references to the 'silly fools who kicked the ball about in the wet.'[55]

This sentiment probably extended beyond York, because rabbit coursing, pigeon shooting, foot racing and knur and spel, a game in which a long-handled club was used to hit a wooden ball as far as possible, all commanded a great deal of support and involvement from the working classes at this time.

Testimony to the popularity and growth of football amongst the middle classes was provided by the playing of the first Yorkshire versus Lancashire match in March 1870. The success of the annual games between Leeds and Manchester, including an exhibition match staged at Huddersfield in 1867, and the rise in the number of clubs on both sides of the county border, led to the suggestion that a county match be arranged. Responsibility for organising the game fell to J. G. Hudson, one of the founders of the Leeds club, who, along with Yorkshire captain Howard Wright, attempted to make the Yorkshire side as representative as possible of the county's foot-balling prowess by inviting players not only from the senior Yorkshire rugby clubs, Bradford, Huddersfield, Hull and Leeds, but also from the dribblers of the Sheffield club, about whom Hudson was later to remark, 'played as if they had never seen a rugby ball.'[56] In all probability, it was the Sheffield players' ineptitude in this match which signalled the end of any serious attempts at collaboration between the rugby and dribbling codes in Yorkshire.

Played on the ground of the Leeds club, the social tenor of the occasion can be gauged from the handbill produced to advertise the game: 'Lanca-shire will be represented by Gentlemen from Manchester, Rochdale, Preston, Burnley and other towns. Yorkshire by Gentlemen from Bradford, Huddersfield, Hull, Sheffield and Leeds.' To add to the prestige of the event, the match was played 'under the distinguished patronage of Sir A Fairburn, Lieutenant Colonel Swinfen and the officers of the 5th Dragoon Guards.' The admission price of sixpence was not so low as to encourage the merely curious, yet the game attracted 'a good attendance of admirers ... there also being a large number of the fair sex who graced the ground with their presence.' Played with twenty men on each side, the game itself was conducted with a characteristically cavalier attention to the rules – the first half lasted 45 minutes and the second was played for an hour. The admissibility of hacking also came under question. The Lancashire captain, William MacLaren, Manchester merchant and uncle of Lancashire and England batsman Archie MacLaren, approached Howard Wright and explained that 'many of his men were in situations and it would be a serious matter for them if they were laid up through hacking, so it was mutually agreed that hacking should be tabooed.' Wright agreed, only to find that the Lancastrians began hacking as soon as the ball was kicked off.

In modern terms, the match was hardly a spectacle. At this time, rugby was played with each side fielding sixteen forwards and four backs, who rarely handled the ball because of the continuous scrummaging by the forwards, the aim being to push the opposing forwards as far back as possible. Heeling the ball out of the scrummage was virtually unheard of. Even at this early stage in rugby's development, it was recognised that the 'dreariness of heavy brigade scrummaging' was hardly an attractive feature of the game. Notoriety surrounded the 1871 Roses game at Huddersfield at which 'the spectators had to be content to hear the shouts and desperate grunts of the huge pack of humanity that struggled for possession of the ball most of the afternoon.'[57] In such circumstances, there were plenty of opportunities for indulging in the less savoury aspects of the game, as Richard Sykes later remembered: 'Anyone who played in the match at Queens Park [in Liverpool] in or about 1865 would remember it as we were overmatched and roughly handled. Some of us had to be helped out of the railway carriage on arrival at Victoria Station.'[58] Passing the ball by hand between players was also extremely rare, the role of the backs at this time being largely confined to punting the ball into the opposition's half to set up another scrummage or, when within range, to attempt to score a goal by drop-kicking the ball. Matches were decided solely on goals scored, which often led to a team that had conceded numerous tries winning a game by kicking a lucky goal. Even then, this anomaly was recognised by the fact that most newspaper reports recorded goals, tries and touchdowns – the latter being the number of times a team was forced to touch the ball down behind its own goal line – in order to give a more accurate assessment of matches.

Football, of whatever code, and violence were inseparable in the public mind from the 1860s onwards, as depicted here in *The Yorkshireman* in 1883.

Unsurprisingly, disputes over scoring or illegal play often arose and, because the rules made no provision for referees, were decided by discussion between the two captains. This apparently gentlemanly method of settling disputes in fact simply gave the upper hand to the more loquacious of the two disputants, as a participant described in the 1890s: 'Some captains would jaw away until they gained their point by sheer blarney, the opposing side giving in merely to get some more play.'[59] As Robert Christison admitted, this necessarily meant that 'the more plausible and argumentative a player was, the more likely he was to be considered as a captain.'[60] Arguments between captains over disputed points had become so common by 1870 that it was accepted practice to add time on to the length of a match to cover the time lost for play.[61] In such an atmosphere gamesmanship, or the art of gaining maximum advantage from the letter of the law, flourished.

15

No greater an exponent existed than Blackburn cotton magnate A. N. 'Monkey' Hornby, captain of England at both cricket and rugby, who became notorious for his behaviour at the 1878 Roses match when, with Lancashire defending a slim lead, he continually kicked the ball into touch. 'Damn it Hornby', protested Yorkshire's Harry Garnett, 'We've come here to play football, not to watch you punt the ball into the next parish,' to which Hornby replied, 'You go to the devil Garnett. We've won this match and we are going to stick to it.' Indeed, the violence and gamesmanship of middle-class football of this period must cast doubt on the reality of the so-called gentleman's code of playing the game purely for the game: the self-image of the middle-class sportsman, who, in Richard Holt's words 'saw himself as someone who could hold his passions in check and for whom the enjoyment of the game was more important than the result,' bore little relationship to the hacking, argumentative and rule-bending ex-public schoolboys who populated the football fields of the 1860s and 1870s.[62] As we shall discover later, they may have articulated these ideals when telling others how to play football, but for themselves winning was the supreme goal.

CIVIC PRIDE AND FOOTBALL'S 'GIGANTIC STRIDES'

The first Roses match was won by Lancashire by the margin of a goal, two tries and a touchdown to nil, but the game's true significance lay not in the result but in the fact that it established football as a respectable recreation in the two counties. The football rivalry between towns and counties mirrored precisely the great growth in civic and commercial rivalry in the decades immediately following 1850. Writing in 1896, Talbot Baines, grandson of the Liberal founder of the *Leeds Mercury*, commented on 'the existence in Northern parts to a degree elsewhere unknown of the "element of local corporate unity." In its most pronounced form it is found in some great towns in Yorkshire, Lancashire, and the neighbouring counties; and its presence begets a public spirit fruitful in all manner of good civic deeds, a wholesome rivalry between communities and a healthy local pride.'[63]

The quest for civic pride, embodied in the erection of town halls and other municipal buildings reached its zenith during this period: Leeds opened its town hall in 1858, Bradford in 1873, Huddersfield in 1879, Wakefield in 1880. Manchester had been accorded the status of a city in 1853, followed by Liverpool in 1880.[64] Nor was this a process confined to the large metropolitan areas: stung by the incorporation of Dewsbury in 1862, the adjoining town of Batley campaigned for incorporation, succeeded six

...iority over its neighbour because
...f this rivalry was based on trade.
...e eastern extremity, textiles were
...lthough areas tended to have their
...g the cotton/woollen cloth division
...wing overseas competition from
...r example, despite specialising in
...turers took the opportunity of a
...3 to capture a portion of the men's
...aller towns between Leeds and
...roduction of 'shoddy' low-quality
...have seen, the vast majority of the
...e region were intimately connected
...ddersfield, Leeds, Liverpool and
...wholly by the sons of textiles manu-
...nited sense, football rapidly became
...and trade rivalry.[65]
...d its identification with inter-town
...hole, no longer formed to be private
...tlemen but were created to represent
...he papers of football matches being
...here, and we thought that Halifax
...he founder of the Halifax club, Sam
...or forming the club in 1873.[66] The
...ormed, under the patronage of the
...st other towns. After six weeks' prac-
tice, they took to the field against Warrington.[67] Four years later Oldham
FC was founded in similar circumstances, the chief constable and a local
peer being present at the founding meeting.[68] In contrast to later years, this
rivalry between towns was highly localised and focused on neighbours or
near-neighbouring towns. At this time there was no suggestion that football
could be a conduit to national prominence, even for the larger towns and
cities such as Manchester or Leeds. The 1870s saw a whole swathe of clubs
formed to represent their towns and led by the sons of textiles manufacturers: Brighouse, Dewsbury, Halifax, Rochdale, Swinton and Skipton
were just a fraction of those clubs founded in this way. Although working
class participants were as yet few and far between, all of these clubs
exhibited a high level of unity among the upper and middle classes which
provided their backbone: Tories and Liberals, merchants and manufacturers were to be found gathered together in virtually all of them. The
strength of local pride and desire for corporate unity can also be gauged

Civic pride in football boots: a caricaturist's impression of the 1884 Bradford versus Manchester game, from *Toby, the Yorkshire Tyke*.

by the contrasting fortune of Cavendish FC which moved from Moss Side to Salford in 1879. They 'wrote to the local gentry for their patronage and support, [but] received the reply that they did not know any of the members of the club or recognise the club as a Salford club.'[69] By 1875, at least 32 towns and cities in Lancashire and Yorkshire had a rugby-playing football club claiming the town's name, not to mention those representing junior teams, local districts, Rifle Volunteer regiments or church organisations.[70]

If the rise in the number of football clubs was spurred by feelings of civic pride, it was facilitated by the works of the municipal age. In particular, the creation of public parks extended the scope for both playing and watching football. Most of the early clubs had relied on either local landowners or the grounds of the local Rifle Volunteers for playing surfaces. One exception to this was the Leeds club, which had played near the centre of Leeds on Woodhouse Moor public park, known as 'the lungs of Leeds.' This had been opened in 1857, followed rapidly by Bradford's Peel Park six years later, Huddersfield's Beaumont Park in 1866 and the more famous Roundhay and Lister parks of Leeds and Bradford in 1872 and 1873 respectively. In Manchester, the first public parks had been opened in 1846. The provision of transport, especially the railways, expanded dramatically during this period, increasing the ability of teams, and spectators, to travel between towns and thus enhancing the nature of local rivalry. On a smaller scale, the widespread introduction by many towns of public transport such as horse trams in the 1870s meant that rivalry between different districts of towns could be indulged in with the maximum of ease.

These manifestations of civic pride were joined in their facilitation of football by that other great passion of the nineteenth century middle classes, cricket.[71] Initially this took the form of out-of-season cricket pitches being used by football clubs – as in the case of Liverpool FC who played on Edge Hill cricket ground until 1879, or York who used the Yorkshire Gentleman's Cricket Ground in the 1880s – but as the popularity of the winter game grew, cricket clubs themselves began to look at it as a complementary form of recreation and formed football sections of their own. Swinton and Widnes were two of the better-known clubs formed in this fashion. In 1876 Halifax, who had originally borrowed Ovenden cricket ground for matches, joined forces with the local Trinity cricket club to form Halifax Cricket and Football Club. Although not all cricket clubs welcomed these developments – the chairman of Oldham's powerful Werneth cricket club warning, a few months after the formation of Oldham FC, that football 'was calculated to irritate the players and when their feelings got wound up it no doubt led to angry displays' – this symbiotic relationship between cricket and football clubs was to continue with increased strength throughout the 1880s.[72]

Cricket, of course, was seen by the Victorians as the highest state which muscular Christianity had yet attained. Many of the public schoolboys who did not follow their classmates into business had gone into the church and taken an enthusiasm for rugby football into their work. The Church of England's attempts to reach out to the working classes in the 1850s and 1860s through 'rational recreation' had continued through the provision of Sunday schools, Bible classes and Young Men's Societies, from which the principles of muscular Christianity were propagated.[73] It appears that two types of clubs were formed by church bodies. The first were those founded by middle-class Sunday-school members themselves, such as that started in 1870 at St John the Evangelist church in Leeds by members of the church cricket team seeking something to do in winter. Its founders were all pupils at Leeds Grammar School, two of them becoming headmasters of public schools, one a partner in a printer's and another a prominent local Conservative politician. In effect, it functioned in the same way as other teams founded by public schoolboys. Its 1874 report contained a catechism of the public school ethic which exhorted members to: 'Let no voice be heard in matches except that of the captain' and 'however much provoked, never to lose temper, but to remember that, as St John's FC they have a character to maintain as well as for good conduct as for good play.'[74]

On the other hand were those clubs started by the clergy to encourage the working classes to participate in church activities? For example, Wakefield's Holy Trinity church provided a wide range of self-improving classes, including bookkeeping, shorthand, languages and 'electricity', as well as running a cricket team. At its annual prize-giving ceremony in November 1872, the Reverend William Madden announced that the Society was to form a football club, after which his colleague Dr Browne spoke of the need to 'preserve to the working class those sturdy thews and sinews which their ancestors possessed and which were supposed to make one Englishman equal to five Frenchmen,' adding that 'science, literature and art would be of comparatively little avail without muscular exercise.' Within the month the new team played its first game against Leeds Grammar School, although the fact that the Trinity side could only muster twelve players to the school's fifteen suggests that, initially at least, not all parishioners shared Dr Browne's enthusiasm for thews and sinews.[75] Founded on similar principles was the Leeds Parish Church club, where the football team was formed directly out of a recreation club attached to the church's 'A' Division Bible Class in 1874. Led by E. H. Dykes, the former

Durham School hacker, the club was held to be 'the embodiment of that sane doctrine of muscular Christianity.' The forerunners of the Salford, Runcorn, Radcliffe and Sowerby Bridge Northern Union clubs also had similar origins.[76]

How successful these exercises were in imparting Christian values to the working class will be seen later, but a foretaste of the problems to be overcome were experienced by Heckmondwike FC. Formed by the vicar of Heckmondwike as part of the church's athletic club, the team became notorious by the late 1870s for the rough play of its team and the violent behaviour of its spectators. In 1876 Halifax walked off the pitch in the midst of a game at Heckmondwike 'owing to the rough and ungentlemanly play' of their opponents.[77] The following year Leeds St John's followed suit only to find themselves come under a hail of stones and clods of earth from the disgruntled crowd.[78] Although at this stage of the sport's development, such behaviour was rare, the church-based sides quickly found themselves having to compromise on the question of club membership. Almost all of them had originally allowed only members of their congregations to play but within a few years, as Dykes was later to ruefully point out, 'force of circumstances led to the introduction of outsiders.'[79]

These circumstances were the massive increases in the popularity of rugby. Just three years after its formation, a note in Wakefield Trinity's cash book commented that 'the interest taken in the club by the public of Wakefield is something extraordinary' and recorded a profit on the season of thirty-one shillings, despite the fact that the club made no charge for admission to games. Such success was now common to many clubs.[80] For major games involving the better-known clubs, crowds could rise to upwards of two thousand people. This growth of interest was given a fillip in 1875 when the RFU decided to reduce the size of teams from twenty to fifteen per side. Other than in county games, fifteen-a-side had been the most common line-up for matches played in the region, but the official sanction to the change gave clubs added incentive to move away from the traditional heavy scrummaging game, making the game a more palatable spectacle for the onlooker. In the 1877 *Football Annual*, it was noted that 'Football in the North of England ... has made great strides during the past season, and in addition to Manchester, Liverpool, Preston, Huddersfield, Leeds, etc, etc, there are many clubs less widely known in Yorkshire and Lancashire which can turn out a fifteen both strong in play and possessing a good knowledge of the science of the game.'[81]

In Yorkshire, the game was also helped by the creation of the Yorkshire County Football Club (YCFC) in 1874, which gave the sport both a structure and a higher profile. Formed at the instigation of Bradford's Harry Garnett, the newly appointed county captain, the YCFC initially set out to ensure the efficient organisation of county games and the selection of the county side. Unlike Lancashire, where the organisation of county matters was firmly in the hands of the Manchester and Liverpool clubs, the YCFC consisted of representatives of the Bradford, Huddersfield, Hull, Leeds and York clubs.[82] Although appointed by no-one other than themselves, as the oldest clubs in the area they possessed sufficient authority to give the burgeoning game a direction it had hitherto lacked. The YCFC's first major action was to organise a trial match for places in the county team in 1875 but it was an idea of Arthur Hudson, the son of a Leeds woollen manufacturer, who had joined the committee a year or so after its formation, which was to change the face of football in the county. Neither original nor revolutionary, it was a proposal to start a knockout cup competition for the leading teams in Yorkshire. The association code's FA Cup had begun in 1871 and three years later in London rugby-playing medical students had begun competing for the Hospitals' Cup. Both had succeeded in bringing their sports to wider audiences and, according to Harry Garnett twenty-five years later, Hudson had convinced the YCFC of the idea by explaining that 'we will make football the game for every boy in Yorkshire and Yorkshire shall be able to play the rest of England and beat it.'[83] Hurriedly organised for December 1877, sixteen teams were invited to compete for the Yorkshire Challenge Cup, although no medals were to be presented to players because it was felt that this smacked too much of professionalism.

In the first round, an unprecedented eight thousand people packed into Halifax's Hanson Lane ground to see the defeat of Wakefield. A week later, five hundred Halifax supporters went by special train to Wakefield to watch their team overcome Trinity. Such scenes were repeated across the county: 'There was so much excitement over the match among the local public that we really were fortunate in getting away from the ground without having to fight our way out ... the spectators swarmed all about the field and there was a scene that up to that time we had not been accustomed to', recounted Hull's William Hutchinson of their second-round tie at Heckmondwike.[84] Three thousand people paid to see the semifinal between Bradford and Halifax, but 'the arrangements for taking the gate money were very inadequate, the result being that a number of those travelling with the Halifax team, rather than bear the infliction of waiting until it came to their turn to pay, leaped over the walls of the field and thus obtained access free of charge.'[85] Unfortunately, due to snow, the final between Halifax and York had to be switched at the last minute from Huddersfield to Holbeck in Leeds, attracting a disappointing crowd of three thousand to watch Halifax, a club not represented on the YCFC committee, carry off the trophy. Nevertheless, no-one could argue with the verdict of the *Yorkshire Post* that 'the object the Yorkshire football committee had in view when they offered this cup – namely, the further development of football in the county – has been fully realised.'[86]

The following season's competition was even more successful. Twenty sides entered and the semifinal – only one was played because Kirkstall were given a bye into the final – attracted 10,000 to Wakefield Trinity's ground to see them overturn their previous season's defeat by Halifax, with special trains bringing spectators from Halifax, Leeds, Bradford, Dewsbury and Huddersfield. Despite expecting a one-sided game, 12,000 turned up for the final at the Halifax ground to see Trinity victorious. Thousands travelled on trains from Wakefield and Leeds, paying sixpence or a shilling to see the match. As soon as the news of Trinity's victory was received in their home town 'the Parish Church bells began to ring in honour of the event. On the arrival at Wakefield of the special train, the victors were met by the Parish Church Association band and an immense concourse of people, and marched from the station to the Woolpacks Inn, the cheering in the streets being again and again renewed.'[87]

This explosion in popularity brought with it a set of entirely unexpected pressures. The first and most obvious was the growth in spectators. As the 1877 Bradford semi-final demonstrated, few clubs could cope organisationally with large crowds. The days when, as in Halifax, crowds could be controlled 'by a few friends parading on horseback', were now gone.[88] The partisanship engendered by the cup competition led to disorderly and rowdy crowd behaviour. As a referee, Harry Garnett had to be escorted from grounds by the police following Yorkshire Cup ties after supporters had sought to dispute some of his decisions with him personally. Most notoriously, the Wakefield Trinity team had been attacked by Halifax supporters after their 1879 final victory in revenge for Trinity's semi-final defeat of Halifax, breaking a window and almost overturning their carriage.[89] The determination of spectators to see their side win was also shared by many of the competing teams. From the beginning of the competition, the YCFC had warned clubs against importing players specifically to play in cup ties but controversy surrounded the transfer of star halfback Rufus Ward from Wakefield Trinity to Halifax in the winter of 1877. His move was variously explained by his falling out with the Trinity committee over an athletics meeting or by the fact that his girlfriend lived in Halifax, but others suspected that he had been offered an inducement to switch clubs, a practice known as 'kidnapping':

Well Rufus hed nobbut nicely gotten browt aht afoor he fell aht wi'
some o' t'Trinity chaps an' fell in wi' Halifax. Nah doan't be sa sharp.
Ah didn't say 'at t'Cup started t'kidnapping bizness. Only this is t'fust
case 'at I knaw, an' it wor just ta help Halifax ta win t'Cup t'fust time,
like. Two an' two, ye knaw – fower. [90]

Whatever the truth of these accusations, it was clear that some clubs were
adopting new methods of improving their chances of cup success. Halifax
held a special training session the night before the 1877 cup final and
Wakefield Trinity began to meet before matches to decide on tactics. Such
methods did not find favour with those players who still viewed the
game purely as a recreation. In contrast to the Halifax team, York captain
Robert Christison spent the night before the 1877 final at a dance in
Harrogate.

The Yorkshire Cup had brought with it an influx of new players, new
spectators and new playing methods. The success of Halifax in the
inaugural final had been followed by 'clubs springing up like mushrooms
on every side. People saw that the "blue and whites", after a paltry
connection with the sport of three years standing, had earned so much
distinction, and why shouldn't they succeed in the same manner?'[91] The
quest for civic pre-eminence embodied in football clubs and the new
competition was also beginning to be embraced by those social strata
normally excluded from its pursuit. Although expressed in a different
manner and often undertaken by different means, the search for civic glory
was enthusiastically taken up by the working classes – indeed, in many
ways, attendance at their town club's football matches was one of the
few practical methods they had of expressing local pride. The Yorkshire
Cup now meant that football and civic honour were now tightly bound
together: 'I copt t'fooitball fever at t'same time as monny a hundred
moor did – when t'Yorkshire Cup wor first laiked for thirteen year sin, and
what's moor – or less, if owt – I've hed it ivver sin,' was how one rugby fan
summed up the impact of the cup.[92] Yet the people who now began to pour
into the game, both as players and spectators, were of a distinctively
different class from the former public schoolboys who had hitherto thought
of the game as their own. Rugby was now poised to reoccupy the position
of mass popularity which had been held in pre-industrial times by folk
football. Slowly but surely, a perceptible threat to the middle-class
exclusivity of the game was beginning to be felt. How they were to deal
with these newcomers was an issue which was to occupy the leaders of
rugby for the next two decades.

NOTES

1. I have chosen the description 'folk football' to describe all the variants of the pre-industrial game because it best captures the traditional, rural-based cross-class popularity of these games. 'Mob' football is a term laden with the value judgements of the nineteenth century fear of the crowd, while mass football doesn't necessarily apply to all forms of pre-industrial football – for example, the Dorking form of camp ball seems to have involved only fifteen men per side. The sometimes used 'rough football' is not only value laden but reeks of the drawing rooms of genteel maiden aunts.

2. Montague Shearman, *Athletics and Football*, London, 1887, p. 260. For recent summaries of the history of folk football, see Robert Malcolmson, *Popular Recreations in English Society 1770–1850*, London, 1975 and Derek Birley, *Sport and the Making of Britain*, Manchester, 1993. Other sources are referred to throughout this chapter.

3. Joseph Lawson, *Letters to the Young on Progress in Pudsey during the Last Sixty Years*, Stanningley, 1887, p. 58.

4. Horatio Smith, *Festivals, Games and Amusements*, London, 1831, p. 122.

5. *Derby and Chesterfield Reporter*, 23 Feb. 1832, quoted in Malcolmson, p. 113.

6. For more on the debate on the decline of folk football see D. A. Reid, 'Folk Football, the Aristocracy and Cultural Change: A Critique of Dunning and Sheard', *The International Journal of the History of Sport*, Vol. 5, No. 2, Sept. 1988.

7. *Stow's Survey*, of 1720, quoted in Horatio Smith, *Festivals, Games and Amusements*, London, 1831, p. 121.

8. Joseph Strutt, *The Sports and Pastimes of the People of England*, London, 1801, p. 100.

9. The White Roding episode is outlined in Birley, p.115. For the Kettering incident see E. P. Thompson's *Customs in Common*, London, 1991, p. 234. Malcolmson lists another three examples.

10. *Derby and Chesterfield Reporter*, 7 Feb. 1845, quoted in Anthony Delves, 'Popular Recreation and Social Conflict in Derby, 1800–50' in E. and S. Yeo (eds), *Popular Culture and Class Conflict 1590–1914*, Brighton, 1981, p. 94.

11. Delves, p. 91.

12. Strutt, p. 100. The claim is echoed in Jehoshaphat Aspin's *A Picture of the Manners, Customs, Sports and Pastimes of the Inhabitants of England*, London, 1825, p. 242. Malcolmson lists 16 local games still being played in the nineteenth century.

13. *Dewsbury Reporter*, 1 March 1884.

14. See for example Stanley Chadwick, *Claret and Gold*, Huddersfield, 1945.

15. *Hull and East Riding Athlete*, 27 Nov. 1889. The question of cultural continuity between pre-industrial and industrial periods is dealt with in Hugh Cunningham, *Leisure in the Industrial Revolution*, London, 1980.

16. Jennifer Macrory, *Running with the Ball*, London, 1991.

17. Despite the impression created by *Tom Brown's Schooldays*, football may not have been as popular as its supporters wished – the 1845 rules note 'the great abuse' of notes to be excused football.

18. Philip Mason, *The English Gentleman: the Rise and Fall of an Ideal*, London, 1993, p. 170 (emphasis in original). The definitive account of the role of games in the English public school system is in J. A. Mangan's *Athleticism in the Victorian and Edwardian Public School*, Cambridge, 1981.

19. Interview with H. W. T. Garnett in *Yorkshire Evening Post*, 12 Jan. 1901.

20. Interview with Reverend E. H. Dykes in *Yorkshire Evening Post*, 9 Feb. 1902.

21. See William Baker, 'William Webb Ellis and the Origins of Rugby Football: The

Life and Death of a Victorian Myth', *Albion*, Vol. 13, 1981. Jennifer Macrory, ibid. is the only serious modern defence of Webb Ellis's claim to posterity. The report of the Old Rugbeian Society can be found in *The Origin of Rugby Football*, Rugby, 1897. The Webb Ellis myth is rivalled for its inventiveness only by the story of Abner Doubleday's 'invention' of baseball, for which see Stephen Jay Gould's 'Creation Myths of Cooperstown' in his *Bully for Brontosaurus*, London, 1991.

22. See John Lowerson, *Sport and the English Middle Classes 1870–1914*, Manchester, 1993. The recreation of rugby as an exclusive pastime is dealt with in Ch. 5.
23. Reverend Frank Marshall, *Football – the Rugby Union Game,* London, 1892, p. 2.
24. A healthy mind in a healthy body.
25. An Old Rugbeian in *Bell's Life*, 22 Nov. 1863.
26. The phrase is Peter Bailey's, from *Leisure and Class in Mid-Victorian England*, London, 1975, p. 68. For more on middle-class culture in the north of England during this period, see Kidd and Roberts (eds), *City, Class & Culture*, Manchester, 1985 and R. J. Morris, 'Middle-Class Culture' in Derek Fraser (ed), *A History of Modern Leeds*, Manchester, 1980.
27. Letter to *Leeds Mercury*, 31 March 1864.
28. For the Volunteer movement in general, see Hugh Cunningham, *The Volunteers*, London, 1975. For demands that the Volunteers take up sporting activities see the *Leeds Mercury*, 7 April 1864.
29. Montague Shearman, *Athletics and Football*, London, 1887, and Peter Lovesey, *The Official Centenary History of the AAA*, London, 1979.
30. See *Leeds Mercury*, 30 April 1864 and Stanley Chadwick, *Claret and Gold*, Huddersfield, 1945. In reversal of usual practice, Leeds Athletic Club was formed out of Leeds FC.
31. See J. R. A. Dalglish, *Red, Black and Blue: The First 125 Years of Liverpool Football Club*, Swinton, 1983. There appears to be little hard evidence about when the club itself was formed however.
32. The three founders were Sykes, Major Tom Brown, a Rugbeian, and Howard Aston, formerly of Cheltenham College. See letter from Sykes to Roger Walker, 14 Feb. 1907, quoted in Len Balaam, *Manchester Football Club 1860–1985*, Manchester, 1985, p. 5.
33. William Hutchinson in *Yorkshire Evening Post*, 1 Dec. 1900.
34. For Leeds Grammar School, see *Football Annual*, London, 1868. No copy of the St Peter's rules appears to have survived, although extracts are quoted in the *Oxford English Dictionary*, Second Edition on CD-Rom, Oxford, 1993, and a summary can be found in A. Raine, *History of St Peter's School, York*, London, 1926, p. 134.
35. See A. M. Crooks, 'County Football – Lancashire' in Marshall, Ch. 19.
36. For Garnett see *Yorkshire Evening Post*, 12 Jan. 1901. The pupils of the other schools are respectively Tom Scarborough, a leading light in the Halifax club, C. Hutton Coates, a founder of Yorkshire Wanderers and E. H. Dykes, the instigator of the Leeds Parish Church club.
37. 'Referee', *A History of Barrow Football Club*, Barrow, 1914, p. 14.
38. *Yorkshire Evening Post*, 22 Feb. 1901.
39. *Yorkshire Evening Post*, 15 Nov. 1902.
40. Source: *Football Annual*, 1868.
41. Interview with J. G. Hudson, *Yorkshire Evening Post*, 8 Dec. 1900.
42. Hull FC Rule book of 1870, quoted in *Yorkshire Evening Post*, 20 Feb. 1904. Huddersfield also decided that it be compulsory for players to wear the team uniform in October 1870.
43. *Yorkshire Post*, 24 Nov. 1874.

44. Details of the school, which folded after an outbreak of fever in 1869, can be found in *Some Account of Bramham College* by 'An Oxford Graduate', London 1854; the *Yorkshire Weekly Post* of 8 June 1904; and in the *Bramham College Magazine*. The school is listed as a member of the FA in the *Football Annual* of 1870.
45. For a discussion on the varying rules of the metropolitan clubs, see Marshall, p. 73.
46. Interview with J. G. Hudson, *Yorkshire Evening Post*, 8 Dec. 1900.
47. *Yorkshire Evening Post*, 22 Feb. 1901. Halifax were even said to oppose tackling below the knee according to the *Athletic News*, 18 Nov. 1876.
48. For Rochdale, see *Football Annual* for 1868. For Sale see M. Barak, *A Century of Rugby At Sale*, Sale, 1962. For Preston see A. Marsden, *Preston Grasshoppers' Centenary Brochure*, Preston, 1969. For Bradford see *Yorkshire Evening Post*, 15 Nov. 1902. For St Peter's see Raine, ibid. For Hull see *Yorkshire Evening Post*, 1 Dec. 1900 and 20 Feb. 1904. The explanation for the strange rule would appear to be that Hull's William Beevor-Lambert had been a pupil at St Peter's where he had presumably been convinced of its efficacy.
49. *Yorkshire Evening Post*, 1 Dec. 1900.
50. Bradford FC 1873/74 Fixture Card, reprinted in *Yorkshire Evening Post*, 5 Jan. 1901.
51. For more on the Sheffield Association, see Percy Young, *Football in Sheffield*, London, 1964.
52. The full text of both the Cambridge and Football Association rules, plus the transcript of the FA's discussion on the rules is in Jennifer Macrory, *They Ran with the Ball*, London, 1991.
53. For reports on Hull FC's soccer adventures, see *Athletic News*, 11 Oct. 1876.
54. *Yorkshire Evening Post*, 15 Dec. 1900.
55. *Yorkshire Evening Post*, 21 Feb. 1903.
56. *Yorkshire Evening Post*, 8 Dec. 1900.
57. Interview with Harry Beardsell, *Yorkshire Evening Post*, 15 Dec. 1900.
58. Letter of Richard Sykes to Willie Parlane, 8 Jan. 1913, quoted in Len Balaam's *Manchester Football Club 1860–1985,* Manchester, 1985, p. 6. Manchester were still playing the occasional game under hacking rules as late as 1879.
59. 'The YRU' by A Wag in *The Yorkshireman Football Number*, March 1890.
60. Robert Christison in *Yorkshire Evening Post*, 22 Feb. 1901.
61. *Yorkshire Evening Post*, 22 Feb. 1901.
62. Richard Holt, *Sport and the British*, Oxford, 1989, p. 174.
63. *The Times,* 30 Oct. 1896. Valuable background to this section can be found in Patrick Joyce, *Work, Society and Politics*, Brighton, 1980.
64. The key text is obviously Asa Briggs, *Victorian Cities*, London, 1963, but see also C. Arscott, and J. Wolff, 'Cultivated Capital', *History Today*, Vol. 37, 1987.
65. In 1895, Brighouse Rangers, a team founded by sons of two of the town's leading textile manufacturers, held a dinner at which the toast was made to 'the town and trade of Brighouse', *Yorkshire Post*, 16 May 1895.
66. See *Halifax Guardian*, 1 Nov. 1873 and *Yorkshire Evening Post*, 9 Feb. 1901.
67. *Wigan Observer*, 29 Nov. 1872 and 24 Jan. 1873.
68. *Oldham Evening Chronicle*, 1 Nov. 1876.
69. James Higson, *History of Salford Football Club*, Manchester, 1892.
70. Source: *Football Annual*, 1868–1876.
71. K. A. P. Sandiford, *Cricket and the Victorians*, Aldershot, 1994, which is also the definitive account of nineteenth-century cricket.
72. S. R. Platt at Werneth CC AGM, *Oldham Evening Chronicle*, 1 Nov. 1876.
73. For more on the organised churches' relationship to the working classes, see K. S.

Inglis, *The Churches and the Working Class in Victorian England*, London, 1963 and Brian Harrison, 'Religion and Recreation in Nineteenth Century England', *Past and Present*, No. 38, 1967.

74. Reprinted in *Yorkshire Evening Post*, 12 Dec. 1903.

75. See the *Wakefield Express*, 2 and 23 Nov. and 14 Dec. 1872.

76. The phrase is A. W. Pullin's, otherwise known as 'Old Ebor', the self-appointed doyen of Yorkshire cricket and football writing and, as the son of a clergyman, a vigorous advocate of muscular Christianity. A summary of Leeds Parish Church clergy's views on the importance of games can be found in a sermon of the Reverend Maurice Ponsonby in *The Leeds Parish Church Magazine*, Dec. 1879, pp. 311–12.

77. *Yorkshire Post*, 11 March 1876.

78. See G. H. Cooper, *Spen Valley Rugby Football Reminiscences*, Cleckheaton, 1920.

79. *Yorkshire Evening Post*, 9 Feb. 1902.

80. Wakefield Trinity FC cash book, quoted in *Yorkshire Evening Post*, 1 Nov. 1903. See also *Athletic News,* 23 March 1877.

81. A. G. Guillemard, 'The Past Season', *Football Annual,* 1877.

82. For accounts of the formation of the YCFC see Ch. 20 in Marshall, and *Yorkshire Evening Post*, 12 Jan. 1901.

83. *Yorkshire Evening Post*, 12 Jan. 1901.

84. *Athletic News*, 22 Dec. 1876 and *Yorkshire Evening Post*, 1 Dec. 1900.

85. *Yorkshire Post*, 26 Dec. 1877.

86. *Yorkshire Post*, 31 Dec. 1877. For an account of Halifax's winning season, see *The Yorkshireman Football Number*, 1890.

87. *Yorkshire Post*, 14 April 1879.

88. Sam Duckitt reminiscing in *Yorkshire Evening Post*, 9 Feb. 1901.

89. *Yorkshire Evening Post*, 12 Jan.1901 and 16 Nov. 1901.

90. 'An Old Trinity Stager', *The Yorkshireman Football Number*, March 1891. A rough translation of this would be: 'Rufus had started to develop nicely as a player when he fell out with some of the Trinity chaps and became friendly with Halifax. Don't go jumping to conclusions. I didn't say the Cup started the kidnapping business. Only this is the first case I know of and it was just to help Halifax win the Cup for the first time. Two and two, you know, make four.' For alternative explanations of Ward's move, see *Yorkshire Evening Post*, 9 July 1901 and 1 Nov. 1902.

91. *The Yorkshireman Football Number*, 1890.

92. 'An Old Trinity Stager', *The Yorkshireman Football Number*, March 1891. This translates as 'I copped [caught] football fever at the same time as many hundreds more did when the Yorkshire Cup was first played for thirteen years ago, and what's more – or less if anything – I've had it ever since.'

2

The Coming of the Working Class: 1879–1886

Beginning with the Ten Hours Act in 1847, the working class had slowly clawed out periods of free time from their employers. In many areas 'Saint Monday', whereby workers would simply not go into work or not work at full capacity on Mondays, was an informal method of reducing the heavy burden of long hours of factory work on working people, but the needs of disciplined, ordered production meant that such informal practices were gradually suppressed and, in effect, replaced by the Saturday half-holiday. In 1850 textile workers were granted a two-o'clock-end to work on Saturdays, which was further reduced to one o'clock in 1874. A year later the August Bank Holiday was institutionalised by an act of parliament. The Saturday half-day holiday became the norm for most, but not all, trades during the economic boom of the early 1870s.[1] This upturn in economic fortunes also saw working-class standards of living begin to rise, providing working-class people with not only the time but also the means to enjoy it, effectively laying the basis for the growth of most modern forms of working-class leisure over the following years.[2] Along with the music hall and seaside trips, football of both varieties became a focus of interest for those with new time to spend, as Moses Heap, a Lancashire cotton spinner, wrote: 'For a while we did not know how to pass our time away. Before it had been all bed and work; now in place of 70 hours a week we had 55½. It became a practice, mostly on Saturdays, to play football and cricket, which had never been done before.'[3]

As we saw in the previous chapter, working-class players had begun to enter the rugby game in the late 1870s, at roughly the same time as the beginning of the Yorkshire Cup. It appears that the first player without a public school background to be selected for the Yorkshire county side was Wakefield Trinity three-quarter Harry Hayley, who made his representative debut against Middlesex in 1878 while still a pupil teacher at a local Wesleyan school.[4] The rapid advancement of working-class players in the game was acknowledged in 1880 by RFU secretary Arthur Guillemard, who somewhat haughtily pointed out that 'the recent foundation of a large number of clubs in the North has resulted in the drafting into club fifteens of a large proportion of tyros, who may know how to drop and place kick, but are unlearned in the various points of the game'.[5] This 'diffusion'[6] of the game down from the middle classes was made possible not only by the increase in working-class leisure time but also by the relative reduction in the class conflict which had prevailed in England since the defeat of the Chartists following 1848. It was a period of 'forty years of slumber' for the English working class, to quote Engels, who described the suppression of previous antipathies in the decades up to the 1880s:

> A gradual change came over the relations between both classes. The Factory Acts, once the bugbear of all manufacturers, were not only willingly submitted to, but their expansion into acts regulating almost all trades, was tolerated. Trades unions, lately considered inventions of the devil himself, were now petted and patronised as perfectly legitimate institutions and as useful means of spreading sound economical doctrines among the workers. Even strikes, than which nothing had been more nefarious up to 1848, were now gradually found out to be occasionally very useful, especially when provoked by the masters themselves, at their own time.[7]

This did not mean that class conflict had been abolished or that the leisure pursuits of the classes were interchangeable, nor did it mean that harmonious relations between the classes were the norm. Practically, it meant that the reduction in social tensions created a greater possibility for members of different classes to play sports together, certainly when compared to the pre- and post-1848 periods. In rugby, this process manifested itself in factory owners and factory workers playing the same game and occasionally in the same teams. The Tyldesley side which won the West Lancashire Cup in 1888 included eight colliery workers and two sons of colliery owners.[8] A flavour of this unusual social mix was captured by Richard Davies, one of the founders of Dalton FC, near Barrow in Furness: 'The occupations [of the players in the 1880s] were varied in the extreme – professional men, mechanics, miners, carpenters, town clerks, butchers, masons, clerks, labourers, landlords, chemists and schoolmasters.'[9] This lowering of barriers between the classes was essentially transient and, in the eyes of rugby's middle-class leadership, dependent on the new working-class participants accepting their leadership and set of values. So while the massive upsurge in rugby's popularity among the working classes of Lancashire and Yorkshire was initially welcomed by the game's rulers, it was also accompanied by tensions and conflicts over the direction the game was taking.

If the growth in leisure time and a reduction of class tensions were the culture media through which the downward diffusion of rugby took place, what were the agencies which facilitated this change? The Yorkshire Cup undoubtedly inspired the formation of countless new clubs; at the beginning of the 1882–83 season the *Yorkshire Post* reported that it had received 120 fixture cards from teams in the region.[10] There were doubtless many others who lacked the means or the ambition to print such cards. By 1886 most large urban regions in west and east Yorkshire also had their own local cup competitions with which to fan the flames of football fever, as did the west Lancashire area, against the wishes of the Lancashire rugby union authorities. Yet it appears that few clubs were formed spontaneously by working-class people – rather, they generally made use of existing clubs or existing recreational channels, such as the church, the workplace or the pub. Many teams were also formed on the basis of local streets and districts, although a district name often concealed a link with a pub or church. Stuart Barlow had identified over seventy such teams in the Rochdale area in 1880s.[11] Typical of this type of side was Hull Southcoates, formed by a local shopkeeper, publican and board school teacher, and based on the Courteney Street area of east Hull. They survived for a decade competing against other local Hull sides and were 'invariably composed of horny-handed sons of toil.' Looking back at their history, an old player proudly remarked that the side had fulfilled at least one useful function, 'and that was in training the manual labourer and in educating his mate to take an interest in the game.'[12]

The spread of church clubs based on muscular Christian principles accelerated in the 1880s, as the clergy sought to capitalise on the football boom and set up their own teams. This growth was not limited to Anglicans; Roman Catholic churches also began teams, such as Wakefield St Austin's which was set up as an alternative to Wakefield Trinity. The names of junior clubs such as Dewsbury Shamrocks and Leeds Catholic Institute also demonstrate the non-sectarian nature of football's popularity. It is also evident that many of these clubs quickly slipped their bonds with the spon-soring church. When the Yorkshire Church Temperance Challenge Shield was started in 1887, one of its rules was that players must be bona fide members of a church, church school or Anglican temperance society, no doubt in order to ensure that the participants' enthusiasm for football was matched by their devotion to the scriptures.[13] Indeed, it was not unusual for churchmen, after having formed a football club, to lose their enthusiasm for the game when faced with the less than Corinthian zealotry of their new recruits, as a Bradford curate discovered after forming a youth side and suffering 'complaints and reproaches from the mothers of his protégés about black eyes, sore bones and all the other luxuries accompanying the game. He was so intimidated that he now wants to back out, but these exuberant youths, having tasted the sweets of victory, insist on going on.'[14] As working-class influence grew, it seems that many ostensibly church clubs were operating under little more than a flag of convenience, with only minimal involvement from the clergy. This certainly became the case with the Leeds Parish Church club and it was also true at a lower level, as the superintendents of Nether Green Sunday School in Leeds admitted after an inquiry into the violent on-field activities of their football club:

> We have not kept a sufficiently close connection with and oversight of the football club which uses the name of the school. Matters have been left too much to the management of the players themselves, with the result that, contrary to the original intention of the officers of the school, the team is largely composed of those who have no connection with it. We feel that it would be incumbent on us to reorganise the club and bring it under more immediate control.[15]

Similar problems affected sides formed for their employees by companies. The most famous works' club was probably St Helens Recreation, formed as the football section of Pilkington Brothers glassworks' recreation club. For a subscription of one penny a week, the recreation club provided football, cricket, bowls and library facilities, but that provision was tightly controlled by the company, who, for example, refused to allow the side to participate in the West Lancashire and Border Towns cup, despite the desire of their players to do so. As captain Monsey Parr explained, Pilkingtons' management 'said we'd better give up cup ties and such things; and you must do as your masters want or else shut up shop … Th' masters don't like us drinkin' and they won't allow committee meetings to be held in public houses.' Indeed, the side was viewed as the personal property of the Pilkington family with established members of the side sometimes having to step down when a Pilkington son decided he fancied a game.[16] More fundamental problems faced the men of Wakefield Glassworks, who, after having made an impressive start to their inaugural season, were forced to disband after their employers decided that they could no longer afford to allow men to take time off work to play.[17] In Huddersfield, a number of employers ran their own clubs, such as Charles Brooke's Meltham Mills' team, or actively helped to subsidise the local junior sides.[18] Other clubs soon broke the link with their benefactors. For example, the apprentice boiler-makers who formed Kingston Amateurs in the west of Hull in 1882, quickly left the control of their employers to eventually become Hull

Kingston Rovers, the city's second senior side. Even more successful was the club formed in 1878 for employees of Barkers' Mill, one of only two factories in the village of Thornes, just outside Wakefield. Although the company donated a field in which to play, those employees wishing to make use of it had to subscribe tuppence in order that the club might buy a ball. Nevertheless, the team advanced so quickly, thanks in large part to the tactical genius of warehouseman and three-quarter Harry Wigglesworth, that in 1882 they produced possibly the greatest upset ever in English rugby by defeating five-to-one-on favourites Wakefield Trinity in the final of the Yorkshire Cup.[19]

Other than the church and the factory, the pub was the most important medium for the entry of working-class players into rugby. Of the forty-five clubs listed in the 1881–82 *Yorkshire Football Handbook*, only five did not have their club headquarters in a pub. By 1885–86 the number of clubs listed had risen to eighty but those without a pub as their headquarters remained at five.[20] While some of these clubs may have chosen pubs for their convenience, the growing importance of the pub in promoting football can be gauged from the fact that, of 20 secretaries of Yorkshire clubs listed in the *Football Annual* between 1877 and 1884, four were identifiable as publicans or beer retailers. Of the rest, six were private residents, two were factory owners, two were textile merchants and the rest comprised of an overseer, a commission agent, a wholesale grocer, a retail grocer, a commercial traveller and a furniture dealer.[21]

The pub had long been the focus for recreational activities in working-class areas and, in particular, the pub landlord often played the role of the recreational entrepreneur, organising sports and sponsoring contests. Unsurprisingly, therefore, pub landlords were not slow to capitalise on the football boom, especially those in possession of land adjoining their pub. Typical, if somewhat hopeful, was a Mr S. Boniface, a licensee at Woodchurch near Dewsbury, who fenced off a football ground behind his pub and 'is now anxiously waiting for the thousands to flock to this place whenever he turned his showy colours on to the field'.[22] History does not record whether, like Shoeless Joe Jackson in *Field of Dreams*, players, or indeed spectators, came to the field. Initially more successful was landlord of the Cemetery Tavern in Hunslet, Mr Cusworth, who in 1883 offered the cricket field behind his pub as a winter pitch for rugby after an unsuccessful foray into soccer. Two local sides Excelsior and Albion merged under the auspices of Woodhouse Hill cricket club to play on the pitch as Hunslet FC. Support for the team grew so quickly that two years after their formation they took over £100 in gate money at a Yorkshire Cup tie in which they defeated Leeds St John's – and Cusworth promptly raised the rent to an unheard of

£365 per year. Although he later relented and asked for only £200, the Hunslet committee decided that if they were going to pay such an astronomical sum, they might as well move and find a ground of their own.[23] A similar falling-out occurred between Woodhouse FC in Leeds and the landlord of their local pub, The Swan with Two Necks, who sued them for non-payment of £39 for beer and cigars he supplied, contrary to RFU regulations, to the players after matches.[24]

Unlike the church and works teams, where football was largely seen as an adjunct to moral or business imperatives, it was in the environment of the pub that working-class cultural practices came to the fore. In particular, sport for money – and for food prizes such as geese and legs of mutton – was an integral part of working-class cultural life across the North of England. Shooting competitions were especially popular. The Crown Hotel in Dewsbury offered '£10 to be shot for at four birds each' in December 1879, one of fourteen pubs offering cash prizes for shooting rabbits, sparrows or pigeons on one weekend. £20 prize money was on offer to the winner of a contest between H. Moorhouse and J. Woodhouse to shoot 21 sparrows.[25] Open foot-racing contests were common; a typical example being at the British Oak Inn at Chickenley Heath near Dewsbury, which offered £7 10s to the winner of a 137 yards race, competitors paying a one shilling entrance fee.[26] Dog racing for money was also highly popular, as was cock fighting; a challenge match between cocks from Chester and Ulverston being fought for £50 a battle.[27] On a larger scale, 1,200 people gathered in 1879 at the Black Horse Hotel at Tyldesley, near Manchester, to watch a wrestling match which was being contested for £25.[28] One of the leading sports in working-class communities at this time was knur and spel, sometimes known as Northern Spel. A long-handled club, similar to those used in golf, was used to knock a wooden ball into the air and, in an almost simultaneous movement, hit it as far into the distance as possible. The best players were able to fire the knur, as the ball was known, between 250 and 300 yards. The sport attracted large crowds and substantial cash prizes were offered to winners of competitions. For example, on one unexceptional weekend in February 1880, J. Wade beat M. Smith at Halifax to win £40, whilst H. Wainwright and R. Beresford battled it out at Barnsley for £50.[29] Needless to say, gambling was an attendant part of all these pastimes.

Consequently, as working-class men took up the rugby game, they brought with them a range of cultural practices which were based on the necessity of selling their labour power in whichever way was the most lucrative, including the utilisation of sporting prowess. 'Spoort's gooid lads, but brass is better,' was how a dialect story of the time summed up this

A NEW PLAYER.

LITTLE AITCHLESS, *a Bradford limb of the law, goes to the Bradford v. Oxford University Football Match, and, hearing all the partisans of the University shouting "'Varsity, 'Varsity,"* asks another limb of the law : "I say, old fellow, which of the players is the fellow called "'Varsity'?' Seems to be a big favourite anyhow."

Across the social divide 1: the cross-class appeal of rugby and its subsequent confusions are captured by this cartoon from *Toby, the Yorkshire Tyke*.

attitude.[30] A greater clash with the ideals of public school sport could not be imagined, especially for those who sought to utilise football as a medium for moral improvement. The centrality of the cash nexus in working-class sport also gave rise to the apparently paradoxical situation of working-class players supporting the operation of market forces in rugby and capitalist mill owners opposing them. In the main, the middle-class leaders of the game saw the working-class professional sportsman as a form of prostitute: 'We shall always view with the gravest apprehensions the introduction of the paid element into a game which up to the present time has been played for sport – or rather for the love of sport – alone,' warned the *Yorkshire Post*.[31] The popularity of the game, and especially the Yorkshire Cup, was therefore viewed with a degree of ambiguity by its leaders. This was both because the sport which they had learnt 'with their Latin grammar' at school was no longer exclusively theirs, but also because increasing working-class involvement was changing the nature of the game itself – as was acknowledged by the secretary of Goole FC in 1882, who wrote to arrange a fixture with York and reassuringly pointed out that 'as our club is pretty nearly free from the working-class element, you have nothing to fear about a rough or noisy game.'[32] The national leadership of the Rugby Union itself had long expressed doubts about the popularity of cup competitions, turning down an offer from the Royal Military Academy to supply a trophy for a national cup competition in 1875. Rowland Hill, the secretary of the RFU, believed that cup ties caused 'an evil spirit to arise, and that sometimes men are influenced more by the desire to win rather than to play the game in the true spirit.'[33] Arthur Guillemard echoed these sentiments in 1880, pointing out that 'the fact that by far the greatest number of disputes occur in the northern counties shows that by the minor clubs the game is far from being properly understood. There is also a great deal of partisanship afloat, and the umpires have by no means a pleasant time of it on occasions.'[34]

The threat which cup competitions represented to the exclusivity of the game was widely understood. Participation in a knock-out cup meant that a club could no longer choose its opponents and the prospect of defeat by ostensibly lesser teams helped to animate the socially exclusive clubs' opposition to cup ties. In Yorkshire, the core of the original Leeds club, now known as Leeds Athletic, transformed themselves into the Yorkshire Wanderers in 1881, refused to play in cup competitions and generally restricted their fixtures to exclusive middle-class clubs. A series of heavy defeats led to them disbanding in 1883. The Rugbeian leaders of Hull FC also gave up the game after a string of crushing losses to the socially open Hull White Star, against whom they had declined to play for some seasons previously, in 1881.[35] The ex-public school leaders of York FC underwent a similar loss of faith in their club, merging in 1882 with their conquerors, York Melbourne, a side 'composed of strong burly workmen, who gradually but surely made a better name for good exciting matches than the old York club.'[36] The YCFC committee even discussed abandoning the Yorkshire Cup in 1880, when its instigator, A. E. Hudson, spoke in favour of its suspension.[37] Although it was decided to continue, doubts remained. In 1882 Dewsbury, Halifax and Huddersfield declined to enter that year's competition. Huddersfield also boycotted the following season's competition and Bradford's annual meetings perennially discussed withdrawing, but the cup exerted such a powerful draw for both players and spectators it was difficult for a club not to compete and retain credibility.[38]

In Lancashire, despite several attempts by clubs to force the county leadership to emulate Yorkshire, the controlling Manchester and Liverpool clubs steadfastly opposed cup football and became notorious for refusing fixtures with clubs they felt to be socially inferior; in Manchester's case this was especially directed against local rivals Salford and Swinton. After years of attempting to arrange a match with their illustrious neighbours, Swinton were finally granted the honour in 1878. In a match that was as significant for Manchester rugby as Blackburn Olympic's 1883 FA Cup final defeat of Old Etonians was for soccer, Swinton, nicknamed the Colliers, won by a try to nil. The disquiet about the stranglehold of Lancashire county rugby by the Liverpool/Manchester duopoly came to a head in March 1881 when Broughton's William Bell called for other clubs to be involved in selecting the county side. Manchester refused the request point-blank and declined to meet with their critics. In May, twelve clubs therefore formed a Lancashire Football Union and arranged representative matches with Lanarkshire and Midland Counties. Sensing that their control of the game could slip away, Manchester eventually reached an arrangement with the rebels in December and the Lancashire County Football Club was formed. Given the nature of the agreement it could hardly be called a compromise: for two years, Manchester were automatically entitled to the positions of president, vice-president, secretary and treasurer, and Liverpool were guaranteed two committee seats. To cap it off, all home county fixtures were to be played at Manchester's Whalley Range ground.[39]

At the time, this refusal to countenance cup competitions and broaden the leadership of Lancashire rugby seemed to have little consequence. Rugby's popularity towered over soccer in the North. For example, in the first week in November 1876 the *Athletic News* published the results of 50 rugby matches and just two association games which had taken place the previous weekend in Lancashire and Yorkshire. At the beginning of the 1877–78 season its directory of football club secretaries listed 141 rugby clubs in Cheshire, Lancashire, Yorkshire, the Northeast and the Northwest, six association clubs, one club playing both codes and thirty-nine playing Sheffield Association rules. While this was clearly an underestimation of the number of active soccer clubs in the region – it named just two clubs in Lancashire – it underlined the lead which rugby had established. Even as late as 1882, the fixtures for the weekend of 11 February listed 133 rugby and 39 soccer matches in the two Pennine counties.[40]

Indicatively, when the *Manchester Guardian* discussed the growth of the two football codes in the same year, it felt compelled to describe the association game, but not the more familiar rugby, for its readers: 'In East Lancashire the dribbling game (kicking the ball along the ground when running) only is cared for.'[41]

Such dominance was not to last. Although at its formation in 1878 the Lancashire FA had just twenty-eight clubs, the overwhelming majority coming from the three towns of Blackburn, Bolton and Darwen, it grew rapidly because of the appeal of the Lancashire FA Cup competition, begun in 1879, and its plethora of local competitions. More importantly, the success of Blackburn's Olympic and Rovers in the FA Cup had demonstrated the nationwide interest it was possible to create through success in a national cup competition and, given the lack of any countervailing attractions in the rugby game, the impact of Blackburn's success on its neighbouring towns was too great to withstand. Preston had been a rugby town at the beginning of the decade but, following the example of Preston North End's conversion in 1881, virtually all its football clubs had switched to the dribbling code by the end of the 1881–82 season. Burnley FC too had begun as a rugby club before changing codes in 1882 and Chorley FC made the same switch in 1883.[42] In fact, many of the key personalities in Lancashire soccer had begun their sporting careers as rugby players, including Scotsman Fergus Suter, possibly one of the first two soccer players to be paid for playing. Other prominent ex-rugbyites included Preston's William Sudell, a key mover in bringing professionalism to soccer, Y. T. Ritson, the founder of Bolton and District FA, and future Football League presidents Charles Sutcliffe and John McKenna and secretary Tom Charnley.[43] While many of them will have swapped their allegiances because of the association game's greater simplicity and openness of play, the stranglehold of the patrician Liverpool and Manchester clubs over rugby in the region may well have proved a disincentive to the entrepreneurial spirit of men like Sudell and McKenna, who, unlike the leadership of Lancashire rugby, were from the less socially exalted echelons of the middle classes and were envious of the prestige that cup competitions and imported players had brought to the Blackburn area. The success of Lancashire clubs in the FA Cup and the civic recognition it brought to towns was the springboard from which soccer became able to overtake and eventually dwarf rugby, as 'The Free Critic' wrote in 1893: 'Up to 1877 there was not a large amount of interest taken in [association] football so far as the North was concerned, and it was not until Darwen made their journey to play the Old Etonians in the English cup ties that we in Lancashire commenced to think of popularising the game.'[44]

By the mid-1880s the growth of soccer in Lancashire had become a cause for concern and at the 1886 LCFC annual general meeting, a number of speakers expressed alarm at its progress. Werneth FC, based near Oldham, had proposed without success that a Lancashire Cup be instituted, modelled on the Yorkshire Cup, in order to rekindle interest in the game.[45] In Liverpool an association cup competition had attracted 20 teams in its inaugural season in 1886 and had shaken the popularity of rugby in one of its bastions. The fear was that Liverpool might go the same way as Preston. Werneth reiterated their call for a cup competition the following spring, their delegate to the LCFC meeting stating that 'the association game was progressing rapidly and [that] the only way to help the rugby game in Lancashire was by a cup competition.'[46] Yet again, the county authorities turned their faces against this move to popularise the sport. But behind this apparent stubbornness lay the hope that soccer's advances could help reassert the social exclusivity of rugby:

> In some districts ... the rugby game is losing ground among the working class and association spreading in its place, owing to the pecuniary advantages to be reaped from the latter game. The loss of followers to the grand old game is regrettable, yet looking at the present state of all professional sports, we cannot but think that this possible loss is far preferable to legalising professionalism.[47]

MONSTER CROWDS AND HOWLING MOBS

As working-class players came into the game, so too did working-class spectators. We have already seen the first five-figure crowds for football matches in Yorkshire in the late 1870s and this growth in crowd sizes continued unabated in the 1880s. It was estimated that in excess of 50,000 people saw the sixteen first round Yorkshire Cup games in the 1882–83 season, with five-figure gates being recorded for the later rounds at Dewsbury and Halifax. The following season, estimates suggested that over 100,000 had seen the first round matches, with the Dewsbury v. Wakefield Trinity tie attracting more than 15,000 spectators paying nearly £354 to get into the ground. This was, proudly boasted the *Dewsbury Reporter*, 'a larger attendance than has ever before been present at a match in Yorkshire.'[48] A few weeks later, the same paper drew attention to the fact that the Blackburn Rovers v. Queen's Park 1884 Cup Final drew only 10,000, while 15,000 had gathered at Halifax to see Bradford's semi-final defeat of Batley: 'It will be noticed that the Yorkshire monster attendances are far in excess of those of the metropolis with its millions of inhabitants.'[49] The crowds continued to grow in subsequent years, 20,000 jamming into Bradford's Park Avenue ground to watch the 1885 cup tie against Hull and 14,000 (with 3,000 locked out) packing Cardigan Fields at Leeds to see the 1886 final between Halifax and Bradford. On a smaller, albeit equally noteworthy, scale were the 5,000 spectators at Thornes, near Wakefield, who watched the local side play Dewsbury in 1883 – despite the fact that, according to the 1881 census, the population of Thornes was less than 3,500! The growth of the game in West Yorkshire was such that the *Football Annual* for 1881 devoted a special chapter to the game in Yorkshire, in which it claimed that 'Yorkshire can boast of being "second to none" in its support of the popular winter pastime.'[50] By 1887 the *Yorkshire Post* could speak confidently of 'the million who follow the game in these parts' and YCFC secretary Arthur Hudson calculated that a total of 350,000 people had attended the 63 ties in that year's Yorkshire Cup competition.[51] Lacking the focus of a county cup competition, attendances in Lancashire were slower to take off but their rapid growth can be seen in the rise in gate money takings of Salford and Warrington during the early to mid-1880s. In 1883 Salford took £160 in gate receipts, rising to £570 four years later, an increase of over 256 per cent. Warrington's growth was even more remarkable, rising from just £34 to slightly more than £1,234 in the same period, due in no small part to the introduction of the West Lancashire and Border Towns cup competition in 1886.[52]

This rise in attendances reflected rugby football's increasing popularity among all sections of society, not just among the working class. Football, particularly during cup competitions, had become a focus for outpourings of civic pride and intertown rivalry which transcended class and political divisions. Describing Warrington's triumphant return from Liverpool with the West Lancashire Cup, the local newspaper stated that 'We have witnessed many processions and receptions in Warrington, but with respect to excitement, enthusiasm and numbers, all have been eclipsed by the monstre [sic] which took place on Saturday evening.'[53] There is no data available for us to determine the exact social composition of the rugby crowd but descriptions of crowds at this time all note the wide social spectrum of spectators at matches.[54] Reporting on the 1884 Bradford versus Manningham derby game, an observer noted that amongst the crowd were 'clergy and ministers, pastors and deacons, very good people and some that were only so-so; lawyers, doctors, magistrates, tinkers and tailors, soldiers and sailors, tag, rag and bobtail.'[55] Further evidence of the cross-class appeal of football can be seen in the behaviour and organisation of the crowds, as this 1881 report of a football crowd in Bradford describes:

On the road near, an endless stream of people goes flowing on. There are enthusiasts munching the last mouthfuls of their dinners and speeding to be in time for the 'kickoff'. From all quarters and directions do they come. Old men and maidens, matrons and children, and young men of every degree. Already the lower walls of the field are surmounted by an unbroken line of spectators, who form a sort of human railing, and, regardless of the drizzle and biting wind, and the somewhat uncertain character of their seats, amuse themselves with pipes, occasional bottles, and the interchange of not too delicate pleasantries with passers-by, while the belligerents in the grandstand strip for the fray.[56]

One piece of evidence which does help us gain an insight into the backgrounds of supporters – rather than spectators – of the game is an 1887 list of subscribers to a fund to commemorate Wakefield Trinity's fourth triumph in the Yorkshire Cup. Supporters of the club were asked to donate upwards of a shilling and the proceeds were used to buy mementoes which were presented to members of the team.[57] The picture which emerges in Appendix Table A.1 is ample testimony to the broad support of rugby across class and occupational lines. Of the 277 subscribers, 198 are traceable today. Of those contributing, 31 per cent came from the gentry and professional classes, while 43 per cent came from the lower section of the lower middle classes, particularly the pub and shop-owning sections. Fully 14 per cent had some connection with the drinks trade. Only 16 per cent were manual workers, either skilled or semi-skilled, yet none appears to have been unskilled. Given the identification, even by 1887, of the game with manual workers, this may seem surprising, but by asking for money over and above admission charges, the fund would automatically exclude members of the poorer sections of the working classes who attended games.

That many spectators were cautious about paying money to clubs can be seen from the common last-minute rushes to get into grounds. Particularly when visiting teams were travelling some distance, the vagaries of the transport system and the unwillingness of some players to make long journeys meant that crowds often waited for confirmation of the opposing team's arrival before parting with their admission money. Financial disaster seemed to be looming at the opening of Wigan's new ground in 1886 when few people had paid admission before kick off time, but as the *Wigan Observer* pointed out, 'It is quite evident that Wigan people are wise in their time and like to see a team turn up before going on the ground, consequently when the [Wakefield] Trinity players arrived in the town there was a great rush to the field.'[58] At most grounds, the cost of attendance for first-class games was usually 6d, with boys being admitted for 3d and women free. Admittance to enclosures or grandstands, which were being erected with increasing frequency at this time, more often than not cost one shilling, the price differential helping both to regulate demand and preserve social distinctions among the crowd. For lower ranking games prices were cheaper: the two junior sides sharing Manningham's Valley Parade ground charged just 3d and 2d to get in. The price of admission was often a controversial topic, and as early as 1880 there were complaints that an admission charge of one shilling for the North versus South match at Halifax 'does not give the working class a chance of patronising the match.'[59] Dewsbury opportunistically doubled their prices for the visit of Bradford in 1886 and suffered a disappointingly low turnout. They did not repeat the price increase. Nevertheless, enterprising supporters were always keen to cut the cost of attendance. Fake Bradford season tickets were discovered in 1886 and many club members indulged in the practice of dropping their season tickets over the perimeter walls of a ground to friends outside, who could then enter for free. Led by Leeds Parish Church, clubs eventually got wise to such activities and introduced a match voucher system for season ticket holders.[60]

For many spectators, the cost of going to a match included travel to a game. From the earliest days of the Yorkshire Cup, when Halifax supporters made the journey to Bradford by train, spectators travelling between towns to support their sides had become commonplace. By 1880 this was such a regular occurrence that a minor controversy broke out when the London and North-Western Railway Company refused to run special trains from towns in Lancashire and Yorkshire for the Roses game at Huddersfield. The ensuing letters of complaint to local newspapers caused them to reconsider their stance and trains were laid on for the North versus South match at Halifax later that season.[61] Bradford in particular were quick to spot the commercial opportunity provided by supporters keen to travel, their regular excursions to clubs in Manchester costing two shillings and threepence for return rail journeys. For one shilling, enthusiastic Huddersfield supporters could, in 1886, travel by train to Leeds to see their side take on Leeds St John's.[62] For those with the time and money to follow their side further afield, Bradford's 1884 journey to Cambridge University was charged at nineteen shillings and elevenpence, while their 1886 tour to London and the Oxbridge Universities cost twenty-five shillings and ninepence.[63] Although it is impossible to estimate the numbers going to away games regularly, it is clear that for important cup matches, travelling supporters could be numbered in four figures. 'Thousands' of Hull supporters were said to have journeyed to Bradford for the 1885 Yorkshire

Cup first round tie, while Halifax laid on six railway coaches for their match at Park Avenue the following year. At the beginning of 1886 it was noted that many West Riding pubs had formed savings clubs to enable patrons to pay for their trip to the forthcoming Yorkshire Cup final. Even an end of season friendly saw St Helens Recreation take two train loads of supporters to Warrington.[64] The scale of regular travelling support can also be judged by the disappointment felt by the local press that only a 100 Dewsbury supporters went with their side to a key game at Halifax.[65] For those who could not afford to travel with their sides, town centre shops and pubs would post regular telegrams reporting the play and results, often as regularly as every ten minutes. Sometimes the crowds awaiting the telegrams approached those at the matches, most notably on the day of finals. Waiting for telegrams to be posted during the Manningham versus Batley Yorkshire Cup final in 1884 in the centre of Bradford, the assembled crowd found themselves harangued by the Salvation Army as it tried to march through the town. The outcome was inevitable: 'Natural result – a collision in which the Army suffered a reverse with the loss of their flag, which was torn up. A football crowd is not to be trifled with.'[66]

It is important to note that football spectating was not an exclusively male activity; women were an integral part of the football crowds of this period. As far back as the first Yorkshire versus Lancashire game in 1870, the presence of female spectators was deemed noteworthy by the press and this continued throughout the 1880s. In 1884 *The Yorkshireman* suggested that one-quarter of a 5,000 crowd at the Manningham versus Hull game were women. The numbers of women attending games may be gauged by the decision of the Bradford committee to start charging women for admission to the grandstand, unless accompanied by a club member, suggesting that some women attended matches without male company.[67] While women's attendance at matches may have been encouraged by the fact that most grounds allowed women into matches free, it is clear that many women were active spectators and keen supporters of their chosen teams. This was pointed out by a journalist at the 1883 game between Yorkshire and Cheshire: 'Don't imagine that all the spectators were men, for they were not. Indeed, the female element was very largely represented and the comments from this portion of the gathering were as numerous and as critical as those of their brothers, husbands and fathers.'[68] In 1885 it was reported that the Bradford captain, Fred Bonsor, had received a letter from 'young ladies' in Wakefield accusing his side of cowardice for their refusal to play Trinity that season.[69] Football clearly appealed not only to young women either: 'It is somewhat surprising that so many mature matrons patronise the sport, and what is even more surprising is the extent of their knowledge of the game and the pitch of enthusiasm to which they work themselves up.'[70] When Pontefract returned home after winning the Yorkshire Cup in 1891, one correspondent noted that the crowd contained a 'great number of the fair sex. Old girls and new, young and pretty, old and, er, well, er, respected.'[71] Although there was a chauvinistic attitude to the reporting of women's involvement as football spectators, often implying that it was somehow unfeminine, that same year the football columnist of *The Yorkshireman* was moved to protest about a 'men only' meeting for Keighley FC 'comrades': 'What about the ladies who patronise the Highfield Lane enclosure? Are they not comrades as well?'[72] Women's behaviour at matches often did not meet Victorian ideals of womanhood, the chairman of Swinton criticising female supporters for their 'bad manners and rowdiness' in 1888. Nor were women averse to participating in hooliganism. After winning a cup tie at Horbury in 1884, the Batley team found themselves being pelted with red hot coals by a woman as they

In the 1880s, women were prominent in northern rugby crowds and were often more than willing to make their presence felt (from *The Yorkshireman*).

left the ground.[73] Yet despite an obvious high level of interest, there is no record of women actually playing the game at this time.

It is also clear that previously exclusive clubs, such as Bradford and Huddersfield, began to open the doors of membership wider. This was spurred on by the growing importance of clubs in a town's civic life and their desire to expand their influence, not to mention the financial benefits which subscription monies brought to clubs: thus many made considerable efforts to recruit new members. Bradford doubled their membership from 1,271 to 2,500 in the three years to 1888, despite the fact that membership cost ten shillings.[74] In preparation for the opening of their new Valley Parade ground, Manningham offered the prize of free membership for seven years for the recruitment of the most members, which was won by a Mr Jackson who recruited 94 new adherents, the next best being 35. This turned out to be a highly successful promotion as it doubled the club's membership to over 1,200. The benefits of membership were usually free entrance to all home club matches and a vote at general meetings, although it seems the former was the motivation to join for most people – for example, less than half of Bradford's membership bothered to attend their 1888 special meeting called to discuss the vital issue of whether to withdraw from the following year's Yorkshire Cup.[75] This indifference to administrative workings was acknowledged by a number of clubs, which, in order to attract more working-class members yet maintain social differentials, introduced tiers of membership. Salford, whose membership grew from just over a hundred in 1883 to over 2,100 in 1890, had four levels of membership: voting honorary members, voting playing members, non-voting season ticket holders and non-voting youths, paying six shillings, four shillings, five shillings, and two shillings and sixpence respectively.[76] Such distinctions often led to resentment, as Halifax discovered when they distinguished between subscribers, who paid £1 per season, and members, who paid half that. This came to a head at their 1887 annual meeting when the chief topic of debate was 'whether the "top nobs" are to be allowed the exclusive use of the large and handsome pavilion' on the ground.[77] This influx of lower-class members into clubs had the overall effect of diluting the control of the game by the upper-middle classes.

The behaviour of football crowds in the North became an increasing cause for concern for rugby's leadership throughout the early 1880s. The prevalence of betting at grounds was a particular source of great disquiet among those who led the game. As early as 1883 it was noted that at the Dewsbury versus Halifax Yorkshire Cup tie 'the amount of betting was enormous' with hundreds of pounds changing hands, and many contemporary reports point to the presence of bookmakers at most senior

FOOTBALL FREAKS.—No. 2.

THE REFEREE OF TO-DAY!   THE REFEREE OF THE FUTURE.

Even in 1895, the referee's lot was not a happy one (from *Toby the Yorkshire Tyke*).

THE COMING OF THE WORKING CLASS

grounds.[78] When Halifax pulled out of the 1882 Yorkshire Cup competition, they cited as a reason 'betting men' who had wanted to see their players lamed, and both Wakefield Trinity and Batley complained that book-makers had tried to influence their players, although no proof was ever produced in any of these cases.[79] At the end of the decade the Yorkshire committee threatened to take legal action against any bookmakers found plying their trade at matches, but, while betting was undoubtedly a common feature at matches, the paucity of the evidence produced by its opponents would seem to indicate that their concern had something of the character of an ongoing moral panic. Writing in the *Clarion*, former Salford and Swinton player A. A. Sutherland pointed to his journeys throughout the football grounds of the North and argued that: 'Of course there are times when a fair amount of money may change hands, but that it would be worth the while of any bookmaker to "square" the players, I am inclined to doubt. The matter is hardly to be taken into serious consideration when discussing the dangers to the game.'[80]

As the partisanship of crowds and the importance of games increased, referees became a regular target for disgruntled crowds and 'sodding', throwing clods of earth at them, became a popular post-game pastime for some supporters. Holbeck, a Leeds team, were barred from the 1885 Yorkshire Cup because of their supporters' anti-referee activities, while Dewsbury almost lost their right to stage a county game at their Crown Flatt ground after a serious outbreak of mud and stone throwing follow-ing a match.[81] Unsurprisingly, many referees made sure that adequate recompense was received, some charging between ten shillings and one guinea to take control of a game, as one club secretary discovered at the conclusion of a match: 'How much are we indebted to you?' Referee: '15/- please.' Secretary: 'Rather high isn't it?' Referee: 'Do you suppose I referee for my health?'[82]

There was some justification for such an attitude, as theirs was not a negligible risk. As can be seen in Appendix Table A.2, of the 24 incidents of crowd disturbances reported to the Yorkshire Rugby Union between 1887 and 1895, 17 involved attacks on referees. The attacks ranged from verbal abuse to the actual beating up of one referee as he made his way home from the ground. The closure of the offending supporters' club's ground for anything between seven days and 12 weeks usually followed such activities. Of the remaining incidents, five involved fights between spectators and players, a phenomenon particularly common among smaller clubs, where spectators were often separated from the action only by a rope. Until 1885, lesser matches were sometimes played without referees, giving rise to similar risks, as Bradford's second team discovered in 1882 when, during an on-field dispute between the two opposing captains, 'spectators crowded on to the ground, hustled the players and the umpires and converted the game into a "fratching" [fighting] match.'[83]

Certainly, in the early 1880s visiting sides and their supporters, especially those who proved to be victorious, could find themselves attacked by crowds. In 1881 the rivalry between Batley and Dewsbury spilt over into fighting after the two teams had disputed the final of a nine-a-side competition in Batley. Similarly violent rivalry led to the 1884 Swinton versus Salford derby match being abandoned. Visiting Hunslet supporters invaded the pitch and attacked Liversedge players and supporters near the end of their 'friendly' game.[84] Pudsey supporters lay in wait for Ossett players and supporters as they made their way back to the railway station after their 1884 Yorkshire Cup match. Batley's retreat from Horbury, a village outside Wakefield, in the same year gives a flavour of the fury generated by supporters of a defeated team:

> The occupants of waggonettes, as well as foot passengers, were assailed by a number of cowardly ruffians who hid themselves behind walls and other barricades, whence they threw large pieces of dross and other missiles. Even the tradesmen could not refrain from venting their spite in a similar manner, a member of that usually respectable body actually coming to the door of his premises in order to fling something at the Batley players as they drove past on their way home.[85]

However, such events may have assumed an importance in the minds of contemporary commentators which their frequency, or lack of it, did not deserve. Indeed, the local constabulary sent only one policeman to the Wakefield Trinity versus Bradford game in January 1884, a match which attracted a crowd in excess of 10,000, suggesting that the threat of violence was not seen as serious by the police.[86] Although, as Robert Storch has pointed out, the role of the police during this time was to act as a 'domestic missionary' in attempting to control and curb working-class leisure activities, they seem to have played little role in regulating the behaviour of the football crowd. Other than escorting harassed referees or teams from the pitch, there is little to suggest that the police sought to impose middle-class values on crowds by, for example, curbing gambling or bad language inside football grounds. Indeed, the presence of significant numbers of middle-class spectators may have meant that the police did not view football crowds as threats to public order.[87] Without exception, judgements about the behaviour of crowds, or more particularly the working-class sections of crowds, were made by middle-class commentators, and it is noticeable that, certainly during the period leading up to 1886, the vast majority of the criticisms of crowd behaviour are not about violence but about the language and enthusiasm of working-class spectators. 'When I say that the home spectators were simply a howling, surging, abusive mob, I don't exaggerate one whit,' wrote a reporter sent to cover a Castleford versus Bradford match, although he was unable to report any violence before, during or after the match.[88] As one might expect, the imagery of the 'mob' loomed large for those unused to, or afraid of, working-class people gathering in their thousands. Although there was neither suspicion nor actual reason to assume that there was any subversive intent behind such gatherings, the sharp contrast in the behaviour of the classes was seen as a disincentive to middle-class players and spectators: 'If "mob law" is permitted to run riot on the football field, however great the provocation, the pastime will become no game for gentlemen,' wrote the *Yorkshire Post* sternly in 1886.[89]

THE FIRST LAWS AGAINST PROFESSIONALISM

The disquiet about the changing nature of rugby was first expressed publicly in November 1879, when it was somewhat breathlessly reported that:

> A certain well-known Yorkshire club has in its ranks a paid man. Such a startling statement as this we can hardly give credence to, since it is so entirely opposed to the hitherto recognised notions of what has hitherto always been considered a purely amateur pastime.[90]

The name of the player in question was not reported, nor was any overt sanction taken against him. The dreaded paid man was in fact Wakefield Trinity's C. E. 'Teddy' Bartram, a cricket professional who had initially played for Harrogate's football team. His prowess with a rugby ball, both drop-kicking and running with it, soon came to the attention of other clubs and he played for York in the 1877–78 season. His experience of the amateur ideal was grounded in the harsh working life of a professional in cricket, and he stopped playing for York when they could not pay for his railway ticket from Harrogate. He resumed playing for Harrogate and, after an outstanding display for the club at Wakefield early in the 1878–79 season, the Trinity committee persuaded him to switch clubs by agreeing to pay his rail fare if he joined them. Although not officially recorded, they also lent him money. Trinity had recently merged with the formerly socially exclusive Wakefield club and were anxious to make their mark among

Yorkshire's leading sides. Teddy was such a key player in helping the club to consecutive Yorkshire Cup victories in 1879 and 1880 that by the end of the following season they invented the position of assistant secretary for him, paying an annual stipend of £52. This remuneration was something of an open secret in Yorkshire rugby circles and there is no doubt that he was deliberately left out of the Yorkshire side in the 1879–80 season because of his status. Despite his outstanding reputation as the best three-quarter in the North – he was probably the most gifted three-quarter to play the game in the region until Dicky Lockwood – he was never selected for England, because, as was noted in 1882, 'there is too much of the professional about him for their [southern selectors'] genteel ideas, football being solely intended, according to their notions, for public school or university players.' He was eventually banned *sine die* from the game in 1889 for professionalism after being found guilty of receiving loans from the club.[91]

Wakefield Trinity's C. E. 'Teddy' Bartram, probably the first rugby player to be paid to play (from *Toby, the Yorkshire Tyke*).

Anxious to maintain the sport's reputation, the YCFC immediately introduced the first rules anywhere in the rugby game – or indeed in any code of football – to outlaw professionalism. Because the RFU had no rules on professionalism at this time, they turned to cricket's governing body, the MCC. On 22 November 1879 the YCFC committee passed a motion stating that 'no player who is not strictly an amateur shall be allowed to play in the Challenge Cup ties, or in any match under the direct control of the County Football Committee; the definition of the term "amateur" shall be the same as that adopted by the MCC,'[92] and quoted the MCC's definition of an amateur:

> That no gentleman ought to make a profit by his services in the cricket field, and that for the future, no cricketer who takes more than his expenses in any match shall be qualified to play for the Gentlemen versus Players at Lords; but that if any gentleman feel difficulty in joining in the match without pecuniary assistance he shall not be barred from playing as a gentleman by having his actual expenses defrayed.[93]

As the YCFC committee was to discover later, such a definition was so broad as to allow virtually any payment as long as it was related to 'expenses defrayed'. Indeed, almost the same form of words was used a decade later by the supporters of 'broken-time' payments. However the real difficulty with the MCC rule was that it served only to define categories of gentlemen and said nothing about working-class players who were not full-time professionals. The structure and deep roots of cricket in English society meant that its distinctions between gentlemen and players could be rigidly maintained, but the rapid development of rugby made similar controls impossible. The main discussions about working-class participation in middle-class sports in the 1860s and 1870s took place in athletics and rowing, where the debate was overtly about whether to exclude the working classes from participation. The 1861 *Rowing Almanack* defined an amateur by listing the educational establishments and institutions to which they belonged and excluded absolutely 'tradesmen, labourers, artisans or working mechanics'.[94] The Amateur Athletic Club, the forerunner of the Amateur Athletic Association (AAA), also explicitly excluded anyone who was 'a mechanic, artisan or labourer' from its definition of amateurism.[95] In 1883 the AAA even barred professional cricketers from its events. On the whole, the tenor of middle-class opinion was opposed to working-class participation on an equal footing in those sports thought of as their own, but in rugby, burgeoning mass working-class interest meant exclusion was out of the question. Instead, the leaders of the sport decided that involvement in the game had to be on their terms:

> The [mechanic, artisan and labourer] must not forget that the rules now governing the game have attained a definite form ... The chief object – we might say the only object – for which the game is fostered by those who, combining ability with responsibility, control its destinies, is a recreation – a pleasure, in fact – that shall produce, in a most acceptable form, relaxation for both mind and body.[96]

Invariably, the word 'professional' was used as a synonym for working-class in both cricket and rugby. The MCC definition of amateurism implied that a middle-class professional was almost a contradiction in terms: as the *Bradford Observer* pointed out, 'The player who has had a [public] school training ... is not likely to develop into the exponent who intends to make a living out of the game.'[97] Of course, many of the leading amateurs of the time found sport a lucrative pastime thanks to expenses payments. In later years W. G. Grace and the high levels of expenses which he commanded became a favourite target of the advocates of broken-time payments to rugby players, as did the Surrey and England cricketer W. W. Read, who on the 1887–88 tour of Australia received £1,137 in expenses payments.[98] On a less lucrative scale, middle-class athletes often competed among themselves for cash stakes. For example, in the 1860s members of the Stock Exchange, civil servants, army officers, solicitors and other professionals competed for money at Brompton, Hackney Wick and Bow.[99] For the middle-class defender of the amateur ethos, therefore, the question of receiving payment for play was secondary to that of the social class of the player who received the money.

The ramifications of the new regulations were not immediately understood and did not stop payments being made to players. In March 1880 A. E. Hudson, secretary of the YCFC, wrote to the *Yorkshire Post* to publicly condemn Heckmondwike FC for offering cash prizes of £5 for a six-a-side rugby competition to be held over Easter. Threatening to ban them from the forthcoming Yorkshire Cup competition, he claimed that the club's offer of money for a game of football was:

> the first that has ever been made, and I do not think that even any respectable athletic club has gone so far as to openly offer money prizes at its annual meeting ... [and] my personal vote would most certainly be given against any club whose proceedings thus (in my opinion) tended, not to the advancement but rather the prostitution of a game which has happily been played for sport alone.[100]

Heckmondwike quickly apologised and substituted gold medals for the cash, but their original offer of cash prizes for a sporting contest was nothing more than standard practice in working-class communities. Indeed, less than three months earlier the same club had advertised for participants to run in a foot race for a prize of £10.[101] Hudson's claim that football had always been amateur was one which was to be taken up regularly over the next decade. Backing the YCFC's stand, the *Yorkshire Post* claimed that since 1300, football 'has stood out in bold relief among the many manly games indulged in by the British youth as being the only example where the competitors engaged are solely and exclusively amateurs.'[102] This was simply not true: in folk football monetary reward was common. In 1773, a 'grand football match' was played at Walton, near Wetherby, in Yorkshire for the not inconsiderable sum of twenty guineas.[103] After the completion of the Workington Shrove Tuesday game, 'the successful party [was] treated with a sum of money.'[104] In 1765, contestants in West Haddon played for 'a Prize of considerable value and another good prize.'[105] At Alnwick, the best players on each side were rewarded with individual prizes, and, as late as 1848, a game was played at Holmfirth, near Huddersfield, for a stake of £5.[106] As they searched for reasons to control the influx of working-class players and attitudes into the game, Hudson and his supporters had engaged in what Hobsbawm and others have identified as 'the invention of tradition' in order to legitimise their authority and instil 'value systems and conventions of behaviour' into rugby.[107] It was this response to working-class involvement in the sport which signalled the start of the development of rugby union's amateur ideology.

The road to amateur purity was however a rocky one. The civic importance now ascribed to football, especially in connection with cup competitions, had increased the pressure on clubs to find the best players and adopt playing methods which enhanced their prospects of a successful team. So, although the leading clubs continued to be controlled by the middle classes which had established them, they found themselves having to adopt many of the norms of working-class sport, albeit surreptitiously, in order to attract and retain the best players. By the early 1880s, payments for time lost from work due to playing and training – what became famous in the 1890s as broken-time payments – were regularly made and regarded in some quarters as legitimate expenses: the *Leeds Mercury* even included such payments as acceptable 'ordinary expenses' in a discussion of the FA's legalising of professionalism.[108] During the time spent training for cup matches or on tours to play teams outside the Yorkshire or Lancashire area, players were often paid expenses for time lost at work.[109] In November 1881, the Wakefield Trinity committee, possibly aware of the attention which was being paid to their activities in the light of the Teddy Bartram affair, passed a resolution stating that 'for the remainder of the football season, no money to be paid out of the funds of the club to any member on account of "broken time" and that a notice be posted in the rooms to this effect.'[110] Hull FC's 1883–84 Report and Accounts actually listed as expenditure £18 spent on 'players' loss of time, through accident and attendance at matches' and the committee minutes for that season, in which they reached the Yorkshire Cup final, show that broken-time payments were paid on at least three occasions during their cup run, including for the final itself when all players were asked not to work on the morning of the game.[111] In December 1885, the York committee decided that, after hearing an appeal from a player who had travelled up to Middlesbrough for a match, 'a day's wage be allowed him in consequence of having to get a man to do his work.'[112]

The YCFC felt sufficiently worried by this situation to further amend the bye-laws of the Yorkshire Cup for the 1884–85 season, tightening the definition of expenses by forbidding players from 'receiving any money over and above expenses actually out of pocket.'[113] Yet in January 1885, *The Yorkshireman*'s rugby correspondent was stating confidently that 'I could mention some dozen players who (if report is to be believed) all receive money over and above their actual expenses.'[114] The Manningham team was so widely believed to be in receipt of cash during its 1886 Yorkshire Cup run that A. E. Hudson felt compelled publicly to denounce the rumour mongers.[115] In the same season it was also reported that there was 'a grave rumour afloat' that Batley had given half the gate money of the match against Barrow to the players to share among themselves.[116] Unofficial rugby competitions for money, like the one organised by Heckmondwike in 1880, also began to be played again – one of the more notable being a full fifteen-a-side contest in Leeds on Whit Monday in 1883 which offered a first prize of £15 to the winning team with 15 shillings to each player and £1 each to every team winning its first round match.[117] Even those competitions which provided winners with medals or other non-monetary prizes, for example clocks or suits, were careful to advertise the precise monetary value of such items.

Cash payments, however, were not the most common form of remuneration for players. They smacked too much of 'hard' professionalism for many clubs and, more to the point, were a drain on club finances. Much more popular were payments in kind. In 1881 Dewsbury began the practice of rewarding players with a leg of mutton for each game won in the cup.[118] This quickly became standard practice, and better performances merited even greater rewards. A two-try performance by a Batley player in 1885 earned him 'one leg of mutton, two bottles of port and two shillingworth of eggs.'[119] Mutton was seen as a vital aid to training for the cup too. A Leeds team was reported to have begun regular training for cup matches and to have given each of their players a leg of mutton every week.[120] Unfortunately, lamented *Toby, the Yorkshire Tyke* in March 1884, 'neither mutton nor Blackpool were any use' to Manningham in their Yorkshire Cup loss to Bradford that year.[121] As *Toby* implied, the more ambitious clubs were also taking their players to the seaside for a week to prepare for important cup clashes, but mutton, port and seaside trips were not the only rewards available. 'There is the providing of a man's outfit and a plan which seems to have been adopted of paying for teas for some poorer members of the team after "at home" matches' reported the *Leeds Mercury* disapprovingly.[122] Such was the importance attached to such payments that, if a team performed badly, doubt was raised as to whether their players were receiving their weekly reward. 'They nobbud want a leg of mutton and two bottles of wine apiece, an' then they'll laik,' allegedly complained one Dewsbury supporter after a poor performance from his side. 'Aye, an' if I had t'brass they sud hev it an' all,' replied his companion.[123]

Inducements to players to leave one club and join another also became a central feature of the sport. In September 1882 *The Yorkshireman* published a rumour that Bradford, one of the game's most patrician clubs, had offered a player 'a free ticket, a new rigout and a place in the County [team],' if he signed for them.[124] Although the magazine was forced to withdraw the allegation in its next issue, the fact that it could confidently be stated that even Bradford were indulging in such practices illustrates the extent to which the rules were being ignored. During the 1884 close season it was reported that a Leeds club had 'sent out invitations to join its ranks to a number of players, offering them a solid inducement, euphemistically termed "expenses".'[125] The following season saw 'kidnapping' become rife. Rumours spread about inducements being offered to players by Wakefield Trinity, Manningham and Bradford. Both the Mirfield and Thornes clubs publicly complained about 'large baits' being offered to tempt players away.[126] In Lancashire, Wigan became notorious for their 'kidnapping' of players from Aspull, causing the local paper to comment sarcastically that 'the most cordial relationships at present exist between Wigan and Aspull ... so much so that the latter have lent the other team one of their very best men for the rest of the season.'[127] The *Leeds Mercury* highlighted the underlying reasons for the growth of inducements, pointing out that 'there may appear no reason whatever why [a player] should suddenly join another organisation, but he is a poor man, and the club which he has joined has found him work in their town at increased wages on condition that he plays for them.'[128]

Nowhere was this more true than in the importation of players from South Wales. Unlike the predominately middle-class southern English and Scottish clubs, South Wales shared a similar social basis for the game with Lancashire and Yorkshire, and links between the two regions had been forged in the early 1880s when the leading Yorkshire teams arranged small tours to play clubs in the Principality. Again evidence is sketchy but the first reported Welsh import appears to have been the international full back D. H. 'Harry' Bowen of Llanelli who signed for Dewsbury in February 1884. Despite being highly regarded, he played only a handful of games for the club before returning to Wales.[129] At the beginning of the 1884–85 season Dewsbury announced that they had signed another Welsh international full back, Alfred Cattell, but he does not appear to have played any games for the club.[130] The following year the Wales and Newport back James Bridie signed for Manningham, after he had independently found work in Bradford. He played one game for Manningham and then turned out for their local rivals, Bradford. Presumably mindful of his original obligations, he then went back to play for Manningham! Bradford's poaching caused so much animosity between the two clubs that it inspired Manningham supporters to bowdlerise the well-known song:

> Bridie was a Welshman,
> Bradford was a thief.
> Bradford came to our house,
> And now we are in grief.[131]

Perhaps the most sensational signing was that of Wales and Cardiff half back William 'Buller' Stadden, along with his team-mate Angus Stuart, by Dewsbury in September 1886. Their stated reasons for signing seemed unremarkable. They were 'out of employment, and having made a few friends during Dewsbury's tour of the Principality, they naturally steered for Yorkshire and got employment and a place in the Dewsbury team.'[132] The amount of lucky coincidence involved in this chain of events was not surprisingly called into question. When it was discovered that Stadden's and Stuart's employer was none other than Newsome, Sons and Spedding (Blanket Manufacturers and Woollen Spinners) of Dewsbury, many smelled a rat. Mark Newsome, one of the sons in the company title, was also president and former captain of Dewsbury FC. Despite widespread condemnation of the club, the Yorkshire committee found itself powerless to act because there was no evidence of money having changed hands and, as Newsome knew, there was, as yet, no rule that forbade players working for members of a club committee.[133]

THE OCTOBER 1886 GENERAL MEETING OF THE RFU

By 1886 the tattered nature of the amateur flag and the increasing influence of working-class players and spectators on the game in the North, and especially Yorkshire, had become a cause for much concern in the leadership of both the RFU and the county rugby unions. In January, the press reports spoke of 'the appearance on the scene of the much dreaded and detested professional footballer – the man who plays not for love and honour but for gain' and disclosed that it had 'an array of convincing evidence' of at least two examples of such players.[134] Sure enough, in what appears to have been a preplanned action, Pudsey appealed against their defeat by Manningham in the first round of the Yorkshire Cup on the grounds that their opponents had fielded J. Birmingham and W. Pulleyn, two players who, Pudsey claimed, 'were being paid over and above expenses actually out of pocket.' Both had originally played for Selby, some thirty miles from Bradford, and, as one witness testified, had 'received broken-time payments, rail-fare and a sovereign' to play for Manningham. Pulleyn had even been heard to state publicly that he 'would play for the club that paid him best' and that 'football paid better than working.'[135] Interestingly, both Pulleyn and Manningham's captain admitted that the club had promised to find him a job, something which was illegal by the end of the year but over which the committee took no action. Manningham reacted by presenting six sworn statements that the two had not been paid and the YCFC committee, unable to find a smoking gun, found the case not proven but thanked Pudsey for bringing the matter before them.

As the 1886–87 season began, the *Yorkshire Post* summed up the mood: 'The professional question last year was assumed to have reached very grave dimensions. It is scarcely possible for matters to continue in the present unsatisfactory condition ... The RFU is determined to purify the game in these parts by the combined legislative action of its members after careful consideration.'[136] The *Bradford Observer* wondered if the game had become 'over-popular' and *The Year's Sport* annual called on the RFU to 'exclude the professional football player from their ranks.'[137] Arthur Budd, a member of the RFU committee, took up the argument in that year's *Football Annual*:

> Only six months after the legitimisation of the bastard [of professionalism] we see two professional teams left to fight out the final [FA] cup tie. To what does this all end? Why this – gentlemen who play football once a week as a pastime will find themselves no match for men who give up their whole time and abilities to it. How should

they? One by one, as they find themselves outclassed, they will desert the game and leave the field to professionals ...

The Rugby Union committee finding themselves face to face with the hydra have determined to throttle it before he is big enough to throttle them. ... No mercy but iron rigour will be dealt out.[138]

Budd was not merely speaking for himself. He was a member of a sub-committee which the RFU had set up to draft new laws to illegalize all forms of payment for the October 1886 general meeting. Along with Budd, the committee consisted of Frederick Currey, the RFU President, James MacLaren of Manchester, William Cail of Northumberland, Rowland Hill of London, A. E. Hudson, the Yorkshire secretary, H. W. T. Garnett of Bradford and George Thomson of Halifax. The presence of three of Yorkshire's leading administrators on the sub-committee – in fact, only Budd, Currey and Hill came from the South of England – underlined the fact that a primary aim of its work was 'to meet the evils existing in Yorkshire.'[139]

As Budd's article implied and the debate before the October meeting made clear, the fact that some players received money for playing the game was not necessarily the major issue. The RFU had sanctioned the payment of second-class rail fares for players travelling to matches as legitimate expenses in 1880,[140] but the amount of expenses payments received by southern teams travelling north for matches had subsequently become a source of great controversy. Rowland Hill had congratulated the Yorkshire clubs for 'doing good work to the cause of football by spending some [of their money] in the necessary expenses of those bodies who have great difficulty in finding money' in 1885, yet the double standard involved was not lost on other commentators.[141] 'People are now asking how it is that over £100 was spent in this way for a team composed of amateurs,' wrote the northern rugby correspondent of *Pastime* about payment received by the Middlesex team before their game against Yorkshire at Dewsbury in 1885. 'Yet, forsooth, Mr Rowland Hill says the Yorkshire Executive is doing good work in this matter, and in the same breath is indignant because several members of a cup team received last season a small recompense for incidental expenses received while in training!'[142]

What animated Budd and the RFU was the fear that the influx of working-class players would mean that gentlemen would no longer be able to dominate the game as they had done in the past. The eclipse of the public school-based Association football clubs was seen as a dreadful warning of the shape of things to come.[143] Professionalism and payment for play would allow the working classes to dominate rugby in the same way. The *Yorkshire Post* rugby correspondent, who generally reflected the views of the YCFC, continued Budd's arguments: 'Rough and unfair play, a disregard to the rules, and abuse of the umpires and referees, can all be traced directly and indirectly to the presence of the paid professional, to whom a love of the game and fair play are of very small importance as compared to the necessity of winning a match.'[144] Working-class players and spectators should know their place:

> Why are so few public school men and clergymen found in our leading fifteens? It is because the associations of the game are now becoming thoroughly distasteful to any gentleman of sportsmanlike feeling. They do not care to be hooted and yelled at as part and parcel of a sixpenny show or to meet and associate with men who care nothing for the game other than as a means to an end. We have nothing to say against the mechanic, the artisan or the labourer, who, as long as they indulge in the game for sport and not for profit, are an ornament to the game.[145]

The proposed rule changes declared illegal any payment, either in cash or in kind, to players for playing or training. The new regulations also forbade the employment of a player in any capacity by his club or by any member of the club. Unsurprisingly, they met with little resistance at the October general meeting. Yorkshire's A. E. Hudson led the discussion, euphemistically referring to 'a small cloud which has appeared on the horizon.' Rowland Hill claimed that 'even in the poorest communities' players opposed professionalism and Budd, in characteristically pointed fashion, prophesied that if they compromised with professionalism, 'the game would eventually resolve itself into a distinct game for both professionals and amateurs, as the latter would be in time completely outclassed.' To a Yorkshire delegate who argued that 'the very existence of his club, composed almost entirely of working men, would be threatened if they were held to the letter of the new laws,' Bradford's Harry Garnett bluntly replied: 'If working men desired to play football, they should pay for it themselves, as they would have to do with any other pastime.'[146]

Horace Lyne of Welsh club Newport, supported by Dewsbury, opposed the new regulations because of the impact they would have on the working-class player. He 'thought the rules too stringent, especially with regard to the payment of expenses. A large number of Welsh clubs were composed of working men and they could not afford to lose time when engaged away from home,' and he went on to 'urge payment for lost time.'[147] An amendment from the Lancashire county club, originating from Oldham, that 'a player receiving compensation for injuries sustained while playing for his club should be excepted from suspension' was accepted, but only four clubs voted against the new amateur regulations.[148]

Thus was laid the foundation stone of the RFU for the next 109 years. In direct response to a flood of working-class participation, the leaders of the RFU had drawn a line beyond which they were not prepared to compromise. Although rugby's leaders were perfectly prepared to allow working-class people to participate in the sport, and many, especially those with a church background, sought to encourage it, such involvement was to take place solely on their terms – hence the codification of amateurism. As Garnett's speech implied, compromise with working-class cultural practices was not part of the RFU's agenda: if the working classes didn't like it, they could leave it. This intransigence reflected the fact that the rational recreation shoe was on the other foot; instead of middle-class reformers attempting to change working-class leisure, the impact of the working class on a formerly exclusive middle-class leisure pursuit was changing rugby. Far from middle-class values being imparted to its new participants, working-class values and traditions threatened to overwhelm the sport, especially given the importance of proletarian players and spectators to clubs which now carried the weight of civic pride and expectation with them.

As the RFU leadership realised in its own fashion, working-class people brought to the sport different ways of participating in football, whether it was on the terraces or on the pitch. While violence, dissent and competitiveness were also integral to middle-class ways of playing rugby, for the working class to engage in such practices – with no little success, it should be added – was to undermine the accepted sporting order. More particularly, working-class expectations of monetary or material reward for their on-field endeavours was directly counterposed to the Arnoldian spirit which underpinned much of rugby's appeal to the middle classes. Thus the reaction of working-class players to the new regulations was summed up by a Batley player who declined to discuss the terms of an offer to switch clubs until he had heard the outcome of the RFU conference: 'Who's bahn to provide t'mutton; becos noa mutton, noa laaking, not me.'[149]

Off the field, working-class spectators also attached alternative meanings to watching the sport. Although they shared with the middle classes the sense of civic pride in their football club, their behaviour at matches – the barracking of the referee, the booing of the visiting side, the resorting to low-level violence when things didn't go their way – all suggest that they saw themselves as participants in the match ritual, rather than mere observers. And, just as working-class players sought monetary value for their efforts, working-class spectators saw the match as a spectacle and demanded value for their monetary outlay. Although not articulated as such, rugby football had become a site of conflict between the expression of working-class cultural practices and the dominant cultural codes of the public school ethos.

NOTES

1. The failure of Bradford hardware store owners to agree to 2pm Saturday closing in 1881 led to a minor protest by young counter clerks who were therefore unable to watch football. *The Yorkshireman*, 2 April 1881.
2. Useful summaries of the development of working-class leisure time can be found in Hugh Cunningham, 'Leisure and Culture' in Vol. 2 of *The Cambridge Social History of Britain 1750–1950*, Cambridge, 1990 and Wray Vamplew's *Pay Up and Play the Game*, Cambridge, 1988. The classic text on Saint Monday remains D. A. Reid, 'The Decline of Saint Monday 1766–1876' in *Past and Present*, No. 71, May 1976.
3. Moses Heap, diary manuscript in Rawtenstall Library, Lancashire.
4. *Yorkshire Evening Post*, 1 Nov. 1902.
5. A. G. Guillemard, 'The Past Season' in *Football Annual*, London, 1880.
6. This is the term used in Eric Dunning and Kenneth Sheard, *Barbarians, Gentlemen and Players*, New York, 1979.
7. The 'slumbers' quote is from Engels' article 'May 4 in London' of 23 May 1890 in Marx and Engels, *On Britain*, Moscow, 1971, p. 401. The quote which follows is from 'England in 1845 and 1885' of Feb. 1885, pp. 387–8.
8. See Michael Latham, *Buff Berry and the Mighty Bongers*, Chorley, 1995, p. 71.
9. Interview in *North West Daily Mail*, 15 Nov. 1919.
10. *Yorkshire Post*, 10 Oct. 1883.
11. Stuart Barlow, 'The Diffusion of Rugby Football in the Industrialised Context of Rochdale 1868–90' in *The International Journal of the History of Sport*, Vol. 10, No. 1, April 1993.
12. W. Corlyon manuscript notebooks in Hull City Archives.
13. *Yorkshire Post*, 15 Oct. 1887.
14. *The Yorkshireman*, 16 Feb. 1884.
15. *Yorkshire Post*, 11 Nov. 1893. For a broader perspective on the relationship between working-class participants and the clerical sponsors of recreation clubs, see Peter Bailey, *Leisure and Class in Victorian England*, Second Edition, London, 1987.
16. *The Lantern* (St Helens), 13 Sept. 1889. See also *Clarion*, 24 Dec. 1892 and *Athletic News*, 9 March 1896. See also J. Arnold, *The Influence of Pilkington Brothers (Glass Manufacturers) on the Growth of Sport and Community Recreation in St Helens*, unpublished M.Ed. thesis, University of Liverpool, 1977. For the paternalism of the company, see John Walton, *Lancashire: A Social History, 1558–1939*, Manchester, 1987, p. 321.
17. *The Yorkshireman*, 11 Oct. 1885.
18. For more on this see S. Bradley, *Leisure and Society in Huddersfield 1868–95*, BA thesis, University of Bristol, 1989.
19. *The Yorkshireman*, 8 April 1882 and *Yorkshire Evening Post*, 21 Nov. 1903.
20. *Yorkshire Football Handbook*, 1881–82 and 1885–86.
21. Source: *Football Annual*, 1877–84. *Kelly's Directory of the West Riding* 1877–84.

This represents the 20 individuals I have been able to trace out of a total of 57 named secretaries of Yorkshire sides.

22. *The Yorkshireman*, 29 Nov. 1884. For an insight into the importance of the pub to recreation in the working-class communities of the English North East, see Alan Metcalfe, 'Organised Sport in the Mining Communities of South Northumberland', *Victorian Studies*, No. 25, Summer 1982.
23. *Yorkshire Evening Post*, 16 Jan. 1904.
24. *Yorkshire Post*, 21 Dec. 1893.
25. For this and many other examples, see the *Yorkshire Post* of 11, 12 and 13 Dec. 1879.
26. *Yorkshire Post*, 12 Dec. 1879.
27. See Bryn Trescatheric, *Sport and Leisure in Victorian Barrow*, Barrow, 1983.
28. *Wigan Observer*, 8 Nov. 1879.
29. *Yorkshire Post*, 10 Feb. 1880.
30. *The Yorkshireman*, 1 Dec. 1887.
31. *Yorkshire Post*, 2 Dec. 1879.
32. A Londoner, 'Metropolitan Football' in Revd F. Marshall (ed), *Football – The Rugby Union Game*, London, 1892, p. 329. The Goole quote is from a letter of 9 May 1882 in the papers of Munby and Scott, Solicitors, in York City Archives.
33. For the story of the declined cup offer, see Marshall, p. 86. Hill's comments can be found in 'The Past Season' in the *Football Annual*, 1882.
34. A. G. Guillemard, 'The Past Season' in *Football Annual*, London, 1880. See also *The Field*, 12 Jan. 1884 for southern-based calls for a national rugby cup contest.
35. For information on the Hull amalgamation, see *Yorkshire Evening Post*, 1 Dec. 1900 and 20 Feb. 1904 (in which the resolution is reprinted) and the *Yorkshire Post* of 11 March and 1 April 1879.
36. *Yorkshire Evening Post*, 21 Feb. 1903.
37. In this they reflected many of the same concerns as the leadership of the RFU who urged an end to all cup competitions. See G. Rowland Hill, 'The Past Season' in *Football Annual* for both 1882 and 1883.
38. *Yorkshire Post*, 20 Feb. 1883. Bradford did eventually boycott the cup in the late 1880s.
39. For an account of the formation of the Lancashire County club, see A. M. Crook, 'County Football: Lancashire', Ch. 19 of Marshall, and Lancashire County Football Club minutes, 22 Dec. 1881.
40. *Athletic News*, 4 Nov. 1876, 1 Sept. 1877 and 8 Feb. 1882.
41. *Manchester Guardian*, 12 Oct. 1882.
42. *Burnley Express and Advertiser*, 21 Oct. 1882. *Football Field and Sports Telegram*, 17 Jan. 1885 for further details. Key texts are Rob Lewis's, *The Development of Professional Football in Lancashire, 1870–1914*, unpublished Ph.D. thesis, University of Lancaster, 1993, *History of the Lancashire Football Association*, Blackburn, 1928, Graham Williams, *The Code War*, Harefield, 1994, David Russell, '"Sporadic and Curious": The Emergence of Rugby and Soccer Zones in Yorkshire and Lancashire c.1860–1914' in *The International Journal of the History of Sport*, Vol. 5, No. 2, 1988, and, more generally, John Bale, *Sport and Place*, London, 1982.
43. For Suter, see Mason, ibid., p. 69 and *Football Field and Sports Telegram*, 10 Oct. 1885. Details of the others can be found in *History of the Lancashire Football Association* above.
44. The Free Critic, 'The Past and the Future' in *Athletic News Football Annual 1892–93*, London, 1892, p. 107.

45. *Wigan Observer*, 6 Oct. 1886.
46. LCFC committee minutes 15 Feb. 1887 and *Yorkshire Post*, 16 Feb. 1887.
47. An Old Player, 'The Rugby Union Game in 1888–89' in *Football Annual*, London, 1889.
48. *Dewsbury Reporter*, 8 March 1884. The preceding figures are taken from the *Yorkshire Post*. It must be stressed that all figures are newspaper estimates, as no accurate records of attendances were kept at this time.
49. *Dewsbury Reporter*, 5 April 1884.
50. 'The Rugby Game in Yorkshire' in *Football Annual*, London, 1882.
51. *Yorkshire Post*, 4 April 1887 and 31 Oct. 1887.
52. The Salford figures are taken from the financial summaries in James Higson's *History of Salford FC*, Salford, 1892. For Warrington, see the *Warrington Guardian*, 8 June 1887.
53. *Warrington Guardian*, 14 April 1886. The club's president was a Tory and two committee members were Liberals.
54. Tony Mason in *Association Football and English Society 1863–1915* is able to give a partial picture of the class and occupational backgrounds of spectators by an analysis of the casualties at the 1902 Ibrox disaster. Fortunately, rugby never suffered such a tragedy.
55. *The Yorkshireman*, 15 March 1884.
56. *The Yorkshireman*, 26 March 1881.
57. *Wakefield Express*, 9 July 1887.
58. *Wigan Observer*, 22 Nov. 1886.
59. *Yorkshire Post*, 16 Jan. 1880.
60. *The Yorkshireman*, 8 Sept. 1887.
61. *Yorkshire Post*, 21 Jan. 1880.
62. *Huddersfield Daily Examiner*, 20 Sept. 1886.
63. For details see *The Yorkshireman*, 18 Oct. 1884 and 16 Oct. 1886.
64. *The Lantern* (St Helens), 9 May 1890. The formation of pub-based clubs to pay for excursions was a common phenomenon in working-class communities. See, for example, the 'Going-Off' clubs described in John Walton's 'The Demand for Working Class Seaside Holidays in Victorian England', *Economic History Review*, Vol. 34, 1982.
65. See *The Yorkshireman*, 17 Jan. and 7 March 1885, 30 Jan. and 18 Sept. 1886.
66. *The Yorkshireman*, 11 April 1885.
67. *Yorkshire Post*, 22 Sept. 1884 and *The Yorkshireman*, 27 Sept. 1884
68. *The Yorkshireman*, 3 March 1883.
69. *The Yorkshireman*, 14 March 1885.
70. *The Yorkshireman*, 20 April 1892.
71. *The Yorkshireman*, 15 April 1891.
72. *The Yorkshireman*, 2 Dec. 1891.
73. *Salford Reporter*, 2 June 1888. *Yorkshire Evening Post*, 29 Nov. 1902.
74. *The Yorkshireman*, 26 Sept. 1886 and 11 April 1888.
75. *Yorkshire Post*, 7 Nov. 1888.
76. Higson, ibid., p. 137.
77. *The Yorkshireman*, 28 April 1887.
78. *The Yorkshireman*, 24 Feb. 1883.
79. *Yorkshire Post*, 27 May 1889 and 28 April 1892.
80. *Clarion*, 10 Feb. 1894.
81. *The Yorkshireman*, 27 Sept. 1884 and *Yorkshire Post*, 8 Nov. 1886.
82. The dialogue comes from *The Yorkshireman*, 21 Nov. 1885. More information on

the charges by referees which were soon to be outlawed by the RFU, can be found in the issue for 10 Oct. 1885.

83. *The Yorkshireman*, 21 Oct. 1882.
84. Higson, ibid.
85. For Batley, see C. F. Shaw, *The Gallant Youths*, Batley, 1899, p. 22. For Pudsey, see *The Yorkshireman*, 6 March 1884.
86. Unfortunately, the lone custodian was not able to prevent several hundred spectators entering the ground for free. *The Yorkshireman*, 5 Jan. 1885
87. Robert D. Storch, 'The Policeman as "Domestic Missionary": Urban Discipline and Popular Culture in Northern England 1850–80' in *Journal of Social History*, Vol. 9, 1976. The broadest historical overview of the behaviour of sports crowds can be found in Allen Guttman, *Sports Spectators*, New York, 1986.
88. *The Yorkshireman*, 14 March 1885. A more extended discussion of rugby crowd behaviour will take place in Chapter Six.
89. *Yorkshire Post*, 8 Nov. 1886.
90. *Yorkshire Post*, 2 Dec. 1879.
91. The *Yorkshire Post*, 17 Feb. 1880. *The Yorkshireman*, 9 Dec. 1882. Wakefield Trinity committee minutes, 4 Nov. 1878 and 1 June 1880, quoted in *Yorkshire Evening Post*, 1 Nov. 1902. The word 'induced' was deliberately used by former Wakefield Trinity and Yorkshire RFU president Barron Kilner in an interview describing Teddy's signing in *Yorkshire Evening Post*, 23 Nov. 1901, in which he admitted that 'in the light of more recent legislation the move would have been taken as one of professionalism by the Rugby Union.' This evidence contradicts the assumption of Eric Dunning and Kenneth Sheard in *Barbarians, Gentlemen and Players*, New York, 1979, that the professional question only emerged as in issue in rugby in the early 1890s.
92. *Yorkshire Post*, 25 Nov. 1879.
93. *Yorkshire Post*, 2 Dec. 1879. For more on the question of professionalism in cricket, see Ric Sissons, *The Professionals: A Social History of the Professional Cricketer*, London, 1988.
94. Quoted in P. Lovesey, *The Official Centenary History of the Amateur Athletic Association*, London, 1979, p. 22.
95. Ibid., p. 24.
96. *Yorkshire Post*, 11 Oct. 1886.
97. *Bradford Observer*, 26 Jan. 1886.
98. See *The Yorkshireman*, 9 May 1888. For details of W. W. Read's expense payments on tour see David Montefiore, *Cricket in the Doldrums*, Campbelltown, 1992.
99. Lovesey, p. 22.
100. *Yorkshire Post*, 6 March 1880.
101. *Yorkshire Post*, 20 Dec. 1879.
102. *Yorkshire Post*, 2 Dec. 1879.
103. *Leeds Intelligencer*, 2 March 1773.
104. William Whellan, *The History and Topography of the Counties of Cumberland and Westmoreland*, Pontefract, 1869.
105. *Northampton Mercury*, 29 July 1765
106. Stanley Chadwick, *Claret and Gold*, Huddersfield, 1945.
107. E. Hobsbawm and T. Ranger, *The Invention of Tradition*, Cambridge, 1983, p. 9.
108. *Leeds Mercury*, 9 Dec. 1884.
109. *Leeds Mercury*, 2 Oct. 1886, and *Yorkshire Post*, 27 Sept. 1886.
110. Wakefield Trinity Committee minutes, 28 Nov. 1881, quoted in J. C. Lindley, *100*

Years of Rugby – The History of Wakefield Trinity 1873–1973, Wakefield, 1973 p. 34.

111. Hull FC Report and Accounts 1883–84 and committee minutes, 10 March 1884, 17 March 1884 and 1 April 1884.
112. York FC committee minutes, 5 Dec. 1885, quoted in *Yorkshire Evening Post*, 21 Feb. 1903.
113. Yorkshire County Challenge Cup rules, point six, quoted in the *Yorkshire Post*, 28 Sept. 1885.
114. *The Yorkshireman*, 10 Jan. 1885.
115. *The Yorkshireman*, 15 May 1886.
116. *The Yorkshireman*, 1 May 1886.
117. *Yorkshire Post*, 28 April 1883.
118. *The Yorkshireman*, 14 May 1885.
119. *The Yorkshireman*, 28 Feb. 1885.
120. *The Yorkshireman*, 1 March 1884.
121. *Toby, the Yorkshire Tyke*, 22 March 1884.
122. *Leeds Mercury*, 2 Oct. 1886.
123. *The Yorkshireman*, 9 Feb. 1884. 'They want no more than a leg of mutton and two bottles of wine each and then they'll play.' 'Yes, and if I had the money they would have it.' To appreciate the importance of such 'presents' to working-class players' diets, see D. J. Oddy, 'Working Class Diets', *Economic History Review*, Vol. 23, 1970, and J. R. Roberts, 'Working Class Standards of Living in Barrow and Lancaster, 1890–1914', *Economic History Review*, Vol. 30, 1977.
124. *The Yorkshireman*, 30 Sept. 1882.
125. *The Yorkshireman*, 13 Sept. 1884.
126. *The Yorkshireman*, 12 and 26 Sept. 1885 and 14 Nov. 1885.
127. *Wigan Observer*, 9 Oct. 1886.
128. *Leeds Mercury*, 2 Oct. 1886.
129. *Dewsbury Reporter*, 22 Feb. 1884.
130. *Dewsbury Reporter*, 20 Sept. 1884.
131. *Bradford Observer*, 21 and 28 Sept. 1885, *Bradford Daily Telegraph*, 22 Sept. 1885, *The Yorkshireman*, 12 Sept. and 3 Oct. 1885.
132. *The Yorkshireman*, 3 March 1885.
133. For details of the Stadden and Stuart affair, see *The Yorkshireman*, 25 Sept. 1886 and *Leeds Mercury*, 12 Oct. 1886. Both diplomatically did not name Stadden's and Stuart's employer. Only the *Evening Express*, 11 Oct. 1886, felt compelled to reveal the most pertinent fact in the case.
134. *Yorkshire Post*, 25 Jan. 1886.
135. Details of the hearing are taken from the *Yorkshire Post*, *Leeds Mercury* and *Bradford Observer*, 2 and 3 March 1886.
136. *Yorkshire Post*, 20 Sept. 1886.
137. *Bradford Observer*, 28 Sept. 1886. A. E. T. Watson (ed), *The Year's Sport: A Review of British Sports and Pastimes for the Year 1885*, London, 1886, p. 246.
138. A. Budd, 'The Rugby Union Game' in *Football Annual*, London, 1886, p. 52.
139. *Yorkshire Post*, 27 Sept. 1886.
140. Minutes of the Rugby Football Union committee, 15 Jan. 1880.
141. G. Rowland Hill, 'The Past Season' in *Football Annual*, London, 1885.
142. *Pastime*, 7 Oct. 1885. Details of expenses paid to southern teams are difficult to ascertain. In the 1887–88 season, Bradford paid a total of £244 15s to visiting teams from southern England and Scotland, made up as follows: Blackheath £57 15s; Richmond £42 10s; Guy's Hospital £30; Oxford University £20;

Edinburgh Institution £30; Fettes-Loretto combined schools side £37 10s; London
Scottish £27 10s. See *The Yorkshireman*, 2 May 1888.

143. For a fuller exposition of Budd's views on the probable need of the middle-class
clubs to separate themselves from working-class-based clubs, see his article in
Marshall, *Football – The Rugby Union Game*.

144. *Yorkshire Post*, 27 Sept. 1886.

145. *Yorkshire Post*, 11 Oct. 1886.

146. See Minutes of the RFU, 4 Oct. 1886, *Leeds Mercury* and *Yorkshire Post*, both
5 Oct. 1886, and the *Bradford Observer*, 12 Oct. 1886. Garnett's words later became
immortalised by Budd, who used almost exactly the same formulation six years
later in his article in Marshall, p. 132. By that time, Garnett, like most of the
Yorkshire leadership, had abandoned this position.

147. As above. Ironically both Horace Lyne and Mark Newsome became presidents
of their respective Rugby Unions and members of the rugby union International
Board after the Northern Union split of 1895.

148. For the wording of the Lancashire amendment see the LCFC committee minutes
of 1 Oct. 1886. Unfortunately the RFU minutes of the meeting are incomplete
and do not record individual votes. The details about the votes cast against come
from the *Leeds Daily News*, of 11 Oct. 1886. The names of the other two clubs
which voted against the motion do not appear to have been recorded.

149. *The Yorkshireman*, 29 Oct. 1886. 'Who is going to provide the mutton? Because
no mutton, no playing.'

R chirolleel

North

Divide

South

3

'King Football': 1886–1893[1]

In the autumn of 1896, Talbot Baines, grandson of the Liberal, non-conformist founder of the *Leeds Mercury*, Edward Baines, published a series of articles in *The Times* on the North of England. In its introduction to the first article, the newspaper summed up popular thought on the matter by stating that 'North of the Trent, it is often suggested are found most of the backbone and manly virtues of the country: south of that line exists what amount of good is consistent with somewhat invertebrate moral strictures.'[2] These mutually interdependent images of the North and South of England had a long history predating the industrial revolution – some have even claimed to have found early manifestations of North–South rivalry in the eighth-century writings of the Venerable Bede – but they had been rekindled and given renewed impetus by the coming of the factory age.[3] The dominant image of the North of England in the nineteenth century had been expressed in literature ranging from Blake's dark satanic mills to Dickens' Coketown and Gaskell's Darkshire – most notably by the words of the latter's John Thornton in *North and South*: 'We are Teutonic up here in Darkshire in another way. We hate to have laws made for us at a distance. We wish people would allow us to right ourselves, instead of continually meddling with their imperfect legislation. We stand up for self-government, and oppose centralisation.'[4] For those living in the South of England, Baines argued that 'many of them still feel that, collectively, the points of contrast to be met with in the North of England produce an atmosphere as really, if not as profoundly, distinct from that of their own native districts as is the atmosphere of one of the continental nations.'[5] These supposed differences in attitudes and perspectives of the geographical halves of England have been summed up by Donald Horne in terms of metaphors:

> In the Northern Metaphor Britain is pragmatic, empirical, calculating, Puritan, bourgeois, enterprising, adventurous, scientific, serious, and believes in struggle ...

In the Southern Metaphor Britain is a romantic, illogical, muddled, divinely lucky, Anglican, aristocratic, traditional, frivolous, and believes in order and tradition.[6]

Yet this was at worst caricature and at best based on attitudes which had more credence in the early to middle part of the century. Certainly the idea that northern industrialists were merely 'pounds, shillings and pence' pragmatists with few interests beyond the factory gate is mistaken, as a glimpse of mid-Victorian architecture and artistic patronage of urban centres of Lancashire and West Yorkshire will testify. Moreover, as Patrick Joyce has demonstrated, the culture of the northern factory itself included a variety of social and recreational activities provided by employers.[7] In fact, by the mid-1890s, northern industrialists of the type described by Dickens and Gaskell were few and far between, if they had ever existed at all, and Baines thought it wise to point out that regional differences 'apply primarily and exclusively to the middle and working classes. Such differences in type as may have existed between the upper ranks of society in North and South have not survived in any appreciable form the fusing of public school and university education.'[8]

Certainly in rugby up to the late 1880s, there was no 'North/South divide' among the RFU leadership, as the framing of the 1886 anti-professional rules had demonstrated. In Lancashire the Liverpool/Manchester axis was firmly based on former pupils of Rugby and Cheltenham, and to a lesser extent Eton and Harrow. The founders of Yorkshire rugby were largely educated at southern public schools. Those who had attended private schools in the north, such as Leeds Grammar School, Manchester Grammar School, St Peter's in York or Bramham College, had been educated firmly in the tenets of the Arnoldian tradition, and many of them, such as Lancashire's J. H. Payne or Yorkshire's W. E. Bromet, had also completed their education at Oxbridge. Nor was opposition to professionalism based on antipathy to an urban, industrial culture. Most of these men represented the northern bourgeoisie par excellence, coming from families which had made their money from industry, particularly textiles, or as merchants. The backgrounds of three of the North's presidents of the RFU, and most determined fighters against professionalism, were impeccably industrial: Harry Garnett of Yorkshire was a paper manufacturer, William Cail of Northumberland was manager of a chemical works and J. W. H. Thorp of Cheshire was a textile manufacturer. However, while they may have been proud of their northern roots, they shared with their colleagues living in the south a generalised disquiet about the growth of working-class self-confidence, demonstrated by a rising tide of industrial militancy and political organisation, and the impact of the working class on their leisure pursuits.

The North/South divide is therefore a seductive yet unhelpful metaphor in understanding the development of rugby. Although there were local and regional rivalries, the erosion of r[egional] [na]tional consensus was, as we shall see in this chapter, caused prim[arily by] the growth of differing attitudes towards working-class partici[pation. G]iven that the vast majority of working-class rugby players w[ere] in Yorkshire and Lancashire, it was inevitable that its geograph[ic focus w]ould be on the northern counties. Similar tensions existed every[where] rugby had a significant working-class following. In the south[west of] England, Gloucester and clubs in Torquay were investigated in [the 1890s] and found guilty of violations of the amateur regulations. In [the Midla]nds, there were investigations into payments for play through[out the]1900s involving the Leicester and Coventry clubs, one of whic[h resulted] in the resignation of RFU president C. A. Crane in 1908 after h[e urged fo]r expulsion of the miscreants. Clubs in the Scottish border town[s were su]spected but never convicted of being more than generous with expenses payments to players, and of course, Welsh rugby union was plagued with accusations of professionalism for almost as long as Lancashire and Yorkshire, eventually managing partially to suppress the contradiction by covertly legitimising informal payments to players. The situation in the North of England differed however because the sheer scale of working-class involvement and the impossibility of controlling payments for play were increasingly perceived by the RFU leadership as a direct threat to their control of the game.

This is not to deny that there were rivalries and jealousies between different regions. However, in the main, these tended to involve Yorkshire and the county's perceived slights by either the metropolitan rulers of the sport or their fellow-northerners across the Pennines. Both Lancashire and Yorkshire had grievances against the southern-based RFU leadership: southern county sides often turned up in the North with sides weakened due to players withdrawing because of the long journeys involved and accusations of southern bias in the selection of the England team were commonplace, even after the RFU had introduced the North versus South game in 1874 as a trial match to make selection fairer.[9] There were also disputes over the rules, Yorkshire seeking stricter offside and penalty laws, but the major source of friction in the 1880s was due to the massive growth of the game in Yorkshire and the county committee's consequent belief that they were entitled to a major place in the national leadership of the sport. This was primarily expressed through the call to hold the Union's general meeting alternately in the North and South. As early as 1881 the

YCFC had circularised its member clubs asking them to meet before that October's RFU general meeting, emphasising 'the importance of Yorkshire clubs acting in unison' and the calls for general meetings to be held in the North continued throughout the 1880s. Relations between the Yorkshire-men and the RFU hit a low point in 1887 when the RFU refused to accept Mark Newsome as a member of its executive and the YRU almost gave its support to Scotland in its dispute with the RFU the following year.[10] Despite this, there was never any suggestion that the leadership was anything less than unswerving in its commitment to the RFU's philosophy, if not its personnel. We have already seen how it was Yorkshire representatives who played a central role in drawing up the 1886 amateur regulations. As this chapter will demonstrate, its pursuit of the 'veiled professionals' among its players was second to none and earned it the respect of the RFU leadership. If anything, the fact of being the nation's leading rugby county meant that Yorkshire leaders felt they had a duty to be 'more royalist than the king.'

The rivalry with Lancashire was not simply due to traditional enmities but was also a result of the County Palatine's greater influence on the game's ruling bodies; throughout the 1870s and most of the 1880s Lancashire were allocated more seats on the RFU executive than the white rose county. The Lancastrians were also felt to be too strong in their support of the RFU. The Lancashire union repeatedly voted against Yorkshire's proposals for alternate annual meetings to be held in the North, most notably in 1891 when a Yorkshire motion for alternate meetings was passed by 143–106 but did not carry because it failed to get the necessary two-thirds majority. Lancashire clubs were conspicuous in voting against the motion, including representatives of future Northern Union clubs Broughton Rangers, Oldham, Runcorn, Salford, Swinton and Wigan.[11] For their part, those to the west of the Pennines felt that Yorkshire rugby was intent on self-aggrandisement and the domination of rugby for its own ends. 'They were trying to make the Union an accessory of Yorkshire' protested a delegate to the 1891 Lancashire AGM.[12] To Yorkshire rugby enthusiasts, it was not a question of North versus South but of Yorkshire versus the Rest. This was the case for Yorkshire regionalism in general during the late nineteenth century, as expressed in the plethora of weekly and monthly magazines with the word 'Yorkshire' in their title during this period: *The Yorkshireman, Toby, the Yorkshire Tyke, Yorkshire Owl, Yorkshire Chat* and *Yorkshire Busy Bee* to name only those which had significant coverage of football. These magazines were concerned to demonstrate the virtues of the York-shire character – *The Yorkshireman* even carried a column entitled 'What Yorkshiremen are inventing' at one point – rather than sing the praises of an abstract North, although this did not stop them denouncing the perfidy of an equally abstract South.[13] A similar point can be made about regionalist feeling west of the Pennines – one can find little trace of northern corporate feeling in Lancashire's journals and newspapers of the time. Unsurprisingly, the Lancastrian partisans felt that they too were a unique entity, with possibly more cause than the latter day Yorkists, as a recent historian of the North has pointed out: 'Always an isolated and insular county, Lancashire never quite got into step with the rest of the North. It moved towards alignment belatedly, as so often in the past; and still never quite got into place in the end.'[14]

Yet despite the misgivings of its leadership, the growth of the sport in Lancashire and especially Yorkshire in the 1880s was nothing short of phenomenal. At the start of the 1885–86 season a Yorkshire journalist remarked that: 'Goal posts and mill chimneys seem in some quarters to vie with each other in profusion. A friend of mine residing in the Girlington district [south-west of Leeds] tells me he can count the goal posts of twenty football clubs within a radius of 500 yards.' Between 1887 and 1890 the number of teams entering the Yorkshire Cup doubled, from 64 to 129, and the number of local and junior cup competitions experienced a similar growth, while the turn of the decade saw almost every sizeable town or district in Yorkshire (except Sheffield and Middlesbrough) able to boast its own cup, including Barnsley, Bradford, Castleford, Dewsbury and the heavy woollen district, Halifax, Huddersfield, Hull, Keighley, Leeds with three, Wakefield, Wharfedale and York. The popularity of these competitions with spectators can be gauged from the fact that the Bradford charity cup was able to hand over a clear profit of £700 to local hospitals in 1887.[15] That same year, the Yorkshire Church Temperance Shield competition began with 32 of the county's church-based teams and in 1888 the West Riding Public Schools Challenge Cup was inaugurated, private schools thus emulating the initiative of their board-school cousins in Bradford, who had begun their own competition in 1886. A cup for board schools in Leeds began in 1891, organised by the local branch of the National Union of Teachers. There were also competitions for members of those trades which still had half-day holidays during the week: ties in the Yorkshire Tradesmen's Cup were played on a Tuesday afternoon, while other half-holiday clubs played on a Wednesday afternoon. As a visitor to the county suggested in 1893, rugby had become the 'national game' of Yorkshire:

> I found the entire population of the place arguing madly about place
> kicks, dropped goals, referees, offside play, tackling, punting, dead
> balls, and I know not what else ... I have travelled through this great

county and from end to end thereof [and] have heard no scrap of rational converse. Nothing, absolutely nothing, but strange weird gibberish until my reason tottered on its throne.[16]

In Lancashire, because of the encroachment of soccer and the complete opposition of the county authorities to cup football, the rate of expansion did not match that of Yorkshire – in 1890 the YRU had 198 affiliated clubs whereas the Lancashire union never had more than 50.[17] Yet despite the lack of a county-wide cup competition to focus popular appeal, at a local level cup competitions flourished. The nearest equivalent to the Yorkshire Cup in Lancashire was the West Lancashire and Border Towns Cup which became the focal point of the season for clubs in its region. Begun in 1886 by the semi-autonomous West Lancashire and Border Towns Rugby Union its later rounds consistently attracted five-figure crowds.[18] The core teams of the competition – Wigan were the most northerly side with the remaining eleven teams drawn from the Merseyside area, including St Helens, Warrington and Widnes – had been stung into action by the growth of soccer and the cup was a deliberate attempt to maintain rugby as the dominant football code by increasing local interest. Such was the enthusiasm aroused that in 1889 a league competition was begun and a knock-out cup for junior sides started, the first year's entrants totalling forty. The South East Lancashire Union, formed in 1884 with members coming from the Manchester district, quickly followed its westerly neighbours. Catering for junior sides in the area, its cup was withdrawn by its sponsors, the *Athletic Journal*, in 1889 after a dispute over the allocation of competition profits and an investigation by the Lancashire Rugby Union into allegations of professionalism against the Union's officials.[19] The trophy reappeared later in the year as the Manchester and District Charity Cup. Although not as widespread as in Yorkshire, town-based competitions also sprang up. Eighteen thousand people watched the final of the Wigan challenge cup in 1886. Sixteen sides contested the first Rochdale Charity Cup in 1887 and thirteen sides contested the Warrington junior cup competition in 1888, by which time it was estimated that 10,000 people watched that year's final of the Rochdale cup.[20] These competitions assumed a double importance for the game, firstly by countering the appeal of soccer's plethora of cup competitions and also by granting a degree of autonomy from the constraints of the Lancashire Rugby Union. Provided their paths did not cross too often, the leaders of the Manchester and Liverpool clubs showed little interest in the activities of these local competitions, allowing the more dynamic and entrepreneurial clubs to explore ways of promoting the sport which were forbidden at county level. Nevertheless, as the captain of Warrington argued after they had won the West Lancashire cup in 1886, what was needed for rugby as a whole in Lancashire was a competition which emulated the Yorkshire Cup.[21]

PROFESSIONALISM ON TRIAL IN YORKSHIRE ...

The impact of the 1886 amateur regulations took time to filter through to Lancashire and Yorkshire – indeed, in Lancashire it was to be another four years before any formal action was taken by the authorities. When the anticipated storm eventually broke in Yorkshire in March 1888, it concerned a factory worker, Jack Clowes of Halifax.[22] Along with fourteen other northern players (and six southern-based players), Clowes had been approached by the England cricket professionals Alfred Shaw and Arthur Shrewsbury to take part in a football tour of Australia and New Zealand, to play both Rugby and Victorian (Australian) rules. Unapproved yet unforbidden by the RFU, the tour was an unambiguously commercial venture from the start, as Shaw conceded openly: 'We arranged the trip in the hope of making money.'[23] Unfortunately for Clowes, Dewsbury's president, Mark Newsome, was determined to feed fat the grudge he had borne against Halifax since 1883.[24] Newsome withdrew Dewsbury tourists Stuart and Stadden from his side to play Halifax in the second round of the Yorkshire Cup, which Dewsbury lost, and then appealed against the result on the grounds that Halifax had fielded a professional: Clowes![25]

When called before the Yorkshire committee, Clowes openly admitted everything and even offered to pay his £15 back.[26] The RFU declared him a professional, but he had already set sail with the touring party, placing him in the unfortunate position of being a tourist yet unable to play in any games, but it was an open secret that Clowes was not the only member of the touring party to receive money. Its most famous player, England rugby and cricket captain Andrew Stoddart, who took over the tour captaincy after the original captain, Broughton Rangers' Bob Seddon, was drowned, had been 'bound' to the tour by a down payment of £50, with more to follow.[27] How much Stoddart eventually received is unclear but can be gauged by the fact that two lesser-known amateurs had been offered £200 in expenses to make the trip.[28] Of those who did go, W. H. Thomas of Cambridge University and Wales was paid £90 for the thirty-week tour and tried to negotiate a further £3 per week when the tour was unexpectedly lengthened.[29] There were other advantages to being a gentleman amateur on tour, as can be seen from Shrewsbury's request to Shaw, who had recruited the players, to identify which 'amateurs you have promised to pay their wine and refreshment account at dinners.' Unfortunately for Shrewsbury, Shaw had failed to organise such social distinctions adequately en route, resulting in an on-board drinks bill of £68.[30] As soon as they arrived down under however, Shrewsbury imposed a hierarchy of players – at one point even threatening to stop sending the wages of Rochdale's Johnny Nolan home to his family unless he 'behaved himself', despite the fact that he was the tourists' leading try scorer. The unfortunate Clowes was at the bottom of the pile: 'He won't be able to play in a single match and we shall have all his expenses to pay ... He is a dead head, and of no use to us at all.'[31] For sharp entrepreneurs such as Shaw and Shrewsbury, the RFU's amateur regulations suited their purposes perfectly, as Shrewsbury admitted before the tour began, 'If the rugby union can get players to come out without paying them anything, all the better for us.'[32]

On their return in November 1888, having won twenty-seven of their thirty-five rugby matches and nine of the nineteen Victorian-rules games, confusion surrounded the tourists' status. The YRU, fully expecting the RFU to take disciplinary action, advised clubs not to play such players until the situation had been clarified. Salford telegraphed Rowland Hill to ask if their four tourists would be allowed to play. To everyone's surprise, the RFU lifted the ban on Clowes and merely called on the other tourists to sign declarations that they had received no money other than expenses while on tour. Needless to say, all of them swore that they had not received a penny and the matter was dropped.

The reason for the RFU's reluctance to act was simple: any investigation into the financial arrangements of the tourists would have implicated Stoddart and the other amateurs on tour. If the charges of professionalism had been pursued, the RFU would have had to ban one of England's leading sportsmen and declare illegal the generous advantages of the gentleman amateur's expenses, while to have maintained the ban on Clowes but taken no action against Stoddart would have been to admit openly that different, unwritten, rules applied to different classes of players. Nevertheless, by ignoring both their own regulations and the overwhelming evidence of payments, the RFU had laid bare the underlying class-bias of the amateur ethos – a middle-class gentleman was by definition an amateur, whether he was paid or not, and was not to be judged by the standards of other, working class, men.

This failure to act against 'one of their own' was met with anger by the supporters of amateurism in Yorkshire and seized upon as the opportunity to promote the county as the most determined and consistent proponent of amateurism.[33] The YRU had been under considerable pressure for some time to clean out its Augean stables and since the unexpected death of A. E. Hudson in January 1888 had been dominated by its newly appointed

THE MRS. PARTINGTON OF FOOTBALL.

With apologies to the Rev. F. Marshall, whose efforts to keep down Professionalism are most praiseworthy, but who does somewhat remind many onlookers of the dear old lady who gallantly endeavoured to sweep back the Atlantic with a broom.

The Reverend Frank Marshall is caricatured trying to turn back the tide of professionalism (from *The Yorkshireman*).

treasurer, the Reverend Frank Marshall, the headmaster of Almondbury School near Huddersfield, apostle of muscular Christianity and scourge of the 'veiled professional'. In October 1888, the committee laid charges of professionalism against Leeds St John's, the forerunner of today's Leeds RLFC, alleging that it had induced F. L. North to transfer from Kirkstall through the promise of a job. This time the case was watertight: St John's secretary George Smith had been foolish enough to send North a letter offering him a job, which the player gave to the Kirkstall secretary. Caught in the act, St John's were suspended for six weeks.

This was a tug at a loose thread which began to unravel the rugby tapestry. Instead of accepting their punishment, Leeds St John's claimed they had been made scapegoats and accused the YRU committee, and especially its president Mark Newsome, of hypocrisy. Other clubs claimed that the suspension was too harsh because it deprived them of lucrative games against St John's.[34] Undeterred, the YRU then suspended Brighouse Rangers for professionalism after they had induced Herbert Hartley, a miner, to join them from Liversedge in exchange for a job in which he would 'learn a trade.'[35] A few weeks later, Cleckheaton also found themselves suspended. Their crime was to have encouraged players to attend training sessions during the summer by offering them cloth with which to make up suits. 'No professionalism is still the cry of the hour – town, village and country being consumed with a zeal for football purity,' proclaimed the *Yorkshire Post* with its usual zealotry.

Purifying or not, it was obvious to all that the suspensions were playing havoc with the season and that serious financial losses would be faced both by suspended clubs and their opponents, and, given the widespread nature of the offences for which the three clubs had been suspended, the direct threat of suspension now hung over the head of virtually every club in the county. Faced with the bitter fruits of the amateur regulations, a number of Yorkshire's leading clubs began to campaign for reform. Led by Captain Bell, vice-president of the Halifax club who had led the defence of Jack Clowes, the dissidents forced a special general meeting of the YRU in February 1889 to discuss the suspensions. Bell called for clubs found guilty of professionalism to be punished by the forfeiting of home games only, thus avoiding the loss of fixtures by their opponents. However, he went on to propose a general solution:

> He yielded to no man in his opposition to professionalism and he thought if clubs established some common ground of action they might do something to prevent it. One of the ways to prevent it in its gross form was to give compensation for loss of time. The idea was

contrary to the present law but he thought it was worthy of consideration. He put it to them whether it would not be better to give compensation for loss of time to the working man, who enjoyed his football in the same way as the rich man ...[36]

The genie was out of the bottle. Although Bell commanded support from much of the meeting, no vote was taken as the YRU committee came up with a compromise scheme. The meeting also heard suggestions that county games should be held on weekdays, to avoid players missing Saturday club matches, and that clubs hosting county fixtures should be entitled to a larger share of the gate money. For the first time, a section of the senior clubs had openly called for change on the basis of commercial, club-centred, interests, denying the primacy of county games and amateurism, the twin pillars of Yorkshire rugby tradition.

Despite the qualms of these leading clubs, the YRU continued to hunt down violators of the amateur code, enthusiastically backed by the RFU – speaking after refereeing the 1889 Roses match, Rowland Hill declared that it was his aim 'to drive a nail into [professionalism].'[37] Perhaps not surprisingly, the next two clubs to be suspended, Wakefield Trinity and Heckmondwike, were among those most involved in the campaign for the February special meeting. Trinity had also been at the forefront of moves to start a Yorkshire league. Their offence was to play Teddy Bartram after he had accepted money from a testimonial, now an offence under the RFU rules. They were suspended for six weeks; Bartram, about whom it was common knowledge that he had been paid by the club for ten years, was barred from playing *sine die*.[38] Heckmondwike were charged with directly paying players, and, although not publicly admitted at the time, one player in particular, Dicky Lockwood.[39] The YRU had overwhelming circumstantial evidence against the club. Their accounts showed that gate money from the grandstand always came to an even amount and that, despite having a successful side with three England internationals in it, in only two games during the previous season did they appear to take more than £20 at the gate. Not only did they not have a bank account but the treasurer confessed that he never counted the gate money. Further questions were also raised as to how three players who had transferred to Heckmondwike all worked at the same dyeing factory in the town. Eventually the club and its players were suspended for three months.

The bloodletting went on. Over the next four years, the YRU held over twenty trials for offences against the amateur regulations. Only twelve of these hearings returned guilty verdicts. Bizarrely, the enthusiasm of the committee to track down miscreants led them to investigate wedding presents given to J. W. Moore of Leeds St John's and George Broadbent of Holbeck. Most disappointingly for advocates of rugby's moral role, the Leeds Parish Church club was suspended in January 1890 for sinning against the commandments of amateurism. Their secretary denied paying the players but, as *The Yorkshireman* revealed, this was rather less than the whole truth: 'The items for cigars, champagne, oyster suppers, drinks, etc., and the comfortable fashion in which they encouraged their players by giving them contracts, shows that the church militant is by no means given to mortification of the flesh, nor meant to allow its players to be left out in the cold when a nice little job was knocking about.'[40]

As the YRU's pursuit of the professional spectre gathered pace, the situation grew more complex as calls for league competitions began to be heard from senior clubs. In May 1889 Wakefield Trinity called a meeting of eleven of the county's senior sides to discuss the formation of a Yorkshire Football League. Although it did not win a great deal of support, the move highlighted the growing realisation that soccer was not going to collapse after legalising professionalism and that the formation of the Football League in 1888 had been highly successful. The growth of local cricket leagues in the North also served to underline the benefits to be gained from formal organisation of the season's competition.[41] By 1892 the pressure to form a Yorkshire league had become irresistible, both because of envy of the burgeoning crowds attracted by the Football League but also because the Yorkshire Cup triumphs of the relatively junior Otley and Pontefract clubs, in 1889 and 1891, were seen as diminishing the cup's credibility as the true championship of Yorkshire.[42] In May of that year ten of Yorkshire's leading clubs – Batley, Bradford, Brighouse Rangers, Dewsbury, Halifax, Huddersfield, Hunslet, Leeds, Liversedge and Wakefield Trinity – met to form the Yorkshire Football Alliance. Based explicitly on the organisation of the Football League and with a paid secretary to ensure efficient proceedings, its declared aim was to create 'a real fight for the Yorkshire championship.'[43] Despite intense opposition from both the YRU and RFU nine of the clubs stood firm for the new venture. The one exception was Leeds, of which YRU secretary James Miller was a leading committee member and which had commercial commitments to the Headingley grounds making them chary of opposing the rugby authorities. Faced with clubs determined to form a league, the YRU backed down and agreed to the formation of a Yorkshire Senior Competition (YSC), the word 'league' being avoided because it was felt to carry too strong an implication of professionalism, on condition that the YRU had ultimate control over its activities. There was then a rush to form lower divisions by the less senior clubs. In a few weeks, the unpretentiously titled Number Two Competition had been formed and by September 1893 almost the whole of Yorkshire rugby was organised on a league basis, with sixty teams participating in county-wide leagues.

As expected, the YSC proved to be an outstanding success. In its first month Bradford, Halifax and Hunslet all attracted five-figure crowds. In fact, just about the only loser in the whole affair was the Leeds club, whose abandonment of the Yorkshire Football Alliance was rewarded by their erstwhile allies with exclusion from the first season of YSC. Naively, the club assumed that it would be able to counter this reversal of fortune by arranging fixtures with the leading London sides, who showed no interest at all, so Leeds was reduced to playing friendly fixtures with some of the North's more junior sides. Needless to say, the season proved to be a financial disaster with losses of more than £800 leaving the club determined never to be placed in such a risky position again, a desire which was to shape the history of the club for the following two decades. For the other senior clubs however, there were no such problems: gates, revenue and public interest grew. At the end of the first season of the league system A. W. Pullin addressed the question of whether competition football had proved a success and answered 'with a monosyllabic "Yes".'[44]

... AND IN LANCASHIRE

In Lancashire, the campaign against professionalism was slower to develop, partly because the sport had effectively been 'socially zoned' for many years: day to day contacts between the public school-based clubs and those which relied on working-class players and support were few and far between, especially given the absence of a county cup competition.[45] The situation in Lancashire also differed from Yorkshire in that the growth of soccer offered an alternative to those seeking rewards for their sporting prowess. As a letter to the *Oldham Evening Chronicle* put it: 'The association game is slowly but surely taking our best men, as it is only likely that they will play where they can be paid.'[46] Nevertheless, by 1890 rumours of payment for play had become so widespread that the Lancashire committee, also under pressure to emulate the zeal of the YRU, was forced to act. Acting in concert with the LCFC, Mossley FC charged Werneth with inducing their star player, Abe Ashworth, to join them in exchange for a job. Conducting the case on Mossley's behalf, LCFC secretary J. H. Payne, a Cambridge-educated Manchester solicitor, described how Ashworth, a weft carrier in Mossley earning a £1 a week, had obtained a job as an iron dresser at Werneth's Hartford iron works for twenty-seven shillings per week. Determined to make an example of their first successful prosecution, the LCFC banned the unfortunate Ashworth *sine die* and suspended Werneth for sixteen weeks. The severity of the sentence, which in the case of the club was greater than anything handed down by the Yorkshire committee, shocked observers and caused outrage in Werneth, where 3,000 people signed a petition calling for the sentence to be lifted.[47]

Invigorated by their success, Payne and the LCFC committee planned a series of investigations into professionalism.[48] However, in October they found their hand forced by the Reverend Marshall, who publicly demanded that accusations of professionalism against Oldham be investigated by the Lancashire authorities. Oldham had long had the finger of suspicion pointed at them, especially given their success in recruiting players from Wales. The first was international three-quarter Bill McCutcheon who signed in 1888, swiftly followed by fellow international Dai Gwyn at the end of the next season.[49] Marshall, keen to build on his reputation as 'the man with bell, book and candle [facing] the evil spirit of professionalism', seems to have believed that the club would make an easy target.[50] However, it soon transpired that Marshall had absolutely no evidence for his, albeit probably correct, accusations and, in a move widely regarded as cowardice in Lancashire, refused to make public his evidence, saying that he would call witnesses to back up his accusations only when the LCFC committee pressed formal charges. After interviewing the club's three Welsh imports, who of course denied any hint of payment, the LCFC committee decided to take no further action.[51]

Marshall's ham-fisted attempt to extend the YRU's war on professionalism effectively halted the LCFC in its tracks. Such was the outrage of the Lancashire clubs that any attempt to pursue further investigations would have been treated with scorn, particularly because the accusers would have been seen as a tool of the Yorkshire rugby authorities. Even the *Manchester Guardian*, a determined opponent of any concession to professionalism, felt it necessary to oppose Marshall's attack on Oldham.[52] Antipathy towards Yorkshire had become intense, and not simply because of the two counties' traditional sporting rivalry; the strength of the white rose county had come to dominate northern rugby, toppling Lancashire's former leadership, with the YRU now commanding more seats on the RFU committee.[53] By causing the fight against professionalism to be identified as a Yorkshire issue, Marshall had so seriously weakened the LCFC's case that it was to be another four years before they felt strong enough to pursue the matter again, although when the battle was finally rejoined in 1894 its purpose was to hasten a split in the union.

Nevertheless, rumours of professionalism in Lancashire continued unabated. The most famous rumours centred on the mercurial brothers David and Evan James and their attempts to transfer from Swansea to Manchester's Broughton Rangers in 1892 for a reputed, and astronomical, signing on fee of £250. As with many Welsh players, the avowed reason for moving north was work, as Broughton's secretary explained: 'They left Swansea in search of work. One of them had been out of employment for some time. The other was in work but you know how things are in Swansea. Trade is bad and the wages the one in work got were not of the highest. So they came to Manchester in search of employment. Is there anything extraordinary in that?' However, a well-placed source in Swansea informed the *Clarion* that 'the talk of them leaving Swansea in search of work is moonshine. They were idolised in Swansea but their demands were too exorbitant.'[54] The LCFC blocked their move after Swansea claimed that the brothers had indeed demanded money from the club. It was also rumoured that Huddersfield, after having had their offer turned down by the brothers, had tipped the wink to the RFU.[55] Six weeks later the RFU overturned the decision and gave them permission to turn out for Rangers, but following pressure from the Welsh Rugby Union to make an example of the brothers, the RFU changed their minds in January 1893 and decided that, even if no money was received, the act of asking for payment was an act of professionalism and promptly banned the brothers as professionals.[56]

As in Yorkshire, the campaign against professionalism was complicated by calls for league competitions, but in Lancashire, the clamour for league competition was even more heartfelt. Here, the astonishing growth in support for soccer caused not only envy among rugby clubs but also fear. Rugby, which in 1880 had dominated the county (with the exception of Blackburn and its hinterland) was by 1892 in danger of being overwhelmed by the popularity of the round ball game. The failure of the county authorities to promote the game was causing it to wither on the vine, as A. A. Sutherland lamented at the end of the 1891–92 season:

> Less than ten years ago not a single association club could be found either in Manchester or district. Now both Newton Heath and Ardwick are high up and making big names for themselves at the dribbling code, and have innumerable imitators in their districts. To go further afield, Preston, Southport, Bolton, Bury, Chorley, Little Lever, Bootle, Walton and other clubs which stood high up in Rugby circles have all been absorbed by the associationists ... The conservatism evinced by rugby footballers in the Palatine is astounding and those who profess to look after the best interests of the game are content to sit still while the tide of association football makes great inroads into the stronghold of the rugby game.[57]

Sutherland himself called for a sixteen-team league to be formed of the best clubs in Cheshire, Lancashire and Yorkshire and in 1891 began to compile his own merit table, 'Muff's Rugby League' in the *Clarion*. Nor was he alone in calling for radical change; the *Salford Reporter* noted that soccer's 'introduction of leagues, alliances and the English association cup, not forgetting the recognised professional, [has meant] that the rugby game has soon received the go-by in public favour, especially in the county Palatine.'[58] Some rugby areas had taken matters into their own hands and set up their own district or regional leagues: the Manchester and District, North West, South East Lancashire and West Lancashire leagues all being in existence by 1892. Yet district leagues alone could not stem the tide of soccer into rugby areas. What was necessary, so the senior clubs thought, was an elite league based on the principles of the Football League. In June 1892 Swinton called a meeting in Manchester to discuss the formation of such a competition. The nine clubs which attended not only included the most senior commercially minded clubs – Swinton, Salford, Broughton Rangers, Oldham, Warrington and Wigan – but also three of the exclusive, public school-based clubs, Liverpool, Liverpool Old Boys and Broughton, which had led the Lancashire Rugby Union since its inception. Faced with almost unanimous support for the introduction of leagues, and with Liverpool and Manchester conscious of the fact that if they tried to oppose them they would simply be pushed aside, in September the Lancashire Rugby Union voted to sanction a league system.[59] Thirty-five of the county union's thirty-eight affiliated teams applied to join the three division championship, the only exceptions being, unsurprisingly, Liverpool, Liverpool Old Boys and Manchester, although Broughton also withdrew a couple of seasons later because, in the words of its committee's statement of resignation, it was 'trying to raise the social tone of the club.'[60]

MASTERS, SERVANTS AND PLAYERS

With the mass popularity of rugby there also came popularity of the players. Like so many other developments in northern football, players had become famous names at the time of the introduction of the Yorkshire Cup. Upon securing the services of Rufus Ward from Wakefield Trinity in 1877, Halifax had put up posters around the town bearing the legend: 'Ward, the great Yorkshire half back, will appear at Hanson Lane today.'[61] As the fame of footballers grew so did their rewards; until banned by the RFU, testimonials for players regularly raised upwards of £100. Weddings of players, in particular, were an occasion for much celebration by their supporters – hundreds of Bramley supporters followed local hero Harry Bradshaw to church for his wedding in 1894, blocking roads and turning the event into a minor civic celebration.[62] By 1889, Bradford's Joe Hawcridge was appearing in advertisements in the local press 'recommending' Goldsborough's herbalist embrocation.[63] The late 1880s also saw the introduction of football cards showing pictures of famous players and the crests of notable clubs, the most well known being those produced by J. Baines and Co. in Bradford, which quickly became immensely popular. Few players could match the claim of Huddersfield's Jack Dyson who, after scoring the winning try in a Yorkshire Cup quarter final, discovered that a local shop had made a model of him out of butter![64] Although public fame for sportsmen was not a new phenomenon, the newly found fame of rugby footballers differed somewhat from the adulation of, for example, W. G. Grace, in that it was predominantly focused on working-class players. While the cult of Grace was seen as a national asset, the cult of the footballer was different: 'Nowadays people make too much of football players,' argued the *Hull and East Riding Athlete* in 1890. 'There is too much "hero worship" knocking about. A crack footballer is looked upon as a little god – his name is never mentioned without admiration, and he cannot take the air in the street without being as much stared at as a model in Madame Tussauds.'[65]

No player was as famous in northern rugby football nor so symbolised the rise of the working-class player in the game as Richard Evison 'Dicky' Lockwood. Born to a labouring family in Crigglestone, near Wakefield, he made his debut as a right wing three-quarter for Dewsbury at the age of 16 in 1884 and rapidly established himself as a sporting phenomenon. Known as 'the Little Tyke' and 'Little Dick, the World's Wonder', partly because of his age and also because of his diminutive stature – he was only five feet four inches tall – Dicky played for Yorkshire, the North and England at the age of nineteen. Fleet of foot and deadly in the tackle, observers praised his knack of being in the right place at the right time. Playing for a losing Heckmondwike side in a Yorkshire Cup tie against Batley, he turned in a performance of such virtuosity that he left the field to the applause of both the winning and losing sides. An astute tactician, he was responsible for introducing the Welsh-originated four three-quarter system into the Yorkshire county team and for popularising the tactic of running after the ball after he had punted it in order to put his forwards on side.

Unlike his nearest equivalent of the time as a regional sporting hero, Welsh rugby union captain Arthur Gould, Dicky was unambiguously proletarian, a serious handicap to gaining the respect of those who ran the game: 'Dicky doesn't sport sufficient collar and cuff for the somewhat fastidious members of the committee,' it was reported in 1891.[66] In 1889 he shocked his supporters by moving to Heckmondwike who, thanks to an aggressive policy of attracting players through match payments and jobs boasted one of the best teams in the county. Despite the club being suspended for professionalism, Dicky survived two trials for the same charge, and the feelings of his supporters could be gauged by the fact that 'hundreds of people collected in Heckmondwike market place and its approaches, and the news of his acquittal was received with an outburst of cheering, the gathering in all respects resembling those witnessed at an exciting political election.'[67] Despite captaining England in 1894, he was barred by the RFU from playing in a club match that season. He had been forced to withdraw from the Anglo-Scots international because he could not take time off work to travel to Scotland but wanted to play for Heckmondwike on the same Saturday. This caused a considerable furore in Yorkshire, especially given the fact that Eton housemaster Cyril Wells had been allowed in similar circumstances to play for Harlequins after pulling out of the Rest of England team beaten by Yorkshire the previous season.[68] Dicky, a man who knew his own worth, had little time for the RFU, commenting in the twilight of his career that 'there was always a strong feeling against us', yet his talent was sufficiently prodigious almost to outweigh blind prejudice and between 1887 and 1894 he was an automatic choice for the England selectors. The tension between Dicky and the game's authorities epitomised however the relationship between the supporters of amateurism who ran the game and working-class players who had come to dominate its playing.

That working-class players made up the majority of Lancashire and Yorkshire rugby players by the mid-1880s is attested to by all contemporary commentators, included those who welcomed and those who opposed this development, but, unfortunately, we have no way of empirically testing this fact. Few players of the time can be traced by address and those club records which are available do not hold details of players' occupations or addresses. The best we can hope to do is to use the scanty evidence available to discover what sections of the working class these players came from. This available evidence (see Appendix Table A.3) tends to suggest that there was no particular occupational stratum from which they were drawn. As could be expected from the geography of the game, miners and millworkers make up a significant proportion of the occupations identified but no clear pattern emerges. Of the 47 traceable players, eight worked in textile mills and six in the mines. Four were unskilled labourers and three unemployed. Two others were shopkeepers. But in general there seems to be no great distinction between the number of players working in jobs classed as skilled, semi-skilled or unskilled. Nor are there any marked differences between players in Lancashire and players in Yorkshire. It would appear that players came from all sections of the industrial working classes in the region. In contrast, Tony Mason has speculated that professional Association foot-ballers were drawn mainly from the ranks of the skilled working classes.[69]

Why the occupational structure of players in the two football codes should differ is not clear, particularly as the two sports drew their players and support from the same communities. Much of the above evidence is drawn from transcripts of hearings into charges of professionalism against players where great attention was paid to the precise occupation of players, which would not allow them to gild the lily by claiming to be skilled tradesmen as would be possible in press interviews. Mason himself notes that none of the soccer players in his samples described themselves as labourers or unemployed, whereas seven players, or almost fifteen per cent, are categorised as such in this sample. The reason for these differences may well be found in association footballers' seeking to appear respectable when faced by the press, something that their rugby cousins could not do when faced by a rugby union kangaroo court.[70]

Slightly broader conclusions can be drawn from an admittedly much smaller sample of Welsh players who 'went North' to play for clubs in Lancashire and Yorkshire prior to the split. Of the thirteen whose occupa-tions can be traced (of which seven were internationals) four were factory workers, three miners, three clerks and the others a boilermaker, a storeman and a teacher. The teacher and two of the clerks came North in the 1880s, which would give a more proletarian hue to those following in the 1890s, as the showdown over professionalism grew near and an air of lack of respectability attached itself to playing in the north. It may also may be the case that the economic difficulties of the 1890s hit South Wales harder than the North of England, forcing players who worked with their hands to look further afield for economic security.

This influx of working-class players seemed to many middle-class rugby followers to put the future of the game in doubt unless a firm hand was exercised, especially when dealing with players who appeared to want to profit from the game. Commercial realities, public-school morality and class prejudices combined in the attitudes shown to players by officials. The great Yorkshire three-quarter Teddy Bartram's suspension from the game in 1889 had been precipitated by his impending testimonial at Wakefield. The club president, and leading YRU executive member, Barron Kilner had approached him and said 'Now Bartram, it's come to this: will you allow our club to head your testimonial with £50 and retire, or will you go on playing as an amateur and have nothing?' Unsurprisingly, Bartram, now in his thirties, opted for the money and a ban.[71] More egregiously, in

85

1892 Tadcaster, captained by Yorkshire captain, Oxford blue and England international William Bromet, suspended one of their own players, who was unemployed, for professionalism. He had sung in the club bar after a match, passed the hat round for a collection and received 12 shillings. The club insisted that he pay it back before he could play again.[72]

These attitudes were thrown into especially sharp relief when players were called to answer disciplinary charges before the YRU committee. The committee was both judge and jury, adopting a high moral stance towards those brought before it. For example, swearing and bad language were considered to be especially serious offences, whether directed at the referee or not. Thus the entire Skipton club was banned from playing for three weeks in 1892 after being found guilty of using bad language ... in their own dressing room, half an hour after their match had ended![73] When a player called Leech was brought before it in October 1890 for playing while suspended, he was asked two questions: 'Are you Leech?' and 'Did you play in this match?', and upon answering in the affirmative was told that he was suspended for the rest of the year. When he protested that he had not had a chance to defend himself, the committee increased his suspension to the end of the season for 'impertinence'.[74] Beechcliffe, the club he had played for, was not even a member of the YRU. The fact that almost all of the players brought before it were working class and that the core of the executive consisted of two public school masters, James Miller and the Reverend Frank Marshall, and three local industrialists, Mark Newsome of Dewsbury, Baron Kilner of Wakefield and Harry Garnett of Bradford, carried distasteful connotations for many. Ted Southall, summoned before it to answer somewhat convoluted charges of professionalism (he was the paid secretary of Leeds cricket club and also played for their football section), refused point-blank, saying that 'I prefer to sacrifice football altogether rather than submit to the indignity of appearing before the county committee.'[75]

The hearings into allegations of professionalism give us an especially rich insight into the relationship between players and officials. Disheartened by the difficulty of turning up hard evidence of payments to players in the cases immediately following the 1886 anti-professionalism rules, Marshall proposed in January 1888 that the burden of proof of innocence should rest with the player.[76] At the start of the 1889–90 season the YRU announced that, if asked, players would henceforth have to show cause for their move to another club, even if no charges were pressed.[77] In effect, players were considered guilty unless they could prove otherwise, because, as the *Yorkshire Post* explained: 'The character of the players themselves has to a very great extent changed, and changed, we are sorry to say, for the worst. A great many players who pass as amateurs are not only professionals, in truth of fact, who make money out of the sport, but, what is more, they are making a living out of it by dishonest means.'[78]

The attitude of the players towards these hearings was shaped by the treatment handed out to Jack Clowes, who, as we saw earlier, had innocently answered his cross-examiners truthfully. Subsequent defendants took this lesson to heart and the practice of stonewalling the inquisitors rapidly developed into an art form. No-one was more successful in this than Dicky Lockwood, who managed to survive two inquiries and the suspension of his club and still emerge with his reputation intact. His second trial lasted for three days and the 'prosecution' case was conducted by the Reverend Marshall:

> Marshall: 'What year were you asked to go to Morley?'
> Lockwood: '1886 about.'
> Marshall: 'What was the inducement?'
> Lockwood: 'Nothing.'
> Marshall: 'Do you know Mr Crabtree of Morley?'
> Lockwood: 'Yes.'
> Marshall: 'What did he offer you?'
> Lockwood: 'He did not offer to apprentice me to him. I was not paid anything. If anyone stated I was paid it would be wrong.'
> Marshall: 'A gentleman has stated that you were paid 10s a week.'
> Lockwood: 'Well, that gentleman is wrong.' ...
> Marshall: 'I want you to be very particular about this. I have positive information that you were paid after refusing to go to Morley.'
> Lockwood: 'I was not, sir.'
> Marshall: 'I understand you were paid £1 for exhibition matches.'
> Lockwood: 'That is wrong.'
> Marshall: 'Were you in a position to go to these matches and lose your wages?'
> Lockwood: 'Then I was, sir.' ...
> Marshall: 'I want to be explicit on this point, as to the meaning of "dinners". Have you ever been told that, seeing that you were not so well off, you could have "dinners" if you went to play with any club?'
> Lockwood: 'No, never.'[79]

In general, those who followed Lockwood's example usually avoided sanction, while those who engaged in detailed explanations were less successful. A former Doncaster player called Foster who had moved to Bradford and sought permission to play for Manningham found himself discussing how his prospects as a painter would be improved by his move and had his request turned down.[80] Teddy Bartram exasperatedly confessed during cross-examination that if he had known that IOUs he gave to the club for a £32 'loan' had to be repaid he wouldn't have borrowed the money in the first place.[81]

Players were also at risk from unscrupulous clubs who could utilise the ambiguities of amateurism to blackmail them: Kirkstall's F. L. North, uncertain of how to react to Leeds St John's written promise of a job if he played for them, gave the letter to the Kirkstall secretary, who told him, 'As long as you remain true to us, no-one shall see this letter.' Needless to say, a few weeks later the player changed his mind and the letter was used against him.[82] Richard Earnshaw, a halfback with Shepley, was told that if he left the club his employer would sack him. Eventually he signed for Huddersfield and, as threatened, was sacked. Any doubts as to the cause of his sacking were dispelled when his job was given to Harry Hill, a former Huddersfield player who had moved to Shepley.[83] Few players would have disagreed with one commentator's 1890 observation that 'the amateurs playing under the Yorkshire Rugby Union laws really have less liberty than the professionals in Association, and a comparison of the rules and bye-laws of each will prove this up to the hilt.'[84]

There was some resistance by players to such treatment, although the amateur status of the players meant that there were never any moves towards the formation of a players' trade union. We have already seen how Ted Southall refused to appear before a YRU investigation into professionalism; his example was followed by Salford captain Frank Miles in 1894 who, accused of being offered thirty shillings a week to play for Wigan, told the Lancashire committee that: 'I do not intend to give any evidence at all in any shape or form. I do not care if I get suspended or not. I am not going to turn Queen's evidence against anybody.' He was immediately banned from the game for professionalism.[85] In 1890 a number of players in the Hull team threatened to go on strike over the levels of expenses payments for a game at West Hartlepool, but were eventually persuaded to play – although it is not recorded if they won an increase in payments.[86] Wakefield Trinity, Harrogate and Armley experienced players' strikes over team selection policies. None was successful and the Trinity strike resulted in six players being expelled from the club the following week.[87] In 1891, a pseudonymous letter writer protested against the YRU executive's decision to stop a player's transfer, despite their admitting that there was no evidence of any inducement, by calling on players and club members to 'declare open war and defy the county committee.'[88] Such activities were rare exceptions however, discontent being more likely to be expressed by individual, albeit illegal, bargaining for better terms or by changing clubs, as for example the player who told the YRU executive that he wanted a transfer because he didn't like being forced to wear a collar and tie at his current club and that 'If I'm noan good enew to laake fooitball wi'em baht collar and "dickey", I'm noan bahn to laake at all.'[89] John Sutcliffe, Heckmondwike's international three-quarter, gave up rugby altogether after the YRU suspended the club for professionalism. He immediately switched to soccer, signing for Bolton Wanderers, and eventually became one of only three men to be capped for England at both rugby and soccer.[90] The capacity for collective action was also seriously undermined by the secrecy involved in remunerating players and the divisions this created among them. As a Northern Union commentator looking back at the days before the split pointed out, 'A player who had it in his power to make things awkward for his club received the lion's share indeed; whereas each member of the rank and file had usually to be content with a half a crown which someone, quite accidentally, let fall into his boot or pocket.'[91]

The one aspect of the relationship between players and clubs where players did make their presence felt was in the pressure towards payment for play. There is little doubt that the vast majority of working-class rugby players favoured some form of professionalism: there was a 'burning anxiety amongst them for compensation and for even more than that, for professionalism outright' and it was confidently stated that 'ninety-nine out of a hundred players in Yorkshire' favoured a system of payments. In Lancashire, Swinton captain and England international Jim Valentine spoke for many players when he said, 'A working man cannot be expected to give his working time for nothing and nobody should ask him to do it.'[92] As the practice of payment in cash or in kind spread, so too did the bargaining power of the players, and, as we saw earlier, with it came a distrust of the motives of those players. There was no doubt that the threat of professionalism came first and foremost from working-class players: 'To men of small means, the question no doubt suggests itself whether football cannot in some way or another be made to pay.'[93]

The 'question' indeed suggested itself most strongly when players changed clubs. Dicky Lockwood was reputed to have said that 'he had got all he could out of Dewsbury and that he was going to Heckmondwike to see what he could get there.'[94] J. H. Gordon of Pocklington baldly told the YRU executive that he would play for the club which found him the best job because every man should do the best he could for himself.[95] In 1885 W. Pulleyn was overheard telling friends in a local pub in Selby that 'he would play for the club that paid him best' before he transferred his services to Manningham.[96] F. L. North allegedly arranged his move across Leeds from Horsforth to Wortley because he believed that the latter were the best club in the city 'for tipping.'[97] The provision of a job on condition a player turned out for a particular club was especially common. The depression of the early 1890s in the textile trades meant that for many players their best chance of finding work was by trading their footballing skills. In Lancashire, Radcliffe were able to attract players because their president, J. C. Hamer, owned a cotton factory employing over 700 people and would give jobs to players through a sub-contractor.[98] Three of the Heckmondwike team suspended for professionalism in 1889 worked at the same textile mill in the town but, apart from their football ability, they were little different from 200 other textile workers who had moved there over the past three years to find work.[99]

Much the same applied to the influx of Welsh players into the game from the late 1880s. Bill Keepings came all the way from Cardiff to Halifax to take up a position as a boilermaker and three Welshmen moved to Leeds to play football for Leeds Parish Church and to work at the nearby Waterloo Colliery in 1893.[100] The appeal of Oldham to Welsh players could be found in the continued success of 'Spindledom.'[101] One enterprising Welsh player even advertised his services in the classified pages of the *Yorkshire Post*:

> General Clerk requires a situation, knowledge of French; highest references; wing three-quarter Welsh team. Address P28, The Yorkshire Post, Leeds.[102]

While advertising publicly was unusual, letters to clubs from players seeking jobs were not. W. Thorne, a Dewsbury player hailing from Cardiff, sent a circular around local clubs asking them to 'kindly inform me if you are in a want of a wing three-quarter back. I am from Cardiff, and have been playing with the Dewsbury club, whose officials do not seem to be in a hurry to find me a situation. I can kick with either foot, and am a sound tackler, and have a good turn of speed. I have been accustomed to office work. An early reply will oblige.'[103] In Cumberland, the transfer of J. Alderson from Whitehaven to Westoe in County Durham was vetoed by the county committee when it was informed of a letter Alderson had written to the South Shields club offering his services if they could find him a job or a pub.[104] To the supporters of amateurism, using football talent in this way was anathema: 'These alien recruits, who are said in one or two instances to be pit men, are striking a hard blow at the pastime. In one way or another, it is made profitable for them to go outside their districts, there receiving a good round sum under the elastic term of expenses.'[105]

In the 1890s, as the game's influence increased, it became a common-place for players transferring their services to another club mysteriously to become pub landlords, where their fame could be sure to attract customers keen to bask in the reflected glory of their heroes. In 1893 Harry Varley, a miner in Liversedge, moved to Oldham and took over a pub, as did Edmund Buckley of Halifax on his transfer to Rochdale. Halifax and Bramley became especially famous for the number of publicans playing for them.[106] Nor was the practice confined to clubs in Yorkshire and Lancashire. In August 1893 the Manningham forward Redman moved to the Leicester club to take up a pub in the city.[107] Out of 35 players who appeared for Yorkshire in the 1892–93 season, ten were publicans.[108] Frank Marshall claimed that Bradford's 1893 Yorkshire Senior Competition winning side contained eleven publicans, and in January 1895 the *Yorkshire Owl* facetiously titled an article 'How to spend a football evening', listing eleven pubs in the centre of Bradford which were run by or connected with players from the city's two senior clubs.[109]

How much players were paid by clubs is difficult to ascertain given the secrecy under which payments were made. In the early part of the 1880s payment in kind, through the ubiquitous legs of mutton, bottles of port and other items of food and drink generally out of the everyday reach of most of the players, colloquially known as 'presents', became the norm. This tradition continued and, as RFU rules on payments tightened, the methods used to recompense players became more inventive. As can be seen in the case of Dicky Lockwood, even the provision of dinners for players came under the scrutiny of the YRU. More imaginatively, Elland ran a prize draw in which each player miraculously won a prize every week and Harrogate players received their Christmas 'presents' from the club via the apparent generosity of a certain Mrs Marsden.[110] For winning the Yorkshire Cup in 1888, Halifax presented their players with gold medals, marble clocks and gold watches worth 100 guineas.[111] And, as the Teddy Bartram case demonstrated, clubs were not above 'loaning' money to players who had little intention, or means, of paying it back. Sometimes items noted in the account books of clubs stretched credibility to breaking point. Heckmondwike's accounts showed 4d per player being allowed as refreshments for players' meetings – unfortunately for the club, the Reverend Frank Marshall pointed out at a YRU hearing that a rough calculation would show that the club must have held 60 players' meetings in December 1888 alone![112]

Although vigorously denied by all, a scale of cash payments prevailed amongst wide sections of the sport by the late 1880s, as a study of the YRU's hearings of alleged cases of professionalism shows. A Manningham player called Birmingham claimed to be paid 28 shillings a week in 1885, but this would seem to be an exaggeration on his part.[113] However, Wortley, a junior club in Leeds, allegedly offered F. L. North five shillings a week to play for them in 1889.[114] The aforementioned England international John Sutcliffe reputedly received 10 shillings a match from Heckmondwike, while household-name Dicky Lockwood could command £1 a match from the same club.[115] These rates compared favourably with those paid by the openly professional Association football clubs, and in some cases were even better. Stoke City paid their players 2/6d a week in the 1885–86 season and when Sheffield Wednesday turned professional in 1887 they paid nine shillings for home games and eleven shillings for those away.[116] By the 1890s the going rate for good players had increased, as was illustrated by the trials which engulfed Lancashire rugby in the autumn of 1894. Salford's Frank Miles, an outstanding but uncapped player of the period, was offered thirty shillings a week in the off-season by Wigan. Leigh paid international forward Tom Coop £1 a game, another player seventeen shillings, their two Welsh imports 12/6d and 7/6d respectively and the rest of the team between five shillings and 2/6d.[117] As these figures demonstrate, rugby had developed a sophisticated, albeit informal, market place in which players, usually acting according to Brecht's axiom that 'time is short and so is money' sought to maximise their earnings potential before the inevitable onset of old age, injury or loss of form.

'SCIENCE' ON THE FOOTBALL FIELD

The profound social changes which had taken place in the world of rugby football could not but be reflected in the way the game was played on the field. We have seen in previous chapters how the game up to the late 1870s had been dominated by scrummaging. Yet by 1887 the passing game was so prevalent in the North that the *Scottish Athletic Journal* could remark that the touring Batley side 'throw the ball boldly, and with as much calculated judgement as a first-class cricketer could throw a cricket ball.'[118] Historically, the credit for developing the passing game and placing the game on a 'scientific' basis has gone to Henry Vassall of Oxford University and England, who introduced passing among the team and dribbling by the forwards to the Oxford University side of the early 1880s. Developing this theme, most histories of rugby state that the first pass from a half back to a three-quarter was made by Lancashire's J. H. Payne to Teddy Bartram during the 1881 North versus South game, and that it wasn't until 1886 that Bradford centre three-quarter Rawson Robertshaw initiated the practice of centres passing the ball to wingers.[119] It is clear that tactical innovation and experimentation became widespread in the mid- to late-1880s, moving the game away from constant scrummaging and kicking towards a 'scientific' playing style, defined by the predominance of passing and running with the ball in order to score tries.

Perhaps most daring of the early innovative teams was the Thornes side of 1882 which overcame the much-fancied Wakefield Trinity in that year's Yorkshire Cup final. Marshalled by warehouseman Harry Wigglesworth, Thornes planned their games in a way previously unheard of. Eschewing the traditional practice of forwards taking whichever position was available when they arrived at the line-out or scrum, known as 'first man up gets his head down', the Thornes forwards were assigned positions which they varied according to where on the pitch play was taking place and what the score was at that particular time. Anticipating the 1905 New Zealand rugby union tourists, Thornes used a form of 'wing forward' play whereby the wing forwards would not pack down in the scrum but waited at the side of the scrum in order to tackle the opposing scrum half or to shield their own. Unusually for the time, they also scrummaged with just three players in the front row of the scrum, enabling them to gain more momentum for pushing. The side also used previously prepared code words and signals to indicate a change of tactics, such as the direction of a kick or a direct heel out of the scrum. Nor were they unaware of the importance of psychological factors, so effectively riling the notoriously short-tempered Trinity captain Barron Kilner, who before the final had facetiously asked 'Who, where, what and which is Thornes?', that his performance was severely under par.[120] Yet despite the success of Thornes, which was ultimately short-lived because of the ease with which richer clubs plundered their players, wing-forward play was widely disliked, one critic calling it 'reprehensible', because it was seen as a spoiling tactic which prevented the ball moving away from the scrum. Nevertheless, it had a long history in Yorkshire, Brighouse Rangers using two wing forwards in conjunction with four three-quarters to defeat Halifax as late as the 1893–94 season.[121]

The rise of the Thornes team highlighted the advantages to be gained from having a well-prepared, organised side. By the mid-1880s clubs had started to develop training techniques to enhance their players' abilities, especially for the Yorkshire Cup competition. By 1885 specialist trainers were employed to improve players' fitness. In 1886 Dewsbury appointed Tommy Conlon, a former professional runner, to train the team, a method emulated by Bowling Old Lane when they took on the famous professional sprinter Harry Richardson a few years later.[122] The following year Batley, one of the first teams to appoint a 'medicine man' to attend to the team, announced that they would be training at night under electric torches.[123] St Helens Recreation trained every Tuesday and Thursday in the late 1880s, combining both dumbbell exercises and boxing. Summer training was popular too, although the providing of incentives to players to attend such sessions was to see Cleckheaton suspended for professionalism. 'Most football teams have a property manager, a trainer and a medicine man' reported *The Yorkshireman* in 1892, which later the same month revealed that Hunslet were using the revolutionary method of a blackboard and chalk for pre-match tactical discussions.[124] Nor was diet neglected. The Batley team raised eyebrows at a celebratory dinner when they refused the pudding because it contained brandy and the club president, himself a medical man, insisted that 'physical training required abstention from excess both in food and drink, and if this was not carried out, there was no chance of going on to victory.'[125]

In contrast, such training was felt to be unnecessary by the middle-class amateurs who led the game. 'The Rugby Union officials, apart from other considerations, have a strong objection to training for football, contending that if a player abstains from foolish excess and takes moderate exercise, he will always be in condition,' it was stated in 1886, but the rise of the working-class player demonstrated that, to remain competitive at least, this was simply no longer the case. How much working in a physically demanding job helped when it came to playing rugby is unclear, but certainly many of the players felt it to be an advantage. St Helens Recreation captain Monsey Parr observed in 1889 that 'only those as are used to working hard can tackle it' and pointed to the decline of middle-class players in the game as evidence.[126] As much was admitted in 1892 by 'Londoner' when he examined the reasons for the North's playing superiority: 'How is it done? Why, by converting the indigenous talent into an enthusiastic machine and by insisting on the fact that that machine is always in working order.'[127]

Fitness and organisation did not necessarily however make for an exciting, open game. Rugby still maintained a large measure of dourness carried over from its early days of mass scrummaging. Under pressure from Yorkshire delegates, the March 1882 general meeting of the RFU ruled that players not in the scrum had to retire five yards behind it in an attempt to open up the game, but the lack of neutral referees (which were not made compulsory until 1885) made this rule something of a dead letter. Another suggestion at this time to make the game more open, touted in both north and south, was to play the game with a round ball to allow forwards more opportunity to dribble the ball as in soccer, although this was never taken up,[128] but as the game became more competitive, the need to develop new tactics and styles of play took precedence and the advantages of the passing game quickly became apparent. By the mid-1880s the growing dominance of passing movement and team play was leading some to question the importance attached to the goal in the winning of games. Before the 1886–87 season, the only way a game could be won was by one side scoring more goals than its opponent, regardless of the number of tries scored by either side. Hence it was not unknown for a team to dominate a game, scoring several tries but no goals, yet lose a game to an inferior team because the latter had scored a lucky goal. In the Yorkshire Cup, 'minors', or touchdowns by a defending side behind its own try line, were used to decide drawn matches but the South East Lancashire Cup competition took the logic to its fullest extent and introduced a points system which awarded four points for a try, eight for a goal, six for a drop goal and one for a minor, the winner being the side which scored the most points rather than the most goals.[129] In October 1886 the RFU decreed that three tries would equal a goal, which still meant that four tries had to be scored to defeat a goal (although in September 1891 this was changed to make three tries superior to a goal). That this marked the beginning of an important change to the traditional nature of the game was noted in 1888:

> The acme of good play is when a skilful three-quarter or half back finishes up a skilful or dashing run by dodging a full back and planting the ball over the line. In the North, no other part of the game is more applauded than this, and anything in the rules tending to lessen the kudos of the same cannot but injure the style of play and make the game less scientific and more of a blind dropping into touch exhibition.[130]

This is not to say that forward play did not change. Northern forwards, especially those from Yorkshire, became noted for their size, mobility, dribbling ability and skills in wheeling the scrum to enable a quick heel out to allow the scrum-half to set up an attack. Internationals Harry Bradshaw and Donald Jowett, nicknamed 'the baby elephant', both weighed over 19 stones yet were famed for their ability to move quickly around the field. Indeed, of forty-four players from Lancashire and Yorkshire who were selected for England between 1886 and 1895, twenty-three were forwards. Against Scotland in 1892, the pack consisted of seven forwards from the two counties, as well as four backs from Yorkshire. Yet despite the considerable success of what was known as the 'fast forward' game, it increasingly came to be felt in the north that too many matches were dominated by forward play, especially cup ties when the necessity to win meant that sides kept the ball tight in scrummages to lessen the risk of their opponents gaining possession. The 1891 Yorkshire Cup competition became notorious for this type of play: in the Batley versus Dewsbury local derby neither half back made a single pass to his backs, and Wakefield Trinity and Ovenden managed 79 scrums and 54 line-outs in their allotted eighty minutes.[131]

Clubs had been aware of this problem from the mid-1880s and various attempts had been made to overcome it. In 1889 Halifax had experimented with three half backs and just eight forwards, using it to good effect to defeat the 1888 touring New Zealand side. However, when faced with the speedier, more skilful forwards of the senior Yorkshire sides, they found their less numerous pack overwhelmed and abandoned the idea, although others continued their experiment up to 1895.[132] Two full backs was offered as an alternative but never gathered much support. The dominating influence of northern forwards also meant that clubs were reluctant to move to the four three-quarter system pioneered in Wales and first used by the Welsh national side in 1886.[133] 'Buller' Stadden had unsuccessfully introduced the system to Dewsbury when he moved there in 1886, but Oldham were the first northern side to use it regularly when Bill McCutcheon joined them in 1888 from Swansea.[134] Even then, there was still widespread doubt in Lancashire and Yorkshire as to its efficacy – despite northern admiration for the back play of clubs like Newport, it was believed that its success in Wales was due to the poorer quality of Welsh forward play, especially in comparison to club football in the north of England. When it came to be widely, although not universally, accepted in the early 1890s, it was partly due to Dicky Lockwood who introduced the system to the Yorkshire county side and captained the 1894 England side against Wales which used four three-quarters to beat the Welsh 'at their own game.' It was also part of a broader move to make the sport more attractive to spectators and counter the increasing threat of soccer. The need for change was well spelt out by a former player in 1891:

> The public ... don't want to witness only scrimmages nowadays but fast, open play, and nothing will tend to bring about this more than playing four three-quarters ... The association game is no doubt in a healthy state and in places has sounded the death knell to Rugby football. Why is this? Simply because the public want a game where they can see plenty of the ball. If four three-quarters is not generally adopted, then I contend that the number of players should be less.[135]

A few months later, addressing a conference of Yorkshire referees, YRU secretary James Miller called for a reduction in the number of players in a team to thirteen. Recalling the improvement to the game which the reduction from twenty-a-side to fifteen-a-side in 1875 had made, Miller argued that the 'pushing age' of dominant forwards had come to an end and that 'instead of admiring the physique and pushing power of those giants which took part in the game in the early stages ... in the future they would be able to admire the skilful and scientific play of the game.' He returned to the theme in 1894 when speaking at a dinner in honour of Manningham, that year's Yorkshire champions: 'Let [the game] be of an open, skilful and scientific character and not the slow monotonous game which people would not go and watch,' and reiterated the need to reduce the number of forwards in the game, 'where most of the illegalities and transgressions occur.'[136] In addition to his native county, where his successor as secretary, William Hirst, had spoken forcibly in favour of thirteen-a-side at Huddersfield's AGM that year, he found much support for his ideas in Lancashire, ranging from staunch defenders of the amateur ethos such as the *Manchester Guardian* to outright advocates of open professionalism like the *Clarion*.[137] More so than Miller, who had just seen soccer establish its first beachheads in Yorkshire, Lancashire clubs were acutely aware of the need to make the game more attractive in order to hold back the tidal wave of soccer now sweeping through their region.

But although the RFU was prepared to travel a little down the road of reform – the deciding of games by points scored instead of solely by goals had been introduced for the 1889–90 season, a goal being counted as three points and a try as one, although this was raised to two in 1891 – radical moves such as those proposed by Miller and his supporters in the north were beyond the pale. There were even those, such as Loretto headmaster H. H. Almond, who advocated a return to the days of twenty-a-side, fearing that rugby had become nothing but spectacle and was in danger of losing its purpose as a means of keeping fit for boys and young men.[138] Although those engaged in the debate had no way of knowing it, it was to be the Northern Union, freed from the constraints imposed by the RFU, which would continue and put into practice the discussion about reform of the game and its playing.

THE BUSINESS OF RUGBY

The sheer weight of interest generated by the game led inevitably to very rapid commercialisation. 'Who would have been believed ten years ago if he had prognosticated that £260 and £270 would be received as "gate money" at Saturday afternoon football matches?', remarked one observer in 1884.[139] Nowhere was this more true than in Bradford. By 1885 Bradford

FC were forced to appoint a second paid part-time secretary due to the administrative burden now placed on the club by its success. In 1887 the club took £2,049 in gate money but was also estimated to have lost another £1,000 due to matches cancelled because of widespread snow that winter. The following season they took £2,500 and their gate money income never dropped below £2,000 until 1892. Although it was undeniable, but not publicly stated, that some of this income was expended on players, it was of such little importance that for nine years, until 1892, annual profits never fell under £1,000 and actually topped £2,000 in 1886. In 1887 the club announced it had paid off a capital debt of £8,000 which had been used to develop the Park Avenue ground and a year later the accounts showed that a cash balance of £4,331 was available at the bank. In 1890 that figure had risen to £7,000. They were, it was claimed with little fear of contradiction in 1887, financially the strongest football club of any code in England, a fact acknowledged in a roundabout way by the Inland Revenue in 1893 when they chose to investigate Bradford and Aston Villa for non-payment of taxes.[140] Other clubs also found themselves in a world of riches which would have been unimaginable in 1880. Manningham's income topped £1,500 in 1888 and continued to rise. In the same season Hull FC took over £1,900 through their gates. Halifax's gate money rose to over £2,000 during the 1888–89 season and the new Headingley-based Leeds club took over £2,200 in gate money in the 1891–92 season. Although such amounts were not generally equalled in Lancashire, at least by rugby-playing football clubs, the growth in gate money receipts was still startling. Salford, despite playing in close proximity to both Swinton and Broughton Rangers, saw their income from gates almost double to over £1,000 in the five years to 1891. Warrington's gate money after 1887 stayed constantly around the £800 mark, with St Helens averaging around £600.

Where did this money go? Some went in one form or another to the players, although such money was not always included in recorded receipts – as the *Bradford Observer* confided, 'The trick [of paying players] can be done by manipulating the gate money before it becomes a cash book item.'[141] However, as many clubs discovered later in the Northern Union, there was a great deal of difference between an informal agreement to pay cash in hand, or in kind, and legal contracts obliging clubs to pay a weekly wage bill. Aside from any ethical attachment to amateurism, most clubs opposed professionalism because of its sheer cost – one look at the wage bills of the professional soccer clubs was enough to persuade any rugby club official of the dangers of 'open' professionalism. Being under no obligation to pay players regularly meant that, at least up until the late 1880s, labour costs were a minor drain on resources. In fact, the greatest source of expenditure was the purchase, improvement and maintenance of grounds. Fuelled by the massive inflow of capital to the game and necessitated by the ever-increasing numbers watching the sport, rugby clubs initiated a ground development boom from the mid-1880s. Halifax, Manningham, St Helens, Leeds St John's, York, Warrington, Swinton, Wigan, Rochdale Hornets, Leigh, Keighley, Hunslet and the two Hull sides were merely the most prominent clubs of the time to have moved grounds in the decade before the 1895 split. Halifax spent nearly £5,000 buying their Thrum Hall site and erecting a pavilion. Hull eventually paid £6,500 to acquire the Hull Athletic Grounds, renaming it the Boulevard.[142] Manningham spent £1,400 to make their Valley Parade ground playable before a ball was passed. Huddersfield spent over £8,500 improving their Fartown complex. By 1896 Oldham had spent almost £3,500 building a pavilion, stand and terraces at their Watersheddings ground. Bowling Old Lane, a successful Bradford junior side, were faced with a bill for £1,000 to develop a new ground before local volunteers and supporters pitched in to help reduce the cost to £300, and, although not directly funded by the Leeds St John's club, their new home at Headingley cost £25,000 to build and develop.[143]

Once installed at an appropriate ground, clubs also faced high levels of expenditure for its up-keep. Bradford and Leeds regularly spent between £100 and £200 per season on straw to protect their pitches from the unwelcome visitations of the northern weather. Advertising costs were also a significant outlay: for example, Salford never spent less than £100 on advertising after 1887 and in 1888 Hull spent over £300 on this item. Turnstiles were probably first used by Hull and Wakefield Trinity in 1883 and by 1890 most senior clubs had installed them, often creating the need to pay gatemen, or 'money takers' as they were known; although an unusual example because of the size of the ground, Leeds paid out £61 in gatemen's wages in 1892. Nevertheless, claims that crowds were under-reported remained constant and the 1892 Widnes AGM saw vociferous appeals for more 'checkers' to be appointed.[144] Those clubs not sufficiently endowed to commission their own purpose-built grandstands would buy them, usually from agricultural shows. Dewsbury bought their original stand from the York Show in 1883 before replacing it with the memorably titled, 130 yards long, 'Noah's Ark', which they bought from Preston for £170 in 1885 and Castleford purchased their two stands from the nearby Pontefract Show.[145]

In fact, commercial reality dictated that once a club had decided to become part of the football world and compete in cup competitions, develop a successful side and attract public support, it found itself caught in a spiral

Even by the mid-1880s, matches at Bradford's Park Avenue ground were still viewed as social occasions for the local middle classes (from *The Yorkshireman*).

of increased crowds and rising expense in order to be able to cope with the growing number of spectators, and from a civic point of view, success was not merely attained through the winning of matches, it also required a ground of which its locality could be proud. Hence the constant rivalry between Bradford, Huddersfield and Leeds for the title of the north's leading rugby arena, and the large amounts poured into the construction of pavilions, access to which was invariably restricted to the more socially exalted supporters of the club. However the exigencies of football economics also meant that this drive for bigger gates and better facilities undermined many of the social exclusivities of the game. Although gate money meant that clubs were no longer dependent on members for the whole of their income, members' subscriptions still played an important part in club finances. As commercial realities began to dominate clubs' thinking, the need to increase membership brought in larger numbers of working-class and lower middle-class members, diluting the social cachet of club membership and further weakening the control of those who had founded the clubs.

Other than gate receipts and membership subscriptions, the most usual ways of attempting to raise additional income were summer sports days and annual balls. Sports days, usually held around Whitsuntide and the August bank holiday, focused on athletic events, not least because the playing of football in the summer months was barred by the RFU regulations (in fact the YRU suspended eight teams for this very offence in 1890), and more often than not offered cash prizes.[146] Even a relatively minor side like Pudsey could offer £40 in prize money for their annual athletics meeting in 1889.[147] How successful these ventures were in raising cash is unclear, Warrington only once making more than £27 from their August Monday sports day in the years up to 1895.[148] Likewise the annual balls which many clubs organised seem to have been at best public relations exercises and at worst excuses to spend club money on the more senior members. In 1887 Huddersfield's annual ball attracted 550 'of the elite of Huddersfield' including such civic worthies as H. F. Beaumont MP, the Lord Mayor, the Town Clerk of Leeds and various titled members of the local community. It is not recorded how much money, if any, was raised for the club. The club also organised a series of smoking concerts for members, which included piano and banjo recitals, but which were abandoned after losses were experienced.[149] After two loss making balls, Warrington dropped them completely in 1890.[150]

Other sources of income available to clubs were, by and large, highly marginal. The sale of franchises to sell refreshments inside grounds was common. Halifax raised £80 this way in the 1887–88 season but this appears to have been an unusually high figure, for when Dewsbury tried to sell their franchise in 1885 for the previous season's price of £40 they found no takers and were forced to settle for £25.[151] Other clubs no doubt used the rights to sell refreshments as a form of payment in kind to players. Jim Slevin, Wigan captain in the mid-1880s and mine host at the Bull's Head, was also the sole agent for the sale of refreshments inside the Wigan ground.[152] Some money could also be made during the summer close season. Hull's ground was used as grazing land for sheep and, at one point, Batley allowed a local farmer to keep poultry under the stand but balked at a request to allow pigs to use the pitch, but again, the amounts which could be made through such enterprise were strictly limited, Hull receiving just £11 for grazing rights.[153]

Despite this high, if not always fruitful, level of commercial activity, there is little indication that any rugby club in the north saw itself, or indeed acted, as a profit maximising institution. Most clubs, and especially the most senior ones, saw themselves as akin to a civic institution, bringing honour to their town and providing a focal point for local sporting endeavour – yet another manifestation of the sense of civic pride which had spurred the formation of clubs. Hence the number of clubs which combined football with cricket and/or athletics, very often with the football section subsidising the less well-patronised cricket sections. As *Athletics News* commented in 1887, 'In ninety-nine cases out of a hundred ... football helps cricket over the stile of financial embarrassment.'[154] Halifax in particular spent considerable sums subsidising their cricket section, which, it was widely admitted, would have gone bankrupt if not for football's helping hand. This sense of a broader civic importance was also manifested in the close relationship between many clubs and local charities. In 1890 Huddersfield donated £2,000 from its profits to local charities, topping its previous best donation by £800. Bradford made similar donations over the years and at one point in the mid-1880s the Bradford committee discussed whether the club should become a charitable institution run solely for the benefit of local good causes.[155] The Yorkshire Rugby Union itself was the epitome of this charitable instinct, devoting on average almost 90 per cent of its profits from county games and the cup final and semi-finals to charities across the county.[156] Salford manifested another aspect of this sense of civic duty in 1891, when it decided to purchase £300 of local corporation stock despite sustaining a loss on the season of nearly £30.[157]

However, the necessity and expense of developing and improving grounds increasingly eroded many of the financial commitments which clubs had made to charitable and civic purposes. By the early 1890s, 'business-like' was becoming a vogue phrase among rugby's administrators, and one of the constant criticisms from the northern clubs of the RFU was that it was 'unbusinesslike' in its dealings.[158] In 1891 Wakefield Trinity discussed merging with Wakefield cricket club partially because their combined resources 'would secure better management' for the club.[159] The year after Huddersfield had made the £2,000 donation to charity, the exigencies of extending its Fartown ground led the club to reduce this amount to just £184. Park Avenue had cost Bradford so much to acquire, a phenomenal £13,000, that its donations to charity slowed to a trickle. The demands of capital investment for ground improvements meant that senior clubs had little choice but to become incorporated and convert themselves into limited liability companies, so as to minimise risk and make the raising of loans easier. Huddersfield had become an incorporated body as early as 1879, but this was not connected with the raising of capital. In practical terms, Manningham led the way in 1886 when, as part of their move to their new Valley Parade ground, they were granted a Board of Trade licence of incorporation. The cost of leasing the ground from the Midland Railway Company and its development into a football stadium cost the club almost £2,000, £1,350 of which was paid off by 1888, thanks to the success and popularity of the club, despite their sharing the city with Bradford, the game's biggest crowd pullers.[160] However even this incorporated status did not lead to a drive for profit accumulation or individual speculation, as Bradford's *Weekly Telegraph* somewhat gushingly explained:

> The club is now, therefore, a corporate body, with a common seal and permanent succession, the funds are protected against misuse, and the profits of the club cannot be divided either amongst the committee or the members, but on the winding up of the club the funds must be divided up among the charitable institutions of the town. It will be seen, therefore, that the work of the committee is pure love, and they cannot receive anything for their services.[161]

In fact, the only direct financial benefit gained by the individuals of the committee due to incorporation of the club was the limiting of individual liability to twenty shillings per member. Again, it can be seen that even in this move to greater commercial awareness and organisation, the articles of association specified that local charities would be the beneficiaries in the unlikely event of the club failing and having assets to distribute.

The success of Manningham's experiment with limited liability and the incessant financial toll of providing facilities for the tens of thousands watching football led others to follow their lead. In 1891 Huddersfield put their company status to work in order to raise capital for ground expansion plans by issuing 5,000 £1 shares bearing 5 per cent interest per annum.

Unsurprisingly, considering the size of the football bubble at the time, the issue was massively oversubscribed.[162] Three months later Bradford announced their intention to incorporate in order to raise money to complete the purchase of Park Avenue. Most notable, however, both for its long-term impact on the history of football and cricket and its demonstration of the tension between commercial realities and the sense of civic duty pervading rugby, was the foundation in 1890 of the Leeds Cricket, Football and Athletic Company Limited, the first rugby football club to be formed as a limited liability company.

Despite being the centre of rugby football in the north of England – for example, on one weekend in 1891 eighty-nine teams from the immediate Leeds area had their match results recorded in the *Yorkshire Post* – Leeds, uniquely, did not have a team which was representative of the whole of the town.[163] Clearly, given the importance football now occupied in the cultural life of Yorkshire, the lack of a team which could carry the honour of the town was sorely felt, not just by football enthusiasts but also by those civic dignitaries eager to promote the virtues of the municipality. For it was not just in football where Leeds found itself lacking. In cricket too, the town had no ground to match Sheffield's Bramall Lane, or Bradford's Park Avenue, and was felt to have conceded by default to Sheffield the title of 'the home of Yorkshire cricket.' On a broader scale, its status as a town, rather than a city, was believed to be injurious to its standing as a commercial centre, especially given the rise to prominence of Birmingham, granted cityhood in 1889, and to a lesser, but probably more keenly felt, extent Sheffield. The Conservative MP W. L. Jackson, who was also a founding member of the Leeds CFA Ltd board of directors, led the town's first attempt to upgrade its status in 1890, the year of the Leeds club's formation, but it was to be another three years before Leeds acquired the title of city.[164]

At the beginning of the 1886–87 season, members of Leeds St John's, which had now established itself as the town's leading club through a combination of playing success and social status, being led primarily by ex-Leeds Grammar School boys, voted in principle for the formation of a Leeds football, cricket and athletics club. In 1887, following the defeat of St John's by Wakefield Trinity in the Yorkshire Cup final, the clamour rose for something to be done about getting 'a club of first-rate standing' in the town.[165] In November of that year, the formation of the Leeds Cricket, Football and Athletic Company Limited was announced, with the intention of raising £25,000 for the purchase of Lot 17a from Cardigan Estates, comprising twenty-two acres of land in the Headingley area. By January 1889 sufficient funds had been raised and the sale was complete, although the issue of 25,000 £1 shares was never fully taken up and the outstanding £8,000 was loaned by a local businessman. A month later 400 members packed into an extraordinary meeting of the St John's club and voted to join the new club as its football section. On 20 September, the new Leeds side played its first game at the Headingley ground, which, with a capacity of 30,000 offered 'unrivalled accommodation to all classes of spectators' according to the club's first annual report, and in June 1891 the Yorkshire county cricket side made its debut on the new ground. Facilities were quickly expanded to include athletics, bowling, tennis and cycling (and also, a little later, soccer) as the club sought to provide a complete range of sporting activities and attractions for the town.[166]

The board of directors of the club was composed of prominent local businessmen, most of whom also played some form of role in the civic life of the town. The chairman was Lord Hawke, the patrician ruler of Yorkshire county cricket for forty years. His vice-chairman was Charles Tetley of the brewing family, and other members included the afore-mentioned MP, W. L. Jackson, John Gordon, former president of the St John's club and a local Tory councillor, two solicitors, a merchant, and the owners of textiles, gas burner and engineering factories. Despite Leeds being a stronghold of the Liberal Party, of the three members whose political affiliations can be traced, all were Conservatives.[167] Two of the directors had a direct commercial interest in the ground: J. Tweedale's architects' firm designed the main stand and George Bray designed the popular south stand. Although it was the most commercially minded of all rugby organisations, even the Leeds club did not have profit maximisation as its *raison d'être*. It never issued a dividend to its shareholders until 1927 and, perhaps inevitably, its football section generally subsidised its other sections, including cricket on occasions, most of which were designed to provide a service to members rather than attract spectators. The size of the debt incurred in the buying and development of Headingley did however put the club under serious financial pressure and there was a constant drive to cut expenditure, the biggest component of which was usually termed 'players' expenses.' In theory this covered travel, medical and outfitting costs but it was of course widely assumed to include payments for play. Indeed, it was only after the formation of the Northern Union that players' expenses showed a significant decrease![168]

As the Leeds example makes clear, although rugby clubs were not run as profit maximising organisations and were viewed more as civic institutions, the exigencies of running a successful football side meant that the rigours of the market place came to bear more and more on clubs. So while it would be untrue to describe even the most cost-conscious club as a classical capitalist enterprise – not least because no director or administrator ever got rich running a club, although some did get poorer – the need to raise funds, to control expenses and to attract new custom were just as great as for any other form of company. As the chairman of Warrington pointed out at his club's annual general meeting in 1887, 'as in cricket and all other exercises, so it was in football, success in the balance sheet meant success in the game.'[169] It was the clash between this commercial reality and the practical implications of the sport's ostensibly amateur ethos which began the unravelling of the ties which bound together the RFU and most of its northern clubs.

NOTES

1. This is the title of a celebratory anonymous poem which appeared on the front page of *The Yorkshireman*, 8 Oct. 1890.
2. *The Times*, 30 Oct. 1896.
3. For the observation on Bede, see H. M. Jewell, *The North–South Divide: The Origins of Northern Consciousness in England*, Manchester, 1994, p. 4.
4. Elizabeth Gaskell, *North and South*, London, 1855 (Penguin edition), p. 398.
5. Talbot Baines, *The Industrial North in the Last Decade of the Nineteenth Century*, Leeds, 1928, p. 17.
6. Donald Horne, *God is an Englishman*, Sydney, 1969. Quoted in Martin Wiener, *English Culture and the Decline of the Industrial Spirit 1850–1980*, Cambridge, 1981, p. 41.
7. For an exploration of the cultural activities of the northern Victorian bourgeoisie, see Janet Wolff and Caroline Arscott, 'Cultivated Capital', *History Today*, Vol. 37, 1987, and R. J. Morris, 'Middle Class Culture 1700–1914' in Derek Fraser (ed.), *A History of Modern Leeds*, Manchester, 1980. For factory culture, see Patrick Joyce, *Work, Society and Politics*, Brighton, 1980.
8. Talbot Baines, ibid., p. 18.
9. It must, however, be pointed out that the idea of the North versus South game was proposed by Hull's William Beevor-Lambert in 1873.
10. Yorkshire County Football Club circular of 10 Oct. 1881. For more on the YRU and RFU at this time see *Yorkshire Post* throughout Jan. 1888.
11. Hostilities were increased by the exclusion of sixteen Yorkshire clubs from the 1891 AGM for irregularities over their payments of subscriptions. Rochdale Hornets were one of the few Lancashire clubs to vote with Yorkshire.
12. *Yorkshire Post*, 16 Sept. 1891.
13. For an interesting discussion of this point see C. Dellheim, 'Imagining England: Victorian Views of the North' in *Northern History*, Vol. 22, 1986.
14. Frank Musgrove, *The North of England: A History from Roman Times to the Present*, Oxford, 1990, p. 310. For a rejoinder, see J. Walton, 'Professor Musgrove's North of England: A Critique', *Journal of Regional and Local Studies*, Vol. 12, No. 2, 1992.
15. The quote is from *The Yorkshireman*, 14 April 1887. The Huddersfield Holliday Cup, founded in 1885, is still played for by local rugby league teams.
16. *The Yorkshireman*, 2 May 1893.
17. *Yorkshire Post*, 3 June 1890. In Dec. 1894 the LCFC had 43 member clubs, see *Salford Reporter*, 1 Dec. 1894.

18. *Wigan Observer*, 6 Oct. 1886.
19. For full details, see *Athletic News*, 8 Oct. 1889.
20. *Wigan Observer*, 22 April 1886. *Rochdale Observer*, 11 April 1888.
21. *Warrington Guardian*, 5 June 1886.
22. Clowes was later badly injured in an industrial accident which almost ended his career. *The Yorkshireman*, 6 Nov. 1889.
23. A. W. Pullin, *Alfred Shaw: Cricketer. His Career and Reminiscences*, London, 1902, p. 102. See also David Firth, *My Dear Victorious Stod*, London, 1977, and Peter Wynne-Thomas, *Give Me Arthur*, London, 1985.
24. See *Yorkshire Post*, 3 April 1883 and subsequent issues for the full story. It was one of the few disputed cases in Yorkshire rugby in the 1880s which had nothing to do with accusations of professionalism – Halifax claimed Jones was not eligible to play for Dewsbury because he had previously been a reserve for the Lancashire county side.
25. Revd F. Marshall, 'Foreign Tours', in *Football – The Rugby Union Game*, Revd F. Marshall (ed), London, 1892.
26. *Halifax Guardian*, 17 and 24 March 1888.
27. Letter of Arthur Shrewsbury to Alfred Shaw, 14 March 1888: 'We sent [Stoddart] a cheque for £50 only a few days since which should bind him.' I am grateful to Peter Wynne-Thomas at Nottinghamshire CCC archive, Trent Bridge and Trevor Delaney for making available copies of Shrewsbury's correspondence.
28. Shrewsbury to Shaw, 14 March 1888.
29. Shrewsbury to Shaw, 22 June 1888.
30. Shrewsbury to Shaw, 29 Feb. 1888 and 5 June 1888.
31. Shrewsbury to Shaw, 22 June 1888 and 5 June 1888.
32. Shrewsbury to Shaw, 18 Jan. 1888.
33. *Yorkshire Post*, 26 Nov. 1888.
34. *Yorkshire Post*, 18, 20, 22, 24 and 30 Oct. 1888.
35. *Yorkshire Post*, 13 Nov. 1888.
36. *Yorkshire Post*, 20 Feb. 1889.
37. An Old Player, 'The Rugby Union Game in 1888–89' in the *Football Annual*, London, 1889 and *The Yorkshireman*, 27 Nov. 1889.
38. *Yorkshire Post*, 8 March and 16 and 20 July 1889.
39. This was confirmed some years later by former Leeds Grammar School and Heckmondwike player Aulay MacAulay in the *Yorkshire Evening Post*, 9 March 1901.
40. *The Yorkshireman*, 29 Jan. 1890.
41. *Yorkshire Post*, 8 and 15 May and 4 June 1889.
42. *Clarion*, 1 Oct. 1892.
43. *Yorkshire Post*, 19 May 1892.
44. A. W. Pullin, 'Competition Football in Yorkshire: Has it proved a success?' in *The Yorkshireman Football Number*, March 1893.
45. The phrase 'social zoning' is from John Walton 'Residential Amenity, Respectable Morality and the Rise of the Entertainment Industry: the Case of Blackpool 1860–1914' in *Literature and History*, Vol. 1, 1975, and many other works, in which he describes the social segregation of Blackpool holiday sites.
46. *Oldham Evening Chronicle*, 13 Oct. 1890.
47. *Oldham Evening Chronicle*, 26 and 29 Sept. and 15 Nov. 1890. Two years later, while playing for Werneth's neighbours Oldham, Ashworth played for England.
48. This is confirmed in an article in the Manchester *Umpire*, quoted in the *Oldham Evening Chronicle*, 30 Oct. 1890.

49. McCutcheon later became a leading Northern Union referee and president of the Oldham club.
50. The description of Marshall is from RFU committee member G. F. Berney in Revd Frank Marshall and L. R. Tosswill, *Football – the Rugby Union Game*, London, 1925 (Revised edition), p. 58.
51. *Oldham Evening Chronicle*, 13 and 30 Oct. 1890. *Yorkshire Post*, 23 Oct. 1890.
52. *Manchester Guardian*, 27 Oct. 1890.
53. *Yorkshire Post*, 17 Jan. 1891.
54. *Clarion*, 29 Oct. and 5 Nov. It is interesting to compare the similarity of the words used by the Broughton Rangers secretary and those used by Dewsbury in 1886 in explanation of Stadden's and Stuart's move from Cardiff.
55. *The Yorkshireman*, 1 Nov. 1892.
56. For more details on the RFU's volte-face see *Yorkshire Post*, 3 Dec. 1892 and 27 Jan. 1893 and *The Yorkshireman*, 31 Jan. 1893. They were reinstated as amateurs in 1896 before signing for Broughton again in 1899, by which time Rangers had become founding members of the Northern Union.
57. *Clarion*, 2 April 1892.
58. *Salford Reporter*, 24 Sept. 1892.
59. *Yorkshire Post*, 3 June 1892, 15 Sept. and 4 Oct. 1892.
60. *Clarion*, 22 Dec. 1894.
61. *Yorkshire Evening Post*, 9 Feb. 1901.
62. *Yorkshire Post*, 18 Sept. 1894.
63. *The Yorkshireman*, 12 Jan. 1889.
64. *The Yorkshireman*, 25 March 1891.
65. *Hull and East Riding Athlete*, 8 Oct. 1890.
66. *The Yorkshireman*, 11 Nov. 1891.
67. *The Yorkshireman*, 27 Nov. 1889.
68. *Yorkshire Post,* 13, 16 and 17 March 1894.
69. Mason, op. cit., Ch. 4.
70. Interestingly, Ross McKibbin, in his 'Work and Hobbies in Britain, 1880–1950', in *The Ideologies of Class*, Oxford, 1990, p. 161, suggests that 'the principal hobby of the unskilled labourer was certainly sport', which seems to add further weight to undermine the case for footballers being predominantly skilled men.
71. *Yorkshire Post*, 16 July 1889.
72. *Yorkshire Post*, 22 Nov. 1892.
73. *Yorkshire Post*, 23 March 1892.
74. *Yorkshire Post*, 14 & 25 Oct. 1890.
75. *Yorkshire Post*, 24 Oct. 1890.
76. *Yorkshire Football*, 24 Jan. 1888.
77. *Yorkshire Post*, 16 Sept. 1889.
78. *Yorkshire Post*, 14 Oct. 1889.
79. *Yorkshire Post*, 20 and 28 Dec. 1890.
80. *Yorkshire Post,* 7 Feb. 1893.
81. *Yorkshire Post*, 20 July 1889.
82. *Yorkshire Post*, 2 Oct. 1888.
83. *The Yorkshireman*, 21 Oct. 1891 and 2 Dec. 1891. *Yorkshire Post*, 28 Nov. 1891.
84. 'The YRU' by A Wag, in *The Yorkshireman Football Number*, March 1890.
85. *Salford Reporter*, 17 Nov. 1894.
86. *Hull and East Riding Athlete*, 29 Jan. 1890.
87. On the Armley strike, see *The Yorkshireman*, 16 Dec. 1891. On Wakefield, see *Yorkshire Post*, 6 Feb. 1893 and *The Yorkshireman*, 14 Feb. 1893. For Harrogate,

see *Yorkshire Post*, 3 Jan. and 1 Feb. 1894.

88. *Yorkshire Post*, 21 Oct. 1891.
89. *The Yorkshireman*, 29 Jan. 1890. 'If I'm not good enough to play football with them without a collar and tie, I'm not going to play at all.'
90. *Yorkshire Post*, 28 Sept. 1889. Sutcliffe's unique career encompassed a try-scoring debut for England in their 1889 match against the Maori tourists, a professional soccer debut for Bolton Wanderers eight months later and an England soccer debut against Wales in 1893. He subsequently played for Millwall, Manchester United, Plymouth Argyle and Southend United before returning to his native West Yorkshire in 1919 as the trainer to Bradford City, the club which as Manningham had made the same switch of codes in 1903.
91. *Yorkshire Chat,* 25 Nov. 1899.
92. *The Yorkshireman*, 13 Sept. 1893 and 1 April 1891 and *Clarion*, 22 Oct. 1892.
93. *Yorkshire Post*, 9 Sept. 1889.
94. *Yorkshire Post*, 20 Sept. 1889.
95. *The Yorkshireman*, 6 Nov. 1889.
96. *Yorkshire Post*, 2 March 1886.
97. *Yorkshire Post*, 13 Dec. 1889.
98. *Salford Reporter*, 10 Nov. 1894.
99. *The Yorkshireman*, 18 Sept. 1889 and the *Yorkshire Post*, 20 Sept. 1889.
100. *Yorkshire Post*, 10 Nov. 1891 and *The Yorkshireman*, 31 Jan. 1893. The three Welsh-men had initially gone north to play for Holbeck but on arrival in Leeds had been 'kidnapped' by the Church club's officials.
101. *Oldham Evening Chronicle*, 27 Oct. 1890.
102. *Yorkshire Post*, 6 Oct. 1893. Unfortunately, we have no way of knowing the identity of this enterprising Welshman – nor if he was successful in finding a situation.
103. *Yorkshire Post*, 9 Oct. 1894.
104. *Yorkshire Post*, 16 March 1893.
105. *Yorkshire Post*, 17 Jan. 1887.
106. *The Yorkshireman*, 29 Nov. 1892 and 11 April 1893.
107. *The Yorkshireman*, 23 Aug. 1893.
108. Figures taken from Trevor Delaney, *Rugby Disunion*, Keighley, 1993, p. 71.
109. *Yorkshire Owl*, 23 Jan. 1895.
110. *Yorkshire Post*, 6 Dec. 1892. *The Yorkshireman*, 29 Oct. 1890.
111. *The Yorkshireman*, 30 May 1888.
112. *Yorkshire Post*, 20 Sept. 1889.
113. *Yorkshire Post*, 2 March 1886.
114. *Yorkshire Post*, 13 Dec. 1889.
115. *Yorkshire Post*, 20 Sept. 1889.
116. These figures come from the chapter on players in Tony Mason, op. cit., p. 95.
117. *Salford Reporter*, 17 Nov. 1894 and *Yorkshire Post*, 8 Sept. 1894.
118. Quoted in C. F. Shaw, *The Gallant Youths*, Batley, 1899.
119. See for example O. L. Owen, *The History of the Rugby Football Union*, London, 1955.
120. *Yorkshire Evening Post*, 21 and 28 Nov. 1903. *The Yorkshireman*, 8 April 1882.
121. *The Yorkshireman*, 11 Oct. 1893.
122. *The Yorkshireman*, 5 March 1889.
123. *The Yorkshireman*, 17 Feb. 1887.
124. *The Yorkshireman*, 6 and 27 Sept. 1892.
125. *The Yorkshireman,* 15 Jan. 1890 and *Yorkshire Post*, 28 April 1892.
126. William 'Monsey' Parr, St Helens Recreation captain in 1889. *The Lantern* (St Helens), 13 Sept. 1889.

127. A Londoner, 'Metropolitan Football' in Revd Frank Marshall, *Football – the Rugby Union Game*, London, 1892.
128. See Revd Frank Marshall, *Football – the Rugby Union Game*, London, 1892, *Yorkshire Post*, 10 Feb. 1880 and *The Yorkshireman*, 9 Dec. 1882.
129. *Athletic News*, 7 April 1890.
130. *Yorkshire Post*, 7 Jan. 1888.
131. *The Yorkshireman*, 18 Feb. and 25 March 1891.
132. *Halifax Guardian*, 2 Feb. 1889. The West Riding club played the three half-back system, albeit unsuccessfully, in their 1894 Yorkshire Cup semi-final.
133. Advocacy of two full backs and eight forwards can be found in the *Yorkshire Post*, 24 Nov. 1892. For the development of the four three-quarter system see Gareth Williams and David Smith, *Fields of Praise*, Cardiff, 1980, p. 61.
134. *Athletic News*, 23 April 1906. *The Yorkshireman*, 3 March 1887.
135. *Yorkshire Post*, 26 Nov. 1891.
136. *Yorkshire Post*, 30 April 1894.
137. *Yorkshire Post,* as above. *Manchester Guardian*, 28 Nov. 1892.
138. H. H. Almond, 'Football as a Moral Agent' in *Nineteenth Century*, Vol. 34, 1893.
139. *The Yorkshireman*, 15 March 1884.
140. *Yorkshire Post*, 22 March 1887. For details of the Inland Revenue, see *Yorkshire Post*, 2 March 1893.
141. *Bradford Observer*, 9 March 1886.
142. For details see *The Yorkshireman*, 8 Dec. 1894.
143. *The Yorkshireman*, 26 Sept. 1886 and 1 Sept. 1887. *Yorkshire Post*, 10 Feb. 1891. Some of this material is taken from Trevor Delaney's excellent and exhaustive *The Grounds of Rugby League*, Keighley, 1991.
144. *Warrington Guardian*, 4 June 1892.
145. *Yorkshire Post*, 30 April 1891, 14 and 19 May 1892, 13 April 1893. Hull FC annual reports and accounts 1883–84 and 1887–88. J. Higson, *The History of Salford FC*, Salford, 1892. *The Yorkshireman*, 2 Jan. 1886.
146. *Yorkshire Post*, 16 Sept. 1890.
147. *Yorkshire Post*, 10 June 1889.
148. *Warrington Examiner*, 25 Nov. 1895.
149. *Yorkshire Post*, 10 Jan. 1887 and *Huddersfield Daily Examiner*, 13 Oct. 1886.
150. *Warrington Examiner*, 4 June 1890.
151. *The Yorkshireman*, 12 Sept. 1885 and 24 April 1887.
152. *Wigan Observer*, 22 Nov. 1886.
153. *The Yorkshireman*, 30 Oct. 1886.
154. *Athletic News*, 11 Oct. 1887.
155. *Yorkshire Post*, 22 Jan. 1887 and 17 April 1890.
156. *Yorkshire Post*, 3 June 1890 and 9 May 1891.
157. Higson, ibid.
158. See, for example, the *Yorkshire Post*, 10 Sept. 1894.
159. *Yorkshire Post*, 21 Jan. 1891.
160. *The Yorkshireman*, 2 May 1888.
161. *Bradford Illustrated Weekly Telegraph*, 25 Sept. 1886.
162. *Yorkshire Post*, 10 Feb. 1891.
163. *Yorkshire Post*, 26 Jan. 1891.
164. An excellent account of Leeds's road to cityhood can be found in Arthur Elton, 'Becoming a City: Leeds, 1893' in *Publications of the Thoresby Society, Miscellany,* Second Series, Vol. 3, 1993.
165. *The Yorkshireman*, 4 Sept. 1886 and *Yorkshire Post*, 10 March 1887.

166. Leeds Cricket, Football and Athletic Company Limited, *Annual Report and Accounts*, for year ending 30 April 1891.
167. *Slater's Directory of Leeds and District*, London, 1890.
168. *Yorkshire Post*, 14 May 1892.
169. *Warrington Guardian*, 8 June 1887. For more on this debate regarding soccer clubs, see Stephen Tischler, *Footballers and Businessmen,* New York, 1981, Wray Vamplew, *Pay Up and Play the Game: Professional Sport in Britain 1875–1914*, Cambridge, 1988 and also his 'The Economics of a Sports Industry, Scottish Gate Money Football 1890–1914', *Economic History Review*, Nov. 1982, Vol. 35.

4

Schism: 1893–1895

By 1893 Britain was a very different society from that which it had been in 1886. Relationships between the classes had changed profoundly. The relative harmony which had characterised British society in the decades following the early 1850s had given way to a social climate in which industrial conflict and class antagonism were to the fore. Beginning with the Trafalgar Square riots of 1886 and followed by the matchgirls', dockers' and gas workers' strikes of the late 1880s, a new tide of class conflict spread rapidly across the country, spearheaded by the 'new union' movement. In 1890 cavalry attacked a demonstration supporting striking Leeds gas workers. Later that year a protracted strike took place at Manningham Mills in Bradford, when over 5,000 men and women struck for almost five months in protest against pay cuts.[1] In 1892 cotton manufacturers in Lancashire locked out their workers. The following year in Hull, striking dockers were confronted by naval gunboats in the Humber. Rugby's heartland of Cheshire, Lancashire and Yorkshire experienced the UK's highest incidence of strike activity in 1892 and 1893, culminating in the 1893 miners' strike, during which troops shot dead two and wounded sixteen more at Featherstone, near Wakefield.[2] On a political level, indications of working-class self-confidence were seen in the growth of the Social Democratic Federation in Lancashire and the formation in Bradford of the Independent Labour Party in 1893. For the upper and middle classes, their old certainties were disappearing and the fear of the mob was rising. It seemed that Matthew Arnold's semi-ironical warning of 1869 was about to bear fruit, 'The working class which, raw and half-developed, has long lain half-hidden amidst its poverty and squalor, and is now issuing from its hiding place to assert an Englishman's heaven-born privilege of doing as he likes, and is beginning to perplex us by marching where it likes, meeting where it likes, bawling what it likes, breaking what it likes.'[3]

Rugby found itself a direct participant in events which symbolised the changing times. Matches were played to raise funds for the Manningham

1893: *The Yorkshireman* depicts the new rugby season starting amidst growing social unrest.

Mills strike in 1891 and three of Bradford's international players were special constables who, along with the Durham Light Infantry, helped to break up demonstrations supporting the strikers.[4] Later that year, striking miners set fire to the glassworks belonging to Pilkington Brothers in St Helens, patrons of the St Helens Recreation football club. Hunslet captain Albert Goldthorpe and Castleford captain Harry Speed, later to become a Liberal councillor, organised a benefit match in Leeds for locked-out Castleford glassworkers in 1893.[5] The Yorkshire Rugby Union (YRU) committee itself was divided over an appeal for aid by striking West Yorkshire miners when Castleford Liberal councillor Arthur Hartley, later to become president of the RFU, called on the YRU to make a donation to the miners' relief committee. In a debate which continued over two days, Hartley was backed by the delegates from Hunslet and Bradford but opposed by Dewsbury's Mark Newsome and the YRU secretary James Miller, whose uncompromising declaration that 'the time had now come when the responsibility for the distress must go back to those who caused it, and ought to be laid at the door of the men themselves' gathered sufficient support to ensure that the miners' supporters were defeated.[6]

These heightened class tensions were manifested throughout the game. As working-class players and spectators continued to flock into the game, the involvement of former public schoolboys continued to decline. By 1892 even Bradford, a club long regarded as having the most socially exalted players in Yorkshire, had a team which with a couple of exceptions was entirely composed of working men.[7] As one commentator declared regretfully in 1889,

> This Rugby football movement, which commenced in Yorkshire with the 'classes' and first drew its strength from the public schools and the middle classes, has finally, like other movements and fashions, good or bad, spread downwards to the 'masses'. It is this which has led to the corruption of the sport, which has in some districts tended to drive gentlemen out of the field.[8]

Not surprisingly, given such attitudes, friction between the classes flared up in various ways. As early as 1886, Bradford's annual general meeting heard complaints that working class players didn't get a fair chance. '"Talent must prevail" is their motto on what is known as the "collar and cuff question",' said *The Yorkshireman*.[9] At Halifax the following year, working-class members of the club complained that they had been barred

114

from the club pavilion, while at Manningham the same year a section of the membership ran a 'working man's candidate.' The following year they called for votes for committeemen who would 'put their hands dahn for t'players.'[10] On a more basic level, class antagonism could also act as a catalyst for violence on the field, as the Otley Clarence team claimed after being accused of 'foul and low' behaviour by the Leeds Good Shepherd team. Clarence blamed 'one of the [Good Shepherd] players, who considering himself a cut above the others, had to be accommodated in a special dressing room' as the cause of the trouble.[11]

Irritation was also regularly expressed that middle-class players allowed their outside interests to interfere with match preparations, the most famous example being Bradford captain and half-back Fred Bonsor's late arrival at the 1885 Yorkshire Cup semi-final, and by the late 1880s the demands of regular training led to a steady stream of middle-class players giving up the game because of business pressures. Throughout the 1880s most of the captains of the leading clubs were ex-public schoolboys, in much the same way as captains of county cricket sides were always amateurs, but even this tradition was now challenged. Much outrage was expressed in 1891 when Dicky Lockwood, the most famous rugby player in Yorkshire, was passed over for the county captaincy in favour of Oxford-educated William Bromet. 'It is simply a case of pandering to social position, nothing more nor less. We thought we were "all fellows at football"; yet an alleged democratic Yorkshire committee can still show a sneaking fondness for persons who are – we had almost said – in a better social position than ourselves,' complained one correspondent.[12] Eventually talent did prevail and Lockwood went on to captain both Yorkshire and England.

Although sometimes trivial, all of these examples highlighted growing working-class self-confidence in the sport and the gradual development among working-class participants of a consciousness that they had contributed as much to the game, if not more, than the middle classes which had hitherto dominated it. The middle classes found their authority challenged on the playing fields and, to a certain extent, in the committee rooms. It was undeniable that it was working-class players which had made the sport so popular in the north, as Robert Blatchford's *Clarion*, founded in 1892, pointed out: 'The prosperity and popularity of the game dates from the time the working man commenced to interest himself in it, both physically and mentally. His success at the game may not be quite suitable to the tastes of the Corinthian, but it is nevertheless a fact that since he poked his nose into the recreation football has come on in leaps and bounds.'[13]

115

THE MIDDLE CLASS, THE WORKING CLASS
AND THE AMATEUR ETHOS

Once again, therefore, the debate about the future of rugby in the 1890s centred on the role of the working man within the game. Characteristically, it was Arthur Budd who put his finger on the central point of the debate: 'Since the working man has become so prominent an element in our game, there are many who advocate the introduction of professionalism *in toto*, and others, the moderate party, who are in favour of compensation for loss of time.' He was not sympathetic however:

> The answer, then, to those who urge that the working man ought to be compensated for 'loss of time' incurred by his recreation is that, if he cannot afford the leisure to play a game, he must do without it … What would happen if stockbrokers wanted compensation for loss of time? Compensation commensurate with earnings would create a scandal. AB, the stockbroker, has therefore to stop at home at his desk because he cannot afford to play, but CD, the working man, is allowed his outing and compensation for leaving work.[14]

Given the level of expenses demanded by middle-class London clubs for matches against northern clubs, this latter point was somewhat disingenuous. Budd re-emphasised his 1886 arguments that professionalism would mean the middle-class player being unable to compete with working-class players, arguing that 'while you allow a man to play for money, you prevent another playing for love of the game without emolument.' It was not hard to see why Budd felt that middle-class players were in danger of being driven from the game. Top-class rugby in England was becoming dominated by the working-class player. The overwhelmingly working-class Yorkshire side's stranglehold on the county championship from 1889, relieved only in 1891 by the equally proletarian Lancashire team, and the growing importance of working-men players to the England team – eleven of the fifteen members of the English side which defeated Scotland in 1892 were from Lancashire and Yorkshire and ten of those were manual workers – only served to confirm his fears. However, as A. A. Sutherland waspishly pointed out in reply to Budd, if playing the game for enjoyment, rather than victory, was the thing, why was the gentleman player so worried about failing to triumph over working-class professionals? 'It might reasonably be said, by the same line of argument, that amateurs who cannot afford the leisure to practise to keep up to the standard of professional play, must do without the game,' he suggested archly.[15] However, the crux of Budd's argument was not, in truth, about payments but about control of the game: 'No professional sport under its own government, and independently of amateur supervision, has ever yet permanently prospered in this country.'[16] In his eyes, sport had to be administered by the middle classes. Professionalism would undermine their control by making them inferior to the working classes on the field of play and thus destroying the credibility of their governance.

Nowhere was this clearer than his reply to those, like Amateur Athletics Association founder Montague Shearman and, by implication, FA and Surrey CCC secretary C. W. Alcock, who pointed to cricket as a sport which had accepted professionalism and not sunk into moral turpitude.[17] 'Our best amateur cricketers devote quite as much time to [playing] as the professionals. As a consequence, while they are able to maintain an equality of play, they are at the same time able to retain a monopoly of government,' he claimed. This, of course, was true, but only because, as many of the supporters of broken-time pointed out, W. G. Grace, Andrew Stoddart and many other of cricket's leading gentlemen amateurs made much more money from sport than any professional cricketer or association footballer. In essence, Budd's position meant excluding working-class players from the higher echelons of the game. Without financial assistance, argued the supporters of payments for play, working-class players could not play at the sport's most competitive levels. England international forward Donald Jowett was one of the better examples of such circumstances. He was forced to step down from representative matches because 'to keep some of these engagements he had to break two or three days' work. His employers took no deep interest in football, and regularly stopped his wages for the time broken. He could not afford to lose this money and hence his request to the authorities not to select him.'[18]

Rowland Hill supported Budd in denying that useful parallels could be drawn between cricket and rugby. Whereas cricket could be played for many years with jobs as coaches, groundsmen or umpires available upon retirement, rugby, he claimed, did not have the same long-term prospects. A professional rugby player would find for a time 'that it is more remunerative to play football than to follow his regular occupation,' but when he retired from the game 'he then realises that football has unfitted him for other work, and finds it very difficult to get any employment; and if he is able to get work it will probably be at a much smaller rate of pay than he would have received if he had from the first stuck steadily to work.'[19] He offered no evidence for this view – indeed, given the boom in rugby and association it was quite probable that the expanding infrastructure of football would provide opportunities similar to those for former cricket players, and, as we

117

have seen in the previous chapter, many rugby players in Lancashire and Yorkshire had in fact discovered that their prominence as footballers had enabled them to acquire employment opportunities previously unavailable.

However weak his argument, Hill's concern for the future prospects of players was not simply cynical. Like the Reverend Frank Marshall and many other supporters of amateurism Hill believed that the middle classes had a debt of responsibility to those below them. It was his duty to protect the lower orders both from themselves and those who would needlessly exploit them. He summed up this belief a few weeks after the Northern Union split in 1895:

> I saw gradually coming up a new class – the working class – taking a deep and great interest in our game. As one who has always held some good old-fashioned Tory notions [in fact he was a Conservative councillor in London for many years], in good friendship to the working classes, I looked with passionate delight upon this development, but unfortunately dangers have come. Those who ought to have led the working men properly have, I deeply regret to say, led them astray. It is for that class that I feel so keenly sorry today – these men who but for a few years will not be able to take payment for broken-time or for anything else.[20]

Hill's view of his relationship to the working classes was exactly that which John Stuart Mill had described thirty years earlier as being a typically English one of 'dependence and protection': 'The relation between rich and poor, according to this theory ... should be only partly authoritative; it should be amiable, moral and sentimental; affectionate tutelage on the one side, respectful and grateful deference on the other. The rich should be *in loco parentis* to the poor, guiding and restraining them like children.'[21] This feeling that the lower orders were child-like was very common among the supporters of amateurism, Frank Marshall being the most explicit: 'I look upon [rugby] for the working man much as I regard the same game for my boys at school.'[22] At the 1893 AGM discussion on broken-time, Lancashire's Roger Walker, a future RFU president, and Mr Hobson from the Midland Counties RFU spoke with gushing condescension of working-class players viewing the game as a 'little holiday' and not desiring payment. The *Rugby Union Football Handbook* for the 1894–95 season spoke in similarly patronising terms, declaring that : 'There is no keener sportsman than the bona-fide working class amateur; he is ready to give time (which is money to him) in pursuit of his amusement, as far as he can, and is the last person to ask for exceptional privileges.'[23]

A GOOD LIVING IN THE CHURCH.

Muscular Christianity meets its match: *The Yorkshireman* highlights the failure of the Leeds Parish Church side to meet its Corinthian ideals.

Much of the philosophy behind this type of relationship between the classes came, of course, from the Church of England, of which Hill was a 'devoted adherent'.[24] Yet by 1893 much of the enthusiasm previously shown by its clergy for northern rugby was beginning to wear thin. The Yorkshire Church Temperance Challenge Shield, begun in 1887 to 'promote an interest in football among the younger churchmen of Yorkshire and, secondly, to keep them out of the public houses', and open only to teams affiliated to Anglican churches, church schools and temperance societies, had rapidly become notorious for its entrants' cavalier attitudes to its rules. In 1888 it was forced to revise its rules to bar clubs which had pubs as team headquarters, but even this didn't stop Hull Britannia from proudly displaying the trophy in a Hull pub.[25] By 1892 it had given up the ghost and abandoned the competition. Leeds Parish Church, arguably muscular Christianity's flagship in the North, were suspended for professionalism in 1890 and later that year had their ground closed for a month after an angry crowd had attacked a referee. The following season Cosmo Lang, the future Archbishop of Canterbury then working as a curate at the church, was forced to appear before the YRU to answer charges of violent play by the team on a tour of Ireland after their hosts had threatened to bring criminal charges.[26] There was little surprise therefore when the Bishop of Chester, on a pastoral visit to Leeds in 1890, chose to use the pulpit to denounce professionalism in football 'even at the risk of giving offence to every working man in England.' Nor was he alone, as a disillusioned muscular Christian, writing under the pseudonym of Orestes, made clear:

> In the brave days of old, in the public games of the Spartans and the Athenians, the victor was crowned with a wreath, not of gold but of the leaves of the wild olive, but in these degenerate days, after 1800 years of the high moral teaching and influence of Christianity, our young city athletes are to be bribed to victory by the secret application of 'palm oil' and to have their morals corrupted and their minds debased ...[27]

Continuing the theme, the vicar of Farsley, near Leeds, denounced football in 1893 as 'a fascination of the devil and the twin sister of the drink system.'[28] Some of this hostility was due to a residual suspicion of sports among the more puritan-minded clergy which dated back to the first half of the century, but it was undeniable that by the mid-1890s muscular Christians had begun to doubt rugby's usefulness as an agent of evangelism among the urban working classes. Although not all clergymen were opposed to the course the sport was taking, Bradford committee member Reverend J. E. Leighton being a notable exception, the exodus of men of the cloth from involvement in the game was such that, speaking at a Church Congress in Exeter in 1894, Rowland Hill called on clergy to stop criticising from the sidelines and 'make their influence felt' by playing a role in the sport once more.[29]

In fact, the RFU was experiencing the same phenomenon which afflicted the Church of England in its dealings with the urban working class and which had frustrated the efforts of the purveyors of 'rational recreation' in their attempt to bring middle-class culture to the masses a generation earlier. As we saw in the previous chapter, dutifully supplicant members of the working class were difficult to find and the feelings of those who thought themselves to be *in loco parentis* were not always reciprocated by their ostensible charges. Marshall himself faced deep hostility from almost all sections of the game, being heckled by players at after-match dinners, confronted at railway stations and regularly stoned by youths on his way to and from Almondbury School.[30] Despite the best efforts of the muscular Christians, working-class culture remained firmly rooted in the pub and the local community, and when the working-class player failed to match up to the idealised vision of him held by those controlling the game, the friendly patronage soon turned to something more vicious. No longer was the rhetoric of the 'honest working man' employed by the purveyors of the amateur ideal. 'Hordes', 'herds', 'howling mobs' and 'seething masses' were commonplace terms used to describe working-class players and spectators who did not fulfil their appointed role. Indeed, such people were viewed in the same light as those subject to British imperial rule overseas: 'I could not expect worse from the heathens of darkest Africa,' claimed J. H. Jones after his refereeing had been hooted and catcalled during a match at Hull.[31] Oft expressed anxieties about large crowds at matches in Lancashire and Yorkshire – although such concerns were rarely voiced about international matches or major games held in the South, where spectators tended to be middle class – were also to a large extent based on a deep distrust of working-class participation. The legalisation of broken-time payments would, as B. F. Robinson put it, force players to 'pander to the howling mobs that crowd the circular stands of some Yorkshire coliseum.'[32] Behind such language lay a fear which had been so alarmingly described by Mark Rutherford in 1885: 'Our civilisation is nothing but a thin film or crust lying over a volcanic pit ... [it is to be wondered] whether some day the pit would not break up through it and destroy us all.'[33]

When it came down to it, a working class which did not accept its place in the social order of the sport was not welcomed at all. 'The Rugby game, as its name implies, sprang from our public schools. It has been developed by our leading London clubs and universities; and why should we hand it

121

over without a struggle to the hordes of working men players who would quickly engulf all others?' asked the dual cricket and rugby international and Yorkshireman, Frank Mitchell.[34] 'Creston' poured scorn on 'those pampered members of society, the British lower classes, who can apparently only regard any form of sport as it assists them to make money. It was an ill day for the game when the northern labourer diverted his attention from quoits and rabbit coursing and pigeon flying and turned it to football', going on to claim that 'the lower-class player is the greatest adept at breaking laws when the referee is not looking.'[35] Nor were such sentiments confined to those residing in Southern England. Writing in the *Yorkshire Evening Post*, an opponent of broken-time payments was moved to write:

> The seething mass of humanity, monopolising the streets, obstructing traffic, shouting and yelling the coarsest language, and behaving like the herds usually associated with prize fights are not necessary for the success of southern football ... If Yorkshiremen cannot afford to play the game they boast so much about, pay them for their services but let them ... start a union of their own, where they can quarrel among themselves, find employment for the many out of work, and indulge in strikes, trades unions, and a general disinclination for honest work so dear to the average North Country working man.[36]

Similar attitudes could also be found across the Pennines: 'If the working man cannot afford to play, he must do as other people have to do who want things they cannot afford – do without. Football is a luxury, not a necessity ... the said working man, by the way, being too often a man whom a thoughtless crowd has spoiled for the dry drudgery of everyday life,' argued a correspondent in the *Salford Reporter*. Even the ostensibly socialist readership of Blatchford's *Clarion* was not immune from such prejudice: 'The individuals who would benefit under professionalism and payment for broken-time would still be the working man who does not work, the cadgers, drawers of ale, ostlers, billiard markers, and that species,' wrote one reader in 1893.[37] As usual, it was Budd who cut to the essence of the argument of the supporters of amateurism when he warned that if 'blind enthusiasts of working men's clubs insist on introducing professionalism, there can be but one result – disunion ... and if this black day comes, which I hope it never will, it will be the duty of the Rugby Union to see that the division of classes dates from the dawn of professionalism.'[38]

ROUGH PLAY, CHIVALRY AND MANHOOD

One of the central issues in this debate was the assertion, made by Rowland Hill and many others, that professionalism would lead to unacceptable levels of rough play, an argument which had also been used against cup competitions. 'The necessity to win will be felt more by the paid player than by the amateur, the necessity to win will create a determination to win at all hazards; this will inevitably result in rough play,' argued the RFU secretary. In the *Fortnightly Review* 'Creston' advanced the same argument, albeit somewhat more colourfully: 'The Rugby Union professional would be the most appalling character seen in England since the Mohocks. A man who collared us for his daily bread would be perfectly unbearable.'[39] The *Manchester Guardian* blamed the allegedly growing roughness of the game for the decline of middle-class players in the North: 'It is undoubtedly a fact that after leaving college many of our finest players have given up the game simply on the ground of the roughness which has been imported into it.'[40] The RFU were acutely sensitive to accusations of roughness and to the emotive power of such accusations on the wider public. In its early years, the game had been haunted by perennial accusations of violent play; indeed, one of the catalysts for the formation of the RFU had been calls in *The Times* for the game to be banned because of its ferocity. Gradually however, as an anonymous contributor to the *Football Annual* of 1881 pointed out, 'as the game began to be better understood, and played with greater perfection, those prejudices were removed.'[41]

As working-class players began to flood into the game in the early 1880s however, the old accusations began to be voiced again. In 1883 Rowland Hill criticised the cup competitions for encouraging rough play and the Reverend E. H. Dykes, captain and founder of the Leeds Parish Church team, had protested about the dangerous use of spiked boots, despite being an enthusiast of schoolboy hacking.[42] Rough play came to be explicitly associated with those clubs seen as working class. Thornes became known as 'the doctors' friends' for their allegedly over-vigorous play, Manningham going so far as to cancel their fixture with them in 1884. Horbury, a mining village team from near Wakefield, gained a similar reputation,[43] but despite such claims, violent play was not the sole preserve of working-class players, nor an outgrowth of recent trends towards professionalism. Indeed, many felt that professionalism would reduce the incidence of rough play. 'With the same stringent regulations in force as at present there would be a minimum of rough play, for the simple reason that the suspension of the professional would mean a matter of life and death,' wrote 'Nomad'.[44] A. W. Pullin also pointed out that the first season of the new Yorkshire

Senior Competition league, held by the RFU to be the next worst thing to professionalism, had seen only two or three players reported for foul play.[45]

In fact, many of those former public schoolboys who now complained at the roughness of their working-class opponents prided themselves on their ability to give and take hacking. As A. A. Sutherland pointed out, 'The football of our school days was a very crude and cruel thing and would not be tolerated for one moment. Time was when it was perfectly legitimate to single out an opponent and hack him over in a style that would have done credit to the "purring" propensities of the corner cads of Liverpool,'[46] and even during this period, violent play was not the preserve of the lower orders. Remembering an 1881 game for Blackheath against a northern club, C. B. Grundy recalled that: 'Their idea evidently was, "There's a team of southern amateurs, let's frighten them by playing rough," and they did play rough! But they never made a greater mistake in their lives. At half-time Blackheath had thirteen men left and the others eleven. The rest had been take in cabs to the nearest hospital.'[47] Similarly, on their 1885 tour of Scotland Bradford encountered 'some of the foulest play ever perpetrated' in 'a display of coarse play far from creditable to the followers of the Rugby code' from the resolutely middle-class Edinburgh Academicals.[48] Testimony to the fact that rough play was not unique to the 1880s was also provided by a veteran of rugby's early days:

> 'Chivalry', they call it! Well I can see no harm in giving pretty names to uncouth subjects; but it seems to me that if the bare-faced (and bare-shinned) hacking prevailed now to the same extent as in the halcyon days that I am speaking of, that little Rule 47 [penalising foul play] in the new rule book would have to be slightly enlarged. At this very moment I possess one of these 'chivalrous' tokens, below the knee, as a memento of a game which took place upwards of fifteen years ago.[49]

The charge that rough play was the fault of the working classes was difficult to sustain not only because it was empirically untrue, but also because violence was an integral part of the 'manly' philosophy of the middle-class administrators of the sport. 'Rough' sports were seen as healthy and character-building – after all, it was only in 1871 that hacking, seen by its proponents as the true mark of the manly game, was made illegal. As early as 1876, following calls to ban the sport after two deaths during matches, *Athletic News* had responded by stating that football could never be outlawed 'as long as English youths inherit the traditional pluck and energy of their race.'[50] The uneasy tension between classes and the aggressive demonstration of masculinity was no better expressed than by the rugby correspondent of the *Yorkshire Post* who, two months after blaming the veiled professional for rough play, denounced those who wished to see 'chances of accident' taken out of the sport and warned that 'our athletic youth and manhood will have to subside into dominoes, bezique, croquet or other gentle crafts and our playing fields will no longer serve to educate in those important elements which have done so much to make the Anglo-Saxon race the best soldiers, sailors and colonists in the world.'[51]

As with payments for play, approval of masculine aggression was dependent on who was doing what to whom. Physical toughness was widely admired among the middle classes. The reputation of J. G. Ashburner, a leading Barrow player of the 1880s and a scion of one of the town's leading shipbuilding families, was based largely on his brute strength and aggression: 'He was set on by a bullock in a loose box, and ... lifted it bodily and downed it. On one memorable occasion, when Barrow were playing Bradford, Fred Bonsor, the international half back, tried to tackle him. Out came that powerful arm, down went Bonsor, minus a few teeth.'[52] Halifax's three-quarter Doctor Robertson was praised for 'an exhibition of true British courage' by the *Athletic News* for playing throughout a game in which he had sustained three broken ribs.[53] For a team of miners from Horbury or textile workers from Thornes to subject a team of former public schoolboys to a rough game was to upset the natural order of class relationships. But for teams of ex-Rugby and Cheltenham boys to hack at each others' legs until the blood ran, as Manchester FC did until the late 1870s, was to stiffen the sinews of the imperial character. This contradiction was unwittingly, but neatly, encapsulated by a former public school pupil in 1886:

> A great many of the Horbury team were artisans and colliers. Now, I don't object to any working man – collier or whatever he may be – as long as he understands the game he is playing, but when in ignorance he puts on his working boots, which, combined with betting on the event [and] brute force ignorance of the game of Rugby Union ... I am not surprised at smashed legs ... it is a disgrace to the prestige of 'Dear Old England' for time-honoured fair play.[54]

Working-class aggression was seen as legitimate only when it occurred within a framework of national, racial and imperial identity as defined by the middle-class leaders of rugby. 'I believe that football is a thing which will encourage men to be brave *in whatever position of life they are placed* [my emphasis],' stated the Warrington president after his team's cup victory in 1886, as if to emphasise to his predominantly working-class players that their superiority on the football field extended no further than the touch line.

This ambiguity towards rough play in the game can be seen in the statistics for players' offences reported by referees to the Yorkshire Rugby Union (YRU) executive in the 1890–91 season. On average, players were suspended for shorter periods for reported acts of rough play than for acts of open violence or dissenting from referees' decisions. Of the 198 teams in membership of the YRU before the start of the season, 46 had players appear before the disciplinary committee. Of 76 offences reported, rough play accounted for 24, yet the average period of suspension handed out by the committee was a mere two-thirds of a week. Fighting, kicking and striking an opponent – violent offences differentiated from rough play in that they were clearly outside the rules of the sport – made up 26 of the offences and, excluding one life ban, carried an average suspension of two weeks. Most surprisingly from a modern perspective, twenty-four players, almost a third of the total, were reported for dissent. This may suggest that referees were seeking to impose standards of behaviour on players which they were reluctant to accept. The average suspension for such offences was a week and two-thirds, but there were also two season-long bans and one life ban for this offence. In fact, the three lengthiest bans were for dissent and only two other players received bans of more than five weeks, for kicking and rough play respectively.[55]

Similar ambiguities towards working-class physicality could be seen in the attitude of the rugby authorities towards insurance schemes set up for injured players. While there were suspicions that such schemes were used as a means of covertly paying players, in many cases justifiably so, there was also a feeling that it was somehow unmanly to receive money for injuries sustained on the football field. The image of the workshy labourer also figured strongly in this world view, as expressed by YRU president and leading glass manufacturer Barron Kilner when cross-examining an official of the Leeds district rugby union about their insurance scheme in 1890: 'Did it not strike you that such payments [of £1 a week to injured players unable to work] might lead to "shamming" for a week or two?' In the early 1880s a number of clubs had taken out insurance policies for their players, to some extent spurred on by the enterprising Employer's Liability Assurance Corporation which in 1882 offered insurance policies at annual premiums of ten and five shillings each. The following year Manningham took out ten shilling policies for their first team, three-quarters of the premium being paid by the club and the rest by the players. For that, an injured player would receive fifteen shillings a week for total disablement or 7/6d for 'partial' disablement. This was certainly not an amount which could support an injured player for any length of time and, perhaps mindful of such problems, in 1883 Salford set up their own insurance scheme for players, contributing 15 per cent of the gate takings from each home match to the insurance fund. In 1886 York voted to pay injured players ten shillings a day insurance money and Warrington took out insurance policies for both its first and reserve teams, the benefits being thirty shillings a week plus the payment of all doctor's fees for injured players.[56] After some debate as to whether receiving an insurance payment was itself an act of professionalism, insurance payments of no more than ten shillings a day were legally sanctioned at the RFU's 1886 annual general meeting, but in order to avoid clubs setting up their own schemes as a means to pay players covertly, it was ordered that only schemes run by bona fide insurance companies would be recognised. Despite these restrictions, suspicions about players 'undeservingly' receiving insurance pay-outs continued, fuelled by the commonly held belief among the leaders of the Rugby Union that players who could not afford to play, and consequently run the risk of injury, should not play. [57]

However as fears of war came to the fore in the 1890s, the controlled aggression of rugby was widely seen to have a military purpose, both for the middle classes and working classes. In 1894 the St Helens team were told by their local MP that 'the Duke of Wellington once said that the battle of Waterloo was won on the playing fields of Eton. That was, of course, when football was largely confined to the public schools. If the Duke had been here today, he would have said that any future battles of Waterloo would be won on the playing fields of St Helens.'[58] B. F. Robinson even praised the sport as an alternative to conscription for the working classes:

> Perhaps the best feature of this enthusiasm for Rugby football which has grown up among working men is the delight in hard exercise and the consequent self-denial that it has taught him. A man cannot spend his nights and his wages in the public house if twice a week he has to face a hard struggle of forty minutes 'each way'. Many foreigners, among whom the German emperor stands conspicuous, have recognised the advantages of artisan athletics, but it must be remembered that they have an excellent substitute in their military system ... It seems probable that without such games as football we should gradually sink from our present premiere [sic] position in masculinity among the European nations.[59]

The practical outcome of this line of thought was to be seen a couple of decades later in a letter from Colonel Davidson of the 1/10th Liverpool Scottish regiment to the sisters of a young lance-corporal, Jack King, who had been killed in action in France in 1916: 'It was a sad day for football. We can ill spare men like these, but if another game of football is never played in Britain, the game has done well, for after two years' command in the field, I am convinced that the Rugby footballer makes the finest soldier in the world.'[60]

The attempts to direct working-class physicality as expressed on the football field towards public school-defined 'manliness' and nationalistic and military ends also meant seeking to marginalise the importance of women to the game. As we saw in the previous chapter, women made up a significant proportion of rugby crowds in the 1880s and 1890s, yet they played no role whatsoever in the structures of the sport. Given the sheer weight of the double social oppression facing working-class women during this time, it is unlikely that there would have been large numbers of women seeking to be involved in the sport, even if they had been encouraged to do so, but, nevertheless, fear of feminine influence ran deep in the minds of rugby's rulers. Even in pursuit of his *bête noire*, the veiled professional, Frank Marshall refused to countenance taking evidence from a woman during an investigation in 1889: 'We have no dealings with women here,' he reportedly told a woman who was prepared to offer evidence of players receiving cash from the Wortley club in Leeds. Marshall himself was described by a former pupil as 'a thoroughly manly man, and one whose manliness appealed to his boys.'[61] In general, there was widespread mockery of women's interest in football, and this increased in the mid-1890s as women's participation in sports began to grow. The perceived difficulty of women participating in such a 'manly' sport, in contrast to cricket for example, was seen as one of rugby's strengths, as the president of Salford explained in 1891: 'It was perhaps the only game that was absolutely masculine in the country. Women took part in cricket and other pastimes but he had never yet heard of them playing football.'[62] The necessity for sexual segregation in rugby in order to develop truly masculine men – and, in a common piece of circular logic, of the necessity of truly masculine men to maintain rugby's manliness – was most perfectly expressed by H. H. Almond who saw rugby as a means to develop 'robust men' with 'manly sympathies', pronouncing in 1892 that 'I have never yet known a genuine Rugby forward who was not distinctively a man.' Whether he regarded backs as 'unmanly' is not recorded.[63]

How violent was rugby in reality? To some extent such judgements are subjective, especially given the absence of documentary evidence about the extent of player injuries. However, in *Barbarians, Gentlemen and Players*, Eric Dunning and Kenneth Sheard quote a set of figures which appear to suggest a horrific rate of 71 deaths and 366 broken limbs among Yorkshire rugby players between 1890 and 1893.[64] To be blunt, these figures are wrong. They were taken from two paragraphs which appeared in the 'Football Notes' column of the *Wakefield Express* of 8 April 1893. The column does not state that the deaths occurred solely in Yorkshire or while playing the rugby code of football. Indeed, the columnist saw fit to reproduce the figures without comment. In fact, although the *Express* didn't mention it, the figures were taken directly from a series of articles which had appeared in the *Pall Mall Gazette* over the preceding three years entitled 'The Butcher's Bill'. These articles were part of a campaign to prove the dangers of football and were widely commented on at the time as being unreliable, not least by the editor of the *Gazette* himself who felt compelled to add a disclaimer to the 1892 article stating that 'neither we nor the author can vouch personally for the accuracy of the following statements.'[65] The articles, which consisted of lists of accidents, covered the whole of the British Isles, and even some football incidents in Australia in 1892, included both association and rugby, and encompassed everything from school games to international matches. Entry to the lists was indiscriminate and arbitrary – one related baldly that an unnamed Blackburn Rovers player 'was hurt' in a November 1891 match while another claimed a death due to peritonitis was 'caused probably by a kick on the football field.' The rigour which was applied to the compilation of these articles can be gauged by the inclusion of an accident of a match at Warriston 'the nature of which was not stated.'[66]

If these figures for Yorkshire are wrong, what is the true figure? Between 1890 and 1893, a total of seven fatalities occurred in Yorkshire rugby, one tenth of the figure quoted by Dunning and Sheard, out of a total of thirteen deaths directly linked to playing the game between 1886 and 1895. Appendix Table A.4 sets out the details – unfortunately, information about serious injuries, such as broken limbs or internal injuries, are not recorded on any systematic basis and levels of insurance payments, given their use as a wages' supplement, are unreliable.

All 13 fatalities were attributed to accidents rather than deliberate foul play and all but one occurred in games involving junior clubs, suggesting that at the higher echelons, with better standards of refereeing and well-disciplined, organised teams, the game was neither more nor less dangerous than before or after this period. Two of the deaths, A. Dougherty and W. Scoley, appear to have occurred as a result of complications setting in after injuries. No deaths occurred in matches in Yorkshire Cup or Yorkshire

Senior Competition matches, supposedly catalysts for rough play because of the high degrees of competitiveness which they engendered. Interestingly enough, in none of the cases of rough play investigated in the 1890–91 season (see p. 126 above) was a serious injury recorded as having occurred to the 'innocent' party.

Nevertheless, even an average of one and a half deaths per season is shocking, yet players and officials tended to be scornful about accusations of roughness, other than when making specific accusations against individual clubs. Possibly with one eye on the class bias underlying many such accusations, the rugby correspondent of the *Wigan Observer* quoted figures showing that ten deaths had occurred during the previous two hunting seasons: 'From a statistician's point of view, it is by a heavy percentage safer to play at football than to ride after hounds or shoot the beasts of the field or the birds of the air.'[67] Lees Knowles, president of Salford, used a similar argument five years later, pointing to figures which suggested that there were more serious accidents in riding, cricket and cycling than in football.[68] John Gordon, a former Leeds St John's player and the first president of the city-wide Leeds club formed in 1890, seems to have summed up the attitude of most players when he claimed that the critics of rough play 'really do not know anything about football'.[69]

BROKEN-TIME OR OPEN PROFESSIONALISM?

For the majority of those who controlled rugby in its northern strongholds, the issue of amateurism was not as simple as the leaders of the RFU believed. As we have seen, the attempts by the YRU to purge itself of all traces of professionalism in the late 1880s had created an atmosphere of paranoia in the sport. Team selections were subject to the arbitrary banning of players and, even worse from the point of view of the club administrators, fixture lists could be decimated by the suspensions of opponents or of the club itself. While the ideal of amateurism was viewed as a noble aim, it was widely realised that the practicalities of implementing it could only result in working-class players being driven out of the game. To embark on such a course was unthinkable, for it would decimate rugby's popularity in Lancashire and Yorkshire, as an anonymous player pointed out in 1891:

> In the North the game is essentially dependent upon working men, both for its exposition and its support. It is a game by the masses for the masses. It is a cosmopolitan institution, in which all have an equal interest ... To carry out such an abstract idea [amateurism] to its

logical conclusion would be to depopularise the game and make it the selfish possession of the silver-spooned classes. Moreover, it would deprive the pastime of its ablest and most numerous exponents, who are essentially the working men of the North, and of its most enthusiastic supporters, who are undoubtedly the wage-earning classes.[70]

Since the early 1880s the fabric of rugby in the North had been woven from the cloth of working-class participation and the day-to-day reality of rugby was rapidly eroding support for the philosophy of amateurism. The mass popularity of the sport meant that the game had become a spectacle, much to the chagrin of amateurists. 'There was too much consideration for the spectators and too little for the players,' argued Scotland's captain after the 1893 Anglo-Scottish match at Headingley,[71] but in the North of England, large crowds and rugby were synonymous. What was good for one was necessarily good for the other and the spectacular nature of the game was freely acknowledged. 'Football now ranks as a popular entertainment, and spectators consequently have the right to get the best article they can for their money. That can only be provided by professionals. No one goes (often) to the theatre to see amateur actors,' stated a supporter of open professionalism, using a line of argument pursued by 'Nomad' of the *Bradford Telegraph*:

> If these [players] are not fit subjects for remuneration, then all I can say is this, namely that the thousands who flock to witness their performance ought not to be charged any admission fee ... those who provide the play ought, if they require it and by every human law (except those framed by the Rugby Union), to receive a share of the spectators' contributions. If it were so the players would naturally return the compliment by giving as good a display as possible.[72]

By the spring of 1891, the discontent over the broken-time issue, combined with the pressure for the formation of league competitions in Lancashire and Yorkshire, had begun to coalesce into a campaign. 'Something must be done in the direction of compensating men for the loss of working time,' pleaded *The Yorkshireman*.[73] 'A Professional in Mufti' issued a call to arms in March of that year: 'I say, therefore, to the clubs of the Yorkshire Union, and to footballists generally, let payment for loss of time be your battle cry and watchword, and what Yorkshire says today, England will accept tomorrow.'[74]

The demand for payment for loss of time, or broken-time, was explicitly not a call for open professionalism on the model adopted by the Football Association. The formula sought a return to the pre-1886 days when payment for time off work for training was more or less an accepted part of the game. Its advocates stopped short of proposing out-and-out professionalism because it was felt in northern rugby circles that soccer-style professionalism would lead inevitably to spiralling costs, wage inflation and regular bankruptcies. It was hoped that broken-time payments could be a middle road between Spartan amateurism and the jungle law of open professionalism. Politically too, it was felt that there would be more chance of broken-time being adopted by the RFU because it was merely a way of reimbursing the expenses of playing the sport yet would not allow a player to earn his living or make a profit from the game. Support for the idea was quickly forthcoming. 'That this meeting is in favour of the payment of football players for broken-time' was carried at Batley's annual general meeting in May 1891. Applause greeted Wakefield Trinity president Barron Kilner's speech in favour at his club's AGM. It was even suggested that the Reverend Marshall might support broken-time payments as a way of preserving the amateur ideal.[75] YRU secretary James Miller made a rousing speech in favour of the proposal at a meeting of Yorkshire club secretaries that same April:

> Football is no longer the pastime of the public schools and the leisured classes alone; it has become the sport of the masses – of the wage-earning classes in our great manufacturing centres. That being so, football legislation ought not to be for the 'silver spoon' fraternity but for working men and the Union clearly cannot legislate on the same lines for the latter as they could for the former classes. It is unreasonable to expect the same 'amateurism' from the wage-earning classes as from public school men. It is unfair to expect working men to break time to play football without their being remunerated.

Yet despite the rhetoric about the rights of the working-class player, the broken-time principle was conceived as one which if implemented would reduce the influence of the players in the game, as Miller made clear. He felt that it was pressure from the players which was leading rugby towards professionalism and therefore proposed three methods to combat the threat; firstly to 'limit the migration of players or transfer of services; secondly to grant reasonable concessions by allowing men to be paid for the loss of wages by breaking time; and lastly to increase rather than diminish the penalties imposed for professionalism. If these three remedies were applied the ground would be cut from under the feet of such players who not only advocated professionalism but were working to bring it about …'[76] That the broken-time proposal was seen as a means for tightening control over players was emphasised in November of that year when the *Yorkshire Post*, whose representative had been made a non-voting member of the YRU committee the previous month, commented on a speech by Miller on broken-time by stating: 'Whether the game flourishes on a deceptive basis or not – and how tired we are of hearing the term veiled professionalism – the time has arrived when players are to be put in their places and kept there.'[77] Indeed, the whole thrust of the arguments of the advocates of broken-time was that its introduction would be a better safeguard against the spread of professionalism than the pristine amateurism of the RFU. Miller and the leadership of the YRU shared the RFU's concern about the growing influence of the working class on the game – the differences were over how to deal with it.

This need to exert greater control over players was also bound up with the developing business exigencies of running a major rugby club. As the clubs became bigger enterprises and sought to secure their long-term futures through the purchase of grounds and through incorporation, so too did they desire to put their relationship with the players on a more businesslike footing. The broken-time scheme would allow clubs to plan their financial futures better by putting the payment of wages on a fixed and orderly basis while avoiding the perils of professionalism. Despite the popularity of the game, financial losses were a common occurrence, especially for those clubs outside the Lancashire and Yorkshire elite crowd-pullers. For example, Batley's profit of £227 in 1887 was entirely due to a bumper attendance at their Yorkshire Cup tie with Wakefield Trinity which brought in over £300. The club only made a profit once more before joining the Northern Union in 1895, when they were forced to hold a bazaar to raise funds to clear off an accumulated debt of more than £600. Throughout the 1890s much concern had been expressed about the ability of players to extract payments from clubs but clubs could not exert financial discipline over players without breaking the RFU's amateur regulations. As the *Bradford Observer* argued in 1893:

> Professionalism is worked on recognised lines. Amateurism simply pretends to be and what the difference amounts to in money today no man can tell. Unless a decided check is put upon the lavish expenditure of clubs a general state of bankruptcy must ensue before long. There will at least be a fixed scale of payment limiting the liability, whereas some of today's amateurs appear to involve their clubs in costs which can never be properly estimated beforehand.[78]

In short, broken-time would help to put the running of clubs on a firm capitalist footing.

This was the key to the apparently contradictory spectacle of middle-class businessmen and professionals making stirring speeches in defence of the rights of the working man. For clubs to become successful and stable businesses the rules of the RFU had to be modified. The sanctions against infringements of the amateur code put clubs' futures at the mercy of the zealots of amateurism. The need for secrecy and behind-the-scenes dealings with players meant that financial planning and wage control were almost impossible. Strictures against cup and league competitions, especially in Lancashire and at a national level, resulted in valuable opportunities for revenue and expansion of the sport's influence being lost. Pure amateurism meant that clubs were not in control of their own destinies, and that, because the RFU's decision-making annual general meetings were always held in London, patronage and social connection played too strong a role in determining the development of the sport. The northern clubs' call for equality for the working man was part of a general desire to see market forces – the equality of the cash nexus or 'bourgeois equality' – play a greater role in the overall administration of the game. Hence the call for broken-time was based both on a desire to control wages tightly and to compromise with an RFU that had declared many times before that it would not relinquish its principles.

Unlike the support for amateurism, the movement for broken-time had no clear ideological basis. Its ranks included those who believed that broken-time would defend amateurism; those who wished to return to pre-1886 practices; those who felt that broken-time was a viable option in itself; and those who felt that broken-time would give the game some breathing space to prepare for the inevitable arrival of open professionalism. For this latter group the discussion was about expediency and economics. 'Pro-fessionalism will come, must come; and when it does arrive Rugby clubs will benefit by the mistakes and the experience of the Association fore-runners,' wrote A. W. Pullin in March 1893. 'But the time has not come yet, and a means to postpone it – not to obviate it, for that is impossible – is to grant payment for bona-fide broken-time.'[79] Much of this debate was informed by Charles Edwardes' widely noted 1892 article 'The New Football Mania', which pointed out that even the most successful soccer clubs were unlikely to make money and that the cost of paying players had proved crippling to many.[80] The following year, *The Times* had also highlighted the detrimental financial effects that professionalism had brought to soccer.[81] Those in favour of broken-time payments argued that their scheme would meet the demands of the players while avoiding soccer-style bankruptcies caused by clubs having to pay wages. 'Yorkshire football supporters ... have no desire to see Yorkshire Rugby football sink to the commercial level of the Association game, to see clubs lose their local connection by the wholesale importation of either Scotch, Welsh or even Irishmen. What they do desire, however, and what they will eventually insist on, is that a working man player shall not be placed under restrictions which make it impossible for him, in many instances, to assist either his country, county or club', argued *The Yorkshireman*.[82] The possible economic impact was explored in detail in an article published just two weeks before the 1893 RFU AGM at which the motion to legalise broken-time payments was to be discussed. 'OPQ' warned that 'professionalism has proved ruinous to Association clubs' and that rugby clubs couldn't afford to pay the huge wage bills professionalism would bring:

> Even Bradford could not afford to pay their men, and that club is the most successful financially in connection with the Rugby game. At the end of last season they had a balance to the good of about £1,164; but supposing they had to pay their men how far would that go? As I have already pointed out, Everton pay £3,529 in wages, Blackburn Rovers £2,156 and so on. It is plain to be seen, therefore, that once professionalism were adopted the balance of even the Bradford club would be as much on the wrong side as it is on the good.

He concluded by saying that 'some reform is necessary, I admit, but the experience of Association clubs warns us from the payment of players as professionals unless we are anxious to rush headlong into bankruptcy. The solution of the difficulty is to be found in the payment for broken-time, and a maximum rate per day should be fixed for that.'[83]

Yet, according to the advocates of open professionalism, the figures quoted by 'OPQ', like many of the assumptions of the broken-timers, did not tell the whole story. 'He quotes figures from the balance sheets of Rugby Union clubs,' argued a knowing critic, 'but does he imagine that these balance sheets faithfully show every penny received? They are cooked, and what is shown is only the balance of what is left after deductions have been made for payments already made.' Where do the funds come from for the many presents given to play,' he asked? 'From the club receipts of course, and there is no difficulty in so arranging matters that there shall not be the slightest trace of them in the books.'[84] Moreover, to the supporters of professional rugby, the experience of soccer was something to be admired. 'Nomad' pointed to the strides forward taken by Association since the introduction of professionalism: 'I noticed the other day that 25,000 spectators assembled at Sheffield to see a cup tie between Sunderland and Aston Villa, two out-and-out professional teams. What a reflection on the alleged "waning interest" and "hopeless state of affairs" which the dribbling game is said to have developed.'[85] To 'Nomad' and his co-thinkers, professionalism had raised the playing standards of soccer and the same would occur in rugby, with the increased wage bills being paid for by larger gates brought about by improved spectacle on the field.

'Nomad' also argued that broken-time payments would not substantially benefit the working-class player. If it was paid just for playing in matches, it would hardly be noticed as most matches were played on Saturday afternoons when no one was at work anyway. Nor would three or four hours' payment at his normal wage rate compensate him for losing the quite valuable food, drink, clothes, etc, which players often received, and mere compensatory payments would not put him on an equal par with the middle-class amateur. 'The pure amateur should accept only his railway fare and the price of his bed, if that, but your "amateur" as a rule takes far more than the working man player does in "expenses". Would the broken-time compensation bring the working man player up to a level with the amateur? Not at all – but under professionalism, legalised and properly regulated, the player would have at least a fair and fixed remuneration.'[86] Others felt that the broken-time proposal was simply a manoeuvre by clubs wishing to postpone the fateful day: 'If we are to have professionalism let us have it and be honest about it, but don't let us go for miserable bastard subterfuges and legalise professional practices in an amateur game up a back street.'[87] A. A. Sutherland, with a clarity shared only by Arthur Budd, his polar opposite in the debate, spoke up for the players: 'We've heard too much rubbish about the working man and his loss of wages, and to talk about the injustice done to him is so much rot. The top and bottom of it is, the working man does not care a rap for the payment for broken-time dodge … what the working man requires is hard cash for services rendered, and in view of the money the clubs make, his demand is fair and legitimate.'[88]

From their own vantage point, the leadership of the RFU understood these arguments well and, despite protestations that it would safeguard amateurism, the broken-time proposal was totally unacceptable to them. Far from being a supporter, as had been hoped, the Reverend Marshall continued to press the YRU to seek out violators of the amateur ethic and at the 1891 RFU general meeting had proposed draconian rules to outlaw inducements to players to change clubs. These laid down that a player suspected of merely discussing such inducements had to prove his innocence of the charge before his county committee. The new regulations 'would not restrict the liberty of the undoubted amateur,' argued Marshall, but 'men under a suspicion of professionalism would not be able to migrate unless they were prepared to give a satisfactory account of themselves.'[89] Three months later the RFU declared its intention to look into the status of insurance payments to injured players, with a view to determining if they allowed players to profit from their injuries. The leadership of the RFU were determined to turn back the tide. Marshall, writing in the 1892 *Athletic News Annual* declared that: 'it is far preferable to have two bodies, one amateur and the other professional, than to have the methods of the Association imitated by the Rugby Union.' When the YRU voted over-whelmingly in the summer of 1893 to put the broken-time issue to that September's RFU annual general meeting it was clear that he and his co-thinkers were not prepared to compromise, and Arthur Budd's 1886 call to arms – 'no mercy but iron rigour' – became their watchword.

THE 1893 ANNUAL GENERAL MEETING OF THE RFU

Nevertheless, the supporters of broken-time payments still felt that they could win over a majority of the Rugby Union. Arithmetically, the clubs in the north were felt to outnumber those in the south, and as the RFU AGM approached, an unprecedentedly high level of unity had been forged in northern rugby around the theme of equality of treatment for the working-class player. Rumours even circulated that Northumberland's William Cail, the RFU president, backed the proposal.[90] The Lancashire annual general meeting voted to support broken-time because 'the game is both supported and played extensively by the working classes, and their players feel as keenly as ours the pinch of the shoe in the loss of broken-time,' with the delegates from Rochdale Hornets, Swinton, Warrington and Wigan going so far as to speak in favour of open professionalism.[91] The issue was summed up in microcosm at a meeting of the Huddersfield District Union five days before the AGM, when a supporter of the Reverend Marshall, speaking as a representative of the Old Almondburians club, spoke against broken-time payments. Responding, 'Mr Crosland [of the Paddock club in Huddersfield] pointed out that the Old Almondburians were in no need of compensation for broken-time, as they were not working men.'[92]

To ensure the biggest possible turn-out, the YRU chartered a special excursion train to take the delegates from Yorkshire to the AGM, to be held as usual at the Westminster Palace Hotel in London. Costing delegates ten shillings for the day or fifteen shillings for a four-day ticket, the train consisted of twelve coaches and stopped at eleven of the major towns in

West Yorkshire. Disappointingly for the YRU, although 'every compartment was well-filled', it was not sold out and some of the tickets were sold off the day before the meeting at five shillings each.[93] The *Evening Post* special correspondent accompanying the delegates on the train reported 'a look of determination about every man which told of his zeal in the cause of broken-time', cataloguing their origins in mock-Carlylean tones. 'From the distant parts of Hull and Goole came the wise men of the East, from the fastnesses of Brighouse, or the lesser-known regions of the Calder Valley, on they came.'[94]

At the meeting James Miller moved the motion, 'That players be allowed compensation for bona-fide loss of time.'[95] He argued that the changed conditions which the RFU now faced were due to the success of the leaders of the game in fostering and popularising it. The sport was no longer confined to the public schools and universities but had been taken up by working men, but 'having introduced the new type of player, the RFU at once did him an injustice. These men were constantly called upon to lose their wages in order to play for their county or their club and at the same time they were debarred from recompense for the loss of time involved. Why should not the working man be able to play the game on level terms with the gentleman?'[96] He cited the case, although he did not name him directly, of Harry Bradshaw, a forward from Bramley and a worker at Newlay Dyeworks in Leeds, who had played for England against Ireland in Dublin the previous season. Although his travel and accommodation had been paid for, he still lost three working days' pay journeying to and from the match. In contrast, the gentlemen who played in the team with him lost nothing. This could not, Miller claimed, be called playing on level terms, 'the game should be played as a sport and not as a source of income but it did not mean that these players should play it at a loss. If it was legitimate to refund expenses, why not refund wages lost?'[97] He concluded by asking delegates not to pooh-pooh the idea because it came from Yorkshire and vote for a 'simple act of justice' which would both satisfy the working man and raise the strongest banner against professionalism yet devised.

William Cail of the Northumberland RFU moved the amendment to Miller's motion, 'That this meeting, believing that the above principle is contrary to the true interest of the game and its spirit, declines to sanction the same.' He claimed that only one of the northern counties fully supported the motion and that Miller's citing of Harry Bradshaw was 'entirely fallacious' because he too had been at the same match and had succeeded in getting back to work on Monday morning. He concluded by asking any of the players present if they would like to become professionals

FOOTBALL FREAKS.

No. I.—THE STRICT GRAMMARIAN.

Scene :—Blackheath, last Saturday. The Bradford v. Marlborough Nomads Match.

Real unadulterated Bradfordian (to very gentlemanly South Country "Nomad") : "Nah then, what's ta jarrin' at ? Fotch t' umpire; *he'll* sooin sattle all this here threeapin' an' fendin' and provin'!" (*Utter consternation of South Country Nomad.*)

Across the social divide 2: social mixing on the field of play did little to break down the mutual incomprehension of southern-based middle-class players and the predominantly northern working-class players (from *Toby, the Yorkshire Tyke*).

to be bought and sold. Mark Newsome of Dewsbury seconded Miller, 'At present the working man was the only man who suffered anything by playing football. He did not play on a level with the other class of players.' The motion 'would put them on an equal footing.'[98] Indeed, the whole discussion revolved around the position of the working-class footballer. Mr Hobson of Midland Counties RFU said that his teams were almost entirely composed of working men who did not desire payment, former RFU president Roger Walker of Lancashire doubted that 'honest working men' wanted any alteration to the rules and from Devon the Reverend Warner opined that the amateur gentleman often lost more playing football than the working man. J. W. H. Thorp, president of Cheshire RFU, declared that 'the pseudo-working man and the bastard amateur do not represent the working man of this country. The latter, and I don't mean the working man who gets a transfer from one club to another which places him in a public house, do not want this miserable subterfuge of broken-time payment.' The Reverend Marshall, who was so roundly heckled by the Yorkshire delegates that the chairman had to tell Wakefield Trinity secretary J. H. Fallas to sit down, told the meeting that the aim of the motion was to allow Yorkshire clubs to continue to break the amateur rules with impunity. Like Walker, he called on those who wanted professionalism to form their own union.[99] Almost unnoticed, Mr Northin of the Bowling Old Lane club in Bradford spoke against the Yorkshire proposal on the grounds that his club could not afford to pay players and that payments would force many small clubs out of existence.[100]

In defence of broken-time payments James Gledstone of Otley appealed to the RFU 'as English sportsmen [to] recognise that it was their duty to place the working man on the same level with the other classes,' and Joe Mills of Swinton explained that 'the working man, who chiefly composed the teams in Lancashire and Yorkshire, felt that they had a grievance' and that the motion would put matters right.[101] Following the Swinton delegate's claim that broken-time payments would help to avert full professionalism, Harry Garnett of Bradford, who at the 1886 RFU AGM had suggested that if working men couldn't afford to play the game they shouldn't play at all, rose to support the motion reluctantly as a way of delaying the inevitability of professionalism for at least a few years. Ominously, virtually all the speakers against the motion, including Rowland Hill, Walker and Marshall, warned that the Union would split if agitation for broken-time or professionalism continued. However, the debate had no material bearing on the outcome of the vote, which went against broken-time payments by 282 to 136. Immediately after the AGM the leadership of the RFU convened a special meeting to amend the constitution, so that henceforth the first bye-law of the Union allowed membership only to those clubs 'entirely composed of amateurs.'

Doubtless intense lobbying and vote procurement played a major role in this result, but is it the case that H. E. Steed of Lennox FC was charged by the RFU with collecting proxy votes from clubs opposed to the motion and raised a total of 120, as claimed by former RFU executive member George Berney in 1925 and by subsequent historians?[102] There is no contemporary evidence for Berney's claim. *Pastime*, the shrillest of all supporters of amateurism, didn't mention any arrangements despite an editorial entitled 'All Hands!' which darkly warned that 'the club which does not send a delegate ... may incur a heavy responsibility.'[103] In fact, most commentators of the time blamed the defeat on the softness of the Yorkshire voting bloc rather than the machinations of the RFU. The *Leeds Daily News* claimed that some Yorkshire delegates had been so disgusted with the insults from their opponents that they had walked out prior to the vote and later pointed to the bad organisation of the vote by the YRU which had seen some of the region's delegates vote against their own motion.[104] The *Leeds Mercury* reported a widely believed rumour that a number of delegates 'took advantage of the cheap excursion to London to enjoy themselves and never went to the meeting.'[105] As to whether a number of Yorkshire delegates lost their way en route to the meeting, as is claimed in Titley and McWhirter's history of the RFU, there is no contemporary confirmation. The ease of the RFU's victory was also assisted by a lack of Yorkshire-style zeal for the motion on the part of the Lancashire clubs. Although a number of them voted for broken-time there was no attempt to mobilise support, possibly because the matter was so identified as a Yorkshire issue.[106] The evidence would suggest that Berney's memory was mistaken and that he was actually referring to the following year's special general meeting. In December 1894 Steed organised a circular signed by eleven supporters of amateurism – including former Yorkshire captain W. E. Bromet and Barbarians founder W. P. Carpmael – which asked those clubs opposed to broken-time but unable to attend the meeting to send their proxies to Steed. The reaction in Yorkshire to this circular was outrage but, significantly, no one in either camp spoke about voting arrangements at the 1893 meeting, implying that such overt electoral planning was a new feature of rugby's civil war.[107]

The reaction of the supporters of broken-time to this defeat was controlled anger. *Clarion* remarked that the arguments of the anti-broken-time speakers were nothing more than 'a reassertion of the typical British snob's comfortable belief that the business of the working man is to work; Providence made him a purpose; play was intended only for us – us gentlemen.'[108] There was no doubt among the advocates of broken-time that the reasons for their defeat revolved around the question of class. 'The AGM', wrote OPQ in *The Yorkshireman*, 'has cleared the ground of many side issues and laid bare the position assumed by those who oppose the payment of out-of-pocket expenses to the working men. We have at last been boldly told the truth ... if a man cannot afford to play he has no right to; that Rugby football is a game for the classes and, in effect, that the masses are neither more nor less than intruders.'[109] While expressing their outrage at the stunning blow they had received, most northern commentators cautioned against splitting from the RFU. 'Fortunately,' said the *Yorkshire Evening Post*, 'Yorkshiremen and Lancastrians, having been beaten at the vote, can take their defeat philosophically.'[110] A. W. Pullin hoped for a 'practical compromise', and OPQ told the Yorkshire clubs that it was their 'duty manfully to stand by the cause they have espoused.'[111]

The door to internal reform was now locked however. Having won the decisive battle, the victors were in no mood to be magnanimous. The *Manchester Guardian*'s comment on the AGM was that 'jerrymandering is not palatable in politics or football, but it is sometimes excusable, and this was a case in point.' *Pastime* gloated that 'it remains to remove suspected clubs, at the discretion of the committee, from membership; to expel all those which avowedly sympathise with professionalism or refuse their heartiest co-operation for its detection and suppression.' 'Creston' waxed lyrical: 'The victorious citadel of amateurism requires to be vigorously defended, and the North and South should combine to hold it, vigorously expelling any club from the Union that directly or indirectly favours money-making at the game. The legislation of Messrs Budd, MacLaren and Rowland Hill ... was at the critical moment admirably strong.' From Scotland, the president of the Scottish Union 'expressed a hope that the watchword with regard to professionalism would be no surrender.'[112] There was to be no repeat of the post-1886 failure to rid the game of the professional threat, as the *Yorkshire Owl* warned darkly:

> The English Rugby Union, as such, comprising the universities, the schools and the many clubs formed afterwards by the old school brigade, will never stand professionalism in the game, whatever name it is cloaked under ... It would have to sacrifice many fine exponents of the game doubtless, but it would not hesitate. It would lose a good many international games, but it would still not hesitate.[113]

THE ROAD TO 1895

Less than two months after the AGM the RFU charged Huddersfield, one of the most senior and widely respected clubs in the North, with professionalism for allegedly offering John Forsyth and George Boak, two players from Cummerdale Hornets in Cumberland, to play for them for thirty and twenty-five shillings per week respectively, plus jobs at the Reed, Holliday chemical works. After an acrimonious hearing lasting five and a half hours, the club was banned from playing until the end of 1893. Only the votes of the Yorkshire representatives on the RFU prevented its immediate expulsion.[114] An uneasy truce prevailed for the following twelve months, as attention in Yorkshire shifted to the matter of automatic promotion and relegation in the Yorkshire Senior Competition, but it was in Lancashire where the first moves took place of the endgame which was ultimately to resolve the conflict in the Union. The social gulf which divided the leadership of the Lancashire rugby union from the majority of its member clubs and the aborting of the 1890 investigations into professionalism had resulted in the build-up of great stores of combustible material on both sides. Amateur zealotry, as personified in the election of Manchester's Roger Walker as RFU president in September 1894, and a well-entrenched system of covert payments, not to mention the successful example of local professional soccer, were the tinder to which the spark of political necessity was added in August 1894.

The week before Walker's election, the Lancashire committee charged Leigh with making illegal payments to players, ranging from £1 to 2/6d, and paying the board and lodgings of their two Welsh players, Dai Fitzgerald and Charlie Wilding. Although the club was suspended for ten weeks, the committee also ruled that they would automatically be placed at the bottom of the first division of the Lancashire Club Championship and barred from charging admission to any games rearranged due to the ban.[115] Three weeks after the Leigh ban, Salford were also charged with professionalism for offering Joe Smith, a Radcliffe player, twenty-five shillings a week to switch clubs. They too were found guilty and received the same punishment as Leigh. James Higson, the Salford chairman, felt that his club was being treated as a scapegoat and promptly escalated the dispute by counter-charging Radcliffe and accusing Wigan, Swinton, Tyldesley, Broughton Rangers and Rochdale Hornets of the same offence.[116] On 13 November Wigan suffered the same fate as Leigh and Salford when they too were found guilty of professionalism for offering the latter's Frank Miles thirty shillings a week to play for them.[117] There were now only three Lancashire first division clubs not involved in the dispute, and the contradiction between the RFU's amateur regulations and the day-to-day commercial interests of the Lancashire clubs was at breaking point. A split appeared to be imminent; the *Wigan Observer* predicted schism in the Union 'within ten weeks'. These explosive events had not gone unnoticed across the Pennines. Rumours of a professional league being formed in Lancashire by the end of November were given credence when reports surfaced of Leigh officials visiting prominent Yorkshire players. Leeds even held a special general meeting to discuss the new situation. Clearly, if Lancashire went professional, Yorkshire would be forced to follow suit to prevent the loss of their best players.

Into this conflagration the RFU threw a six point 'manifesto' on amateurism, which announced that henceforth, clubs or players charged with professionalism would be treated as guilty unless they could prove otherwise. Guilty clubs would be expelled from the Union. The key clauses read:

> 2. That offences committed by clubs after the issue of this circular, whether through themselves, their agents, officials, members or ticket-holders, shall be punished by the expulsion of such clubs and the permanent suspension of all their members and officials. ...
> 4. That having regard to the notorious methods of concealment hitherto adopted by offending clubs, this committee will, in dealing with future cases, consider that the burden of proof of innocence lies on the club or person charged.

It was, commented the *Yorkshire Post*, 'draconian and unbending in [its] severity.'[118] The manifesto was sent to all member clubs, with the request that they sign a declaration announcing their support for the measures. Only the Yorkshire representatives on the RFU executive voted against the manifesto but it was greeted with opposition not only in Yorkshire and Lancashire but also in Durham, Gloucestershire and the Midlands, all of whom voted it down. On 21 November, the leading twenty-one clubs in Lancashire and Yorkshire met to organise opposition to the manifesto and called for a special general meeting of the RFU at the end of December to vote on the document. Despite H. E. Steed's attempts to organise pro-manifesto proxies, the outcry against the 'un-English' clauses transferring the burden of proof proved to be so strong that the RFU dropped the contentious fourth clause two weeks before the special general meeting, but at the meeting, held on 28 December 1894, it was made clear by the RFU that this was merely a tactical retreat. Rowland Hill explained that they had backed down because 'they did not want to have a split with those they believed to be favourable to the cause of amateur football and that if they could bring such clubs into line with them by the sacrifice of some points not of a fundamental character, the cause they had in view would be aided.' 'Keep your nerves strung up,' advised former RFU president William Cail, 'as, although it is only a sparring match tonight, it may be that when we next meet the gloves will be thrown aside and we shall be called upon to hit out as hard from the shoulder as we can.'[119] He announced that a subcommittee was to be formed to redraft the anti-professional laws, on the lines of the original manifesto, for introduction in September 1895. The tenor of the meeting can be gauged from the fact that an unsuccessful motion to offer £20 to anyone providing information about alleged acts of professionalism, proposed by Philip Maud and W. P. Carpmael of the Barbarians, gained 163 votes. Whether those receiving money for informing would thereby professionalise themselves was not stated.

For the supporters of payment for play, in any form, there were now only two options: succumb or secede. This future was clear to all, as was pointed out by the *Yorkshire Post*, 'If the obnoxious "class" feeling introduced at last Friday's meeting by men who should know better is allowed to have its full sway, the inevitable result is a split in the Union.'[120] For some, such as A. A. Sutherland of the *Clarion*, it was time for the northern clubs finally to grasp the nettle:

> There's either a lamentable want of brains or honesty – perhaps a want of both – in all [the Lancashire and Yorkshire clubs'] movements and people are getting heartily sick and tired of the whole thing. There are two courses open for the clubs to take – either amateurism or professionalism ... What we do want and pine for is the honest official bold enough to give prominence to the wishes of the majority of the working men players, and strike out for professionalism.[121]

Throughout January meetings of the leading northern clubs took place to decide on the next steps to take. Various schemes to form a northern rugby league were suggested and on 30 January the George Hotel at Huddersfield hosted a meeting of representatives of Brighouse Rangers, Batley, Dewsbury, Huddersfield, Hull, Leeds, Liversedge, Manningham, Wakefield Trinity, Broughton Rangers, Leigh, Oldham, Rochdale Hornets, Salford, Swinton, Tyldesley, Warrington and Wigan. Bradford, Halifax, Hunslet and St Helens sent their support to the gathering, which voted to form a 'Northern Union', a 'sort of mutual protection society', to organise the playing of an annual challenge match between the Lancashire and Yorkshire club champions and regulate transfers between member clubs.[122]

No one was fooled by these apparently innocent intentions and it was no surprise when details leaked out of the meeting's secret resolution:

> In the event of any club in this Union being expelled, or in any way punished by the English Rugby Union or the respective county Unions, such club shall have the right to appeal to this committee, who shall investigate the matter, and if it be decided that they have been unfairly dealt with, this Union will support the club so treated.[123]

Seeking to follow the letter of the RFU's constitutional law, if not its spirit, the new body, which had officially titled itself the Lancashire and Yorkshire Rugby Football Union of Senior Clubs, submitted its rules, minus the secret caveat, to the RFU for its approval. In doing this, some clubs hoped the RFU would accept them in the same way that the Football Association had accepted the Football League. The outcome, however, was inevitable, as had been predicted by an increasingly hysterical *Pastime*, which opined that the clubs must 'forever renounce that particular form of professionalism to which they once pledged themselves – broken-time. They must profess their obedience to the county unions ... On the whole, it seems to be a beautiful case for the Everlasting No!'[124]

As the hostility towards the new organisation grew, so did the doubts of some of its participants. Bradford, Huddersfield and Leeds – the three most wealthy clubs in Yorkshire – distanced themselves from the project by the device of signing the new union's agreement but not affixing their company seals, thereby rendering their agreement not legally binding. Salford and Swinton also withdrew their support.[125] The murky waters of the battle were further muddied by the coming to a head of the disputes over automatic promotion and relegation which had been brewing in the Yorkshire Senior Competition and the Lancashire Club Championship.

From its formation in 1892 the YSC had been a self-elected body, entry to which could only be granted by a vote by its clubs. The subsequent creation of the second, third and other junior Yorkshire leagues had put pressure on it to allow automatic promotion for the winners of the Second Competition, and consequently relegation of the bottom side. While accepting the principle in theory, the YSC had voted against any changes at the end of its first season in 1893. Unsurprisingly, this did not go down well with either the Second Competition clubs or the YRU, which had taken up the cudgels for the smaller clubs in order to reassert its own power. When the same thing happened at the end of the 1893–94 season the YRU pressurised the YSC to accept the playing of a test match between the bottom YSC club and the top Second Competition club to decide the issue.

However, when the YSC came to incorporate this change into its own rules, a rider was added stating that a club finishing at the foot of the table because of 'unforeseen circumstances' may be excused the necessity of playing in the test match. In truth, this clause was added to guard against a club finishing at the bottom of the table due to its suspension for professionalism, as had almost happened to Huddersfield and which was to happen to three Lancashire clubs the following season. This dispute allowed the defenders of amateurism to pose as the protectors of the little clubs. Speaking at a Liberal rally during the 1895 general election, Castleford's Arthur Hartley, a future President of the RFU, railed against the 'unelected House of Lords which the YSC has become' and denounced its refusal to accept the YRU's call for 'equal rights for all.'[126]

Although this issue became a bitter struggle, which some have claimed was the real reason for the 1895 split, and directly resulted in the YSC clubs resigning *en bloc* from the YRU in July 1895, it was in fact a battle for position before the inevitable showdown over payment for play.[127] This was demonstrated by the moves in Lancashire by the attempts of the First-Class Competition clubs to assert control over promotion to and relegation from their ranks following the suspensions of Leigh, Salford and Wigan in 1894. Although automatic promotion and relegation had been accepted from the start of the Lancashire league system in 1892, the suspensions and the placing of the miscreant clubs at the bottom of the First-Class league meant that clubs found guilty of professionalism found themselves facing economic ruin through relegation and the resulting loss of attractive fixtures. Perhaps not as prescient as their Yorkshire counterparts, the First-Class clubs now fought a rearguard action to avoid being picked off one by one by the Lancashire authorities. Eventually, in July 1895, the First-Class clubs, with the exception of Salford and Swinton but with the addition of Widnes, resigned from the competition.

These resignations effectively cleared the way for the formation of a rival rugby union, the necessity for which was underlined on August 12 when the RFU published a draft of the new rules on professionalism which it was to present for ratification to that September's annual general meeting. They were simply a more thorough rendering of the previous year's manifesto and, despite hopes by some in the YRU that some arrangement could be reached, represented the RFU's final nail in the coffin of compromise. Nevertheless, the waverers in Bradford, Leeds and Huddersfield still remained to be convinced. Bradford's hand was forced by their players threatening to strike if the club did not support the new union and by petitions, many of them prominently displayed in the pubs of Bradford players, raised by supporters calling on the committee to back the split.[128]

At Leeds a special general meeting was held which voted decisively to support the splitters, resulting in the resignations from the club of W. A. Brown and James Miller, current and former secretaries of the club respectively, the latter having made a passionate but forlorn appeal to the club's players. A disgruntled Leeds shareholder captured something of the class dimension of the decision when he complained that 'it is questionable if any of the football committee are shareholders of the club and, at any rate, it may be safely assumed that they do not hold £50 of shares among them; yet they by their conduct may, and are, jeopardising £30,000.'[129] Any hopes the vacillators may have had of a sympathetic hearing from the Rugby Union were dashed by a letter from the RFU secretary, Rowland Hill, which told them that even if they remained loyal they could not expect any fixtures with the leading southern clubs.[130] Faced with their two allies joining the rebels and, like them, fearful of being unable to generate sufficient revenue to protect the large investments made in their ground, Huddersfield issued a statement announcing their decision to join the new union, blaming it on the RFU's new laws against professionalism, which they characterised as 'too drastic in nature, and make an apparently small offence magnified into one of the gravest kind.'[131]

At 6.30 pm on Thursday, 29 August 1895, at the George Hotel in the centre of Huddersfield, representatives of Batley, Bradford, Brighouse Rangers, Broughton Rangers, Dewsbury, Halifax, Huddersfield, Hull, Hunslet, Leeds, Leigh, Liversedge, Manningham, Oldham, Rochdale Hornets, St Helens, Tyldesley, Wakefield Trinity, Warrington, Widnes and Wigan met and unanimously adopted the resolution 'That the clubs here represented decide to form a Northern Rugby Football Union, and pledge themselves to push forward, without delay, its establishment on the principle of payment for bona-fide broken-time only.' Although not at the meeting, Stockport were asked to join and immediately dispatched a representative to take part in the gathering. All the clubs present, except Dewsbury whose committee had not had time to discuss the matter, handed their letters of resignation from the RFU to Oldham's Joe Platt, who had been elected acting secretary, for him to forward to Rowland Hill. There was now no going back – the game of rugby was utterly and irrevocably split.

NOTES

1. H. Hendrick, 'The Leeds Gas Strike', *Publications of the Thoresby Society, Miscellany*, Vol. 16, Part 2, 1993. Cyril Pearce, *The Manningham Mills Strike*, Hull, 1975.
2. For detailed statistics on strike activity for this period see the Board of Trade's *Report of the Chief Labour Correspondent on the Strikes and Lockouts of 1896,*

London, 1896. For the shooting of Featherstone miners see J. J. Terrett, *H. H. Asquith and the Featherstone Massacre*, London, not dated. For Hull dockers see E. Gillett and K. A. MacMahon, *A History of Hull*, Hull, 1980.

3. Matthew Arnold, 'Culture and Anarchy', in Gordon Haight (ed), *A Victorian Reader*, New York, 1972, p. 209.
4. *The Yorkshireman*, 21 Jan. 1891 and Pearce, ibid.
5. *Yorkshire Post*, 20 April 1893.
6. *Yorkshire Post*, 7 and 14 Nov. 1893.
7. See Bradford's Jack Toothill in *Clarion*, 26 Nov. 1892.
8. *Yorkshire Post*, 14 Oct. 1889.
9. *The Yorkshireman*, 8 May 1886.
10. *The Yorkshireman*, 28 April 1887 and 9 May 1888. 'Put their hands in their pockets for the players.'
11. *Yorkshire Post*, 15 and 19 Dec. 1888.
12. *The Yorkshireman*, 11 Nov. 1891.
13. *Clarion*, 7 Oct. 1893.
14. Arthur Budd, 'The Past and Future of the Game', in *Football – The Rugby Union Game*, Revd F. Marshall (ed), London, 1892, pp. 132–3.
15. *Clarion*, 6 Oct. 1894.
16. Marshall, p. 135. This view was also propounded by H. H. Almond, Headmaster of Loretto school in Scotland. See his two articles, 'Rugby Football in Scottish Schools' in Marshall, and 'Football as a Moral Agent' in *Nineteenth Century*, Vol. 34, 1893.
17. Montague Shearman, *Athletics and Football*, London, 1887.
18. *The Yorkshireman*, 28 March 1893.
19. G. Rowland Hill, 'The RFU 1880–81 to the present', in *Football – The Rugby Union Game*, Revd F. Marshall (ed), London, 1892, p. 106.
20. Speech at the 1895 AGM of the RFU, *Yorkshire Post*, 20 Sept. 1895.
21. John Stuart Mill, 'Principles of Political Economy' (1865 edition), quoted in John Golby (ed), *Culture and Society in Britain 1850–1890*, London, 1986, p. 134. Similar attitudes could also be seen among the southern slave holders in the United States in the nineteenth century; see Eugene Genovese, *Roll, Jordan, Roll: The World the Slaves Made*, London, 1974.
22. Revd Frank Marshall, 'Payment for Broken Time at Rugby Football' in *Athletic News Football Annual, 1892*, Manchester, 1893, p. 149.
23. 'The Past Season' in *The Rugby Union Football Handbook 1894–95*, London, 1894.
24. Hill's devotion is attested to in *The Times*, 25 April 1929.
25. *Yorkshire Post*, 5 Dec. 1887 and 18 July 1888.
26. *Yorkshire Post*, 30 Sept. 1890 and 9 March 1892.
27. *Yorkshire Post*, 27 Oct. 1890 and 14 April 1891.
28. *Yorkshire Post*, 22 March 1893.
29. *Clarion*, 20 Oct. 1894.
30. The Anglican church's troubles with the working class in this period are detailed in Keith Inglis, *The Churches and the Working Classes in Victorian England*, London, 1963. On Marshall's troubles with the locals, see Gerald Hinchliffe, *A History of King James's Grammar School in Almondbury*, Huddersfield, 1963, p. 183.
31. *Yorkshire Post*, 21 Feb. 1893.
32. B. F. Robinson, *Rugby Football*, London, 1896.
33. Mark Rutherford, *Deliverance*, London, 1885, p. 85, quoted in W. E. Houghton, *The Victorian Frame of Mind*, London, 1957, p. 58.

34. Frank Mitchell, 'A Crisis in Rugby Football' in *St James's Gazette*, 24 Sept. 1897.
35. Creston, 'Football' in *Fortnightly Review*, Vol. 55, 1894.
36. Letter from 'An Old Player' to the *Yorkshire Evening Post*, 30 Sept. 1893.
37. *Salford Reporter*, 27 Oct. 1894. *Clarion*, 7 Oct. 1893.
38. Arthur Budd, 'The Past and Future of the Game', in *Football – The Rugby Union Game*, Revd F. Marshall (ed), London, 1892, p. 137.
39. Creston, 'Football', ibid. The Mohocks were aristocratic ruffians who terrorised the night-time streets of eighteenth-century London.
40. *Manchester Guardian*, 18 Sept. 1893.
41. 'The Rugby Game in Yorkshire' in the *Football Annual*, London, 1881.
42. *Yorkshire Post*, 27 Feb. 1883.
43. *The Yorkshireman*, 27 Dec. 1884 and 3 Oct. 1885. Middle-class hostility to miners in a sporting context can also be seen in Alan Metcalfe's 'Organised Sport in the Mining Communities of South Northumberland', *Victorian Studies*, No. 25, Summer 1982.
44. Nomad, 'The Future of Rugby Football: Professionalism and the League' in *The Yorkshireman Football Number*, March 1892.
45. Old Ebor (A. W. Pullin), ' Competition Football in Yorkshire: has it proved a success?' in *The Yorkshireman Football Number*, March 1893.
46. *Clarion*, 7 Oct. 1893. 'Purring' was an informal test of strength which involved kicking an adversary's shins and was common around the Merseyside area. See John K. Walton, *Lancashire, A Social History*, Manchester, 1987.
47. C. B. Grundy, quoted in John Lowerson, *Sport and the English Middle Classes*, Manchester, 1993.
48. *The Yorkshireman*, 7 Nov. 1885 and *The Scotsman*, 8 Nov. 1885.
49. 'The YRU' by A Wag in *The Yorkshireman Football Number*, March 1890.
50. *Athletic News*, 30 Nov. 1876.
51. *Yorkshire Post*, 29 Nov. 1886. For the same reasons, the paper also opposed the RFU's introduction of sending-off for foul play in 1888.
52. 'Referee', *History of Barrow FC*, Barrow, 1914, p. 5.
53. *Athletic News*, 23 Oct. 1888.
54. *Yorkshire Post*, 2 April 1886.
55. These figures are taken from the reports of the YRU executive committee appearing in the *Yorkshire Post* for the 1890–91 season.
56. See *The Yorkshireman*, 21 Oct. 1882 and 3 Nov. 1883. J. L. Higson, *History of Salford Football Club*, Salford, 1892. *Yorkshire Evening Post*, 21 Feb. 1893. *Warrington Guardian*, 8 June 1886.
57. *Yorkshire Post*, 10 Oct. 1890.
58. Sir Henry Seton-Karr quoted in Alex Service, *Saints in their Glory*, St Helens, 1985, p. 15.
59. B. F. Robinson, *Rugby Football*, London, 1896, pp. 49–50.
60. Quoted in Kenneth Pelmear, *Rugby Football: An Anthology*, London, 1958, p. 344.
61. Gerald Hinchliffe, *A History of King James's Grammar School in Almondbury*, Huddersfield, 1963, p. 231.
62. *Pendleton Reporter*, 28 Nov. 1891.
63. The latter quote can be found in H. H. Almond, 'Football as a Moral Agent' in *Nineteenth Century*, Vol. 34, 1893 (emphasis in original). The other two phrases are from his chapter in Revd Frank Marshall, *Football – the Rugby Union Game*, London, 1892, p. 55. For a broader perspective on women's participation in sport during this period see J. A. Mangan and Roberta J. Park (eds), *From 'Fair Sex' to*

Feminism: Sport and the Socialisation of Women in the Industrial and Post-Industrial Eras, London, 1987.

64. Eric Dunning and Kenneth Sheard, *Barbarians, Gentlemen and Players*, New York, 1979, p. 220. These figures are also quoted by A. J. Arnold, *A Game That Would Pay*, London, 1988, Greg Ryan, *Forerunners of the All Blacks*, Canterbury NZ, 1993, and, implicitly, in John Walton, *Lancashire, A Social History*, Manchester, 1987, pp. 319–20. Dunning and Sheard found the clipping from the *Wakefield Express* in scrapbooks, sadly now lost, formerly belonging to founding Northern Union president Harry Waller at the Rugby League headquarters in Leeds (conversation with Kenneth Sheard, July 1995).

65. *Pall Mall Gazette*, 23 March 1892. For criticism of the figures see the *Yorkshire Post*, 6 April 1891 – 'the list is inaccurate in more than one instance' – and H. H. Almond, a stern opponent of professionalism and leagues and someone who could have been expected to point to such figures as proof of the correctness (and safety!) of amateur values, in 'Football as a Moral Agent', *Nineteenth Century*, Vol. 34, 1893.

66. *Pall Mall Gazette*, 30 March 1891 and 23 March 1892.

67. *Wigan Observer*, 2 Oct. 1886.

68. *Pendleton Reporter*, 28 Nov. 1891.

69. Speech at the first AGM of Leeds Cricket, Football and Athletic Club, *Yorkshire Post*, 2 May 1891.

70. *The Yorkshireman Football Number*, March 1891.

71. *Yorkshire Post*, 6 March 1893.

72. XYZ in *The Yorkshireman*, 4 Oct. 1893. Nomad, 'The Future of Rugby Football: Professionalism and the League' in *The Yorkshireman Football Number*, March 1892.

73. *Oldham Evening Chronicle*, 13 Oct. 1890. *The Yorkshireman*, 1 April 1891.

74. A Professional in Mufti, 'A Plea for Legitimate Concessions' in *The Yorkshireman Football Number*, March 1891.

75. See *The Yorkshireman* and the *Yorkshire Post* throughout April, May and June of 1891.

76. *Yorkshire Post*, 11 April 1891.

77. *Yorkshire Post*, 2 Nov. 1891.

78. *Bradford Observer*, 18 Sept. 1893.

79. Old Ebor (A. W. Pullin), 'Competition Football in Yorkshire: has it proved a success?' in *The Yorkshireman Football Number*, March 1893.

80. Charles Edwardes, 'The New Football Mania', *Nineteenth Century*, Vol. 32, 1892.

81. *The Times*, 25 Sept. 1893.

82. *The Yorkshireman*, 28 March 1893.

83. OPQ, 'Professionalism in Football', *The Yorkshireman*, 6 Sept. 1893.

84. A letter from 'Straightforward' in *The Yorkshireman*, 4 Oct. 1893.

85. Nomad, 'The Future of Rugby Football: Professionalism and the League' in *The Yorkshireman Football Number*, March 1892.

86. Ibid.

87. *Yorkshire Owl*, 27 Sept. 1893.

88. *Clarion*, 24 Nov. 1894.

89. Minutes of the RFU, 16 Sept. 1891. Marshall's comments are in *Pastime*, 23 Sept. 1891.

90. An unsubstantiated rumour circulated that Cail had originally supported the broken-time motion but turned his back on it when offered Rowland Hill's support to continue as president for a second year. See *Yorkshire Post*, 6 Feb. 1909.

91. *The Yorkshireman*, 20 Sept. 1893.
92. *Leeds Mercury*, 16 Sept. 1893.
93. *Leeds Mercury*, 19 Sept. 1893.
94. *Yorkshire Evening Post*, 20 Sept. 1893.
95. Minutes of the RFU, 20 Sept. 1893. No full transcript of the meeting exists and the minutes only list the clubs present. I have therefore reconstructed the debate with the help of the daily papers of the time.
96. *Leeds Mercury*, 21 Sept. 1893.
97. Ibid.
98. *Yorkshire Post*, 21 Sept. 1893.
99. All quotes are from *Leeds Mercury*, 21 Sept. 1893.
100. *Yorkshire Evening Post*, 21 Sept. 1893.
101. *Leeds Mercury*, 21 Sept. 1893.
102. G. F. Berney, 'Progress of the RFU from the Season 1892–93 to the Present Time' in Revd Frank Marshall and Leonard R. Tosswill, *Football – the Rugby Union Game*, London, 1925 (Revised edition).
103. *Pastime*, 6 Sept. 1893.
104. *Leeds Daily News*, 21 and 25 Sept. 1893. Trevor Delaney in his *Rugby Disunion* estimates that at least 22 Yorkshire clubs voted against the broken-time motion.
105. *Leeds Mercury*, 23 Sept. 1893.
106. Indeed, the meeting attracted little attention in the Lancashire press, and the local newspapers in Barrow and Oldham, at least, didn't even mention the momentous events.
107. The text of H. E. Steed's circular of 1894 can be found in *Yorkshire Post*, 8 Dec. 1894.
108. *Clarion*, 23 Sept. 1893.
109. Ibid.
110. *Yorkshire Evening Post*, 25 Sept. 1893.
111. OPQ, 'Payment for Broken Time' in *The Yorkshireman*, 27 Sept. 1893.
112. *Manchester Guardian*, 25 Sept. 1893, *Pastime*, 27 Sept. 1893, Creston, 'Football' in the *Fortnightly Review*, Vol. 55, 1894 and *Yorkshire Post*, 14 Oct. 1893.
113. *Yorkshire Owl*, 4 Oct. 1893.
114. *Huddersfield Daily Examiner*, 5, 9 and 27 Oct., 15 Nov. and 4 Dec. 1893. Not only were Forsyth and Boak banned from playing by the RFU but they were also fined £3 and £1 respectively by Carlisle Magistrates Court for leaving their jobs at Cummerdale Print Works without giving notice.
115. Lancashire Rugby Union minutes, 28 Aug. 1894 and *Yorkshire Post*, 8, 12 and 28 Sept. 1894.
116. *Salford Reporter*, 20 Oct. and 10 Nov. 1894. Lancashire Rugby Union minutes, 17 Oct. 1894.
117. Lancashire Rugby Union minutes, 13 Nov. 1894 and *Wigan Observer*, 17 Nov. 1894.
118. *Yorkshire Post*, 5 and 17 Nov. 1894. The *Bradford Observer* speculated that the manifesto had been written by Frank Marshall, 3 Dec, 1894.
119. *Yorkshire Evening Post*, 29 Dec. 1894.
120. *Yorkshire Post*, 31 Dec. 1894.
121. *Clarion*, 8 Dec. 1894.
122. *Yorkshire Post*, 21 and 31 Jan. 1895.
123. *Yorkshire Evening Post*, 19 Feb. 1895.
124. *Pastime*, 8 Feb. 1895.
125. *Yorkshire Post*, 28 and 29 March 1895.

126. *Yorkshire Post*, 19 July 1895.
127. This view has been expressed most notably in Michael Latham and Tom Mather's *The Rugby League Myth*, Adlington, 1993. The *Yorkshire Post*, 9 Sept. 1895, effectively answered it when it said that 'questions of promotion and relegation in the Yorkshire Union have been shown to be but the outward and visible methods of offering resistance to the rigid amateurism that the authorities desired to enforce, and it has been made clear that the real wish of the Senior clubs was to control the county organisation so as to find shelter for themselves in the time of the Rugby Union's visitation.'
128. *Bradford Daily Argus*, 26 Aug. 1895 and *Yorkshire Post*, 27 Aug. 1895.
129. *Yorkshire Post*, 29 Aug. 1895.
130. Letter from G. R. Hill, published in *Yorkshire Post*, 27 Aug. 1895.
131. *Yorkshire Post*, 30 Aug. 1895.

5

The Rise and Decline of the Northern Union: 1895–1905

The Northern Union was born into a world in which the pace of change was becoming increasingly rapid. English society was becoming much more centralised, and culture, of whichever class, became increasingly nationally based. New levels of economic integration and the growth of the role of the state undermined regionalism and activities of a purely local character. Industrial conflict in the 1890s, for example the 1893 miners' strike, quickly took on a national dimension, a development which was highlighted by the growth of national trade unions and employers' federations, and also by the keenness of the state to intervene in disputes. This keenness was not only due to national considerations but also to international ones; the decline of Britain's trade position relative to its major competitors meant that serious industrial troubles at home could affect its economic position abroad. Also, of course, the increasing weight of London in national affairs was a reflection of its position as the centre of a global, and still expanding, empire.

This centralisation of British life was demonstrated in myriad ways. The rise in working-class living standards during this period had created a market which saw the growth of national retail chains, such as the Co-op stores, Boots the Chemists and Lipton's grocery stores. The advertising and branding of goods became nationally based, so that many items available in shops in Manchester, especially newly mass-produced clothing, footwear and food, were also likely to be available in shops in London. Partly due to the growth of literacy after the 1870 Education Act, weekly magazines, such as *Tit-bits*, *Answers* and *Pearson's Weekly* began to sell in hundreds of thousands across the country. More importantly, the launch of the *Daily Mail* in 1896 signalled the beginnings of the national newspaper, and the concomitant decline of the previously popular regional and dialect press.[1] Made possible by the development of rotary presses and mechanical typesetting, the *Mail* symbolised the creation of a national, albeit London-led, medium and, as if to underline this, was by 1900 being printed simultaneously in the capital and in Manchester. Nowhere was this growth of a nation-wide culture more apparent than in the unprecedented rise of soccer, spurred by its national FA Cup and Football League competitions, and in the ubiquitous influence of the music hall, possibly best high-lighted by the popularity of the song 'Ta-ra-ra-boom-de-ay', which, as an Edwardian commentator wrote, 'lit at the red skirts of Lottie Collins, spread like a dancing flame through the land, obsessing the minds of young and old, gay and sedate, until it became a veritable song-pest.'[2]

Yet this was not simply a structural change. As institutions and activities took on a national dimension, so too did many become suffused with a nationalist fervour. From the late 1880s there had been a growth of militaristic patriotism throughout society, based on the growth of empire and an awareness that Britain's hegemonic world position was in decline. 'Nowadays, nothing goes down better than a good patriotic song,' said music hall star Vesta Tilley in 1888, and, at the other end of the scale, J. A. Mangan has identified a shift by the mid-1880s towards the glorification of the 'warrior-patriot' in public-school magazines.[3] By the close of the century and the outbreak of the Boer War, nationalistic jingoism was at its height: songs, novels, boys' stories, poetry and the national press, in particular the *Daily Mail*, were sodden with the shrill and baying glorification of war and empire. Sport was central to this ethos. Sir Henry Newbolt's *Vitaï Lampada*, with its injunction to 'Play up! play up! and play the game' on both the cricket field and the battle field, was only the most famous of works drawing the explicit links between sport and its use as a form of military training. While the focus of exhortations such as Newbolt's was towards the public schools and the next generation of the officer class, the importance of rugby to military preparedness among the working classes, as we saw in the previous chapter, was not forgotten. It was, explained a letter to *The Times*, 'the game of all games that calls for all the qualities that go to make a true Briton' and 'the best trial of the relative vigour and virility of any two or more opposing countries.' The fact that Cecil Rhodes himself had underwritten the expenses of the 1891 tour of South Africa was ample testimony of the importance of rugby to the imperial mission.[4]

It was therefore unsurprising that the formation of the Northern Union met with accusations that its actions were at best damaging to the national interest and at worst downright unpatriotic. According to Arthur Budd, the NU was embarking 'on a policy of revolution' which 'depreciated the value of the game as a means of muscular culture.'[5] A. W. Pullin asked 'are all the Yorkshiremen of the future, therefore, to sacrifice their birthright – the right to their national affairs and the national honours – for a mess of six bob pottage?'[6] Even those who did not invoke patriotism against the

NU deemed it guilty of practices which marked it out as 'un-English'. In the North, so described Ernest Ensor, 'a system began of petty treachery, mean cheating and espionage, which almost passes belief ... The miserable game was played until convictions became too numerous. The defected ones met together ... [and] ... left the old school, and started one in which bribery might be not only unpunished, but compulsory.'[7] The use of such language became the dominant form of discourse when the NU was discussed by its opponents. 'Purity' and 'cleanliness' were popular ways of describing the RFU and its policies, whilst 'evil' and 'mercenary' sufficed for the professionalism of the NU and its players. Faced with growing numbers of local players opting to join NU clubs, the Cumberland Rugby Union President Roger Westray declared that 'such men might be an advantage to the Northern Union but they were a disgrace to their own county' as his union sought to 'scrape its keel of mercenary barnacles.'[8] Tom Broadley, England international and Yorkshire rugby union captain, crossed over to Bradford NU club in late 1896 and was consequently described by James Miller as being 'wanting in the chief characteristics of a man and a sportsman.'[9] By such denigration, its critics sought to prove that the NU's actions, indeed its whole existence, were inimical to traditional English values as expressed through the ethos of public-school games. This was not based solely on class prejudice towards the NU's overwhelmingly working-class players and spectators, but also on a belief that the new union undermined the importance of the role which rugby played in British national life. In the eyes of its critics, the Northern Union no longer played the game for the physical training and moral development but for pounds, shillings and pence.

Of course, the Northern Unionists were no less patriotic than Arthur Budd and his co-thinkers, but the effect of such rhetoric in a period in which the framework for much of modern British national identity was being established, coupled with the new organisation's lack of links with the public schools and other national institutions, was to lock it out of the mainstream of British sport. The Amateur Athletics Association barred NU athletes from taking part in its meetings, despite the fact that its rules outlawing the receipt of any expenses whatsoever also technically excluded rugby union athletes.[10] In 1898 policemen were forbidden to play NU by order of the Conservative Home Secretary Sir Matthew White Ridley, because, as the Chief Constable of Halifax pointed out on his behalf, 'it would be highly derogatory to the best interests of the service for police officers to be allowed to play as professionals in football matches, considering the rowdyism and betting that are carried on in connection with football matches.'[11] The RFU even held talks with the Football

Association to discuss the possibility of banning NU players from playing soccer.[12] The importance of national interest and identity to rugby union's attempts to undermine the NU game can also be seen in the later 1900s when the new game was spreading to Wales and New Zealand. The surge of interest in NU football in Wales in 1907 and 1908 was dismissed by a Welsh Rugby Union official with the comment that 'the quarters affected are not those in which the Welsh national sentiment is fairly reflected. The mining districts of the Principality are the natural quarters for the development of the professional element, but these are not the localities whence the strength of Welsh international football is derived.' Similarly, a denial that the NU game could be genuinely representative of a nation was made by New Zealand Agent-General C. Wray Palliser about the 1907 New Zealand NU touring side: 'It will in not the slightest degree represent either the rugby union football of New Zealand or the sporting community of the colony ... it comes with no sort of credit from the colony of New Zealand.'[13] Although such attempts at exclusion were to play a central role in the formation of a distinct Northern Union ideology, they more importantly succeeded in questioning the legitimacy of the sport and pushing it into a position where it could be portrayed as an aberrant strand of national sporting culture.

FROM SPLIT TO DOMINATION

The leaders and supporters of the NU were well aware of the disapprobation that the split would bring, if not its long term effects. Their response was to argue that they were the ones who had washed their hands of subterfuge and hypocrisy. At last, their dealings were honest and above board. 'The clubs who have struck a blow for freedom are to be commended for throwing off the cloak of hypocrisy, conceit and subterfuge, and standing out for those essentially English characteristics – honesty and straightforwardness,'[14] said a correspondent to the *Hull Daily Mail*. 'Freedom from the thraldom of the Southern gentry was the best thing that could happen,' was the *Wigan Observer*'s comment, while an unnamed Northern Union supporter wrote to the *Yorkshire Post* to proclaim, 'I say with Mark Twain's bold, bad boy, that we glory in the sentence of outlawry pronounced on us, as freeing us from the tyrannical bondage of the English union, and we breathe pure air in being freed from the stifling atmosphere of deceit in which we previously existed.'[15] George Harrop, a referee who volunteered to officiate at one of the first Northern Union matches, 'expressed his delight that he would thus be the first member of the

Huddersfield club to fall under the ban of the English Rugby Union.'[16] Brighouse's Harry Waller, the textiles manufacturer who had been elected the NU's first president, spelt out the necessity for the split later that season: 'Rugby football in the North – for every part of the Kingdom in fact where there was a preponderance of working-class players – could not be honestly carried out under the existing bye-laws of the English Union.'[17]

The formation of the NU was undoubtedly popular with players. As we have seen, Bradford were effectively forced into joining by the actions of their players. At Broughton Rangers, the motion to join the NU was moved by the club captain and seconded by another senior player. Harry Barker, captain of Liversedge, said 'I think the Northern Union is a champion move and I think the committee should have been justified in making the move a year ago.' Echoing the call for honesty, Bradford's international three-quarter Tommy Dobson stated 'All Yorkshire owes a debt of gratitude to the seniors [ie, the senior clubs] for speaking out so plainly in favour of what should be the leading element in sport – truth.' Dewsbury's decision not to join the NU was met by one of their players with the question 'What wages are yer paying up here?', and upon receiving the reply 'None', he responded 'It's no use me stopping here then.' In Huddersfield, it was reported that 'the players naturally champion the [Northern] Union and a very large section of spectators of matches take the same side.'[18] This was also reflected among members and supporters of clubs throughout the new organisation. Hunslet, St Helens, Manningham, Hull, Leigh and Broughton Rangers all recorded unanimity at general meetings called to vote on joining the NU, while most of the other member clubs tallied only a handful of votes against. In Dewsbury, despite the club committee's reversal, a local journalist reported that 'there wasn't a single supporter who wouldn't say "Let us have the Northern Union and the sooner the better".'[19] The clamour for the NU was demonstrated at a special meeting of the Hull and District RFU in September, which voted 33–24 to resign from the RFU in support of the NU, even though the NU had as yet no means by which district bodies or junior clubs could affiliate.[20] The only club at which significant opposition was encountered was Bradford, which still clung to remnants of its patrician past, where three committee members and four senior players, one of whom, Edgar Dewhurst, was also a committee member, resigned in protest.[21]

Despite this acclamation by players and spectators, the new body firmly denied that it was about to introduce professionalism to rugby. Indeed, the six shillings broken-time payment had been fixed to equal the maximum daily insurance payment allowed by the RFU professionalism rules. Ernest Gresty, Broughton Rangers secretary and member of the NU Emergency

Committee, asked 'How can it be professionalism? The man that receives bare recompense for the loss of his wages makes no money by so doing. It is no more than saving him from losing anything.' William Hirst, secretary of Huddersfield, stated that he was 'as strongly opposed as ever to professionalism' but 'held that payment of working men players for loss of wages through playing in a match was not professionalism.'[22] In September, to demonstrate its fealty to the amateur ideal, the NU turned down applications to play from Sam Hall of Swinton and J. Smith of Radcliffe, both of whom had been banned as professionals the previous season by the Lancashire Rugby Union. Indeed, it is apparent that at least some sections of the NU hoped that an accommodation could still be reached with the RFU on the lines of the FA's relationship with the Football League; Tony Fattorini, Manningham's representative on the NU committee, told a meeting of his club that 'if the new union were properly conducted, the Rugby Union would have to recognise professionalism in some form or another in the future or they would find ere long the only support they received would be from the universities and the public schools.'[23] Given the attitudes of the RFU this hope was forlorn in the extreme, yet it was to be a recurring theme over the next decade.

Despite the hostility of the rugby union authorities and their desire not to appear too radical, the NU's first season was highly successful. Although Joe Platt's claim that 20 of the 22 NU clubs made a profit in the first season seems to be an exaggeration, there can be no doubt that most of the rebel clubs experienced higher crowds and increased profits. Platt's own club Oldham was the most successful, returning a record £1,148 profit. Hull also made their highest ever profit, thanks to an increase of over 50,000 spectators. Halifax increased their gate takings by 50 per cent, and even bottom club Rochdale Hornets made a profit of £96, despite winning only four of their forty-two games. This was an important vindication for the NU. The sketchy evidence available suggests that the senior Northern clubs had seen a decline in profitability in the period up to 1895; although crowds appear to have remained stable, the expense of ground refurbishments and covert player payments had taken a heavy toll. Without the qualitative leap in attendances which soccer was experiencing, many clubs found themselves on shaky financial foundations. This applied most particularly at the extreme ends of the spectrum: Bradford and Leeds, with large capital investments in their grounds, faced a constant battle for financial success, while clubs based on small towns, such as Brighouse Rangers and Tyldesley, found it difficult to generate enough revenue to justify their places among the elite. Even at the height of their success, winning their respective county leagues in 1895, both clubs made a loss. These economic realities did not excuse even the most pristine custodians of the amateur cause: Manchester FC voted to wind the club up in March 1895 after it was revealed that they had accrued liabilities of £409, although the decision was later rescinded.[24]

The success of the NU's first season was crucial in attracting the second wave of splits from the RFU. For Salford and Swinton, the North's most successful clubs to remain aloof from the splitters, the lack of quality opposition in the reconstituted Lancashire Club Championship and the potential financial boost of joining the NU were overwhelming arguments to jump ship. Both had been involved in the initial discussions about a new rugby body but had dropped out due to a combination of personal antagonism and organisational jealousy. In April 1896 Salford held a special general meeting at the request of members to discuss joining the NU. J. Daniels moved the motion to join the NU, pointing out that the club had lost £713 over the last four years: '[As] Salford was a working-class club and didn't contain any so-called gentlemen, he considered that it would be very nice for the players to have a present of six shillings worth of silver every week. If they continued on amateur lines they would go to smash. They all knew that working-class clubs were better supported than clubs such as Liverpool or Manchester.' Out of a gathering of 400 people, only three opposed the switch.[25] Following a season in which they had lost £450, Swinton's move to the new body received similar acclamation at their general meeting, at which it was pointed out that over the previous four seasons, annual gate money had slumped from £1,016 to £383 and the number of season ticket holders had halved. Vindication of their decision was quick in coming: in their first two seasons in the NU they made record profits of £450 and £529.[26] Over the summer of 1896 a steady stream of Lancashire's junior and local clubs followed into the NU; Rochdale St Clements, Radcliffe, Werneth, Morecambe and others tearing the heart out of an already emaciated Lancashire Club Championship. At a local level, the effect was no less cataclysmic and that summer saw most of Warrington's local clubs go over to the NU, as did around 50 clubs which formed the Oldham Junior Rugby League.[27] In July, at its first annual general meeting, Platt announced that the NU now had 48 members and fully expected that number to increase substantially.

In contrast, by the following summer the Lancashire Rugby Union had only 13 member clubs, focused on the traditional ex-public schoolboy sides.[28] Their last base of popular rugby, in the northwest of the county, had evaporated when promises of fixtures with Manchester, Liverpool and Liverpool Old Boys made to Barrow and Ulverston, the leading clubs in the area, failed to materialise. By April of 1897 Barrow had voted unanimously to join the NU and a petition was circulating in Ulverston calling on the club to make the switch. At the beginning of July, Ulverston, Millom and the rest of the North West League voted to join the NU. Ulverston's general meeting was told that James Higson, who had become the LRU secretary after Salford's departure to the NU and who was one of the NU's most vociferous critics, had secretly told an Ulverston committee member that 'the best thing they could do was to join the NU' because middle-class clubs wouldn't play them.[29] The loss of the northwest Lancashire clubs had a knock-on effect on Cumberland and Westmoreland clubs, who generally looked south for their better fixtures. The success of Millom's first season in the NU – after seeing gate money slump to just £107 in their last rugby union season, they had taken almost £300 at the gate and made a record profit of £81 – had given the impetus to other clubs in the region to abandon the RFU. At the start of the 1898–99 season *Athletic News* commented that rugby union in Cumberland had been reduced 'to an almost vanishing quality' and by January 1899 there was not a single rugby union club left in west Cumberland, a former hotbed of the game.[30]

The effect in Yorkshire was no less devastating. Regardless of earlier pledges of loyalty to the YRU, the majority of the county's Number One Competition, the Yorkshire leagues' first division, went over to the NU in the summer of 1896. Holbeck's chairman, George Chapman, summed up their plight when he stated bluntly that 'when it came to be a serious question of finance, they should follow the example of the majority of leading clubs.' Leeds Parish Church, that year's champions, recorded only five votes against their switch of allegiance.[31] Unfortunately for the YRU, the spectacle of their senior league members decamping at the end of the season was something to which they would grow accustomed. In June 1897 Hull Kingston Rovers, that year's Yorkshire cup and league champions, went over and the following summer most of what remained of the Number One and Number Two Competitions resigned *en bloc* to reconstitute themselves as the NU's Yorkshire Number Two Competition. In 1899 Hebden Bridge, Ossett, Kirkstall and Alverthorpe flew the nest and in the summer of 1900 Keighley, Otley and Bingley decided that 'the interest has gone out of rugby union' and joined the NU.[32] This pattern was repeated locally as one by one the existing local leagues and unions lined up with the NU. By June 1897 there was not a single rugby union club in the Halifax district, which was described by a Sowerby Bridge rugby union supporter as being 'a hotbed of Northern Unionism and bigotry'; at the start of the following season the *Yorkshire Post* reported that 'in Leeds, rugby union football is practically non-existent', while the NU 'is at the height of its popularity.'[33] The Bradford and Huddersfield district rugby unions simply voted to disaffiliate from the YRU and affiliate to the NU. At its opening round in 1901, the Yorkshire Cup, once one of the biggest football competitions of any type, a symbol of rugby union's domination of Yorkshire winter sport and capable of attracting at its height 132 entrants, could boast a mere eleven clubs. The mighty had been felled.

Although the NU undoubtedly presented a highly attractive alternative for many clubs, it was not solely responsible for the collapse of Yorkshire rugby union. The YRU and the RFU each played a critical role in the destruction of their own power base. The RFU's September 1895 general meeting had attempted to cast out the NU devil by declaring that any contact with an NU club or player on the football field was an act of professionalism, punishable by a life ban from the Rugby Union. Initially, loyal clubs had asked Rowland Hill if it were possible for them or their reserve sides to play their NU equivalents, believing the situation to be analogous to Football League sides playing the Corinthians, who were members of the RFU as well as the FA. Hill replied by saying that any RFU club which played an NU side would professionalise itself and be expelled.[34] This immediately posed problems at a local level: for example, Beverley FC were left with virtually no fixtures after clubs in the Hull District Union, with whom they played most of their matches, voted to support the NU. Eventually they admitted defeat and played matches with NU supporting clubs, whereupon the YRU expelled them for professionalism. More corrosively, the RFU's insistence that any contact with NU football automatically contaminated a player, and the zeal with which this edict was pursued, meant that any player who had any contact with the NU was thrown out of the Rugby Union. In February 1896, the YRU banned a Wyke player who travelled with Brighouse Rangers to a match at Leigh. He didn't play but the fact that Rangers paid his third-class rail fare was enough to condemn him. The following month the Horbury club were suspended because one of their players had earlier played for a Wakefield junior side against a team which contained an NU player. Elland had two players banned for the same offence and Primrose Hill's G. A. Cliffe was banned for playing in a game staged at Huddersfield's Fartown ground. The YRU was faced with numerous requests for reinstatement as amateurs from players who had played occasional games with NU sides, the vast majority of which had to be refused. Most bizarrely of all, in January 1898 the YRU ordered Goole FC not to play a charity rugby match against a touring Little Red Riding Hood pantomime troupe; this was deemed to be an act of professionalism because earlier on its tour the troupe had played in a charity match with the NU's Batley! Clearly, no-one was safe from the contagion – one unnamed RFU official allegedly even being of the opinion that anyone who watched an NU game, let alone played in one, should be barred from taking part in rugby union.[35]

Such antics seemed arbitrary and irrational to most clubs, even those loyal to the RFU. However, there was method in this apparent madness. The RFU truly believed that the danger of working-class professionalism was, in Arthur Budd's words, a hydra and that a policy of Laudian 'Thorough' had to be pursued in order to root it out. In response to those who said that the RFU's action would leave only a remnant of their game in the North, A. W. Pullin, generally an accurate guide to RFU thinking, said, 'Possibly the Rugby Union would like to see that result, believing that the "fit but few" principle is conducive to a cheerful and settled state of mind.'[36] From its own vantage point, the RFU leadership's belief that a continued purge of the game in Yorkshire was necessary was not hard to substantiate. It was common knowledge that players in Yorkshire still received payment for play – indeed, immediately after the split some of the clubs remaining in the YRU boasted of how they would pay more than the NU clubs' six shillings a day – and problems with overly boisterous working-class crowds remained, despite the declining interest in the Union game.[37] In the four years following 1895 the YRU suspended ten grounds and reprimanded six other clubs for crowd trouble, most notoriously at Sharlston, near Wakefield, when on Christmas Eve 1898 a fight broke out between two players: 'The referee intervened and a general melee ensued. The spectators broke into the field and joined in the fighting. The Kippax players had to be guarded by the police from the field. Some of them could not get dressed and two of them had to run two miles to escape their assailants.'[38]

In fact, the central core of the YRU leadership – James Miller, now a virulent opponent of broken-time, Mark Newsome, Harry Garnett, Barron Kilner and Arthur Hartley – had a conscious strategy of reconstructing Yorkshire rugby union on the same public-school basis as it had been in the 1860s and 1870s, but this time freed from the danger of contamination by the working classes. The YRU's actions were part of the general growth of exclusive, middle-class leisure activities which was taking place in late Victorian society. As John Lowerson has pointed out, the growth of golf and tennis clubs in particular were among the most visible examples of the development of discrete leisure spheres for the middle classes. Eric Hobsbawm has also pointed to the fact that, while only two golf courses were built in Yorkshire before 1890, twenty-nine golf courses were built in the county between 1890 and 1895. The 1895 split was seen as an opportunity for 'clubs to be formed on the same lines as the clubs of fifteen to twenty years ago, when members played for the pure love of the game, found their own clothing and paid all their own expenses (except, perhaps, third-class railway fares), besides paying the annual sub to the club.'[39] Thus nostalgia for a lost golden age intersected the generalised growth of an exclusively middle-class sporting culture. By 1900, when it had been abandoned by the great majority of its working-class-based clubs, the YRU was confidently predicting 'a turn of events caused by the public schoolboys and others taking part in the game' as it sought to 'encourage the class of players who hitherto have been elbowed out in the evolution of pro-fessionalism.'[40] Clubs began to be formed by ex-public and grammar schoolboys. Old Dewsburians was formed 'by some of the better class Dewsbury and Batley residents'; the creation of the Hull and East Riding club was 'taken in hand by the sons of Hull and district's leading citizens' and Wakefield RFC was founded by 'Grammar School old boys and others.'[41] In Lancashire, the Furness, Oldham, Leigh and Vale of Lune rugby union clubs were formed in a similar fashion during the same period. The most prominent of this new wave of clubs in Yorkshire was Headingley FC in Leeds, which had been formed in 1892 on strictly amateur lines and was to dominate Yorkshire rugby union from the early 1900s onwards, thanks to its ability to attract the county's best Oxbridge and ex-public school players and its uncannily close relationship with the YRU committee – the latter most notoriously demonstrated at the 1909 Yorkshire Cup final, when Skipton walked off after a controversial Headingley try. It was later revealed that the referee was a member of the Headingley club.[42] By 1907, when the YRU formed the Yorkshire Wanderers side to promote the game in public schools, it was estimated that over 180 of those currently playing rugby union in the county were former public schoolboys, which, considering that the YRU had barely twenty clubs, accounted for at least half the players in the county.[43]

This drive towards middle-class exclusivity was not a linear process. Many in the YRU sought to preserve the all-encompassing basis of the YRU which existed from the mid-1880s. There was consequently a running battle with the RFU and its supporters in the YRU over the question of reinstatement of those who had played Northern Union football, with the majority of the YRU continuously appealing for a more lenient attitude: 'The English Union, instead of assisting us when they know we are fighting their battle in the face of great odds, do all they can to thwart and hinder us,' complained YRU committee member Harry Brown in 1897. Requests for flexibility from the RFU were met with a brick wall of indifference: an RFU report on the situation in Yorkshire in January 1898 stated unequivocally that 'no help can be given to the Northern clubs without sacrificing all the principles of amateur football.'[44] As well as the reinstatement issue, the suspension of Hull KR in 1897 and the RFU's compromise over the Arthur Gould case in the same year animated the disillusionment of YRU loyalists with the RFU. Hull KR had been found not guilty of professionalism by a YRU investigative committee but this had been overturned by the RFU and a secret hearing had suspended the club for a month. This was viewed as a serious slight on the YRU committee. Just as damaging was the RFU climbdown over the Arthur Gould case. Gould, the most famous and talented player in Wales, had been presented with the deeds to a house as a testimonial by the Welsh Rugby Union. This had been denounced by the RFU and the International Board as an act of professionalism and, in protest, the Welsh had withdrawn from the Board. A split appeared to be imminent. However, at its September meeting of 1897, the RFU backtracked and declared that, although he had committed an act of professionalism, 'the exceptional circumstances' of the case meant that he would not face a ban. Rowland Hill admitted openly that it 'was a question of expediency' because it would be 'a serious strain on the loyalty of the West Country clubs of England if those fixtures [against Welsh sides] were prohibited.' F. E. Smith, later Lord Birkenhead, the future Conservative cabinet minister and avowed supporter of amateur sport, candidly admitted in *The Times* that a compromise had been reached to 'prevent the great accession of strength to the Northern Union which would have followed had the Welsh Union been driven into their arms.'[45] The decision seemed so blatantly hypocritical that even Harry Garnett was moved to complain that 'the Rugby Union should not cause a feeling that they had one mode of dealing with a working man professional and another method where the person indicated happened to belong to another class.'[46] Unfortunately, this was exactly the way the RFU did operate, a fact not lost on the embattled YRU loyalists. Indeed, such was the anger and frustration that the YRU committee discussed joining the NU or forming an independent Northern Amateur Union several times in the late 1890s. Neither proposal amounted to much as clubs simply voted with their feet and went over to the NU.

Those seeking a third way between the burgeoning professionalism of the NU and the contracting exclusivity of the RFU could not succeed. The social conditions which had led to the rise of rugby in the 1880s no longer existed. Between middle-class exclusivity and mass, working-class-based forms of entertainment there was no middle ground. In fact, it was the NU that was the natural successor to the community-based, populist traditions of the mass-supported rugby of the 1880s, recreating the network of locally-based cup and league competitions and continuing the intense discussions about the direction of the sport which had characterised Lancashire and

Yorkshire rugby union. The NU immediately revived the debate on the need to make rugby more attractive, although the evolution of NU rules into an entirely separate and distinct sport from that of rugby union was to take another ten years. Most notably, the inauguration of the Northern Union Challenge Cup in 1897 was a conscious decision to emulate, on a grander scale, the success of the Yorkshire Cup. With 52 entries in its first year and an average crowd of around 6,000 per game, the cup fulfilled all expectations, not least for the eventual winners Batley, for whom it helped to return a record profit on the season of £879. The return of the victors to their home town recalled the triumphant homecomings of Yorkshire Cup winners in years past:

> The first notification of their arrival in Batley was the discharge of no fewer than 160 fog signals, the deafening cracks of which were ably seconded by thousands of hoarse-voiced, lusty-lunged enthusiasts, who crowded all available space along Station Road and Hick Lane; these two, and in fact all other principal thoroughfares, presenting to the lookers-on nothing but a heaving, restless sea of animated faces. A procession was formed and headed by the Batley Old Band, and, as it paraded along the thickly-populated streets, coloured lights, torches, and numerous other methods of illumination were employed in order to manifest the enthusiasm of the delighted followers of the successful team.[47]

Throughout the next few years the Challenge Cup presented ample evidence of the health of the new organisation. While not on the scale of the monster attendances which now marked FA Cup ties, crowds of between ten and twenty thousand were commonplace, with over 20,000 for semi-finals in 1897 and 1899, and for the 1900 quarter final at Leeds Parish Church club. The 1898 final, held at Headingley, set a record for English club rugby crowds with 27,941, while this was exceeded in 1901 and 1903 with 29,569 and 32,507 respectively.

Despite the confident assertions of failure by its opponents, the NU's first years were unequivocally successful. By 1899 the former northern strongholds of rugby union had gone over wholesale to the new body, leaving a small rump of largely exclusive clubs based on former public schoolboys. The NU's senior clubs were, to a large extent, profitable and their crowds were the equal of, if not larger than, those of northern rugby union's heyday in the late 1880s and early 1890s. In the working-class communities of the northern towns on which the split was based, rugby football had retained and possibly increased its popularity. The NU even appeared to have held back the challenge of soccer. No greater witness to its success could be found than F. E. Smith, who wrote in late 1897:

> We who live in the North of England see clearly that at least in Lancashire, Yorkshire and Cheshire, the success of the movement is now assured. Undoubtedly there have been and there will be financial difficulties in individual cases – such difficulties are not unknown in association football, but they have not, I am sorry to say, placed professionalism in danger. There is a verve about the game as it is now played in the disaffected districts, there is a degree of public interest about the competitions, and there is a keenness among the players themselves, which teach those who have eyes to see that the revolt will be both permanent and successful.[48]

PROFESSIONALISM AND PLAYERS

Although the NU initially disavowed any intention of introducing professionalism, it was clear to all that this state of affairs could not last. From the initial announcement of the six shillings per day limit on broken-time payments, widespread doubt was expressed as to how players would be attracted to play for such a small amount, especially from Wales, when covert payments in rugby union were known to be higher. The simple answer was, of course, that many clubs paid more than the maximum allowed, and with no effective means of policing broken-time payments the Union could do little to stop it. Stockport were widely rumoured to be offering players £2 a week during the season and a job at thirty shillings a week during the summer just three weeks after the split.[49] The payments entered in club accounts varied widely: in the 1896–97 season, Challenge Cup winners Batley recorded payments of just £59, while Leeds, who had a mediocre season, paid out £553 for broken-time.[50] At a maximum payment of four pounds and ten shillings per match and thirty-five games in the season, Leeds's first team total should not have exceeded £160, especially when four of that season's away games were with other clubs in Leeds. As a disgruntled Leeds member had pointed at the previous year's annual general meeting, the figures didn't add up.[51] Presumably in an attempt to deflect such criticism, the club actually understated players' expenses by two-thirds in 1898, recording a more acceptable £193 when the actual total was £579.[52] As this, and club officials' experience in covering their tracks under the RFU regime, proved, even those clubs returning low broken-time figures were not necessarily telling the whole truth.

As we saw in chapter four, one of the underlying reasons for the call for broken-time was to improve the control of payments to players. In the first few weeks after the split, many clubs had tried to implement the broken-time regulations rigorously and only pay a proportion of the six shillings maximum with one club paying its men just four shillings for three games. However, this met with widespread opposition from the players and payment of the six shillings became seen as, at the very least, the minimum payment.[53] The steady flow of Welsh players into the game and the need to provide them with wages and jobs was also a key factor in the undermining of broken-time. By 1897 it was clear that, as a system for controlling wages, it was not working and that widespread abuses were taking place: 'It does not seem likely that the Northern Union officials will long be able to shut their eyes to the existing state of things in their own clubs. Either they must constitute searching enquiry and punish clubs that have practised professionalism or openly embrace the payment of players,' commented the London-based *Mascot*.[54] In November of that year, the NU appointed a seven-man committee to look into this state of affairs and examine the options in a move towards open professionalism. Two months later it presented a majority and a minority (of one) report, the former supporting the introduction of professionalism, albeit with residential and occupational restrictions, and the latter opposing professionalism.[55] The debate flourished throughout the next six months, with Bradford proposing the introduction of a maximum wage of one pound a week. This was rejected as being both impossible to police and, as had happened with the six shillings broken-time payment, likely to become a standard wage which few clubs could afford.[56]

When the new regulations were unveiled in the summer of 1898, they began with the fateful words 'Professionalism is legal' but proceeded to detail such stringent conditions as to make its operation unique. Defining a professional as anyone in receipt of remuneration over and above travelling expenses, the 'work clauses' of the rules specified that every professional player must be in 'bona-fide employment' and that any change or loss of employment, including such due to fire, strike or lock-out, must be notified to the NU secretary, who would decide if a player was eligible to play. Examples of employment not regarded as 'bona-fide' were given as 'billiard markers, waiters in licensed houses, or any employment in connection with a club.' Players could register with a club for one season at a time but, unless they had special permission, could not transfer during a season. No professional was allowed to receive wages during the close season and no professional could serve on a club or Union committee. In any case of alleged contravention of the new rules, the burden of proof was to lie with the accused player or club. Those found guilty would be suspended.[57]

To a great extent, the rules were a quite-conscious amalgam of the experience of soccer, rugby union and the labour relations codes of the factory. From soccer, the lessons learned were largely negative, hence the outlawing of payments to players during the close season and, albeit overlaid with a large dose of paternalism, the insistence that players have work outside football. These measures were felt to be vital in keeping down wages. From rugby union was taken the definition of professionalism, the objection to professionals playing any part in the governance of the game (which was also an FA rule) and the placing of the burden of proof on the accused rather than the accuser. From the factory was taken the complex registration and reporting systems designed to control the activities of the players and the paternalistic rationale that the rules had been introduced for the welfare of the players. Harry Waller justified the new regulations with the argument that

> the Northern Union was anxious to make football the means of improving the positions of players. They would do what they could to find positions for players as they were able to under the rules. He did not think that anyone would like to join a football club for the sake of playing the game on Saturdays only and idling during the remainder of the week.[58]

Because of such statements it has been argued that the central motivation for the introduction of the work-clause regulations was to impose a form of 'social control' on players and to transmit bourgeois values to the working class.[59] While it is true that the regulations did tighten control over players and exclude some forms of pub-based employment, the underlying reasons for this were to regulate the economic conditions in which the NU operated. For example, working as a pub waiter or billiard marker was specifically outlawed because it was a common method used by clubs to give virtually work-free employment to players. Although declining in importance since the early 1890s, the drinks industry had a close relationship with football and the NU was no exception. During this time many leading NU officials were publicans, the 1895–96 'Official Guide' of the Hull & District RFU carried a one-line advertisement for Hull Brewery products at the head of every page and the chairman of the Leeds club was C. F. Tetley, a member of the famous Leeds brewing family. Similarly, although the insistence on players having 'real' jobs may have been based on a concern for the long-term prospects of the players, it had

" SAINTS " AT THE CARDIGAN ARMS. THE CONSOLATION OF
DEFEAT.

As this cartoon of the Leeds St John's side illustrates, alcohol, public houses and rugby
had been inseparable since the late 1870s (from *Toby, the Yorkshire Tyke*).

been a particular criticism made by rugby followers of soccer's professionalism that the latter's economic difficulties were caused in part by
paying players a full week's wages for only a few afternoons' work of
training and playing.[60]

Although not a true cartel, many of the NU's concerns resembled those
of a cartel and, until the turn of the century at least, much of its regulatory
work was aimed at establishing equality of competition. Thus the minutiae
of the work clauses were drawn up in order to stop clubs finding ways
around the rules and gaining an unfair advantage. This even extended to
the employment of private investigators to check the veracity of a player's
story.[61] There were therefore numerous additions and caveats added to the
regulations over time, which sought to restrict even further the actions of
players. By 1903, it had been decided that a player who was ill and off work
on the Thursday, Friday or Saturday morning could not play in that
Saturday's match; he must work three days after being off work before
being allowed to play again. Players who had as much as a half-day holiday
during the week had to apply to the NU for permission to play. Eventually,

any absence from work during the season meant that a player had to apply for permission to play.[62]

In justifying the new rules the leaders of the NU found themselves repeating many of the concerns about professionalism expressed by the leaders of the RFU a few years earlier. 'The Northern Union,' said Waller in 1899, 'although it had adopted professionalism, could congratulate itself that its management was in the hands of amateurs.'[63] Budd and Hill's arguments that the professional footballer was a man who was sacrificing his future for short-term gain were alluded to by Hull chairman Charles Brewer when he argued that the work clauses would prevent that from happening:

> The clause was provided solely for the benefit of the players them-selves. While the men are playing football they are receiving a certain return for it, and if they followed their ordinary occupation, as the committee expected them to do, they were making a nest egg for future years. The committee put the working clause before the players in the latters' own interests, and asked for their loyal co-operation in carrying out the rule.[64]

It is impossible to say whether the work clauses succeeded in their professed goal of raising the long-term prospects of the players. One must doubt it, if only because of the silence of the architects of the policy on the question. As with pre-1895 working-class rugby union players, the tenancy of a pub was probably the best a player could hope for, although the availability of these sinecures had diminished sharply since the early 1890s. Even then, a pub was far from a passport to a supposed life of indolence: in 1897 Dicky Lockwood, now playing for Wakefield Trinity, was declared bankrupt after accumulating debts of £300 in running the Queen's Hotel at Heckmond-wike, and later that year Oldham and Lancashire stand-off Harry Varley disappeared from his pub because of financial difficulties.[65] In general, players continued the occupations they already had outside football, partly because the work clauses forced them to stay in regular employment and forbade club payments outside the season, but mainly because the low level of remuneration available in the NU could do little more than supplement their non-football wages.

Although a critic of the work clauses claimed that most NU players were unskilled labourers, this seems to have been an exaggeration. In line with pre-split times, there appears to be no particular pattern to the occupations followed by the players, with the geographically dominant industries of mining and textiles heading the list of occupations.[66] As can be seen in Appendix Table A.5, eight of the 36 players whose employment can be identified were miners, four textile workers and three dockers. Two each were brass moulders, bottle makers and general labourers. Indeed, the occupational pattern of working-class rugby players seems to have altered little in the 25 years following 1886.

In reality, the paternalism expressed by the NU's Waller and Brewer towards working class players was no different from that of the RFU's Rowland Hill. Their differences were about the ways to protect players from themselves. As Waller himself said: 'The English Rugby union legislated for clubs as they would like them to be; and the Northern Union for the clubs and the players as they were today. The Northern Union, in a word, went with the times.'[67]

The exclusion of professionals from NU committees was ample demonstration of their determination not to let working-class players gain too much influence over the game, and when it came to implementing the work clauses, the trials of players accused of infractions brought forth eerie echoes of the 1880s rugby union trials. This is illustrated by the following extracts from the cross-examination of J. Trowell, a player from Beverley FC accused of playing in a game against Bridlington while not working:

> J. Clifford (Chair): It is reported to us that Trowell had not worked for two weeks previous to playing in this match.
>
> Trowell: I was working under the same stevedore all that time. This week I started to work on Monday morning and finished on Wednesday night.
>
> Welsh: The stevedore is really your employer?
>
> Trowell: Yes.
>
> Lister: What did you draw last week?
>
> Trowell: 15 shillings.
>
> Clifford: And what the week before?
>
> Trowell: 27/6.
>
> Clifford: And what the week before that?
>
> Trowell: 16 or 17 shillings.
>
> Clifford: And what this week??
>
> Trowell: 14 shillings.
>
> Platt: And have you had a permit from this committee when you have lost any time?
>
> Trowell: Yes.

Evidence was then presented from a private investigator, employed by the NU, who said that he had gone to see Robert Middleton, Trowell's stevedore, but found that he didn't live at the address given by Trowell.

Trowell introduced the investigator to Middleton who could show him neither a wages book nor when Trowell last worked for him:

> Clifford: When did you last work for Middleton?
> Trowell: This week.
> Clifford: Did you work for him last week too?
> Trowell: Yes. Monday, Tuesday and Wednesday.
> Clifford: What was the ship you took our representative to?
> Trowell: It was a fresh one we were going to start working on the Friday. We did not work on the Thursday.
> Clifford: What ship did you work on the Monday, Tuesday and Wednesday?
> Trowell: The Bouradina.

The inquisition continued later:

> Platt: Why did you not wire your secretary (Mr Simpson) [about not working on Thursday]?
> Trowell: I can't afford to send wires to Beverley.
> Platt: You can afford to get your club into trouble.
> Houghton: Where does Middleton live?
> Trowell: I don't know.
> Lister: You say Holland's, the stevedores, pay your wages?
> Trowell: Yes, and Middleton bullies us.
> Lister: I suppose Holland's will keep an account of the time? Are you paid by the hour?
> Trowell: Yes, Middleton has a book which he gives in after every ship ...[68]

As can be seen, the work clauses signalled the NU's determination to institute an iron rule over its players. In the first few months of the new regulations' operation, Swinton had two league points deducted because their star Welsh player, Owen Badger, took time off work to visit his sick child in Wales but did not receive NU permission to play in the following Saturday's match. A Hull player was banned for a month for not telling the NU that he had changed jobs. Most famously, Dai Fitzgerald, Batley's Welsh international three-quarter, was banned for eighteen months in 1898 when a private detective working for the NU discovered that his job as a coal agent didn't actually involve any work. The following season Hull KR fullback H. Sinclair received a similar suspension when the sub-committee found that he was not 'following regular employment.' In 1902 Hunslet had two league points deducted after one of their players accidentally submitted the wrong form to the NU. That same year the NU General Committee stopped Broughton Rangers' Willie and Sam James, younger brothers of the famous James Brothers, opening a tobacco shop together and ordered them to find alternative employment within two weeks.

The activities of the NU leadership were accompanied by ever-tightening control over players by their clubs. In November 1895 Bradford captain Jack Toothill was forced to resign from the club committee after he had declared himself unfit to play in a game due to his job in a dye house. Wigan summarily transferred John and Joe Winstanley to Leigh after they had argued with club selection policy. Alf Mann was forced to miss playing for England against Wales in 1908 after his club suspended him for 'insubordination and using bad language to members of the committee.' Bradford even refused to agree to a player's transfer to Batley until he had repaid the insurance money they had given him after he had broken his leg playing for them.[69] Little wonder that one commentator was moved to remark that 'we are unable to discriminate between the mailed fist of the Rugby Union and the knuckle-duster of the younger body. Each is equally bent on having its own rule obeyed.'[70]

The response of the players to the discipline imposed on them veered from acceptance to resignation to resistance. In the first month after the split, Warrington players had gone on strike for two matches against the club committee for not paying them the full six shillings per day for broken-time and disputes on this matter were common in many clubs. In December Leigh forwards refused to play unless they received a higher rate of broken-time payment. The following January Huddersfield suspended four players who had objected to receiving their usual 2/6d tea money in kind rather than in cash. These strikes and other actions by players were important factors in making the maximum six shillings broken-time payment the standard, and indeed the minimum, payment. It appears to be the case that, as with the introduction of covert payments into northern rugby union, the pressure to increase wages came directly from the activities and expectations of the players themselves. In all, 15 strikes took place in the NU in the first decade of its existence and all were over issues of wages. Although, as can be seen in Appendix Table A.6, all were short-lived and lasted no more than one or two games, the regularity with which they occurred indicates a relatively high level of unrest among players.

There is other evidence of concern among NU leaders about the state of player relations: a few weeks before the introduction of the work clauses, Waller called for a reduction in 'friction' between players and club officials. In 1899 Wigan officials blamed their poor run of results on the 'considerable trouble with some of the players' which they had been having. At Leeds's annual general meeting in 1903, club chairman Joshua Sheldon asked that players 'consider some of the difficulties the management of clubs laboured under, instead of putting obstacles in the way of committees by making great demands.'[71] It is difficult to gauge how successful strike actions were, although players in the early years of the NU were more likely to succeed in demands for higher payments simply because there was more money in the game at that time. In 1898 the Lancashire and Cheshire county organisations agreed to players' demands for one pound wages for playing in county games, even though Yorkshire only made six shillings broken-time payments.

Others were not so fortunate. D. Rogan, the leader of the Leeds strikers, was banned from the game for life for 'insubordination'. The five leaders of the Castleford strike suffered a similar fate, although all were reinstated within two years.[72] Paradoxically, the NU's insistence on having work outside the sport probably meant that players were more willing to take action than the full-time professionals of the Football League, who ran the risk of losing their livelihoods if they went on strike. Conversely, this was also probably the reason that NU players didn't develop any form of trade union organisation until after World War One, because, apart from the obvious problem of sportsmen recognising that they had a commonality of interest, they had a sense that their real economic interests lay at the workplace rather than at the football club. In fact, there were a number of instances of players accepting pay cuts because of the parlous economic state of their clubs: for example, Keighley, Batley and Leigh players did so in 1905 and 1907, and Lancaster players voted to continue with their club after the committee had resigned, saying they were unable to pay players, in June 1905.[73]

Although it is difficult to assess general wage levels because of the paucity of club records, a general indication can be gained from newspaper reports. At the highest echelons of the game, wages were comparable with those in the Football League; one unnamed Lancashire club being reported in 1898 as paying its players between thirty shillings and four pounds per week, with bonuses of 50 per cent for a win and 25 per cent for a draw, which would put the top earning players comfortably above the Football League's maximum wage of four pounds a week. Dai Fitzgerald was paid two pounds a week by Batley before he was suspended. In 1903 Leeds said that their players were paid an average of thirty shillings per match, although this is on the low side for the first team because the figures also included 'A' team players. At the same time, Halifax were paying one pound and ten shillings a win to the backs but five shillings less per win to their forwards. By 1908 Wigan paid their backs two pounds ten shillings a win and two pounds after a loss. In common with Halifax and many other clubs, they also paid less to their forwards, who had to make do with one pound, seven shillings and sixpence a win and one pound, two and six after a loss. Justified on the basis that backs deserved more because they attracted spectators, this differential unsurprisingly caused much resentment and, as can be seen from Appendix Table A.6, was the direct cause of at least three strikes by forwards.

However, as the NU was forced to come to terms with its economic difficulties at the turn of the century, few clubs could afford such high wages. Even by 1899, Manningham were claiming to pay players only between ten shillings and twelve shillings and sixpence a match, while a local rival was offering Elland players sixteen shillings a win, twelve shillings a draw and eight shillings after a loss. The Rochdale Hornets strike in 1902 was caused by the committee's non-payment of the team's wages of seven shillings and sixpence for an away game at Millom. In 1904 Swinton, one of the game's leading sides, were forced to reduce wages to ten shillings for a win and five shillings after a loss. In dire financial straits, Castleford were only paying players five shillings a match in 1906, less than the previously scorned broken-time limit. For the lucky few, a good run in the Challenge Cup usually meant bonuses for winning teams – when they won the cup in 1900 Swinton players received ten shillings extra for winning their first round game, one pound for winning subsequent rounds and five pounds for winning the cup, as did Halifax when they lifted the trophy in 1904.[74]

Of course, star players were normally able to demand higher wages than the team average. Halifax full back Billy Little commanded four pounds and eleven shillings a game in 1905 and at least two other players received at least twice the average pay of their team mates. Warrington's legendary winger Jack Fish was the only man in his side to receive a pound a week in the early 1900s. New Zealander Lance Todd received a straight £250 per season when he signed for Wigan in 1908, and, at the outer reaches of the NU's wages' universe, Hull's centre three-quarter Billy Batten, a future founding member of the Rugby League Hall of Fame, was reputedly earning £14 a match shortly before World War One, which probably made him the highest paid professional footballer in Britain, if not the world.[75] Curiously enough, there is no evidence of resentment towards such players by their team mates, presumably because they were seen as benefiting other players due to their ability to win matches and draw crowds.

Welsh players also regularly received more than their native team mates, although this was often because of the large cash sums they were paid when signing for NU clubs. Many, like Llanelli captain and Wales three-quarter Owen Badger, found themselves in a position to negotiate significant amounts from suitor clubs: 'The bidding started at £20 and a weekly salary, which sum daily increased, and on Tuesday Badger's price had reached £75. The brilliant three-quarter back held out for £100 and two pounds, ten shillings per week standing wages, until the end of the season, and at these figures he was invited to meet a deputation of Swintonians at Shrewsbury.'[76] When Cardiff and Wales scrum-half Dicky Davies signed for Wigan in 1907 he received £200 down, two pounds and ten shillings weekly wages and another thirty shillings per win. The highest signing-on fee paid to a Welsh player was the £300 received by Swansea's Dan Rees from Hull KR in 1905, although the £155 paid in 1913 to George Hayward, also of Swansea, was the highest received by a Welsh forward, demonstrating again the difference in the commercial potential of forwards as perceived by NU clubs. Gwyn Nicholls, future Welsh captain in the historic defeat of the 1905 All Blacks, felt sufficiently confident of his future that he turned down Hull's offer of £500 and 'a substantial weekly salary' to stay with Cardiff in October 1901.[77] The signing-on fee was particularly important in tempting players to 'Go North', not only because it was probably the largest amount of cash a working-class player would ever see, but also because many players in the Principality were already in receipt of regular monies from their ostensibly amateur Welsh clubs. Indeed, some may even have been earning more in the 'amateur' game than many 'professionals' in the NU. Treherbert were accused of offering Pontypridd's Dawson £1 a week to play for them in 1901 and in 1907 allegations were made that players were commonly paid between a sovereign and six shillings per match.[78]

The fortunes of Welsh players in the NU varied widely. Many were undoubted successes, like Wigan's Johnny Thomas and Bert Jenkins, who became the fulcrum of the club's successes in the late 1900s, Thomas eventually becoming a director of the club. Others were not: a year after signing for Swinton, Badger had left for Wales after being disciplined under the NU's work-clause rules. Dicky Davies played just sixteen games for his £200 and Gwyn Nicholls' brother Garnett signed for Wigan but never played for them. Such behaviour gained Welsh players the reputation of being both work-shy and overly expensive for the standard of play they provided: 'It appears that a man has only to say he comes from Wales to be put into some Northern Union team straight away, sometimes to the detriment of promising young local players,' complained *The Yorkshireman* as early as 1895.[79] The introduction of the work clauses was widely perceived as an attempt to stop Welsh players from taking advantage of easy jobs on offer from clubs and make them work in real jobs. At its extreme, this resulted in Hull and Wigan taking legal proceedings against players who had received signing-on fees but never showed up at their new clubs, Wigan receiving £65 compensation from the courts for the £120 they paid to Aberavon's Tommy Thomas.[80]

This growing self-confidence of the clubs in dealing with their players and in controlling wages reduced the need for the work clauses. The static attendances and economic decline of the sport in the early 1900s drastically reduced inflationary pressures, leaving little leeway for clubs to emulate their spendthrift soccer cousins of the 1890s, and, as can be seen, apart from star performers, players could not earn enough playing the game to allow them not to have a full-time job. Indeed, within the first few months of the introduction of the new rules, complaints were being raised that they were heavy-handed and counter-productive. This was partly due to the large administrative burden placed on clubs and the NU in regulating the system. On one Friday in January 1900 the Professional Sub-Committee dealt with 167 cases, a total exceeded by the work of the committee on 4 October 1901, when they looked at 203 applications, including the entire Brighouse Rangers' team and thirteen of the Leigh side. The sum total of their deliberations was to refuse permission to play to just four players.[81] Many of the decisions of the committee appeared to be both bureaucratic and arbitrary: Hunslet had requested exemption from the need to receive permission to play after a half-day holiday for the eleven miners in their side, whose working patterns gave them a mid-week half-day, but the committee refused. Leeds's T. D. Davies was barred from playing after being sacked as a pub landlord on a Thursday and being unable to find new employment on the Friday. R. Petrie of Seaton found himself investigated for missing work despite the fact he did not receive any wages from his club. Most egregious was Broughton Rangers' fine for a number of their players not working on the morning of the 1902 Challenge Cup final.[82]

The severity of the punishments handed down to clubs for breaches of the work clauses also caused much resentment. Swinton lost two league points over the Owen Badger affair and the following season both Broughton Rangers and Rochdale Hornets received the same sanction. In the 1901–2 season six of the clubs in the fourteen-team Northern Rugby League had points deducted for transgressing the clauses. In order to maintain strict adherence to the rules, the NU had little choice but to adopt such measures. Fines could simply be regarded as trading losses but the deduction of points struck at the heart of a club's existence. Unsurprisingly, most of the leading clubs resented not only the interference in their affairs but also the undermining of the league competition which points' deduction caused. As with the YRU's attempts to stifle professionalism in the late 1880s and the Lancashire suspensions for professionalism in 1894, such harsh discipline meant that, ultimately, a side was being judged by off-field criteria rather than on-field performances and posed a threat to the integrity of competition, which would consequently affect spectator interest. This had happened in the 1901–2 season when Swinton's playing record would have made them runners-up in the championship but for the deduction of four points which placed them in fourth position.

By 1901 there was significant opposition to the work clauses, and support for outright professionalism was expressed by a large minority of the senior clubs which formed the elite Northern Rugby League that year. They were able to exert enough pressure in 1902 to force the ending of punishment by points deduction but attempts to introduce open professionalism at the 1904 NU annual general meeting, backed by Broughton Rangers, Salford, Swinton, Oldham, Hull and Hull KR, failed, largely due to the residual fear of poorer clubs that it would mean that their players would be prey for the richer clubs. Opposition was also voiced by those who maintained that the work clauses fulfilled a wider social role by discouraging work-shy attitudes among players: the Hunslet committee supported the clauses because 'open professionalism would be detrimental to the players by encouraging loafing', as did Leeds and Bradford, whose chairman, Fred Lister, threatened to refuse his turn as NU president for the 1904–5 season if the clauses were abolished.[83] It is notable that these latter two clubs were also those which looked most hopefully for some form of rapprochement with the RFU, suggesting again that the paternalistic attitudes embodied in the work clauses were not so far removed from those of the RFU. A majority for their abolition was only gained for the start of the 1905–6 season, after they had been fatally discredited by the events surrounding the Leigh versus Wigan Challenge Cup tie. Two weeks after Leigh had beaten Wigan and the day before they were due to play Halifax in the next round, Wigan complained that one of the Leigh players had played without a permit. The NU ordered the game to be replayed, which Wigan won, and were then faced with a Leigh complaint that a Wigan player had taken part in the match in contravention of the work clauses. Faced with the postponement of yet another cup-tie the NU allowed Wigan to play Halifax but ordered them to forfeit their share of the gate money, thus admitting Leigh's charge.[84] The affair managed to encapsulate both the administrative nightmare of the system and the threat to the credibility of the NU's competitions posed by the work clauses. It therefore came as no surprise when the regulations were finally struck from the rule book at the 1905 general meeting. Finally, open professionalism had been introduced by the Northern Union, yet the poor financial state of the sport meant that the momentous decision had little, if any, impact on the game.

THE RISE OF SOCCER AND THE DECLINE OF THE
NORTHERN UNION

The chief reason for the NU's change in fortune from the late 1890s to the middle of the 1900s could be summed up in two words: association football. As early as 1893 the Manchester FA was arguing that it should have its own seat on the FA council because of its success in popularising soccer in 'the stronghold of Rugbyism' and the 50,000 attendance at Fallowfield in Manchester for that year's FA Cup final had shocked rugby supporters.[85] By the mid-1890s, soccer leagues had been established in most traditionally rugby towns and in Lancashire by 1897 professional sides had been formed in Oldham, Rochdale and Wigan. None of these clubs lasted more than three years as financial difficulties quickly overcame what were essentially speculative ventures, yet the growth of the game in schools and communities was rapidly undermining the bedrock of rugby support. In Lancashire's north-west, the rise and decline respectively of the two sports was such that rugby had completely disappeared from Ulverston by 1906 and neighbouring Barrow could boast only nine local rugby sides as opposed to twenty-three soccer clubs. As the *Athletic News* pointed out, 'for all practical purposes that famous recruiting area for Northern Union football [from Lancaster to Barrow] in the northwest may be considered wholly "soccerised".'[86] In Yorkshire, the former rugby town of Barnsley had been completely swamped by association, so much so that in December 1898 the Beckett Cup, the district rugby knock-out competition trophy, was handed over to the local FA because there were no longer any rugby teams left to play for it. The two Bradford clubs found themselves out-flanked by soccer enthusiasts who had persuaded the local board schools to take up the 'dribbling code' after a boy had broken his leg in a rugby game and Leeds also developed a thriving schools competition. In Hull the decade following the split saw the number of local soccer sides grow from just seven to ninety-six. Despite continual organisational problems, soccer leagues in the East and West Ridings of Yorkshire continued to attract new sides and by 1904 there were 436 clubs affiliated to the West Yorkshire FA.[87] Nor was the eclipse of rugby by soccer confined to the hinterland of the NU. In 1900 Bristol RFU were refused permission to form a local league to counter the growth of soccer in the city and in 1902 the Northumberland RFU called on the RFU to institute a national cup competition to hold back the tide. In 1908, West Hartlepool, the leading rugby union club in the north-east disbanded and reformed itself as Hartlepools United AFC.[88]

As many of the leaders of pre-1895 Lancashire and Yorkshire rugby had recognised, soccer had more appeal to spectators because of its more open style of play. The administrators of the NU were also exceptionally conscious of this, as could be seen from the debates on the rules of the game throughout the union's early history, but soccer's attraction was not simply due to its mode of play: in an era of national culture and national consciousness, soccer was a truly national sport. By 1906, it could claim over 7,500 affiliated clubs, approximately fifteen times the number of clubs claimed by the NU and the RFU combined.[89] The superseding of old regional ties by growing centralisation, the popularity of national newspapers and the importance of national events to localities previously untouched by them; all of these factors gave soccer's national pre-eminence an unassailable advantage in the struggle for football dominance. As the *Leeds Mercury* pointed out in 1905:

> The public want a national game rather than a code peculiar to a circumscribed area ... Thus, while the Northern Union has too limited an area to be really a great force, and the Rugby Union is to some extent discredited as a purely amateur combination and is weakened through the loss of the cream of the clubs of the north, the Association game is national in scope and influence, and is yearly becoming more powerful and more popular.[90]

Soccer was also a national sport in more than just a geographical sense. Despite the dominance of the working-class professional player and spectator, it still remained a game of all the classes, even if they rarely played it together. Soccer was widely played in the public schools and by teams of ex-public schoolboys. In the armed forces, it enjoyed total domination, the FA in 1906 recording 578 teams in the army, where it was the only recognised football code until 1907, and 180 navy sides.[91] It therefore suffered none of the social disadvantages which the NU faced, despite the apparently similar proletarian base of the two sports. Indeed, the attitude of many northern RFU supporters to soccer's untrammelled professionalism was in very marked contrast to that which they displayed towards the NU. James Higson, Lancashire rugby union secretary following the split, became a director of Newton Heath AFC (later to become Manchester United) in 1897. Mark Newsome, who despite his advocacy of broken-time payments in 1893 remained a loyal supporter of the RFU and became its president in 1906, saw no contradiction between his support for amateurism and his club, Dewsbury, abandoning rugby union and concentrating on soccer in 1897. A. W. Pullin, journalistic scourge of the Northern Union and intransigent defender of the RFU, became the founding vice-chairman of Leeds City AFC. This doublethink was no better demonstrated than by the response of a rugby union supporter to the NU's establishment of a schools competition who stated that 'it will be a great pity to introduce NU ideas into the minds of school-lads beyond what they know already. I consider it unhealthy for boys to grow up with the idea that they are going to play a game for which in the future they are going to receive wages,' and went on to call on schools to play soccer![92] Unlike the Northern Union game, soccer was not perceived as being aberrant or at odds with English national identity – in fact, its hierarchical pyramid of upper-class national administrators, middle-class controlled clubs and working-class players and supporters fitted the nationalist framework of late Victorian and Edwardian society perfectly.[93]

The NU was therefore at a structural disadvantage about which it could do very little when faced with the soccer threat. Its clubs had initially responded to the round ball game's popularity in its strongholds by co-opting it. At the time of the split, Bradford, Halifax, Huddersfield and Leeds had formed soccer sections of their clubs and in 1896 eight of the West Yorkshire FA's twenty-seven members were NU clubs; Hudders-field's secretary, William Hirst, even became its president. The initial success of the NU's competitions however led most of the clubs to aban-don soccer by the late 1890s, especially as the soccer sections almost invariably made a loss, in some cases quite substantially, and attracted poor attendances.[94] There was another reason for their abandonment too. In the period up to the split, when the clubs were menaced by the RFU's professionalism rules, the existence of a soccer section was regarded as an insurance policy, whereas, if a club was expelled from the RFU on its own, the association game offered a way in which it could continue its footballing activities. The consolidation of the NU removed this need.[95] The shock of the soccer explosion in their own backyards also stimulated many clubs to form new local competitions or sponsor existing ones. Warrington had begun a rugby competition for local factory sides in 1895, from which they both recruited players and made a profit by staging the finals at their ground, and in 1899 Halifax had reinvigorated their local rugby league by providing financial backing of five pounds to each club and offering a cup to be competed for, albeit with the proviso that all 350 players in the league were to be registered as Halifax players.[96] Both initiatives were copied by other clubs as they attempted to recreate the thicket of local league and cup competitions which northern rugby had established in the late 1880s. Stung by the strides made by soccer in local schools, in 1902 the Yorkshire NU committee started a schools' competition which embraced schools across the county, all of them board or council schools. In Leeds, twenty-four schools participated in the local schools' league and the final of their knockout competition attracted crowds of up to 3,000 people.[97]

The major initiative to secure the NU dam against the tidal wave of soccer was however to prove more controversial. In April 1901 Halifax called a meeting of twelve of the leading clubs in Lancashire and Yorkshire – Batley, Bradford, Broughton Rangers, Huddersfield, Hull, Hunslet, Oldham, Rochdale Hornets, Runcorn, Salford and Swinton – to consider the formation of an elite Northern Rugby League. They felt that the prevailing fixture system whereby each club played opponents from its own county provided too few top-class fixtures and sought to establish a fixture system whereby the best clubs would play each other regardless of county location. The NU had tried such an arrangement in its inaugural year, with each club playing every other club, but the volume of fixtures, each club played forty-two matches that season, coupled with the costs of travelling, forced them to switch to a county-based system. The twelve NRL clubs felt that the original system could be reconstituted but with fewer clubs. There was also a strong minority of the clubs, led by Broughton Rangers and Hull, who favoured open professionalism. Most revolutionary, the twelve sought to expand their number to include rugby union teams from the northeast and the Midlands. South Shields rugby union club joined in June, after having sounded out the NU about joining the previous year, but Leicester, which had been approached because of their notoriety for covertly paying players, declined, largely because, it was commented, 'they have been extensively patronised by the English Rugby Union, as well as by the crack southern clubs, and really do not need any attraction in the way of the Northern Union.'[98] The new league was forced to expand its numbers anyway, but for reasons of constitutional politics. In order to get a majority on the NU committee to sanction the formation of the Northern Rugby League (NRL), Brighouse Rangers and Leigh were offered places in the new venture. Such horse trading won the new league no friends among those excluded from its plans and the non-NRL clubs in Yorkshire voted to boycott all matches with them. The rancour continued until the beginning of the 1902–3 season when the thirty-six leading clubs were incorporated into a two-division structure. Three seasons later this was abandoned in favour of a return to a single league with a county-based fixture system after clubs in the second division complained about high travelling costs and declining gates due to unattractive fixtures. The entire exercise had proved to be 'an unqualified failure' in the words of the Hull committee, and had seen the disbanding of the NU's only outpost in the north-east, after the clubs had voted against South Shields's inclusion in the NRL at the end of the 1903–4 season because of the costs involved in travelling to Tyneside.[99]

The failure of the NRL and the continued erosion of its base by soccer only served to deepen demoralisation within the sport. The cross-class composition of soccer and the overt appeal of middle-class exclusivity from the RFU had helped to 'proletarianise' the NU, making it difficult for clubs to attract businessmen to the game and serving to increase the disillusionment of many of its existing middle-class patrons. As early as 1898 A. D. Penny, the chairman of Leeds, had complained about the lack of support the club was receiving from the city's employers and the same concern was expressed by Hull, Hull KR and Hunslet officials over coming years.[100] This disillusionment with the NU was also accompanied by a desire in some quarters to abandon professional rugby and return to amateurism and the RFU. Significantly, although for reasons not apparent at the time, Manningham's outgoing chairman, James Freeman, had called in 1900 for his club to 'go back to that free and independent style of amateur play' and in 1902 Leeds's president, Joshua Sheldon, declared, 'I don't appreciate a sport for which men have to be paid for its promotion, and I wish that Leeds had stayed a strong amateur club.' In the same year, and most damaging of all, Herbert Hutchinson, Wakefield Trinity's leading committee member and a former NU president, resigned from his club to rejoin the RFU, calling on the leading clubs of the NU to do the same.[101]

Another symptom of the haemorrhage of middle-class support for the NU was the abandonment of the sport by the Church of England, signified by the abrupt closure of the Leeds Parish Church club in 1901. Even before the split the church's belief in the evangelising power of rugby had been waning and the Leeds Parish Church side in particular, with its reputation for rough play, covert payments to players and violent crowds, was an acute embarrassment to the church to which it was nominally attached. The fact that the club was also heavily supported by members of Leeds's immigrant Jewish community, which was situated near the club's ground, also confirmed for the church that rugby was no longer a useful means of extending its influence among the lower classes.[102] Nevertheless, at the turn of the century, the club was, after Hunslet, the leading force in Leeds rugby, and certainly put its richer rival at Headingley, to the north of the city, in the shade. In 1900, 20,000 packed into its ground to see the Challenge Cup quarter-final with Runcorn, one of two quarter-final appearances it made, and crowds of ten thousand were not uncommon for important games. The club finished above Leeds in the league on four out of its five years in the NU, including being fourth in its penultimate season, but its death knell was sounded with the appointment of Sidney Gedge as a curate at the church in 1900. All curates were automatically made vice-presidents of the club, but rarely concerned themselves with its activities. Gedge, however, was a Scottish rugby union international, a personal friend of Rowland Hill and an active RFU referee; he played a role in the financial management of the club and was a key member of the committee which decided to shut it down. The ostensible reason was that the lease on their ground could not be renewed but as even A. W. Pullin admitted, the club had had ample time to relocate and had even been offered a ground nearby, but had done nothing. Within eight weeks of voting to disband in July 1901, the club had disappeared without trace, its effects being auctioned off in early September.[103] Other than through local Sunday schools, this ended the church's involvement with the NU at a national level, with future links being limited to the referee, the Reverend Frank Chambers, and a handful of appearances for St Helens by the Reverend Christopher Chevasse, the son of the Bishop of Liverpool who was a curate at the local church.[104] In another example of the relationship between rugby union and soccer in the North, Leeds Parish Church became a bastion of local soccer.

Yet the biggest blow came two years later, when Manningham, winners of the NU's first championship in 1896, voted to go over to soccer and joined the second division of the Football League. As we saw above, the leadership of the Manningham club had expressed their disquiet at the direction of the NU before the turn of the century, and this had continued as their playing fortunes declined. In 1901, when Bradford, Halifax and Leeds were winding up their soccer sections, Manningham had told the West Yorkshire FA that 'we are doing all we possibly can to help the Association game' and that they would look again later at the question.[105] This was something of an understatement and may well have been deliberately so: rumours had circulated in West Yorkshire since about 1900 that the Football League was keen to establish a side in Leeds or Bradford, if possible without links to an NU club. At some point towards the end of 1902 it appears that the Manningham committee approached the Football League and formed a relationship with Bradford's leading soccer evangelists, James Whyte, a Scotsman who was a sub-editor on the *Bradford Observer*, and Charles Brunt, a headmaster prominent in the promotion of soccer in Bradford schools. A series of semi-official meetings took place in the early months of 1903 and in May the club was sensationally accepted into division two of the Football League, by 30 out of 35 votes, without ever having played a game of soccer. In hindsight, it seems unlikely that such a coup could have been carried off so smoothly without guarantees having been made by the Football League. Having been accepted into soccer's elite, the club committee then moved to sever all links with the NU. At the general meeting which endorsed the committee's decision to switch to soccer and abandon rugby, committee member and textiles manufacturer Alfred Ayrton summed up the mood by expressing a dissatisfaction which managed to combine nostalgia for rugby union and support for soccer: 'I will never be a member once more, in any shape or form, of the Northern Union. As at present constituted, it is badly managed. The game has been tampered with, tinkered with and spoilt, and we are trying to substitute for it a game which will be attractive.'[106]

As can be seen, there was more to Manningham's decision than simply to find a game which would pay.[107] In fact, the club had made profits in four of its eight years in the NU but in its first three years as Bradford City AFC it made an aggregate loss of £1,638, almost its total NU losses, £1,687, but the difference was in the crowds attracted to the new club – in its first season under association rules it took £4,546 at the gate, easily doubling Manningham's best ever receipts in a season. Manningham had become a middling club in a regional competition of a declining sport; Bradford City were the most talked-about club in the national competition of a sport which was conquering the nation. The civic mission which had inspired the formation of northern rugby clubs in the 1870s was being repeated, but this time on a national scale with a different sport. The centralised and unified nation which England had become by the turn of the century meant that civic ambition could no longer be fully satisfied within a regional framework. Even Manningham's dropping of their district's name in favour of their city's seemed to signify the entrance of the club on to a new, national stage.

The success of Manningham's switch quite naturally led other NU clubs to investigate their options. Throughout 1903 and 1904 rumours abounded of other clubs following their example: Hull held meetings with Bradford City to discuss a possible switch, but this only eventuated in them sharing their ground with the newly formed Hull City;[108] Salford and Swinton were also rumoured to be considering taking the plunge, although again this resulted only in Salford sharing their ground with Salford United AFC.[109] At the end of the 1903–4 season the Leeds-based Holbeck club disbanded after losing their promotion play-off game to determine if they were to be promoted to the first division of the NRL. Six days later, the newly formed Leeds City AFC rented their Elland Road ground and announced their intention to buy it for £5,000.[110] The NU General Committee sought to flush out any remaining soccer sympathies among clubs in June 1905, when its annual general meeting decided 'that no club shall be represented on the Union committee whose interest in football is not solely devoted to the Northern Union game' but, although this appeared to steady the ship, the alarm bells started ringing once again three months later when the *Yorkshire Post* reported that 'indications are that before very long we shall have an association club in opposition to the one at Valley Parade.'[111]

That club was Bradford, the self-proclaimed flagship of Yorkshire rugby's power in the 1880s and 1890s. Again, it appears that much covert planning went on behind the scenes, but whatever the final mechanics of the rupture, the forces underlying it had been at work since before the 1895 split. These centred on the debts which had been incurred in the purchase and development of the club's Park Avenue ground, itself a symbol of civic pride and of the competition between the county's senior clubs to have the most prestigious sporting amenities in Yorkshire. Even in the NU's first season the club reported an outstanding debt of £10,300 on the ground and had defaulted on the 1895 and 1896 instalments of their £1,000 annual payments. Despite making a profit every year in the NU except their last, including one of £1,319 in 1900, by 1904 they were still £7,000 in debt.[112] It is also probable that those who lent the club the money to buy the ground – three knights of the realm, a local MP, a colonel who was also a companion of the order of Bath, and two local firms – no longer felt the same attachment to a club which had ceased to be the embodiment of the town's leadership and their civic values, as it had been when they first lent the money. Public subscriptions and bazaars were held to reduce the debt, but they only made a small dent. In an example of how profit maximisation did not operate as the driving principle of the NU, the club never considered selling off the adjoining cricket pitch, despite the fact that cricket invariably made a loss and attracted generally woeful gates; in 1904 only £70 was taken during the entire cricket season. To have sold off the cricket pitch would have deprived Bradford of its county cricket ground, an unthinkable option which would have been a disastrous blow to the prestige and civic standing of the town throughout Yorkshire.[113]

Indeed, it was the desire for social prestige combined with the club's long-term economic problems which underpinned the eventual split. The success of Manningham's switch to soccer and the national attention it brought to the town was felt deeply by the Bradford committee, used to being the city's premier sporting club. When viewed in the context of the NU's increasing marginalisation and its image as a purely working-class sport, the pressure to act became intolerable, regardless of the club's winning of the Challenge Cup in 1906. This sense of thwarted social superiority was captured by Mr H. Geldard of the club committee when he stated that 'the downfall of the Northern Union game had been brought about by the election of men from small unknown places to represent the Union,'[114] but the club itself was deeply split about the course it should take. Led by former player Laurie Hickson and the Reverend J. E. Leighton, the club committee voted in December 1906 to leave the NU unless it reverted to RFU rules, which was clearly impossible, and Hickson received assurances from the RFU that the club would be welcomed back with open arms, although not the players because they were professionals.[115] Three months later, it was reported that the committee were in favour of applying to join the Football League and a special meeting of members was called to vote on the future of the club. After acrimonious debate the meeting ignored the committee's vote for soccer and voted to return to the RFU by 'a good majority.' Unimpressed by the decision of the meeting, the committee sent out voting papers to members, which resulted in a majority for soccer, and a week later had the members' meeting declared illegal and contrary to the club's articles of association. On 7 May the Finance and Property Committee, the club's ultimate decision-making body, voted 18–2 to switch to soccer, 'recognising that association is the best paying game from a financial point of view.' The die was now cast, despite a rearguard action by NU supporters, who three weeks later founded Bradford Northern at a meeting of 300 people. Bradford's difficulties were not over however; their application to join the Football League was rejected and, to prevent their venture being stillborn, they successfully applied to join the Southern League, along with the newly formed Oldham Athletic. Ironically, in view of the club's quest to recapture its social standing of the 1880s, throughout its life as a soccer club it was destined to play second fiddle to Bradford City until its eventual demise in 1974.[116]

Because it was expected, Bradford's breakaway came as something of a relief to the NU. Indeed, it had come out of the episode relatively well, with a new club, a committed layer of supporters and with the district league unscathed by the machinations of the senior clubs. Just as important, Bradford had not been joined by other clubs, despite the prevalent rumours that Leeds, who shared many of the same aspirations and dissatisfactions with the NU's direction, would follow them. Despite club president Joshua Sheldon's desire to return to the RFU fold, economic reality and the election of Leeds City AFC to the Football League in 1905 dictated that Leeds would remain an NU club, because, as Sheldon himself admitted, 'something more than the game as played by rugby union clubs was required.'[117] In short, the Headingley grounds could only remain open through the regular cash flow provided by the NU club: without it, the grounds, and in particular the nationally renowned cricket pitch, would close.

Other signs of demoralisation within the NU seemed to have dissipated too. Hull and Barrow had raised the question of opening discussions with the RFU in 1905 but had received no support. Indeed, by mid-decade the NU probably had more adult clubs affiliated to it than the RFU.[118] As the first decade of the twentieth century passed its mid-point, the NU, buffeted by a world which was forcing it to change and abandon its old certainties, stood at a crossroads.

NOTES

1. This is particularly true of the weekly and monthly journals dedicated to regional interests, such as *The Yorkshireman*, *Yorkshire Owl*, the *Manchester Monthly* and Manchester's *Ben Brierley's Journal*, all of which failed in the 1890s. See Margarèt Beetham, 'Healthy Reading: The Periodical Press in Late Victorian Manchester' in *City, Class and Culture: Studies of Cultural Production and Social Policy in Victorian Manchester*, A. J. Kidd and K. W. Roberts (eds), Manchester, 1985 and *Lancashire and Cheshire from AD1540* by C. B. Phillips and J. H. Smith, London, 1994. On the impact of contrary effect of national newspapers being printed in the provinces, see D. Read, *The English Provinces*, London, 1964, p. 272.
2. Holbrook Jackson, *The Eighteen Nineties*, London, 1913, p. 28. For more on the centralisation of British society during the 1890s, see Asa Briggs, *Victorian Cities*, London, 1963, R. Williams, *The Long Revolution*, London, 1961 and E. J. Hobsbawm, 'The Making of the Working Class 1870–1914' in *Worlds of Labour*, London, 1984.
3. The Vesta Tilley quote is from Gareth Stedman-Jones, 'Working Class Culture and Working Class Politics in London 1870–1900: Notes on the Remaking of a Working Class', *Journal of Social History*, Vol. 7, No. 4, Summer 1974. Useful commentary on this period can also be found in Penelope Summerfield's 'The Effingham Arms and Empire' in E. and S. Yeo (eds), *Popular Culture and Class Conflict 1590–1914*, Brighton, 1981. For the warrior-patriot see J. A. Mangan, *The Games Ethic and Imperialism*, London, 1986, p. 60. See also J. A. Mangan, 'Duty unto Death: English Masculinity and Militarism in the Age of the New Imperialism' in *International Journal of the History of Sport*, Vol. 12, No. 2, Aug. 1995. David Cannadine's 'The Context, Performance and Meaning of Ritual: The British Monarchy and the "Invention of Tradition", c. 1820–1977', in E. J. Hobsbawm and T. Ranger (eds), *The Invention of Tradition*, London, 1983, also makes important points about the importance of this period to the growth of nationalist symbolism and ritual.
4. P. A. Vaile writing to *The Times*, 10 Oct. 1905. For Cecil Rhodes, see Revd Frank Marshall and Leonard R. Tosswill, *Football – the Rugby Union Game*, London, 1925 (Revised edition), Ch. 23.
5. Arthur Budd, 'The Northern Union', in *Football*, 1897, p. 32.
6. Old Ebor 'The Northern Union in Yorkshire' in *Athletic News Football Annual 1896*, London, 1896, p. 187.
7. Ernest Ensor, 'The Football Madness', *Contemporary Review*, Vol. 74, Nov. 1898, p. 756.
8. *Yorkshire Post*, 29 May and 26 Oct. 1896.
9. *Yorkshire Post*, 3 Nov. 1896.

10. After much controversy, the AAA passed the motion 'No professional footballer can be allowed to compete under AAA rules' in May 1899. *Yorkshire Post*, 15 May 1899.

11. *Athletic News*, 5 Dec. 1898. Technically the ban was on policemen playing any form of professional football but as the vast majority of soccer professionals were full-time and unlikely to indulge in part-time policing, the ban was actually directed at the semi-professionals of the Northern Union. In 1907 the same regulation was used to discipline P. C. Arch, an Aberdare player who had been suspended by the Welsh Rugby Union for receiving payments. See *Yorkshire Post*, 14 Sept. 1907. It may simply have been coincidental that this suspension was handed down in precisely the same month in which the new Welsh NU clubs were launched.

12. In a pre-emptive strike the RFU reached an agreement with the FA in Nov. 1894 to honour each others suspensions, including those for breaches of the professionalism rules, see *Yorkshire Post*, 5 Nov. 1894. Discussions continued after the split but the FA decided not to implement the RFU's ban on players with NU clubs, due to the opposition of the Football League and the adverse impact such a ban would have on the prospects for the growth of soccer in West Yorkshire. See the *Yorkshire Evening Post*, 25 Sept. 1895, *Yorkshire Post*, 21 Nov. and 18 Dec. 1895 and the *Bradford Illustrated Weekly Telegraph*, 31 Aug. 1895. However, H. Milnes was prevented from playing for Hunslet AFC by the FA in 1898 because he had previously been found guilty by the RFU of signing for Holbeck Northern Union club. See *Yorkshire Post*, 28 January 1898.

13. *Yorkshire Post*, 20 Jan. 1908 and 12 Sept. 1907. In Australia, rugby league was also for many years accused of being unpatriotic in rugby union circles for its allegedly ambiguous attitude to the outbreak of the First World War – see Murray Phillips, 'Football, Class and War: The Rugby Codes in NSW 1907–18' in J. Nauright and T. Chandler, *Making Men*, London, 1996. For a slightly more modern comment on the exclusion of rugby league from the English national sporting pantheon, see Angus Calder, *The Myth of the Blitz*, London, 1991.

14. 'The Case for the Belligerents', *Hull Daily Mail*, 4 Sept. 1895.

15. *Wigan Observer*, 7 Sept. 1895 and *Yorkshire Post*, 21 Sept. 1895.

16. *Yorkshire Evening Post*, 6 Sept. 1895.

17. Harry Waller speaking at a dinner for the NU's first champions, Manningham. *Yorkshire Post*, 29 April 1896.

18. *Salford Reporter*, 7 Sept. 1895. *Yorkshire Chat*, 4 Sept. 1895. *Bradford Daily Argus*, 31 Aug. 1895. *Leeds Evening Express*, 30 Aug. 1895. *Bradford Observer*, 29 Aug. 1895.

19. *Leeds Daily News*, 27 Aug. 1895.

20. *Hull Daily Mail*, 20 Sept. 1895.

21. *The Yorkshireman*, 14 Sept. 1895.

22. *Salford Reporter*, 7 Sept. 1895. *Yorkshire Post*, 31 Aug. 1895.

23. *Yorkshire Post*, 7 Sept. 1895.

24. See L. Balaam, *Manchester FC 1860–1985*, Manchester, 1985.

25. *Athletic News,* 20 April 1896. *Salford Reporter*, 18 April 1896.

26. *Salford Reporter*, 2 May 1896. *Swinton FC: Souvenir History of the Club*, Swinton, 1929.

27. *Yorkshire Post*, 17 April 1896.

28. *Yorkshire Post*, 31 May 1897. The clubs were: Manchester, Manchester Free Wanderers, Liverpool, Liverpool Old Boys, Waterloo, Sale, Broughton Park, Broughton, New Brighton, Birkenhead Park, Blackley, Little Borough and

Castleton Moor. The following year Castleton Moor joined the NU and Broughton disbanded.

29. *Barrow News*, 10, 4 and 24 April, and 1 and 3 July 1897.
30. *Athletic News*, 14 and 21 March and 24 Oct. 1898. Millom's figures are in *Yorkshire Post*, 25 May 1898.
31. *Yorkshire Post*, 20 and 21 May 1896.
32. Keighley President, W. R. Elgie, in *Yorkshire Post*, 13 April 1900.
33. *Yorkshire Post*, 10 July 1897, 3 and 13 Sept. 1898.
34. *Salford Reporter*, 7 Sept. 1895.
35. *Yorkshire Post*, 18 Feb. 1896, 10 March 1896 and 31 March 1896. Somewhat unsurprisingly, later that month Horbury voted to join the NU. The pantomime story is in *Yorkshire Post*, 25 Jan. 1898. The story about the RFU official is told in a letter from A. R. Meek, a RFU supporter, in *Yorkshire Post*, 21 Jan. 1901. A recently published history of rugby league in London alleges that the RFU did indeed threaten to ban rugby union players who attended matches of the London Highfield club in 1933: see D. Farrar, P. Lush and M. O'Hare, *Touch and Go*, London, 1995, p. 77.
36. *Athletic News*, 7 Feb. 1898.
37. *Bradford Daily Argus*, 31 Aug. 1895.
38. *Yorkshire Post*, 4 Jan. 1899. Sharlston, the ground and twelve players were expelled from the YRU.
39. Letter to *Yorkshire Post*, 5 Nov. 1895.
40. YRU President James Hall in *Yorkshire Post*, 26 June 1899. *Yorkshire Post*, 1 Jan. 1900.
41. *Yorkshire Post*, 24 Oct. 1900 and 2 July 1901. *Hull Daily Mail*, 15 Jan. 1901.
42. The Headingley club published a centenary brochure in 1978, claiming descendency from various clubs which had called themselves Headingley in the 1870s and 1880s. In fact, the club itself originally dated its foundation as 1892, as attested to by their celebration of fifteen years existence in 1907. See 'The Headingley Club – Fine Fifteen Years' Record' in *Yorkshire Post*, 18 Sept. 1907. For complaints about YRU favouritism towards the club, see especially *Yorkshire Post*, 19–24 April 1909.
43. *Yorkshire Post*, 10 Dec. 1907.
44. *Yorkshire Evening Post*, 4 March 1897 and *Yorkshire Post*, 11 Jan. 1898.
45. *The Times*, 18 Oct. 1897.
46. For a details of the RFU discussion, see *Yorkshire Post*, 17 Sept. 1897. For a full background to the Gould case, see Gareth Williams, 'How Amateur was My Valley: Professional Sport and National Identity in Wales 1890–1914' in *The British Journal of Sports History*, Vol. 2, No. 2 (Sept. 1985). Ironically, Gould was from a working-class family but his fame and the channels of social advancement available in Welsh rugby union had given him a respectability unattainable to northern rugby stars. I am grateful to John Jenkins and Gareth Williams for letting me see their research into Gould's background.
47. Figures from *Yorkshire Post*, 30 April 1897. Description from C. F. Shaw, *The Gallant Youths*, Batley, 1899, p. 77.
48. *The Times,* 18 Oct. 1897.
49. *Yorkshire Evening Post*, 16 Sept. 1895.
50. *Yorkshire Post*, 30 April 1897.
51. *Yorkshire Post*, 30 June 1896.
52. See *Yorkshire Post*, 27 May 1898 for the incorrect figure and *Yorkshire Post*, 26 May 1899 for its correction. No explanation was offered for this action.

53. For an example of this see *Yorkshire Evening Post*, 30 Sept. 1895.
54. *The Mascot*, 26 Dec. 1896.
55. I have been unable to confirm the identity of the author of the minority report, but the available evidence suggests that it could have been NU secretary Joe Platt of the Oldham club.
56. *Yorkshire Post*, 14 Jan. 1898.
57. The full text of the regulations can be found in *Athletic News Football Annual*, 1898, Manchester, 1898, pp. 198–9.
58. Harry Waller speech at presentation of Yorkshire county medals in *Yorkshire Post*, 23 May 1898.
59. See, for example, Eric Dunning and Kenneth Sheard, *Barbarians, Gentlemen and Players*, New York, 1979, p. 205, and Paul Greenhalgh, 'The Work and Play Principle: The Professional Regulations of the Northern Rugby Football Union 1898–1905', *The International Journal of the History of Sport*, Vol. 9, No. 3, Dec. 1992. For a critique of the use of the term 'social control' in the context of leisure, see Gareth Stedman-Jones, 'Class Expression versus Social Control?', *History Workshop*, 4, Autumn 1977.
60. On the latter point, see particularly *Clarion*, 5 Jan. 1895.
61. On the notion that the NU was an economic cartel, see Brian Davies, 'Bifurcation in Sport: Some Preliminary Thoughts on the Case of Rugby League' in *The Journal of Regional and Local Studies*, Vol. 8, No. 1, Spring 1988 and Wray Vamplew, *Pay Up, Pay Up and Play the Game: Professional Sport in Britain 1875–1914*, Cambridge, 1988. Paul Greenhalgh makes a convincing case that the NU was not a genuine cartel in his *The History of the Northern Rugby Football Union 1895–1910*, University of Lancaster Ph.D. thesis, 1992.
62. See 'Rulings of the Professional Sub-Committee' in the NU's *Official Guide*, 1903–4.
63. Waller speech at Batley in *Yorkshire Post*, 24 April 1899.
64. Charles Brewer after the Yorkshire versus Lancashire match in *Yorkshire Post*, 6 Nov. 1899.
65. *Yorkshire Post*, 7 Jan. and 21 Nov. 1897. Harry Varley later reappeared to captain Leeds for a season. An anonymous contributor to *Pastime* (4 Oct. 1893), who may well have been the Reverend Frank Marshall, argued that players were often given poorly performing pubs with little support from the breweries concerned.
66. *Hull Daily Mail*, 25 Jan. 1899.
67. *Yorkshire Post*, 24 April 1899.
68. Northern Union Professional Sub-Committee Minutes, 20 Feb. 1903 and 13 March 1903. Unfortunately, there is no record of whether Trowell was found guilty.
69. *Athletic News*, 25 April 1898. *Yorkshire Post*, 28 Dec. 1908.
70. For Badger, see *Athletic News*, 7 Nov. 1898. For the Yorkshire cases, see *Yorkshire Post*, 3 Nov. and 8 Dec. 1898, 7 Oct. 1899 and 22 Feb. 1902. For the James Brothers see NU General Committee minutes 7 Dec. 1902. The quote is from *Yorkshire Post*, 2 Jan. 1899.
71. *Yorkshire Post*, 23 May 1898, 19 Jan. 1899 and 28 May 1903.
72. *Yorkshire Post*, 5 Dec. 1898 and 9 March 1900. NU General Committee minutes 11 June 1902, 8 Sept. 1902 and 8 Nov. 1904.
73. *Yorkshire Post*, 11 Jan. and 10 June 1905, and 9 Jan. 1907.
74. *Athletic News*, 26 Sept. 1898, *Yorkshire Post*, 23 Jan. 1899, 31 May 1899, 28 May 1903, 27 Feb. 1906, 29 July 1908. The Halifax details are in Andrew Hardcastle, *The Thrum Hall Story*, Halifax, 1986. For a comparison with soccer wages, see Mason, pp. 96–104.

75. Billy Batten's wages were attested to by his son Eric, himself a rugby league great, in an interview in 1988 for the video *Rugby League Tours*, Micron Video, Wigan, 1988. For independent confirmation see *Yorkshire Evening Post*, 9 Feb. 1928.
76. *Yorkshire Post*, 3 Dec. 1897.
77. *Yorkshire Post*, 7 Oct. 1901. For more details about Welsh players' journeys to the Northern Union, see Robert Gate's superb *Gone North*, Ripponden, 1985.
78. *Yorkshire Post*, 31 Jan. 1901 and 13 June 1907. For confirmation that some Welsh clubs paid wages comparable to NU clubs up until the 1920s, at the very least, see Dai Davies' autobiography in Phil Melling, *Man of Amman*, Llandysul, 1993.
79. *The Yorkshireman*, 2 Nov. 1895.
80. *Yorkshire Post*, 21 Jan. 1900 and 19 July 1908. On the impact of the work clauses on Welsh players, see *Athletic News*, 12 Dec. 1898.
81. Northern Union Professional Sub-Committee minutes, 4 Oct. 1901 and *Yorkshire Post*, 6 Jan. 1900.
82. Northern Union General Committee minutes, 14 May 1902. Cumberland Professional Sub-Committee minutes, March 1903. *Yorkshire Post*, 4 Jan. 1904.
83. *Yorkshire Post*, 3 and 11 June 1904.
84. *Yorkshire Post*, 18, 24 and 25 March 1905.
85. The quote is from Graham Williams' fascinating *The Code War*, Harefield, 1994, p. 123.
86. *Barrow and District Yearbook*, compiled by E. Foster, Barrow, 1906. *Athletic News*, 6 Aug. 1906.
87. *Yorkshire Post*, 15 May 1904 and 30 May 1905.
88. See the reports of the RFU general meetings in the *Yorkshire Post*, 21 Sept. 1900 and 1 Sept. 1902.
89. See the minutes of the FA Council meeting of 12 March 1906.
90. *Leeds Mercury*, 2 Oct. 1905
91. FA Council minutes, 12 March 1906. Neither the army nor the navy affiliated to the Amateur Football Association, which was formed in 1906.
92. *Yorkshire Post*, 6 Dec. 1902.
93. The question of the social composition of the leadership of the NU and its supporters is examined at the beginning of the following chapter.
94. Both the Leeds and Bradford soccer sections lost over £180 in 1896 and 1897 respectively. See *Yorkshire Post*, 24 June 1896 and 28 May 1897.
95. Although this was not explicitly stated by the clubs for obvious reasons, circumstantial evidence suggests that soccer was viewed as a 'get-out' option. See *Huddersfield Daily Examiner*, 14 Oct. 1893, *The Yorkshireman*, 7 Sept. 1895 and *Athletic News*, 20 April 1896.
96. Such mass signings of junior players was outlawed in Nov. 1899 by the NU, which placed a limit of 75 registered players on each club and laid down that they pay 2/6d to the junior club from which the player was signed.
97. Minutes of the Leeds Schools (Northern) RFU, various dates. The creation of a schools' Northern Union competition was the direct stimulus for the formation of the English Schools Rugby Union, which was proposed to the RFU committee in 1904 by Mark Newsome in order to counter the threat of the NU.
98. *Yorkshire Post*, 22 May 1901. Leicester were investigated for alleged professionalism but the RFU, despite overwhelming evidence, never found them guilty, presumably because they would have immediately joined the NU. RFU president Charles Crane resigned in disgust at the RFU's inaction in 1908.
99. Hull FC, Annual Report and Accounts 1905–6.

100. *Yorkshire Post*, 23 April 1898, 31 May 1902 and 21 May 1908. Hull Kingston Rovers, Annual Report and Accounts 1903–4.
101. *Yorkshire Post*, 24 May 1900, 31 May 1902 and 3 July 1902. Hutchinson became a member of the Headingley club, for which his son, a future England international, played.
102. The high level of Jewish support for the Leeds Parish Church side had been noted in the early 1890s, so much so that *The Yorkshireman* uniformly referred to the club's supporters by the anti-Semitic epithet 'sheenies'. See *The Yorkshireman*, 29 Sept. 1894.
103. *Athletic News*, 22 July 1901. *Yorkshire Post*, 10 Sept. 1901. Gedge's position as a vice-president of an NU club was an expellable offence under the RFU's professionalism laws but, as he explained, Rowland Hill had confirmed that the rules 'were not intended to apply to cases' such as his. *Yorkshire Post*, 6 Dec. 1900.
104. For Frank Chambers and his own brand of muscular christianity, which was not above punching rowdy spectators, see Gerald Hinchliffe, *A History of King James's Grammar School in Almondbury*, Huddersfield, 1963. For Chevasse, see Alex Service, *Saints In Their Glory*, St Helens, 1985 and J. R. A. Dalgleish, *Red, Black and Blue, The First 125 Years of Liverpool Football Club*, Swinton, 1983.
105. Letter from Manningham's S. S. Naylor to the West Yorkshire FA committee, *Yorkshire Post*, 12 Dec. 1901.
106. See *Bradford Observer* and the *Yorkshire Post* throughout May 1903. The quote is from *Yorkshire Post*, 30 May 1903. Background information can also be found in A. J. Arnold's 'Shall it be Bradford or Leeds? The Origins of Professional Football in the West Riding Textile District', *Publications of the Thoresby Society – Miscellany*, Vol. 19, 1990.
107. For the argument that it was the quest for profitability which took both Manningham and Bradford from rugby to soccer, see A. J. Arnold, *A Game that would Pay*, London, 1988.
108. *Yorkshire Post*, 3 and 9 Dec. 1903.
109. *Yorkshire Post*, 13 June 1904.
110. *Yorkshire Post*, 14 Sept. 1904.
111. Minutes of Northern Union annual general meeting, 14 June 1905. *Yorkshire Post*, 6 Sept. 1905.
112. *Yorkshire Post*, 9 June 1904.
113. For details of the 'benefactors' see *Yorkshire Post*, 20 March 1896. For cricket losses see *Yorkshire Post*, 22 Oct. 1904. The same point about cricket income can be made about all NU clubs which also had a cricket ground. Halifax lost over £1,000 in the 1898 and 1899 cricket seasons and even Headingley struggled to make a cricket profit: in 1901 cricket made a loss of £455.
114. *Bradford Observer*, 16 April 1907.
115. How the players could be guilty of professionalism but not the club which paid them was a riddle which remained unanswered by the Rugby Union. As with the Gould case and Sidney Gedge, it was no doubt a matter of 'expediency'.
116. For details of the club's switch see the *Bradford Observer* throughout April, May and early June 1907. The quotes are from *Bradford Observer*, 16 and 17 April 1907. The club's discomfiture at being denied membership of the Football League was increased when Oldham Athletic were offered Burslem Port Vale's second division Football League place two weeks after their acceptance into the Southern League. Bradford were eventually accepted into division two of the Football League in 1908. In yet another example of the links between rugby union and soccer in the North, Bradford's chief spokesman at the meeting which

accepted them into the Southern League was the RFU-supporting Reverend Leighton.

117. *Yorkshire Post*, 15 Oct. 1906.
118. For moves to begin a rapprochement with the RFU, see NU General Committee minutes, Oct. 1905. For the respective sizes of the two rugby organisations, see the *Northern Union Official Guide 1904–5,* Manchester, 1904 and O. L. Owen, *The History of the RFU*, London, 1955. In 1906 Widnes's J. H. Smith claimed a figure of 420 clubs, including juniors and schoolboys, for the NU, see *Athletic News*, 19 Feb. 1906.

6

A Revolution in Rugby:
1905–1910

Late Victorian and Edwardian working-class life was, it has often been argued, a 'life apart'.[1] The rapid expansion of trade unionism and the concomitant anti-trade union measures of the early 1900s led to social and political tensions unparalleled since the age of the Chartists in the 1840s. The formation of the Labour Party in 1900 marked the organisational break of the trade union movement from its long-standing political alliance with the Liberal Party. As the middle classes moved out of the towns and cities and into the suburbs, the working classes found themselves segregated by geography. Exclusive middle-class leisure activities, such as golf and tennis grew in popularity and served to increase further the division between the classes in the social sphere. In a sense, the turn of the century was marked by a return to the harsher, more adversarial social climate of the mid-nineteenth century, when the lack of contact between the classes had been one of the spurs to the creation of the rational recreation movement, but unlike earlier times, there was no movement by sections of the middle classes attempting to bridge that gulf. Despite differences of degree and regional variations, the working class increasingly occupied a sphere of existence outside the knowledge and experience of the middle classes. Not only were the classes segregated, they were also alienated from each other. As Ross McKibbin has argued, 'the British ideology, for in effect that is what it was, ensured a high degree of social cohesion but not social integration. Associations, groups and classes lived and let live; they knew there were certain boundaries that could not be crossed and rights which could not be infringed.'[2]

The chasm between the classes was brilliantly illuminated by the consequences of the split in rugby. In the decade following the rift, the social nature of rugby in the north changed dramatically. Public and grammar school old boys took refuge in the exclusivity of the rugby union, many of the civic worthies formerly associated with rugby transferred their patronage to soccer and by 1905 the Northern Union itself had been almost entirely deserted by the upper middle-class manufacturing and professional classes which were the backbone of northern rugby in the 1880s and 1890s. As we saw earlier in the discussion on the north–south divide in rugby, the 1895 split was not about southern gentry and northern industrialists: the supporters of the RFU had as many, and probably more, industrialists and textile manufacturers in their camp as the splitters. In fact, the NU found it extremely difficult to stem the haemorrhage of the middle classes, and especially the employing classes, from the game.

As Appendix Table A.7 makes clear, factory owners actually made up a very small percentage of the leadership of the NU. The handful of manufacturers who joined the NU, with the exception of Huddersfield's William Hirst, had not played prominent leadership roles in rugby union previously and the four who sat on the NU General Committee – Hirst, John Clifford, Richard Collinge and Harry Waller – had all left the game by 1906, although Clifford was appointed joint manager of the first NU tour to Australia in 1910.[3] The majority of the leaders of the NU were in fact drawn from the lower middle classes, especially smaller retailers such as publicans and shop owners, and, to a lesser extent, the 'respectable' upper working classes. A similar pattern can be found in the table of shareholders in NU clubs detailed in Appendix Table A.8 – although the Leeds club, formed at the height of rugby's cross-class popularity in 1890, unsurprisingly shows a significant variation – and in Greenhalgh's analysis of Northern Union club directors, where he found almost two-thirds could be classified as proprietors, publicans or skilled proletarians. As if to underline the NU leadership's confinement to the less socially prestigious sections of the middle classes, the two schoolmasters who were members of the NU committee were teachers at board and church schools, rather than middle-class private schools. Indeed, most of the listed occupations entailed continuous contact with the working classes through shops, pubs and schools, not to mention as foremen and managers, and were part of the daily structure of working-class life. As Robert Roberts pointed out in his description of working-class life in Edwardian Salford, publicans and shopkeepers were commonly viewed as members of the highest echelons of the working class, rather than belonging to the middle classes.[4] Yet even if not of working-class origin themselves, the day-to-day economic interests of the proprietors and retailers who led the NU meant that they were less liable to join the flight from the sport of the more socially illustrious members of the middle classes.

The social composition of the NU leadership also helps to explain the development of a distinct and separate ideology of the sport, with its emphasis on the supposed rights of players and its self-proclaimed democracy, which was to prove as deep-seated and durable, and almost as capable of international diffusion, as the RFU's commitment to amateurism. In part, this was a reflection in microcosm of a broader social shift affecting the northern middle classes at the turn of the century, which, as John Walton describes in the case of Lancashire, 'left Liberalism and Dissent increasingly, though never exclusively, the preserve of the smaller and newer employers, the shopkeepers, traders and artisans, and the politically articulate segments of the working class, [and] was matched by a growing tendency to cultural homogeneity among late Victorian and Edwardian urban elites.'[5]

Much of the NU's ideology had been carried over from the rhetoric of the campaign for broken-time, which sought to place the working man on an equal footing with middle-class players. The NU was also forced to accept the way its opponents portrayed it as a sport fit only for the working classes, a view most graphically expressed in 1903 by Crawford Finlay, the Scottish rugby union referee, who 'was surprised that Wales selected miners, steelworkers and policemen for their international teams and suggested that these players should join the Northern Union.'[6] The NU's attempts at expansion in the latter half of the Edwardian period were explicitly based on forming clubs which would appeal to the working class – the initiators of the Coventry NU club in 1909 were said to 'propose catering for the working-class population with the offer of single shares of one pound.'[7] This ideology was acceptable to the leaders of the NU because of the position they occupied in society. As members of the lower middle classes, they desired opportunities for themselves greater than their economic power could provide (hence, in many cases, their involvement in the sport) and were frustrated by the power exerted over their lives by those with greater access to privilege and power.

Despite its emphasis on equality however, the NU's ideological framework had nothing to do with socialist, or even trade union-based, ideas. Indeed, it was oppositional only to the extent that the stance of others, and in particular the RFU, forced it to oppose the *status quo*. Unlike that of amateurism, the NU's ideology was inclusive, seeking to include all sections of society in the sporting life of the nation. In this, to expand on Walton's observation, it followed Gladstonian Liberalism, with its belief in the removal of all barriers which affected political, liberal or economic life. Gladstone's rallying cry of 1865, 'the interest of every class is to have justice done to all' would have served equally well as the NU's motto.[8] This was no accident. While it would be an exaggeration to say that the 1895 split divided the leadership of northern rugby into Tory supporters of the RFU and Liberal supporters of the NU, there is some truth in this statement. Harry Waller, the NU's founding president, was a prominent member of the Liberal Party in West Yorkshire. Waller's successor as president, Warrington's James Warren, was also a member of the Liberal Party. So too was the president for the 1904–5 season, Rochdale's Richard Collinge, who, like Waller, was a textile manufacturer. By contrast, the NU's most vigorous opponents in the RFU were Tories. James Higson, Harry Garnett, Barron Kilner and Mark Newsome (the latter three being personifications of the gruff northern businessman stereotype), as well as Rowland Hill and Arthur Budd in the south, were all leading members of their local Conservative Parties.[9] Similarly at a local level in 1897 at Wakefield Trinity, club secretary and Liberal councillor J. H. Fallas no doubt took great pleasure in informing the club's former chairman, and future Tory town mayor, Barron Kilner that his name was to be 'struck from the list of vice-presidents and that he be asked to return his membership ticket.' A similar split took place in Manchester in 1895 when Broughton Rangers, with strong links to their local Liberal Party, joined the NU, while Salford, with equally strong connections to the Conservative Party, initially stayed loyal to the RFU.[10]

With the exception of A. A. Sutherland's football column in Robert Blatchford's *Clarion*, the socialist movement took little interest in rugby or in the NU, despite the fact that the Independent Labour Party's birthplace was the Bradford and Keighley area of West Yorkshire and that Salford was one of the strongholds of H. M. Hyndman's Social Democratic Federation. To a large extent this was due to the fact that the majority of British socialists viewed professional sport through the same spectacles as the supporters of amateurism, seeing it as a commercially-inspired corruption of play and recreation for enjoyment.[11] Nevertheless, it was not unknown for players to organise benefit matches for striking workers. Dicky Lockwood was involved, along with Castleford's Harry Speed and Halifax's Fred Firth, in organising games to raise funds during the 1897–98 engineering employers' lock out, and Speed, a surface worker at Glasshoughton Colliery and a local independent councillor of Liberal sympathies, also organised games for striking miners. Even so, there is no evidence that the NU game or its ideology became seen as a component of broader working-class political activity. While there was an overwhelming consciousness of class within the culture of the sport, there was no class consciousness which saw the working class having interests fundamentally opposed to capitalism – at best there was a belief that rugby demonstrated how society was divided into 'us and them'.

To take as a point of departure the work of Patrick Joyce, the culture and customs of the NU became a component of the 'master narrative' of the working classes, a confirmation in sporting terms of how the 'true people' of England had been excluded from their birthright. It is striking how, in the discourses of almost all of those connected with the game, the dominant theme is the identification of themselves as ordinary people or decent Englishmen, who, to borrow Joyce's words, 'showed respect and [were] respected but who were yet refused their proper place in the scheme of things.'[12] For the supporters of the NU that feeling was especially acute, for they had almost taken their proper place at the high table of rugby union, only to be driven from it by those who were, in their eyes, less worthy than themselves – hence the overwhelming desire of the NU to stress their honesty as apposed to the RFU's hypocrisy. This seemed to be confirmed by the NU's confinement to the northern counties of England and fed into what Joyce has called 'a radical populism conceiving of the true England as the industrial north in struggle with Privilege.'[13] Thus the NU combined a parochial pride in its Northernness with a belief that the wider world was not as it should be. It was through these processes that the NU became to its players and supporters one of the many elements of working-class cultural activity which were largely sealed off from the rest of society but whose uniqueness and underlying values were an important factor in the development and articulation of working-class identity in the communities where the game was played.

THE GAME AND ITS SUPPORTERS

Throughout the early 1890s, Lancashire and Yorkshire rugby union crowds were drawn from all sections of the local community, from the gentry to factory workers. 'It was very agreeable', said one correspondent about the 1891 Yorkshire Cup final, 'to notice doctors, lawyers, parsons and even the magistracy swelling the immense crowd by their presence,'[14] but the 1895 secession was the catalyst for the flight of much of the middle class from mass-spectator rugby. Although available evidence makes this impossible to quantify, contemporary commentators were agreed on the growing absence of the middle classes from rugby grounds. Just a year after the split, it was noted that 'the "tone" of football is being gradually but perceptibly lowered ... The repeated scenes of rowdyism, the hooting and coarse language that also too often disgrace the public part of football enclosures are likewise driving away self-respecting patrons of the game week by week.' By 1899 *Yorkshire Chat* could argue that 'I doubt if anyone will venture to deny that the tone of Yorkshire football has lowered distinctly during the past decade. "Gentlemen Players" ... are very few at the present time, and so are spectators from the ranks of the middle and upper classes. It is a pity.'[15]

This contraction of its social base of support does not appear to have led to a long term decline in attendances compared to pre-1895 levels. In fact, the NU's problem was that, overall, average crowd sizes remained relatively static and did not expand in the dramatic fashion of soccer. This point was captured by the chairman of Leigh in 1906 when he remarked that the population of the town had increased by 50 per cent since 1890 yet his club's attendances had not grown at all – indeed, in their championship-winning season of 1905–6, the side had an average attendance of just 3,176.[16] However, for important matches, especially those in the latter stages of the Challenge Cup or the Championship race, the drawing power of NU clubs easily exceeded that which they experienced before the split. Before 1895, attendances of twenty thousand or more were extremely rare, but the NU recorded at least thirty-one instances before 1910, seventy per cent of them in the Challenge Cup.[17] The realisation that cup competitions generated large crowds was instrumental in the NU's decision to begin Yorkshire and Lancashire Cup competitions in 1905. With the exception of Leeds, all the major NU clubs also established new record attendances during this period. Bradford, formerly the best supported club in the rugby union, recorded their highest ever attendance of 27,000 in March 1906, ironically just a year before they abandoned the game. In November 1909, 28,600 broke the Huddersfield ground record by cramming into Fartown to see the Yorkshire Cup semi-final with Halifax. Nor had the new sport any difficulty in easily outdrawing local rugby union, most notably on one Saturday in March 1903 when 22,000 spectators watched a Hunslet versus Leeds cup tie while just 3,000 showed up to see England play The Rest in the city. Occasionally, NU games even drew larger gates than major soccer matches, for example in 1909 when 22,000 people watched that year's Yorkshire Cup final, almost three times those at the previous week's England versus Ireland soccer international at Elland Road. Yet these large crowds were the exception rather than the rule, and average club attendances rarely exceeded ten thousand.

Like the playing personnel of the Northern Union, the game's spectators were drawn very largely from the working class. Again, lack of data makes this impossible to quantify, although there is some evidence which can give an insight into the composition of crowds. For example, of the 800 people who attended Whitehaven's replayed Challenge Cup tie with Idle in 1902, 582 of them were miners, over 72 per cent of the entire crowd. In 1901, season ticket holders at Hull FC fell from 1,454 to 992, a fall blamed by the club on the closure of the nearby Earle's shipyard works, 'amongst whose employees the club had a large number of supporters.'[18] Speaking at a reception for the Batley side after it had won the Challenge Cup for the second time running, the town's mayor noted that the club's supporters were predominantly working class, and, from a more jaundiced perspective in 1897, James Miller denounced Northern Union spectators as 'the same crowd which formerly followed rabbit coursing, dog fighting and matters of that description.'[19] The only other statistics relating to club support are those to be found in the shareholder records of those clubs which became limited companies. While these are useful in highlighting the dominance of shopkeepers, publicans and minor employers in the control of clubs, it is impossible to gauge the relationship of such figures to the composition of crowds. Certainly, paying a pound or ten shillings for no tangible return was a luxury few working-class households could afford, and would therefore probably militate against all but the most deeply committed working-class supporter becoming a shareholder. Indeed, if a working-class family did have any spare money to spend on football, it is probably more likely that the cash would go on a season ticket, as implied by the impact of the shipyard closure on Hull FC, and which was invariably cheaper than buying a company share – for example, a Leeds season ticket for the 1896–97 season cost five shillings to stand in the uncovered terraces, reduced to three shillings and sixpence for women and boys.[20]

We have even less information on the breakdown of crowds by gender. Although women made up a sizeable proportion of Lancashire and Yorkshire rugby crowds in the 1880s and early 1890s, very little reporting of their presence at matches is evident towards the end of the century. *Yorkshire Chat* in 1898 thought that there had been a decline in the number of women spectators since the 1880s, largely because 'women will not mix among men who use such foul language as one hears so repeatedly at football matches.'[21] Shareholders' lists reveal a bare handful of women shareholders, most of them listed as 'married women.' While the apparent decline in women's attendance may well be related to the NU's lack of 'respectability', the 1890s were also a period in which women's interest in football, of whatever code, was frowned upon and mocked by football's administrators, as they sought to assert football's masculinity in a society increasingly preoccupied with preparations for, and actual participation in, war. The fact that by the turn of the century most clubs now charged women for attending games, reversing the old practice of allowing them in free, also probably had an adverse impact on their attendance. We can say a little more about the proportion of boys under fourteen who attended games, mainly thanks to Hull FC's diligent record keeping. Between 1895 and 1910, boys attending Hull FC home games amounted to between seven and twelve per cent of the total paying for admission.[22] Throughout the game, boys were commonly charged three pence, half the sixpence admission price for adults, although in 1897 the NU had ordered Rochdale Hornets to charge boys the full admission price after a referee had complained about rowdy behaviour by young spectators at the ground.

Northern Union crowds differed from soccer crowds most obviously in one key aspect: soccer attendances were bigger – much bigger. As can be seen from the figures in Appendix Table A.9, both Bradford City and Bradford Park Avenue recorded average attendances far in excess of those in the NU, and both Hull City and Leeds City consistently exceeded those recorded for Hull FC and Leeds, although Leeds NU edged ahead slightly in their Challenge Cup-winning 1909–10 season. These latter two examples are, however, not so straightforward because both cities had more than one senior NU side, and given the success of both Hunslet and Hull KR during the mid-1900s the total number of people attending NU matches in these cities still surpassed those going to Football League games. Indeed, Hunslet, the nearest NU club to Leeds City, actually saw a rise in gate receipts in the soccer side's inaugural season.

It would therefore be too simplistic to assume that the new soccer clubs merely siphoned away supporters from their NU rivals, although this did happen to some extent. A fuller explanation of the soccer clubs' larger crowds lies in the fact that they were able to tap into broader sections of the local population than could their NU rivals. Although it is probably impossible to gain an accurate picture or comparison of the structure of the crowds of the two sports, we can gain an insight into their supporters by comparing the shareholders' registers of Leeds City and Holbeck NU, the original owners of City's Elland Road stadium.

Holbeck had joined the Northern Union in 1896 and, despite being overshadowed by its rivals in the city, rapidly established itself as a middle-ranking NU side, forming a limited company in 1897 to facilitate the purchase of Elland Road. In 1904, they were runners-up in the second division but lost to St Helens in the play-off game to decide who should be promoted to the first division. They promptly resigned from the NU, whereupon Leeds City immediately acquired their ground. Although not remarked upon at the time, it cannot have been coincidence that the major shareholder in Holbeck, local foundry owner Joseph Henry, also became the key director of the new soccer club. The following year, Leeds City were elected to the Football League's second division.[23]

In comparison to Holbeck, Leeds City drew far greater numbers of shareholders from the upper and professional classes, but significantly lower levels from manual workers, as Appendix Table A.10 demonstrates. Holbeck, a fairly typical NU side, drew its shareholders largely from the working class and the publican/shopkeeper stratum of the middle classes. Leeds City, being the only professional soccer club in the city, also had a wider catchment area than any of the local rugby clubs, which each had a limited area from which to draw spectators. We have too little information to speculate profitably about possible differences between working-class NU supporters and working-class soccer supporters but, in Leeds at least, there may have been occupational differences, soccer traditionally being strong in the iron and steel industries to the south of the city. On a more general level, it is more probably a reflection of the diversity of working-class culture at the time, for as others have pointed out, Hobsbawm's picture of the emergence of a unified working-class culture emerging in the period 1870–1914 is somewhat simplistic and, taken literally, would certainly exclude the variety of sporting affiliations which this work has sought to explore.[24] City's wealthier supporters came from similar sections of society to those which had set up rugby sides in the 1870s and 1880s – reinforcing the conclusion that the civic pride of the upper middle classes, such as Leeds City director N. R. Hepworth, of the mass production clothing company Hepworths, was now being expressed through the national forum of soccer. The soccer club could therefore be seen as representative of the entire city and able to command support from virtually all sections of the local community.

In general, it seems that crowd disturbances increased under the Northern Union. Certainly in comparison to Yorkshire rugby union in the decade prior to the split, disturbances were more frequent, greater in intensity and took place at more senior levels of the game. Appendix Table A.11 shows that, in the fifteen years following the split, the NU General Committee investigated no less than thirty incidents at the grounds of senior clubs, ordering disciplinary action in all but two cases. Of these disturbances, sixteen were directed at referees, eight at opposing teams and two at both, with four categorised as general 'rowdiness.' The variety of the offences against referees ranged from the largely innocuous, such as the referee who was snowballed by Bradford supporters, to the positively menacing, as experienced by Mr Slevin, the referee at the 1896 Rochdale Hornets versus Brighouse Rangers match:

> At the conclusion of the game the spectators rushed on to the ground and mobbed the referee, and but for the presence of some of the players and the police and private detectives he would have been very roughly handled. He was struck several times with sticks and umbrellas, and at length hustled into the dressing room. An attempt was made to get him out of the ground by a private entrance but he

was intercepted by the crowd. At last he was got into a cab, and was driven off with a detective and one of the Hornets' players. The cab was followed by the mob and stopped, and another route had to be taken. The detective fell out of the hansom, but fortunately was not seriously hurt. The referee was afterwards driven to Heywood, a distance of three miles. In anticipation of the referee returning by train a large crowd had assembled at the railway station at Rochdale, but after waiting some time they dispersed.[25]

The throwing of stones and mud was an occupational hazard for NU referees, and many of them also had to face being punched and kicked by home supporters as they left the pitch. Nor was the experience of the unfortunate Mr Slevin unique – in March 1899 a policeman had to drive a decoy cab away from Swinton's ground in order to fool a large crowd waiting to remonstrate with the match referee. Mr Farrar, refereeing at Keighley, found himself denuded of even police protection in 1903 when a certain Sergeant Dickinson took it upon himself to encourage a disgruntled crowd to exact its own justice on the official.[26] Violence directed against opposing teams usually took the form of stone throwing, either directly at the end of the match or later as they made their way from the ground. This too could range from the relatively harmless, such as the throwing of sods of earth at departing buses, to the frighteningly intimidating. Leaving the Leeds Parish Church ground in 1900 Brighouse Rangers' Charlie Denham was struck by a one and a half inch steel nut and his team mate Eli Robinson was hit between the eyes by a heavy cinder. The fact that many grounds did not possess integral dressing rooms, forcing teams to walk from the ground to the changing facilities (more often than not to be found in a nearby pub), unfortunately gave spectators an opportunity to harry their side's opponents at will. To counter this, the NU sought to encourage clubs to build dressing rooms on their grounds, in 1909 going so far as to order Keighley to do so as soon as possible following an assault on a visiting team. Although there are no instances of fighting between players and spectators at the senior level of the sport, such incidents were not unknown during reserve team games. In 1906, a fight broke out between players in the match between Sharlston and Wakefield Trinity 'A' team, whereupon a large number of spectators invaded the pitch, knocking one Trinity player unconscious and severely biting the hand of another. Similar scenes were witnessed the following year during a game between Huddersfield 'A' team and Stanningley.[27]

Mann and Pearce, supported by Vamplew, have identified five specific causes of crowd disorders in soccer: frustration, when the crowd perceives a grievance related to access to the game or the way in which it was played or refereed; outlawry, when anti-social or criminal elements are violent to property or rival supporters; remonstration, when disorder results from political causes; confrontation, due to ethnic, religious or nationalist differences; and emotional expression, where disturbances are caused by the emotional intensity of victory or defeat.[28] Most NU crowd disturbances in the above list are directly attributable to frustration or emotion following a home side's loss, which was then directed against the referee, the opposing team or both. Whether one can distinguish precisely between the frustrational and expressive categories of disorder is largely a matter of semantics. What is noticeable is the almost complete absence of attacks on rival supporters or simple acts of criminality. Unlike the pre-1895 period, I have been unable to locate a single assault on a group of opposing supporters in the first fifteen years of the NU. This could not be through lack of opportunity: large numbers of supporters regularly travelled to their team's away games, especially for cup ties and Christmas and Easter 'Derby' games between local sides. For example, at the 1905 Challenge Cup final between Warrington and Hull KR, ten thousand people had travelled from Hull and another five thousand from Warrington.[29] Similarly, the only recorded instance of criminal damage taking place other than in the immediate aftermath of a game took place in 1905. Leeds supporters travelling back by train from a game at Hull KR broke windows, straps and communication cords, and somehow managed to uncouple half of the carriages during a stop at Selby. Nevertheless, the local police made no arrests.[30]

The NU sought to curb crowd disorders through the closure of grounds and the fining of clubs. When they felt an offence warranted it, they would also encourage a club to take out prosecutions against spectators identified as causing trouble. As one might expect from a body keen to enhance its respectability, it paid great attention to attempts to stamp out bad language at grounds. In January 1897 the General Committee circularised all clubs with instructions to eject spectators who were being rowdy or using bad language.[31] In 1900, Mr Oakland, who was refereeing a game at Leeds Parish Church (by now a by-word for the most disorderly of spectators, much to the chagrin of the institution whose name it bore), stopped play in the second half and asked the police to remove from the ground a man 'using filthy and abusive language.'[32] When a club was ordered to post notices at its ground or in its town, they invariably warned spectators to mind their language. As part of this desire to be seen as respectable, assaults on referees by spectators were treated far more harshly than similar attacks on players. For the former, as can be seen from the table, the usual punishment was the closure of a club's ground for a specified period, whereas for the latter, a fine or an order to post warning notices was more likely to be handed down. Despite their best efforts however, the rate at which crowd disorders were investigated by the General Committee stayed constant throughout the first fifteen years of the sport.

Why was there such an increase in crowd disorder? Other than pre-season training matches, all NU games were competitive, being played either for league points or knock-out cup advancement. This contrasted sharply with games under the rugby union regime, where until 1892 at least the majority of games were 'friendlies', and this competitiveness may well have contributed to higher levels of tension and volatility among spectators, as mistakes by referees or advantages taken by opponents could result in the loss of important matches, but this is only a partial reason, and does not explain why disorder was directed primarily at referees, less so at opposing players and rarely at rival supporters. A broader explanation may be that the referee was seen as a symbol of authority and that more generalised feelings of frustration were being vented on him.[33] The NU's claims to represent the interests of working-class players must also have had a resonance among supporters, increasing their self-confidence about their ability to influence the game – which was, in fact, no greater than it was before 1895. This contradiction between perception and reality was most readily expressed through anger towards the referee. The crowd's distrust of authority can also be seen in the alacrity with which supporters backed their clubs when the latter were faced with sanctions from the NU's ruling bodies. After being fined £60 and £50 respectively for breaches of the professional rules, both Batley and Hull KR appealed to their supporters to raise the money through public appeals. In contrast to other appeals for monetary support from clubs in times of financial difficulties, which rarely met their targets, both clubs found their appeals oversubscribed, with Hull KR supporters raising over £30 in just two days.[34] The common view of the NU as a working-class, democratic sport would also explain the lack of violence between rival supporters, who perhaps felt a greater affinity with each other because of the sport's ideological under-pinnings, as well as its emerging status as a minority taste. Furthermore, as we shall see when discussing the changing pattern of violence in the game, working-class conceptions of masculinity often involved a view of 'fairness' which was based on openness and honesty among themselves, coupled with indifference or hostility to those in authority. Thus the culture of the game became infused with the attitudes of its working class-players and spectators, regardless of the craving for respectability of its administrators.

207

'A GAME WITHOUT MONOTONY'

The transformation of the Northern Union game from a professionalised version of rugby union into a separate and distinct sport with its own rules and playing style was a long process. The foundations for the change had been laid in the early 1890s when northern rugby clubs debated calls for a move to thirteen-a-side and consequently the 1895 split was accompanied by expectations of radical rule changes to the game. Within two weeks of its birth, the NU engaged in an in-depth discussion about the future direction of the game as the Halifax and Leeds committees proposed moving to thirteen-a-side, with Leeds also calling for the abolition of the line-out and the replacement of the oval ball with a soccer-style round ball. The rationale, explained Leeds committee member Harry Sewell, was that 'we want to do away with that scrummaging, pushing and thrusting game, which is not football, and that is why I propose to abolish the line-out and reduce the number of forwards to six. The football public does not pay to see a lot of scrummaging ...'[35]

Initially, the thirteen-a-side proposal was greeted with almost unanimous support, including from Yorkshire rugby union loyalists Mark Newsome and Barron Kilner, the latter claiming that former RFU president William Cail had also supported such a move in the past. The abolition of the line-out received a more mixed response, especially from the players. Dicky Lockwood wanted it replaced by a soccer-style throw-in, but many others worried that without line-outs the game would become too fast and, as Liversedge captain Ben Sharpe put it, would mean that 'the great and almost only qualification required to make an effective player would be speed.' The introduction of the round ball was opposed by almost all because of the difficulty in passing or drop-kicking it. The only advantage to the round ball was that it was easier to dribble, a skill which was then highly prized by forwards, who would attempt to break away from a scrum with the ball at their feet and dribble towards the opposition's line, gaining such momentum that only an extremely brave or foolhardy opponent would dare to recover the ball with his hands. The round ball proposal was therefore somewhat at odds with the general feeling that more should be done to give the backs greater scope, a view which was confirmed at the two experimental matches sanctioned by the NU in October and November 1895. Although they suffered due to the players' unfamiliarity with the new rules, both matches tended to give support to the thirteen-a-side proposal and underline the possibilities for back play opened up by the abolition of the line-out, as one observer pointed out: 'The line-out must be sacrificed, not merely because it is as a rule an unattractive incident succeeded by a scrimmage, but also because it is a piece of play which is undesirable in a scientific and sportsmanlike sense.'[36]

Despite the groundswell of support for change, the NU's special general meeting in December 1895 voted decisively against any major alterations to the rules. Anticipating the future of the game by eleven years, Halifax's Joe Nicholl proposed that: 'The Rugby game of football as played by the Northern Rugby Football Union should be played by thirteen players on each side, and to consist of six forwards, two half backs, four three-quarters and one full back,' only to see his motion lost by eighteen votes to nine. In his speech, Nicholl made much of the financial savings which the reduction in players would bring but, given the self-confidence of the new organisation and its desire not to appear radical, even this appeal to monetary self-interest failed. Indeed, the Hunslet representative spoke against the motion because he felt that it would 'make a difficulty with the players,' presumably a reference to players' fears that the game would become too fast.[37] The one rule change to which the meeting agreed was the introduction of 'the half back rule', which forced scrum-halves to stay behind their forwards until after the ball came out of the scrum, in order to stop the constant obstruction by the scrum-halves which was a feature of rugby union scrums.

With hindsight, it is clear that the NU's failure to grasp the nettle cost them dearly over the coming years. At the end of the first season, concern was expressed at the lack of tries scored by clubs, no side averaging more than nine points per game, and the following year saw the reduction in value of all goals to two points, regardless of how they were scored. This placed the emphasis firmly on the scoring of tries, which brought three points, and, unlike in the rugby union game, were now more valuable than any form of goal. Nevertheless, the problems caused by the domination of the game by forward play continued to haunt the sport. At the same time as the value of goals was reduced, the line-out was abolished and replaced by a 'punt-out' from touch, whereby a ball going over the touch line would be kicked back into play. Although this was felt to open up greater possibilities for attractive play, it more often than not produced speculative high kicks into opposition territory, increasing the possibilities of illegal charging and rough play, which, because of the difficulty in gathering such a ball, resulted in either a scrum or a penalty – exactly the same criticism made of the line-out.[38] Just two years after its introduction, the NU general meeting discussed replacing the punt-out with a scrum, a proposal which was finally introduced in 1902. While the replacement of the punt-out by the scrum removed the scrappy play which the former had brought, it also drastically increased the amount of scrummaging in the game, a problem which had been exacerbated even further by an 1899 rule change, which decreed that, if a tackled player could not release the ball, a scrum had to be formed. The combination of these rules led to matches like Hunslet's 1902 encounter with Halifax, in which there were 110 scrums.[39] It was even claimed that the excessive amount of scrummaging in the game was turning young players towards soccer.[40] Indeed, the same criticisms of the game were being made as had been made of rugby union in the 1890s, one spectator claiming of the 1905 Challenge Cup semi-finals and final:

> [They] were between clubs which are supposed to play the most attractive style of football and yet they were simply one succession of scrummages from beginning to end, with very few redeeming features to break the monotony. If it had not been that the results of these matches were important I can scarcely imagine people remaining to see the finish ... Northern Union football is being completely ruined by the almost incessant scrummaging, which under present rules not only takes place, but is to a large extent unavoidable.[41]

Although they do not appear to have been aware of it, the NU was wrestling with the same problem as had been faced by American football after it had discarded rugby union rules in the 1870s – how to get the ball back into action after play had broken down. In the US the solution had been found in the invention of the 'snap' at the line of scrimmage, itself a sort of ersatz scrum, but NU thinking was at that time based on traditional rugby union beliefs, which saw the struggle for possession of the ball as being of equal importance to the use of the ball once possession had been gained.[42] Many in the NU therefore thought that the way to decrease the number of scrums was simply to reduce the number of forwards on the field, which would allow backs more room to use the ball. In December 1900, Halifax and Oldham played an experimental twelve-a-side game and, gradually, twelve-a-side became the norm for schools and workshop competitions. In 1901 a twelve-a-side England versus Wales match was played as a testimonial for Broughton Rangers' Evan James and in June 1903 the NU General Committee voted in favour of teams of twelve, made up of six forwards, two half backs, three three-quarters and a full back. 'The essence of our existence is a game without monotony,' said Hull chairman C. E. Simpson in support of the changes.[43] At that year's annual general meeting, Widnes's J. H. Smith moved the motion for change, noting that forwards had become scrummaging machines and that defences were so well organised that 'it was almost impossible to break through,' ending with the observation that 'a reduction in players was imperative as long as they wished to hold their own with the association code.'[44] Despite a majority of fifty-four votes to twenty-four, the motion failed by just five votes to gain the requisite three-quarters majority to enter the rule book. Even so, it was agreed to allow county and junior league games to play twelve-a-side and by the beginning of the 1904–5 season, virtually every NU competition except the Northern Rugby League and the Yorkshire Senior Competition were played under twelve-a-side rules.[45]

The decision not radically to change the playing of the game left the NU in limbo: it was neither satisfied with what it had nor prepared to initiate radical change. Into this vacuum came suggestions that the NU should revert to rugby union rules. This had been reflected in Barrow and Hull's 1905 desultory call to open discussions with the RFU but was pursued in earnest by Bradford in 1906 when they proposed a complete return to RFU rules, with the sole exception of the NU's half back rule. Largely motivated by the club's disenchantment with the NU, it was also partly inspired by the impact of that season's historic rugby union tour of the British Isles by the New Zealand All Blacks, who, claimed Bradford's Fred Lister, had demonstrated 'what fine football could be produced with fifteen-a-side'.[46] When it convened in June 1906 the AGM of the NU was therefore confronted with four different motions to determine its future direction: Bradford's embrace of RFU rules, Whitehaven Recreation's call for twelve-a-side, Warrington and Leigh's advocacy of thirteen-a-side and St Helens' previously unheard of proposal for fourteen-a-side. Indicatively, no-one called for a continuation of the *status quo*. After a decade of indecision, thirteen-a-side was adopted by forty-three votes to eighteen with very little controversy. In moving the motion Harry Ashton of Warrington stated that the change would introduce a better, faster game and 'in addition, it would mean a saving of fully £100 a year to many clubs.'[47]

In order to solve the problem of endless scrummaging, the meeting also voted to introduce a new rule for playing the ball after a tackle. Now, instead of a scrum being formed, the tackled player was allowed to get to his feet, put the ball down in front of him and play it with his foot, usually to a team mate standing behind him. Although this was seen as a reversion to an old rugby union rule, whereby the tackled player had to use his feet when releasing the ball while still on the ground, it actually marked a revolution in the game as profound as the switch to thirteen-a-side.[48] As with American football, the NU had accepted that the struggle for possession of the ball was secondary to the use of the ball in open play. The new 'play the ball' rule meant that the skills of scrummaging, although still important, were now subordinated to those of passing and running with the ball. In 1908, as if in afterthought, the break with the past was formalised when Law 1 was changed from that of rugby union, amending 'the object of the game shall be to kick the ball over the crossbar and between the posts' to 'the object of the game shall be to cross an opponents goal-line to score tries and kick the ball over the crossbar and between the posts.'[49] The adoption of the thirteen-a-side and play the ball rules, combined with the earlier elevation of tries above goals, marked a decisive rupture with the old rugby game and created the distinct and separate sport of Northern Union football. The impact of this revolution became obvious as soon as the 1906–7 season began – over 800 points were scored in the first two weeks, far and away an NU record, and an *Athletic News* headline was able to proclaim: 'The New Rules Completely Vindicated.'[50]

The fundamental nature of the change which had taken place was widely recognised, not least by the 1906 South African rugby union tourists, whose officials gracelessly took the opportunity of the post-match meal after their game against Yorkshire at Headingley to attack the sport of their hosts, calling it 'the revised version of Rugby football – which, it cannot be too often insisted upon, is not Rugby football at all.' *The Times* claimed that Northern Union football was 'an incoherent parody of rugby football.'[51] In this, they echoed earlier critics of the NU's rule innovations, such as Arthur Budd and Frank Mitchell who had seen such changes as departures from the traditional playing philosophy of rugby. Budd had denounced the NU's diminution of the value of goals in 1897, reasoning that 'the very fact that try-getters are plentiful while goal-droppers are scarce shows that the latter art is very much more difficult of acquirement. Now this being so, why, I should like to ask, ought the more skilful piece of play to be depreciated, while a premium is placed on mere speed of foot?'[52] Frank Mitchell felt that line-outs had been discarded simply because Northern working-class players weren't up to them: 'The Northern players are so bad out of touch that the law was infringed in every instance and scrummages were constantly necessary,' and went on to dismiss the NU's other changes by saying that 'the play of the working classes has not, on the whole, gained one whit in the finer points which distinguish the intelligent player from him who relies on his stamina and physique.'[53]

Other rugby union supporters were not so condemnatory: the Reverend E. H. Dykes, the founder of Leeds Parish Church FC and committed advocate of muscular Christian amateurism, expressed his admiration of the NU style of rugby; of the four reasons given by Elland rugby union club as to why they were switching codes the first was that the new 'game was more open and pleasant to watch.' In 1909, the secretary and committee of the Coventry rugby union club, recently suspended by the RFU amidst allegations of professionalism, saw their first Northern Union game and were amazed: 'The swiftness of the play quite carried them away; nothing like it had ever before been seen ... it was in fact, regarded as a more scientific game than is seen under ordinary rugby rules, except on rare occasions.'[54] A similarly effusive reaction was also experienced by a reporter on the London *Daily Graphic*, who travelled 'up North' to watch the 1910 Challenge Cup final:

> The spirit of Rugby is not dead, nor does it sleep. The true spirit of Rugby is as alive as ever in England, and the ancient glamour of a glorious old sport has not yet departed from the hearts of the people. A journey to Huddersfield on Saturday, where Hull and Leeds fought out a gallant struggle for the much coveted honour of the Northern Union Cup, would have been sufficient to convince any reasonable person of this fact ... It was a thrilling and delightful spectacle.[55]

For the NU leadership, the 1906 rule changes were also recognised as being a watershed and, once initial scepticism had died down, celebrated their innovation. 'The game as now played,' said Hunslet's T. V. Harrison, 'was the best that had ever been played by either the Northern Union or the Rugby Union.' Leeds vice-president J. W. Wood echoed this, declaring that 'the rules of the Northern Union were the best ever seen in the rugby game', while NU President J. B. Cooke cast aside modesty and congratulated 'the men who had been connected with the NU. Through many bitter criticisms, they had brought forward the finest game of Rugby football that had ever been conceived.'[56]

The new game was certainly faster, more open and greatly exciting, but had it become 'more dangerous and less enjoyable to the players' in order to be 'brisker and more enjoyable to the man behind the ropes,' as was claimed by its amateur critics?[57] The little evidence we have from players would suggest not. The concerns of many players in 1895 that the game would become too fast seem to have disappeared by the 1906 reduction in team size, although the introduction of the punt-out in 1898 led to some disquiet about the amount of off-the-ball charging which accompanied it.[58] But it seems that most players welcomed the opportunities to run with the ball in their hands which had been opened up by the NU rule changes: Albert Goldthorpe, Yorkshire county representative at both games felt that 'the alteration of the rules has made accidents to players less liable, especially so when the referee rules with a stern hand; and, so far as I am concerned, I can assure you that I prefer the Northern Union in every way to the fast declining old Yorkshire rugby union.'[59] Hull captain C. C. Lempriere, one of the few public-school educated players to welcome the formation of the NU, compared the new game with the developments in soccer: 'In four years [the Northern Union] has made rapid strides; she is becoming scientific and skilful too.'[60]

Certainly deaths in Northern Union matches were less frequent than in rugby union games in Yorkshire before the split. As can be seen from Appendix Table A.12, of the twelve deaths recorded between 1895 and 1910, only three took place at senior level, the remainder occurring in junior leagues. Two of those deaths, of Green and Hanson, were not directly attributable to the playing of the game: Green died of lockjaw which set in after he had been injured in a match and the unfortunate Hanson became possibly the only man ever to die of drowning during a football match when he tried to rescue the ball from a nearby canal and fell in. The most famous death was that of Cumberland county full back John Richardson, who died playing against Yorkshire at Headingley. According to match reports, the fatal injuries were sustained when Richardson ran into one of his own players when trying to field a high ball. Discounting these latter three incidents, the aggregate nine deaths in fifteen years represents a significant decrease from the period of rugby union rules examined in Chapter Four.

What of non-fatal injuries and players subjected to disciplinary measures because of rough play? As with the rugby union period, there is no way of discovering the number or extent of injuries to players. Harry Waller certainly tried to make capital out of the lack of rough play in the NU compared to Yorkshire rugby union. Speaking after the first Challenge Cup final in 1897, he claimed that in 900 games that season, the NU had only 45 players (thirty in Yorkshire and fifteen in Lancashire) reported by referees for rough play, whereas the YRU had 150 players reported for roughness during the same season. 'Not bad for uneducated working man players,' he was moved to say sarcastically.[61] The following season he presented a more detailed breakdown of players reported by referees in the NU version of the Yorkshire Senior Competition. In 480 games thirty-four players had been reported, of which seven were acquitted, twelve found guilty of rough play and fifteen of 'foul charging', most of which were probably committed during the rushes to catch the ball following a punt-out.[62] However, figures from 1903–4, the first season for which reliable Northern Union General Committee minutes can be found relating to disciplinary offences, paint a less rosy picture. In 647 senior games played, 111 players were reported by referees for a variety of offences, the majority of which, eighty-seven, were for kicking, striking, fighting or wrestling with an opponent. Ten were for acts of rough play, six were for arguing or insulting the referee and four were for tripping. Foul charging and retaliation accounted for the remaining four offences.

Compared with broadly equivalent figures for Yorkshire rugby union in the 1890–91 season (see Chapter Four), these figures indicate a steep decline in incidences of rough play and dissension from referee's decisions. Whereas in the 1890–91 season these offences constituted almost sixty-five per cent of the total reported, by 1904 they had plummeted to just over sixteen per cent. In contrast, individual acts of violence between players had increased dramatically. Why this should be so is unclear. It may be the case that definitions of offences altered over time and that what was once rough play was now defined as, for example, wrestling, but it is unlikely that such a change would have led to such a dramatic shift. More likely, the growth of individual violence was perhaps linked to the increased effectiveness of tackling and defensive tactics of NU teams, giving more scope for individual clashes. The rise may also have been due to the 'proletarianisation' of the sport and the emergence of working-class conceptions of masculinity within it. Certainly, within rugby league up to the 1970s, it was common for games to start with a 'softening up period' during which the opposing forwards would seek physically to intimidate their opposite numbers through fair and, more often than not, foul means. One to one confrontations to establish physical domination in a particular position were expected. Striking an opponent, although illegal, was seen as semi-legitimate because it was done in the open and no subterfuge was involved, yet tripping was viewed as being beyond the pale because of the danger to a man running with the ball. Punching was not necessarily an offence for which the culprit would be sent off, tripping inevitably resulted in dismissal. The rise in individual violence in 1903–4, coupled with the disproportionately small percentage of tripping offences, may well indicate that traditional rugby league conceptions of masculinity and violence held sway less than a decade after the birth of the game.[63] The revolution in rugby had taken place not only in the NU's rule book, but also in its culture.

What does this tell us about the application of Norbert Elias's theory of the 'civilising process' to the development of rugby?[64] Leaving aside the problem of defining 'civilised' modes of behaviour and the virtual impossibility of quantifying incidents of injury and violence – not to mention the fact that, to the historian, the thesis appears to suggest a 'Whig interpretation of sports history' in which sports gradually evolve to a plateau of peaceful competition – the evidence hardly seems to fit neatly into the theory. While deaths decreased in the NU, individual violence between players increased, and, as referees of the time could testify, crowd behaviour also appeared to become less 'civilised.' Yet, paradoxically, the players believed that the game was less dangerous than under rugby union rules. Individual violence between players was not viewed as 'uncivilised' by the NU's supporters; the fact that it was controlled, in the open and confined to the playing arena demonstrated that it was merely part of a game. In fact, it was the rucking and mauling of rugby union, with its opportunities for stamping anonymously on one's opponents – acts which were anathema in the league game – which came to be seen as gratuitously violent by rugby league people. The concept of the 'civilising process' also ignores changes in modes of play and the impact of medical improvements in treating injuries and their effects. Rather than being part of an historic process, violence within rugby, as we have constantly seen throughout this work, was to a large degree defined by the cultural context of those who were doing the defining.

1907: THE WORLD TURNS UPSIDE DOWN

If the rule changes of 1906 had set the Northern Union on a new course, the events of 1907 saw it discover a new continent, both literally and metaphorically. Ironically, much of the impulse for the expansion of the sport into the southern hemisphere lay with the 1905 New Zealand rugby union tour of the British Isles. The All Blacks lost just one game, conceded only 39 points and racked up 830, vanquishing all the English, Scottish and Irish teams by huge margins. By laying waste the cream of rugby union in the mother country, they caused much soul searching among those who saw rugby as a measure of British national fitness – although the fact that the drubbings were at the hands of colonial subjects steeped in British imperial ideology helped to sweeten the pill.[65] In the southern hemisphere, the tour helped to cement the national identity of white, or *pakeha*, New Zealand, seemingly confirming the youthful vigour and optimism of the colony. Indeed, seeing it as an opportunity to boost the status of their nation, the New Zealand government had invested heavily in the tour, both in political and financial terms: prime minister Richard Seddon went out of his way to associate himself with the team and the touring party itself was subsidised by the state to the tune of £1,963.[66] The return of the side was greeted with a patriotic fervour normally associated with the return of a conquering army and the All Blacks became synonymous with the manly spirit of the farthest reaches of the British Empire.

Beneath the surface however, the knots of social cohesion by which antipodean rugby was bound were fraying. Even without the government subsidy, the tour was an incredible financial success, recording a profit of £9,962. Yet the players, lauded as national heroes and pioneers of a new era in rugby union, received only three shillings per day expenses. An 'Original All Black', writing in 1908, highlighted the dissatisfaction abroad:

> That they, the All Blacks, could scarcely raise £10 in the whole team on their return passage home to New Zealand is well known, and the fact made a great impression in colonial circles. This brought the question before the colonial public and it was generally admitted that the team were not well treated. Several were men of means, and could well afford the loss of time, but the majority were working men.'[67]

Not only that, but the levels of disquiet among the players were matched by the tour's confirmation that rugby could be a profitable business. The New Zealanders had also witnessed at first hand that the Northern Union not only paid players but attracted much larger crowds than the vast majority of rugby union clubs in Britain. They had seen that there was an alternative way for rugby.

Similar rumblings of discontent were also being heard in Australia, where a more ethnically diverse and urbanised working class had come to dominate the playing and watching of rugby in a way similar to that in northern England. By the early years of the new century it was an open secret that leading players were being paid: for example, in 1904 Harry Hamill of the Newtown club was paid fifteen shillings by the New South Wales Rugby Union (NSWRU) to play against the England touring side after he told them that he couldn't afford to take time off work.[68] In the same year, there had been widespread dissatisfaction in Sydney over the treatment of Alec Burdon, who had broken a shoulder playing against England but had received no insurance or compensation payments from the NSWRU, causing him significant financial hardship. Given the lower levels of social deference and the ostensibly more democratic norms of Australian society (at least for whites), it was clear that the imposition of the amateur ethos could not last. In February 1906, the NSWRU called on the RFU to create an Imperial Board to run the game internationally, and many hoped that this would be the impulse for change in the game. Blair Swannell, a tourist to Australia with the 1899 and 1904 English sides and now living in Sydney, warned that there was a danger that 'the players will take the matter into their own hands, and go from one extreme to another, electing to office officials pledged to what every lover of Rugby football should strive to prevent – professionalism.'[69]

Although there is no hard evidence, it appears that George Smith, the All Black winger, stopped off in Sydney in the Spring of 1906 on his way back home from the tour and discussed the situation in antipodean rugby and the Northern Union with his Australian rugby contacts.[70] Certainly in New Zealand, the return of the tourists must have been quickly followed by discussions about the Northern Union, because just twelve months later, in March 1907, Canterbury postal clerk Albert Baskerville blew apart the national euphoria by announcing that a professional All Black side would tour England to play Northern Union clubs. No mean player himself, Baskerville was known in New Zealand rugby for his book 'Modern Rugby Football.' Rugby league folklore has him picking up a stray copy of the *Athletic News* and being inspired by reports of the new union's success, but it seems that he was the public face of a significant movement of New Zealand players dissatisfied with their position and seeking to make the most of their football talents.

The response in English and New Zealand rugby circles to Baskerville's announcement could not have been greater if the Kaiser had declared himself the rightful claimant to the British crown. The New Zealand Rugby Union (NZRU) banned Baskerville from all rugby grounds in New Zealand and demanded that players nominated for that year's North Island versus South Island game sign a declaration stating that they were amateurs and had not been approached to tour. Those who actually played in the match had to affirm a further five clauses saying that they would help the rugby union authorities to identify tourists and stop the tour taking place. The Anglican Bishop of Auckland denounced the tour from the pulpit and the New Zealand Athletic Association called on the country's parliament to outlaw professional sport. In England, C. Wray Palliser, the Agent-General of New Zealand in the UK, assured the RFU that any touring player would be banned from the sport, and ludicrously called the tour 'some kind of sensation to save the Northern Union' which he portrayed as under threat from 'the renewal of the spirit of real Rugby.' 'It is a phantom side,' he stated with a conviction borne of ignorance and hope. For its part, the RFU announced that if there was the slightest hint of support for the tourists from the NZRU, all relations would be broken.[71]

Despite this barrage of opposition, Baskerville gained significant support from New Zealand players. Duncan MacGregor, a railway worker who had become a national hero by scoring four tries against England in the 1905 international, was one of the first players to refuse to sign the authorities' ultimatum. Twelve Auckland representative players refused to sign and Baskerville claimed to have received requests to join the tour from 160 players, including eighteen of the 1905 tourists.[72] Even the *New Zealand Post* was moved to concede that 'the promoter of the scheme in this colony has met with even more success than he anticipated.'[73] Of the twenty-eight strong party, nine were All Blacks, including four of the 1905 side, and eleven other players had gained representative honours. H. R. 'Bumper' Wright, the captain of the side – the registered title of which was 'The New Zealand All Black Rugby Football Team' – was confident that his team had been picked on merit and that it was 'thoroughly representative and consists of the cream of New Zealand football.'[74]

Meanwhile in Australia, an even greater cataclysm was cleaving rugby union. On 8 August 1907, the New South Wales Rugby Football League was founded by legendary Australian test cricketer Victor Trumper, entrepreneur James Giltinan and Labour Party politician Harry Hoyle. Combining, as the New Zealanders had, the dissatisfaction of players over their poor treatment by the authorities and the opportunity to cash in on the commercial possibilities of professional rugby, the new organisation quickly announced a three-match test series against the professional All Blacks and the support of over a hundred and thirty prominent NSW players, including Dally Messenger, the most famous rugby player in Australia. Although played under rugby union rules, because the Northern Union rule books failed to arrive in time, the test series proved to be a financial success and provided sufficient impetus for Sydney's leading club sides to abandon rugby union for the new league at the start of the following season.[75]

Slightly closer to home, fractures had also begun to appear in the Welsh Rugby Union (WRU). Ever since the compromise over the Arthur Gould case, the tension between Welsh rugby's nominally amateur status and its system of covert payments had led the WRU sporadically to make examples of clubs and, more usually, players who had transgressed the amateur code too openly. Yet unlike in the antipodes, players could express their dissatisfaction simply by going north to join an NU club, so the impulse for the formation of NU clubs in Wales came primarily from the more entrepreneurially-minded among Welsh club officials. The announcement of the professional All Black tour in March 1907 seems to have been crucial in stimulating the movement, reviving memories of the commercial success of the 1905 tour, and in May 1907 E. H. Rees, a former secretary of Aberdare RUFC, placed an advertisement in the *South Wales Daily News* asking for players to join a new NU club at Aberdare. Although Rees was implicated in a WRU inquiry into professionalism, his confident declaration that 'the days of sham-amateurism are over' clearly touched a chord and rumours of the formation of other Welsh NU teams circulated throughout the summer.[76] As it was, Aberdare could not secure a ground in time for the start of the season but Ebbw Vale and Merthyr Tydfil made their way into the Northern Rugby League, to be joined the following season by Aberdare, Barry, Mid-Rhondda and Treherbert.

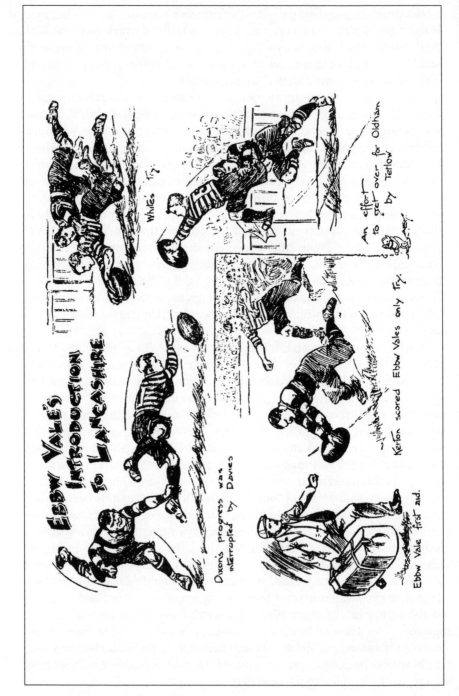

EBBW VALE'S INTRODUCTION TO LANCASHIRE.

Dixon's progress was interrupted by Davies

Wales try.

An effort to get over for Oldham by Tetlow

Kerton scored Ebbw Vales only try.

Ebbw Vale first aid.

One can only imagine the reaction of the marginalised and embattled Northern Union to the events which were unfolding around the world. Much to their surprise, they now found themselves at the head of a worldwide rugby revolution. When Baskerville's proposal arrived, the NU General Committee cautiously polled clubs to see if they accepted his tour terms of £3,000 or seventy per cent of the gate receipts, whichever was higher. Of course, the enthusiasm was boundless, so much so that in May the General Committee felt compelled to warn clubs against signing any of the players while the tour was in progress.[77] When the All Blacks finally arrived in Leeds at 8pm on October 1, their reception was overwhelming. In scenes reminiscent of victorious cup winners returning home, thousands of people turned out to greet them at the city's Midland Station:

> When the players appeared the crowd burst into tremendous cheering, which continued until the men had got into their charabanc. Then Wright, the New Zealand captain, called for 'three cheers for the people of Leeds', which were followed by the stirring Maori war-cry and further cheering. The players were escorted to the Grand Central Hotel by the Hunslet charabanc and the Northern Union officials in carriages, together with the still cheering crowd. The crush was so dense in Boar Lane and Briggate as to cause the stoppage of traffic.[78]

As the scale of the reception indicated, the tour was about much more than a team of overseas rugby players: the crowd was celebrating a triumph over the forces of the establishment. After months of disparagement and denunciations from the press, the RFU and New Zealand government officials, the tourists had arrived. The Northern Union teams, for years semi-pariahs in their own nation, had turned the tables on its enemies and scored a stunning victory.

The New Zealanders more than fulfilled the hopes of their hosts. Playing a sport which they had never before seen, let alone played, they were unbeaten in their first eight matches, including a famous victory over Broughton in front of 24,000, eventually losing at Wigan before an even bigger crowd of 30,000. They won the test series against the Northern Union but lost against both Wales and England. Despite dips in performance owing to the sheer length of their tour – it lasted five months and comprised thirty-four games – well over 300,000 people watched their matches, including 14,000 at the second test match at Chelsea's soccer ground in London.[79] When they finally began their journey back to New Zealand in February 1908, gate receipts in Britain totalled £12,625 and the tourists had a profit of £5,641 to distribute among themselves.[80]

The 1907 New Zealand tourists conquer Huddersfield. Note that they are called All Blacks (from *Athletic News*, 14 October 1907).

How good were the professional All Blacks? Unfortunately, it is impossible to compare them with their 1905 forerunners, not least because the standard of opposition facing the 1907 side was far greater than anything the 1905 side encountered outside Wales. They also found it difficult to adjust to NU rules, as the *Yorkshire Post* commented during the first month of the tour: 'It is the fashion to say that the difference between the Northern Union rules and the RFU rules is so slight that it can be easily overcome, but this is very far from being the case.'[81] Initially, the tourists tried to use classical New Zealand wing forward play, only to find it useless against the wily NU forwards, and their attempts to play two five-eighths and three three-quarters suffered a similar fate. Bumper Wright, one of the most experienced of the tourists, was amazed at the defensive and scrummaging qualities of NU players, adding that 'for pace and cleverness, the professionals were much superior to the amateurs; in fact, as regards bustling play and determined methods there was no comparison between the two.'[82] Wright's comments were echoed by Fred Bonsor, the former Bradford half back, a stalwart of Yorkshire rugby union and no friend of the NU: unlike the 1905 side, the professional All Blacks were 'meeting their equals at all parts of the game, and instead of facing untrained and half-hearted amateurs, they have to tackle the cream of northern athletes ... men of great physique, speed and stamina, full of resource, and up to every move on the football board.'[83]

As if to underline the fact that the NU was now an international force, the following season saw the first visit of an Australian touring side, inevitably nicknamed 'the Kangaroos' after they arrived at Tilbury docks with a silver grey kangaroo in tow. The tour was a victim of its own ambition – lasting six months and taking in forty-five matches, the tourists lost half their matches and made a financial loss of £418.[84] James Giltinan, tour manager and promoter, found himself declared bankrupt when he returned home. To some extent circumstances got the better of them as their tour coincided with one of the worst industrial slumps to hit the north of England in a generation, although their insistence on charging a minimum one shilling admission to all games, double the normal price, did them no favours in communities wracked by sudden unemployment. Yet even the hostile *Yorkshire Post* was sympathetic to their plight: 'No-one will deny that they are the unluckiest football team who have yet visited the British Isles. One match after another has been ruined by adverse weather. Rain, frost and fog have all united to make the financial success of their tour more questionable.' At just over six thousand spectators per match, attendances averaged only two-thirds of those for the New Zealand tour, although twenty-two thousand attended the second test match, held with expansionary zeal at Newcastle.[85] Nevertheless, by proving that the All Black tour was not a flash in the pan, the Australian tour helped to cement the NU's new found international credibility.

The defining moment for the Northern Union was 1907. The arrival of the All Blacks, the creation of the NSW Rugby League in Australia and the breakthrough in Wales at last confirmed for the NU and its supporters the correctness of the course they had taken. Not only had the new rebels accepted the professionalism and playing rules of the NU, they had also accepted its ideological underpinning of equal rights for working-class players. At the welcoming dinner for the All Blacks, their spokesman, Jim Gleeson, denounced the 'pseudo-amateurs, who received their bonuses and obtained what they called in New Zealand "billets"' and said that the tourists 'by coming into the limelight as professionals, were doing what any honest man should do.'[86] Indeed, the side itself was organised as a players' co-operative with each player contributing between £50 and £200 towards the cost of the tour and receiving an equal share of the profits, regardless of how many matches they played in. In Australia, the links between the new game and the rights of the working-class player were even more explicit: current and future Labor Party politicians were prominent as leaders of the new rugby league (as the Australians already called the sport) from the start. Harry Hoyle even likened the movement to the campaign for the eight-hour day.[87] In Wales, the *Western Mail* noted that 'to the colliers especially, the Northern Union code, with its faster play, undoubtedly appeals', whilst another Welsh newspaper, writing about Mid-Rhondda's 1908 game against Australia commented approvingly that 'the Mid-Rhondda team consists of miners and workmen engaged in the collieries. Democracy is more strongly represented among the Kangaroos than among any previous touring teams. The total absence of the "swank" … makes them appear a cut above the ordinary.'[88]

In Australia, the social strictures of amateurism were largely incompatible with the organisation of daily life, as Harry Hoyle argued in 1907: 'The set of conditions controlling the football union are not suitable to the democracy and social conditions of the Australian people.' The ideology of the NU therefore fitted well with Australian society's ostensibly more egalitarian and urbanised culture and helped the new sport grow rapidly,[89] but in New Zealand and Wales, the success of the 1905 All Blacks and the Welsh defeat of them effectively locked out the NU from their respective national cultures. In these countries, the events of 1905 so tightly integrated rugby union with national identity that at best the NU would be marginalised, as in New Zealand where it became an urban game of sections of industrial workers and of Maori and Polynesian peoples, or almost completely exorcised, as in Wales.[90] Welsh rugby union, which because of large working-class support is often compared to rugby league, also differed fundamentally from the NU in social composition. Unlike the NU, whose almost mono-class proletarian base and fringe of petty bourgeois administrators made it unique as a mass sport in Britain, support for Welsh rugby stretched right across society, as highlighted by the Welsh national side's victory over the 1935 New Zealand tourists: 'Wales ... is particularly proud of the fact that Welsh peers and Welsh labourers, with all the intervening strata of society, were united in acclaiming and cheering the Welsh team,' said the *Western Mail*, a statement of cross-class social solidarity which it would be inconceivable to apply to any activity of the NU.[91]

However, in England, the tours and the reciprocal visit by the NU to the Antipodes in 1910 were crucial in giving the sport a legitimacy it had hitherto lacked, for its matches against Australia and New Zealand meant that it could now lay claim to be a representative of the British nation. Regular international competition, and the importation of players from down under, freed the game from the geographical constraints of the north of England and allowed it to express on the international football field its distinct ideology, which was, to quote Patrick Joyce's phrase, 'the idea of the true unadorned England of the north [which] was a variant of the broader mythology of the true political nation of the excluded English.'[92] This allowed it to create its own niche in the British sporting pantheon, acknowledging its working-class base yet accepting a socially deferential position. It may have been proudly proletarian in composition but it was most definitely not oppositional: 'We have as loyal a body of sportsman in the NU as they have in the rugby union,' said Harry Ashton when attacking the lack of press coverage of the NU in comparison to that of their rivals. The sense of deference was also expressed by Joe Platt, speaking at a farewell dinner for the 1910 tourists:

> They were sending out men who represented a democratic union for the first time. There had been many teams sent out to Australia and New Zealand from this country, but they had generally been composed of men of high social standing. The Northern Union team had been chiefly selected from the artisan class. He hoped the players making the tour would do honour to the occasion.[93]

This sentiment was most vividly encapsulated by a poem written for the departing tourists, which attempted to render the public school imperative of the *Vitaï Lampada* into a form appropriate to the 'artisan class'.

> You're not of the bluest blood, boys,
> Not aristocrats, what then?
> You're something that's quite as good, boys,
> You're honest young Englishmen.
> And what does it matter the rank, boys,
> 'Tis better that you should claim
> That you are straightforward and frank, boys,
> And keen upon 'Playing the Game'.[94]

To ensure that the message was not missed, the other two verses ended with the couplets 'So ever be true to the core, lads,/To the principle "Playing the Game"' and 'We'll put it in the form of a toast lads/"The NU" and "Playing the Game".' The NU's discovery of a national role for itself also gave it the confidence to seek royal approval. Proposing a toast to the new king George V in May 1910, J. B. Cooke told his audience that he 'thoroughly believed that if [the king] saw one or two Northern Union games he would be a convert to the game,' and in April 1911 the king acceded to the NU's request that he become patron of their sport. Despite a well-known fondness for rugby union, the new patron never bothered to watch a game of NU football.[95] Like Kipling's 'Tommy', the NU may have been looked down upon, but it believed that it was just as responsible for upholding British honour whatever its social superiors might think of it. Put crudely, it saw itself as the sporting equivalent of the NCO, in contrast to the RFU's officer class.

The international dimension added by the events of 1907 was as vital to the development of the NU as the rule changes of the previous year. As well as increased influence and credibility from international matches, the NU's competitions gained a cosmopolitan flavour unknown in British sport – ten of the Australian tourists stayed behind to join English clubs, as had a handful of 1907 tourists, and they started a pattern of international movement by rugby league players which exists to this day. Indeed, two of these early imports, New Zealander Lance Todd and Australian Albert Rosenfeld, etched their mark so deeply on the game that they are still household names in rugby league circles. With regular international competition and the constant importation of overseas players into the game, the NU now had its alternative to the glamour of soccer's nationwide competitions and the national kudos of rugby union. Out of necessity and while retaining its northern insularity, the NU had become the most international of domestic sports.

NOTES

1. See, for example, Standish Meacham, *A Life Apart: The English Working Class 1890–1914*, London, 1977 and Eric Hobsbawm's 'The Making of the Working Class 1870–1914' in *Worlds of Labour*, London, 1984.
2. Ross McKibbin, *The Ideologies of Class*, Oxford, 1990, p. 166.
3. To be fair, William Hirst's departure from the NU was caused by his committing suicide in 1899 (as his father had done previously).
4. Robert Roberts, *The Classic Slum*, Manchester, 1971, p. 18.
5. J. K. Walton, *Lancashire: A Social History 1558–1939*, Manchester, 1987, p. 233.
6. David Smith and Gareth Williams, *Fields of Praise*, Cardiff, 1980, p. 124.
7. *Athletic News*, 22 Nov. 1909.
8. Quoted in Patrick Joyce, *Visions of the People*, Cambridge, 1991, p. 56.
9. There were exceptions to this: the YRU's Arthur Hartley, president of the RFU in 1913, was a Liberal while the leaders of the Leeds and Bradford clubs were predominantly Tories. Hartley's allegiances may be explained by his freemasonry links and we have already seen how Leeds and Bradford were the most reluctant of the clubs forming the NU but were forced to join by economic exigencies.
10. The correspondence between Fallas and Kilner is reprinted in *Yorkshire Post*, 4 Feb. 1897.
11. See Chris Waters, *British Socialists and the Politics of Popular Culture*, Manchester, 1990, especially Ch. 6.
12. The final chapter of Joyce's *Visions of the People* is especially relevant to the study of the development of the Northern Union and its culture. The quotes are from p. 332. Intriguingly, despite his concern for popular culture and the meanings given to it by the working class in Lancashire and Yorkshire, Joyce has almost nothing to say about rugby or soccer.
13. Joyce, ibid., p. 329.
14. *Yorkshire Post*, 17 April 1891.
15. *Yorkshire Post*, 26 Dec. 1896. *Yorkshire Chat*, 18 Nov. 1898.
16. *Athletic News*, 9 July 1906.
17. This is the number I have been able to trace but there may well have been more, as even by the end of the Edwardian period, rugby crowds were not accurately reported. A sense of perspective of comparative crowd sizes can be gained by the fact that in their first two seasons in Football League Div. 1 in 1908–9 and 1908–10, Bradford City had 23 crowds in excess of 20,000.
18. For Whitehaven, see Northern Union General Committee minutes, 4 April 1902. For Hull, see the club's annual report for 1900–1.
19. Alderman Nettleton quoted in *The Gallant Youths*, C. F. Shaw, Batley, 1899, p. 88. The James Miller quote is from *Yorkshire Post*, 18 Jan. 1897.
20. See advertisement in *Yorkshire Owl Cricket Annual* for 1896.
21. *Yorkshire Chat*, 18 Nov. 1898.
22. Figures taken from Hull FC annual reports, 1895–96 to 1909–10.
23. As with Bradford, Leeds Parish Church and Manningham, one does not have to be a conspiracy theorist to recognise powerful coincidences involved in the demise of Holbeck NU club, not least the fact that the club's 1897 lease on Elland Road specified that rugby had to be played on the ground for seven years; that is, until 1904.
24. For a relevant discussion of the diversity of working-class culture in Manchester during this period see Andrew Davies and Steven Fielding (eds), *Workers' Worlds: Cultures and Communities in Manchester and Salford 1880–1939*, Manchester,

1992. There is also evidence that, certainly during the inter-war period, some people watched both games regularly; see, for example, W. R. Mitchell, *By Gum, Life Were Sparse!*, London, 1981, p. 181.

25. *Yorkshire Post*, 15 Feb. 1896.
26. *Yorkshire Post*, 28 March 1899. NU General Committee minutes 8 and 29 Dec. 1903.
27. *Yorkshire Post*, 22 Oct. 1906 and 5 Oct. 1907.
28. See L. Mann and D. Pearce, 'Social Psychology of Sports Spectators', in D. Glencross (ed), *Psychology and Sport*, Sydney, 1979; W. Vamplew, 'Sports Crowd Disorder in Britain 1870–1914', *Journal of Sport History*, Vol. 7, No. 1, 1980; N. L. Tranter, 'The Cappielow Riot and the Composition and Behaviour of Soccer Crowds in Late Victorian Scotland', *The International Journal of the History of Sport*, Vol. 12, No. 3 Dec. 1995.
29. *Yorkshire Post*, 1 May 1905.
30. *Yorkshire Post*, 4 April 1905.
31. *Yorkshire Post*, 14 Jan. 1897.
32. *Yorkshire Post*, 3 Dec. 1900.
33. Such a view is supported by Richard Hoggart in *The Uses of Literacy*, London, 1957, p. 109.
34. *Yorkshire Post*, 24 Sept. and 3 Nov. 1898. *Athletic News*, 8 Dec. 1898 and 1 May 1900.
35. *Yorkshire Evening Post*, 13 Sept. 1895.
36. *Yorkshire Evening Post*, 16 and 17 Sept. 1895. *The Yorkshireman*, 19 Oct. 1895.
37. The report of the NU SGM can be found in *Yorkshire Post*, 10 Dec. 1895.
38. For confirmation of this, see the letter from the unnamed Northern Union player in *Yorkshire Post*, 21 Sept. 1897.
39. Hunslet president T. V. Harrison speaking at his club's 1903 AGM. *Yorkshire Post*, 16 June 1903.
40. See *Athletic News*, 23 April 1906.
41. *Yorkshire Post*, 18 May 1905.
42. The centrality of the snap at the line of scrimmage to the development of American football as a distinct sport from rugby union is attested to by Michael Oriard, *Reading Football: How the Popular Press created an American Spectacle*, Chapel Hill, 1993, p. 27.
43. *Yorkshire Post*, 30 May 1903.
44. Report of 1903 Northern Union AGM, *Yorkshire Post*, 15 July 1903.
45. The Lancashire Northern Union Combination league played twelve-a-side with five forwards and four three-quarters.
46. Report of 1906 NU AGM, *Yorkshire Post*, 13 June 1906. The NU's J. H. Smith was also an admirer of the 1905 tourists, *Athletic News*, 15 Jan. 1906.
47. Ibid.
48. For a discussion on the play-the-ball rule, see *Athletic News*, 18 June and 3 Sept. 1906.
49. 'Rules of the Game', *Northern Union Official Guide 1908–9*. The similarity with American football was noted, uniquely, by *The Times*, 3 Dec. 1907.
50. *Athletic News*, 16 Sept. 1906.
51. *Yorkshire Post*, 22 Oct. 1906. *The Times*, 3 Dec. 1907.
52. Arthur Budd, 'The Northern Union' in *Football*, London, 1897, p. 34. See also his comments in *Athletic News*, 7 March 1898.
53. Frank Mitchell, 'Forward Play' in Montague Shearman, *Football*, London, 1899, pp. 210 and 276.

54. *Athletic News*, 28 Nov. 1898. *Yorkshire Post*, 6 May 1898 and 10 Nov. 1909.
55. *Daily Graphic*, 18 April 1910.
56. *Yorkshire Post*, 24 Jan. 1907, 30 May 1908 and 6 May 1910.
57. H. Graves, 'A Philosophy of Sport' in *The Contemporary Review*, Dec. 1900. Ernest Ensor also made the same point in 'The Football Madness' in the same journal's Nov. 1898 issue.
58. See the *Yorkshire Post*, 21–27 Sept. 1897 for the punt-out debate.
59. *Yorkshire Chat*, 1 Nov. 1899.
60. *Yorkshire Chat*, 7 Oct. 1899.
61. *Yorkshire Post*, 22 April 1897.
62. *Yorkshire Post*, 2 May 1898.
63. Little work on the rugby league and masculinity has been carried out and much of the knowledge of the game's traditions is retained as oral culture. Much of the latter section of this paragraph is drawn from anecdotal experience. For a decidedly non-academic view of violence in Australian rugby league see Tony Adams, *The Hit Men*, Sydney, 1994.
64. Norbert Elias, *The Civilising Process*, Oxford, 1978. The theory is developed in the context of rugby by Eric Dunning and Kenneth Sheard in *Barbarians, Gentlemen and Players*, New York, 1979. For a critical examination of the thesis, see Daryl Adair's 'Competing or Complementary Forces? The "Civilising" Process and the Commitment to Winning in Nineteenth Century English Rugby and Association Football', *Canadian Journal of the History of Sport*, Vol. 24, No. 2, Dec. 1993
65. For the impact and wider implications of the 1905 tour see John Nauright's 'Colonial Manhood and Imperial Race Virility' in J. Nauright and T. Chandler, *Making Men*, London, 1996 and his 'Sport, Manhood and Empire' in *The International Journal of the History of Sport*, Vol. 8, No. 2 (Sept. 1991). *The Complete Rugby Footballer*, written by tour captain David Gallaher and W. J. Stead, London, 1906, gives the official New Zealand view of the tour.
66. *Yorkshire Post*, 30 June 1906.
67. 'Rugby football in the Colonies' by 'An Original All Black' in *Yorkshire Post*, 13 Nov. 1908.
68. See Ian Heads, *True Blue*, Sydney, 1992, p. 17.
69. *Australian Star*, 8 Oct. 1907
70. Ian Heads provides convincing circumstantial evidence of Smith's visit.
71. For the response to Baskerville see *Athletic News*, 14 Sept. 1907, *Yorkshire Post*, 10 April and 12 Sept. 1907, and John Coffey, *Canterbury XIII*, Christchurch, 1987.
72. Although this claim was dismissed by the NZRU, Fred Marsh, 'Forward', the *Athletic News* rugby correspondent, claimed that the 1907 tourists' captain, H. R. Wright, had shown him letters from fourteen of the 1905 touring party and that another four had enquired verbally. *Athletic News*, 7 Oct. 1907.
73. Quoted in *Yorkshire Post*, 5 Sept. 1907.
74. *Athletic News,* 7 Oct. 1907. The disparaging title 'All Golds', as the 1907 side has become known to history, appears not to have been used at the time of the tour, at least in Britain. When not called the All Blacks, NU circles referred to them as the 'Phantoms', an ironic reference to C. Wray Palliser's comment.
75. For accounts of the formation of the NSWRFL see Ian Heads, ibid.; Chris Cuneen, 'The Rugby War: The Early History of Rugby League in NSW 1907–15' in R. Cashman and M. McKernan (eds), *Sport in History*, Queensland, 1979; and Murray Phillips, 'Football, Class and War: The Rugby Codes in NSW 1907–18' in J. Nauright and T. Chandler, *Making Men*, London, 1996. The text of letters

from Baskerville and Giltinan describing the NSWRFL's foundation can be found in *Yorkshire Post*, 24 Sept. and 2 Oct. 1907.

76. For the background to Rees's move, see 'How Amateur was my Valley' in Gareth Williams's *1905 and All That*, Llandysul, 1991 and the *Yorkshire Post*, 27 May 1907, from which the Rees quote is taken. The WRU's official 1907 report into professionalism is reprinted in *Athletic News*, 9 Sept. 1907.

77. NU General Committee minutes, 25 March and 30 May 1907.

78. *Yorkshire Post*, 2 Oct. 1907.

79. The England versus Ireland rugby union international held on the same day attracted between 15,000 and 18,000. The success of the Chelsea game gave rise to moves to form a London NU club. See *Yorkshire Post*, 25 Feb. and 7 and 27 March 1908.

80. For the figures, see *Yorkshire Post* of 12 June 1908. This does not include the takings from their games in Australia or their one game in Ceylon. The 1905 All Blacks realised receipts of £14,571, although they played two more games, including one in France and two in North America. *Yorkshire Post*, 30 May 1906.

81. *Yorkshire Post*, 10 Oct. 1907. The unsympathetic *Times*, 3 Dec. 1907, compared the tourists to a reasonable home international side.

82. *Athletic News*, 14 Sept. 1907

83. *Athletic News*, 23 Dec. 1907. It is often forgotten that the 1905 All Blacks struggled on the Welsh leg of their tour, losing to Wales and beating Swansea by only one point and Cardiff by just two, scoring a mere twenty-nine points in five games.

84. Ian Heads, *True Blue*, p. 83.

85. *Yorkshire Post*, 5 Feb. 1909. For fuller accounts of the 1908–9 tour see Robert Gate, *The Struggle For The Ashes*, Ripponden, 1986 and Ian Heads, *The Kangaroos*, Sydney, 1990. The Australian national rugby union side, the 'Wallabies', toured England and Wales at the same time as the Kangaroos and proved to be an even greater financial disaster, losing £1,500, although their playing record, on a shorter tour, was better. *Yorkshire Post*, 6 April 1909.

86. *Yorkshire Post*, 7 Oct. 1907

87. Quoted in Heads, p. 38.

88. Quoted in David James, 'The First Ever Northern Union International' in *Code 13*, Sept. 1989. D. M. Messenger, *The Master*, Sydney, 1982, p. 50.

89. Ian Heads, *True Blue*, p. 49.

90. For the impact of the 1905 tour on the respective national identities, see Jock Phillips, *A Man's Country: The Image of the Pakeha Male, A History*, Auckland 1987 and '1905 and All That: Sporting Success and Social Function in Wales, 1880–1914' in Gareth Williams's *1905 and All That*, Llandysul, 1991.

91. *Western Mail*, 23 Dec. 1935, quoted in David Smith, 'Focal Heroes: A Welsh Fighting Class', in Richard Holt (ed), *Sport and the Working Class in Modern Britain*, Manchester, 1990, p. 201. Faced with intransigent hostility from the Welsh Rugby Union and its supporters, a lack of entrepreneurial skills and the high costs of travelling regularly to the north of England, the Welsh Northern Union clubs struggled to survive into the next decade, Ebbw Vale being the longest lasting Welsh club before collapsing at the end of their fifth season in 1912.

92. Joyce, ibid., p. 329.

93. *Yorkshire Post*, 15 April 1910.

94. *Athletic News*, 28 Feb. 1910.

95. *Yorkshire Post*, 26 May 1910. It was thirty-seven years before a reigning monarch actually went to a match, the first being the 1948 cup final.

Conclusion: The Northern Union and Working Class Culture

In April 1910, a new journey began for the Northern Union when twenty-six of the NU's finest players left England for the Union's first-ever tour of Australia and New Zealand. Flushed with the self-confidence of a successful new code of rules, firmly established in the southern hemisphere and buoyant in its heartlands, the Australasian tour was for the NU the final piece in the jigsaw which became the pattern of rugby league for almost sixty years. A new era had begun, and, although the NU wasn't to change its name until 1922, the setting out of the tourists on the high seas marked the beginning of modern rugby league.

Symbolically, the tourists' departure marked the end of the odyssey which working-class rugby had made since the miners and millworkers of the north of England first ran with an oval ball in their hands. From now on, the northern working classes' relationship to rugby was based entirely on a different sport and a different culture from that which the rugby union had provided. It was the culmination of a process which had begun in the 1870s as the working class brought their numbers and culture to the public schoolboys' game. Neither simple class expression nor mere passive diffusion, working-class culture contained strong elements of commercialism and sought to utilise existing leisure outlets for its own purposes. The ultimate outcome was by no means inevitable – given the advantages the sport had over soccer at the time, the possibility existed for it to become the dominant football code – but fear of working-class domination saw the development of an amateur ideology which was ultimately incompatible with either mass working-class participation or the growth of a commercial, mass-based leisure industry. This was the rock which split asunder the consensus of rugby's leaders. However it was the desertion of most of rugby's middle-class supporters to rugby union and soccer and its exclusion from the pantheon of national sport that left the NU an almost exclusively working-class game, albeit with a fringe of administrators from the marginal sections of the middle classes. The road to the formation of NU was as much a case history in the formation of middle-class culture as it

231

was of working-class culture. In a sense too, the wheel had turned full circle: the working classes' leisure activities of the pre-football mid-Victorian period had been largely unknown to and unknowable by the middle classes; now the NU occupied a position in society which was similarly beyond the pale of middle-class comprehension and experience.

Given the varying levels of conflict in rugby, how useful is the concept of hegemony in understanding its development? John Hargreaves, a leading proponent of the theory of hegemony, has argued that the development of mass spectator sports in the late nineteenth century 'signified also a degree of depoliticisation within the working class which commercial interests were quick to exploit,'[1] but the question of commercialism is much more complex and contradictory than the hegemony theorists allow. Far from being counterposed to it or 'accommodated' by it, working-class participation in rugby both spurred on and was facilitated by commercialisation. Working-class players' demands for remuneration were the motive force for the professionalisation of the sport. Indeed, in the debate leading up to the split, the most vociferous champions of open professionalisation of the game were the supporters of players' rights, not the industrialists who occupied leading positions in the game. As Eileen and Stephen Yeo have argued, 'there was a formidable working class, even socialist, case for the professionalisation and capitalisation of sport.'[2] A similar point could be made about soccer: those who were most in favour of the operation of laws of supply and demand in the sport were the players. By and large, it was the working-class participants in both codes of football who were the most committed to 'pure' bourgeois values.

This is not so contradictory as it may appear. To survive in daily life, working-class men and women were forced to sell their labour power to the highest bidder. So in a market where a premium was on football talent, it was inevitable that players would desire the freest operation of that market, shorn of the restrictions of amateurism, enforced semi-professionalism or professionalism bounded by a maximum wage. 'Freedom' for working-class males to play sport at the highest levels could only be achieved by the commercialisation of football. Herein lies the problem posed by rugby for the hegemony theory: all of the demands of working-class players in the 1880s were eventually met by the Northern Union, yet the working class exerted no greater control over the new body than it did over the avowedly anti-working-class RFU.

Was this because they were defeated ideologically by the commercially minded middle classes or because they 'consented' to such an arrangement? Neither solution provides a satisfactory answer in my opinion. Society is not a blank page upon which differing ideologies or value systems compete for dominance. Any struggle for hegemony is unequal from the start – consciousness, of whatever class, is formed in an environment in which the necessity of day-to-day economic survival under capitalism is accepted as the 'natural order.' Leisure activity is necessarily shaped by the economic imperatives of capitalism which seep into every corner of life. Thus working class players were prepared to accept the leadership of the Northern Union because it provided the most equitable solution available under capitalism to the problems they faced from the RFU and its amateur ethos. This does not imply an endorsement of a crude base/superstructure theory, but it does stress the importance of economics to the relationship between rugby and the working class – indeed, from the earliest pressures for covert payments in the 1870s to the players' strikes of the 1900s, the wage relationship played a critical role in the sport. Into this were woven varying degrees of civic pride, regional patriotism, consciousness of class, feelings of injustice and political ideology, from which were woven the fabric of the Northern Union.

Central to the culture of the Northern Union game and its claim to national importance were the regular test match series with Australia for which the 1910 tour set the pattern. As could be expected, preparations for the tour had been fraught with difficulty. Negotiations with the Australians over the share of the gate takings had been long and arduous, and at one point the entire venture had been in jeopardy. In order to reach Australia in good time, the tourists had to set sail before the end of the season, forcing the NU to play the two championship semi-finals on the same day as the Northern Union cup final. Fortunately none of the cup finalists were championship contenders, although, as if beset by fate, the cup final was drawn for the first time in its history and had to be replayed two days later, forcing five members of the touring party to leave a week late. The five were joined at the last minute by Hunslet's star centre three-quarter Billy Batten, who had been selected to tour but had aggravated a knee injury received in the tour trial match at Headingley. Despite the Northern Union committee announcing that he had withdrawn, Batten was determined to prove his fitness and, three days before the final party was to leave, turned out for Hemsworth in a Wakefield League match. Perhaps inevitably, given his renowned drive to succeed, he scored three tries and was passed fit to tour on the spot by watching Northern Union officials. Amazingly, the tour proceeded as planned and went on to be an outstanding success, both on and off the pitch.

Billy Batten himself had a significance for the Northern Union which extended far beyond his outstanding prowess on the field. He was symbolic of what the new game had become. Unlike earlier stars, he had played no other code: his character and playing style were entirely shaped by the demands of the NU game. As if to emphasise the centrality of physicality to the sport, his strength, speed and power as a centre three-quarter were unprecedented: he became famous for leaping over, or more often than not through, opponents. His determination and will to win – nearly ninety years on, one only has to look at the intensity of his expression in photographs and film footage to realise that 'mental focus' is nothing new – encapsulated the attitude of the new generation of professional rugby players.

Off the field, he embodied all of those traits which were to characterise generations of rugby league players. A man who was still part of the community which had raised him – he gave £350 of his testimonial fund to mining families in his home village of Kinsley near Wakefield during the 1921 miners' lock-out – he was also acutely aware of his own value and saw to it that he squeezed the last drop of cash out of those who employed him to play rugby. When Hunslet failed to meet his demands in 1912 he was transferred to Hull FC for £600, doubling the previous NU transfer record, and received an astronomical £14 per match. His relationship with the sport's administrators was similarly tense. In 1920 he refused to play in a trial match and so sacrificed the chance to join that year's touring party to Australia, arguing that if the selectors didn't know whether he was good enough to tour after fifteen years in the game, one trial match wouldn't make a difference. In contrast to contemporaries in other sports, such as soccer's Billy Meredith and cricket's Sydney Barnes, who shared both Batten's brilliance and hostility to authority, Batten was not marginalised or viewed as a maverick. He was accepted by supporters, fellow-players and, albeit grudgingly, officials, as a phenomenon: Hull FC would stick strips reading 'Batten Certain To Play' over posters advertising their matches, guaranteeing a large attendance at games in which he played.[3]

Although not specifically referring to him, it was in unconscious recognition of the achievements of players such as Batten that the saying 't'best in t'Northern Union' came into being across the north of England in the period around the First World War.[4] Used to denote that something was of the highest quality, the phrase carried with it the unspoken assumption that if whatever was referred to was the best in the Northern Union, it was the best in Britain. It therefore carried into popular parlance – of both men and women, it must be stressed – the belief of the NU and its supporters that their players and their game were superior to those of the RFU, binding this up with the broader assumption of the superiority of the Northern way of life. It also expressed the different relationship to their communities of soccer and NU rugby; logically, it would have made greater sense to say 'the best in the Football League' given the national spread of soccer, yet that would have been to lose that sense of apartness and regional pride which the NU gave the phrase. Other phrases relating to the game also slipped into regional language: 'to nip around the blind side', referring to a movement where the ball was passed to the side of a scrum furthest from the referee, became used to denote a shortcut to avoid a queue or an obstruction; 'to sell a dummy', whereby a pass was faked to fool an opponent, became a synonym for a dodge or ruse.

The way in which the terminology of the game slipped into everyday use demonstrates the role of the NU in the construction of a 'Northern' regional identity. Despite the fact that the NU was initially forged from national forces in which regionalism played a subordinate role, as the NU sought to develop its own identity it naturally assimilated the customs and culture of its location. In doing so, it largely transcended the county-based regionalism of the pre-1895 days, and unlike in the rugby union era, when the sport in the North identified itself as 'Lancashire rugby' or 'Yorkshire football', the new game prided itself on being 'Northern.' This decline in county patriotism is also to be seen in the fall in attendances at county matches from the early 1900s and the lack of importance attached to them. Less than ten years after the split there were even calls to abandon them completely, while working class civic pride in town or city, of which support for a rugby or soccer team had been an integral part since the 1870s, remained a potent force, this too had merged at some points, but not completely, with a sense of corporate northernness. In an era of increasingly national culture and identity, the development and meaning of the NU demonstrated not only that regionalism survived but also how it changed and reformulated itself in new circumstances. Equally, the NU itself became part of northern identity. Not only did it become part of everyday language, but it became part of the symbolism of northern working-class history and identity. Supporter or not, everyone knew that, like their own communities, the NU was the best at what it did, that it suffered from discrimination by the establishment and that it was one of 'us' against 'them.' It took its place 'in the realm of everyday practice,' to quote Patrick Joyce, in which its sayings, personalities and culture came to symbolise northern life.[5]

However, a note of caution must be sounded about placing too much emphasis on cultural significance. Commercial exigencies were central to the origins and development of the game and the relationship between the players and club officials was inevitably that of employee and employer. While significant elements of working-class practices were reflected in the overall culture of the game, especially in relation to physicality, crowd behaviour and the meaning assigned to the sport in cultural life, other elements of working-class life, such as distrust of employers and the desire to secure the highest level of wages, were a constant source of tension. The stance of Billy Batten and many other players to the clubs for which they played was often portrayed as disloyal or mercenary but their attitudes were simply those of working class people seeking to secure the best possible return for their labour power. As the not uncommon occurrence of player's strikes demonstrated, far from being an island of northern working-class unity, the NU was subject to the same conflicts between employers and employees as any other branch of industry.

For the supporter, identification with the NU allowed him or her to stand both inside and outside society. It was a confirmation of what Richard Hoggart has called a feeling 'in their bones that the public and the generalised life is wrong.'[6] Part of its appeal was the fact it was almost entirely separate from the middle and upper classes, and, because of its marginalised position in wider society, not wholly part of national public life.[7] In this, it was a cultural expression of what Tom Nairn has described as the working classes' sense of being 'something of an exile inside the society which [they] supported.'[8] The NU was a self-contained world in which the participants could demonstrate to themselves that their code of football rules and players were better than those of the establishment RFU. In the Northern Union, there was no need to prove themselves in the techniques of social advancement or the niceties of etiquette: as in life, what counted was how you performed on the field. This emphasis on ability and merit, partially drawn from working-class attitudes to life but also based on the fact that the sport was an entertainment business, would allow the game to develop a higher level of racial integration than most other sports in Britain, giving rise to a cosmopolitanism which saw white English working men playing with and against black Welshmen, Maoris, Aboriginals and Fijians, not to mention white working class Australians, New Zealanders and Welshmen.[9]

It was this combination of working-class alienation from society, Gladstonian Liberalism, persecution by the rugby union authorities and geographic restriction which moulded the NU. The game's appeal of brilliant handling and running skills and hard physicality were combined with a sense of injustice and righteousness to produce a potency of sporting ideology equal to that of any fuelled by national or racial pride. For working men and women who thought that the order of society was not how it should be, the Northern Union was living confirmation of their suspicions. Like the English populists' vision of Merrie England before the imposition of the Norman yoke, they had seen justice snatched from their hands by the RFU,[10] but, like socialists, they knew that the future lay with them, that ultimately right would prevail and that their game would be recognised in all its superiority for what they believed it truly was: the greatest game of all.

NOTES

1. John Hargreaves, *Sport, Power and Culture*, London, 1986, p. 83.
2. Eileen and Stephen Yeo, 'Perceived Patterns: Competition and Licence versus Class and Struggle' in their edited collection *Popular Culture and Class Conflict 1590–1914*, Brighton, 1981, p. 278.
3. Sadly, like his predecessor Dicky Lockwood, Billy was also declared bankrupt after running into difficulties running a pub shortly after his retirement from the game – see *Yorkshire Evening Post*, 9 Feb. 1928. His contribution to rugby league was heightened by his being the first of a family dynasty. His son Eric was a record-breaking try scorer and his great-nephew Ray was an international loose-forward. For more on Meredith, see J. Harding, *Billy Meredith*, Derby, 1985. For Barnes, see D. Birley, *The Willow Wand*, London, 1979. Richard Holt has made a number of relevant and suggestive comments about the lack of English soccer national heroes in the pre-World War I period: see his 'Contrasting Nationalisms' in *International Journal of the History of Sport*, Vol. 12, No. 2, Aug. 1995.
4. As with many other examples of oral culture, the specific origins of the saying are impossible to pin down. Despite the fact that the Northern Union became the Rugby Football League in 1922, the phrase continued to be used and can very occasionally still be heard today. For example, in the Salford-based soap opera *Coronation Street* in an episode broadcast on 17 June 1996.
5. Patrick Joyce, *Visions of the People*, Manchester, 1991, p.170.
6. The phrase is from Richard Hoggart's *The Uses of Literacy*, London, 1957, p. 94. Hunslet, the community about which Hoggart writes and in which he was brought up, was of course home to one of rugby league's most successful clubs.
7. Alan Metcalfe makes a similar point about the appeal of soccer to Northumberland miners in his 'Football in the Mining Communities of East Northumberland', *International Journal of the History of Sport*, Vol. 5, No. 3, Dec. 1988.
8. Tom Nairn, 'The English Working Class', in Robin Blackburn, *Ideology in Social Science*, London, 1972, p. 198.
9. It appears that the first black rugby league player was Hunslet's Lucius Banks, a black American serviceman signed in 1912.
10. See Christopher Hill 'The Norman Yoke' in his *Puritanism and Revolution*, London, 1958. Curiously enough, the Norman Yoke theory survived during this period primarily thanks to Robert Blatchford's *British for the British*, published in 1902. Blatchford's *Clarion* was, of course, the most outspoken advocate of a split with the RFU in the 1890s. The phrase 'the greatest game of all' was first used as part of an Australian advertising campaign for the game in the 1950s. Its encapsulation of the self-esteem of the game and its supporters meant that it rapidly became rugby league's unofficial motto – and, indeed, the title of a rugby league magazine in the 1990s.

Appendix

Private resident	30	Barber	1
Publican	20	Beer retailer	1
Butcher	8	Builder	1
Clerk	6	Cab owner	1
Joiner	6	Carting agent	1
Draper	5	Cattle dealer	1
Solicitor	5	China dealer	1
Blacksmith	4	Clerk of corn exchange	1
Maltster	4	Eating house owner	1
Manager	4	Engraver	1
Chemist	3	Farmer	1
Coal agent	3	Fish dealer	1
Glass manufacturer	3	Flyposting proprietor	1
Rates collector	3	Furniture dealer	1
Shopkeeper	3	Hatter	1
Tailor	3	Horse dealer	1
Tobacconist	3	Hosier	1
Wholesale grocer	3	House agent	1
Baker	2	Insurance agent	1
Building company owner	2	Insurance superintendent	1
Civil engineer	2	Ironmonger	1
Confectioner	2	Journalist	1
Corn merchant	2	Leather worker	1
District registrar	2	Livery stable keeper	1
Dyer	2	Lodging house owner	1
Grocer	2	Member of Parliament	1
House painter	2	Music teacher	1
Iron foundry partner	2	Music warehouse owner	1
Married woman	2	Newspaper publisher	1
Painter	2	Organ builder	1
Photographer	2	Outfitter	1
Print worker	2	Plasterer	1
Shoemaker	2	Railway inspector	1
Surgeon	2	School inspector	1
Wine and spirits merchant	2	Servant	1
Woollen manufacturer	2	Smallware dealer	1
Accountant	1	Stationer's assistant	1
Aerated water mfctr	1	Stonemason	1
Architect	1	Tin plate worker	1
Assistant overseer	1	Toy dealer	1
Auctioneer	1	Upholsterer	1

*Breakdown according to occupational category**

Category		Number	Percentage
A.	Aristocracy and gentry	42	21
B.	Upper professional	13	7
C.	Lower professional	6	3
D.	Proprietors and employers associated with the drinks trade	27	14
E.	Other proprietors and employers	58	29
F.	Managers and higher administrators	4	2
G.	Clerical	9	5
H.	Foremen, supervisors and inspectors	4	2
I.	Skilled manual workers	26	13
J.	Semi-skilled manual workers	7	3
K.	Unskilled manual workers	–	–
L.	Unspecified (Married women)	2	1

Sources: *Wakefield Express*, 9 April and 9 July 1887. *Slater's Directory of the West Riding of Yorkshire 1887*, London, 1887. *Kelly's West Riding Directory 1889*, London, 1889. *White's General and Commercial Directory of Wakefield 1888*, Wakefield, 1888. J. C. Lindley, *One Hundred Years of Rugby*, Wakefield, 1973. Of the 277 subscribers' names I have been able to trace 198, 71 per cent of the total.

* Occupational categories are those used by Vamplew in *Pay Up and Play the Game.*

TABLE A.2

CROWD DISTURBANCES AT YORKSHIRE RUGBY UNION MATCHES 1887–1895

Club	Date	Offence	Punishment
Leeds St John's	Nov 1887	Crowd attacked opponents after game	Unknown
Shipley	Sept 1888	Crowd 'jostled and hustled' referee after game	Unknown
Liversedge	Sept 1888	Visiting fans invaded pitch after players' fight	Unknown
Mytholmroyd	Nov 1888	Crowd attacked referee after game	Ground closed
Bradford Rgrs	Nov 1889	Spectators and players fight during game	Unknown
Castleford	March 1889	'Spectator violence'	Ground closed – four weeks
York	Nov 1889	Crowd threw mud at referee after game	Ground closed – four weeks
Normanton	Jan 1890	Crowd mobbed referee after players walk-off	Ground closed – four weeks
Mirfield	Jan 1890	Crowd 'abused referee'	Ground closed – two weeks
Ingrow	March 1890	Crowd subjected referee to 'ill-treatment'	Ground closed – two weeks
Leeds PC	Sept 1890	Crowd attacked referee after game	Ground closed – four weeks
Otley	Feb 1891	Crowd abused referee and touch judge	Ground closed – one week
Yeadon	Oct 1891	Crowd invaded pitch after spectator punched player	Ground closed – six weeks

Wortley	Jan 1892	Spectator attacked opposing player during game	Ground closed – three weeks
Mirfield	Oct 1892	Crowd attacked referee after game	Ground closed – one week
Ingrow	Oct 1892	Crowd attacked referee after game	Ground closed – one week
Featherstone	Nov 1892	Ref. beaten up by 20 youths after leaving ground	No action taken
Hull	Feb 1893	Crowd attacks referee after game	Severe reprimand
Dewsbury	March 1893	Spectators seize referee by throat after game	Reprimand
Saltaire	Jan 1894	'Hostile demonstration' against referee after game	No action taken
Bailiffe Bridge	March 1894	Three fights between players and spectators	Match replayed
Leeds	Nov 1894	Crowd jostle referee after game	Club censured
Beeston	Dec 1894	Crowd threw stones at referee after game	Ground closed – one week
Hunslet	April 1895	300-strong crowd attempts to assault ref. after game	Ground closed – twelve weeks

Sources: These are the incidents reported to the committee of the Yorkshire Rugby Union from its foundation to the year of rugby's split. The primary source is the *Yorkshire Post*, supported by *Athletic News*. Incidents not brought to the attention of the YRU have not been included. Unfortunately, the minutes of the Lancashire County Football Committee do not record crowd disturbances and the *Athletic News* is not comprehensive enough to be used as an accurate guide.

TABLE A.3

OCCUPATIONS OF WORKING CLASS RUGBY PLAYERS 1886–1895*

Textile worker	8	Draper	1
Miner	6	Iron dresser	1
Cricket professional	4	Iron moulder	1
Labourer	4	Machine foreman	1
Unemployed	3	Painter	1
Boilermaker	2	Plumber	1
Cabinet maker	2	Printing worker	1
Shopkeeper	2	Railwayman	1
Apprentice joiner	1	Stone breaker	1
Boilermaker	1	Telegraphic operator	1
Bricklayer	1	Tailor	1
Brushmaker	1	Travelling salesman	1
Builder	1	Weaver	1

Sources: *Athletic News, Clarion, Salford Reporter, Oldham Evening Chronicle, Yorkshire Post, Yorkshire Evening Post, Leeds Daily News, Bradford Observer, The Yorkshireman, The Yorkshire Owl* and R. McWhirter and U. A. Titley, *The Centenary History of the RFU*, London, 1971.

* These figures have been taken from 49 players whose occupations I have been able to identify. I have deliberately excluded from the sample some 20 players who were publicans or waiters, on the grounds that, more often than not, these positions were gained as a result of their footballing prowess and would not shed any light on their backgrounds.

TABLE A.4
DEATHS IN YORKSHIRE RUGBY 1886–1895*

Date	Name	Club	Cause of death
January 1888	A. Mann	Manningham Rgrs	Injured kidneys
September 1888	A. Dougherty	Huddersfield	Pelvic abscesses
February 1889	T. Greenwood	Primrose	Damaged spinal cord
March 1889	L. Wade	Shipley	Severe concussion
September 1890	J. Walker-Smith	Lockwood	Abdominal injuries
November 1890	W. Armitage	St Albans (Leeds)	Ruptured liver
November 1890	W. Scoley	Buslingthorpe (Leeds)	Blood poisoning
December 1890	W. Middleton	Harrogate	Internal injuries
March 1891	J. Featherstone	Hull Britannia	Unknown
September 1892	M. Hutchinson	Harrogate	Unknown
February 1893	J. Kirk	Shepley	Broken neck
March 1894	J. W. Speight	Kirkstall	Unknown
September 1894	B. Hudson	Idle	Spinal injuries

* These figures have been obtained through a reading of *The Yorkshireman*'s rugby column from 1882, in which the first reported death at a Yorkshire football match occurred in 1886 – at soccer in Keighley, the *Yorkshire Post*'s reports of YRU executive committee meetings and the *Pall Mall Gazette*'s lists of injuries. I have excluded one death reported in the *Pall Mall Gazette* – in Keighley in 1891 – as I have found no other record of it.

TABLE A.5
OCCUPATIONS OF NORTHERN UNION PLAYERS 1895–1910*

Miner	8	Engineer	1
Textile worker	4	Gas stove fitter	1
Docker	3	School master	1
Brass moulder	2	Steel shearer	1
Glass bottle maker	2	Stone mason	1
Labourer	2	Tailor	1
Blacksmith's striker	1	Tobacconist	1
Boiler maker	1	Wagonette driver	1
Boot maker	1	Waiter	1
Clerk	1	Window cleaner	1
Colliery engine winder	1		

Sources: *Athletic News, Salford Reporter, Evening Chronicle, Yorkshire Post, Yorkshire Evening Post, Yorkshire Chat, Bradford Observer, Wigan Observer, Pontefract and Castleford Express, Hull Daily Mail* and minutes of the Northern Union Professionalism Sub-Committee.

* These figures have been taken from 36 players whose occupations I have been able to identify. As before, I have not included occupations which were the result of foot-balling largesse, such as publicans. To avoid skewing the details, I have also excluded the 11 miners who played for Hunslet and another 11 who played for Normanton. Interestingly, the one schoolmaster was a Welshman from Swansea playing for Hull KR.

TABLE A.6
STRIKES BY NORTHERN UNION PLAYERS 1895–1905

Date	Club	Reason
September 1895	Warrington	Unpaid broken-time
December 1895	Leigh (forwards only)	Wanted nine shillings broken-time payment
October 1896	St Helens (forwards only)	Wanted more broken-time
December 1896	Wakefield Trinity 'A'	Non-payment for broken-time
December 1898	Ulverston	Low pay
May 1899	Oldham	Dispute over bonuses
January 1900	Leeds (five players)	dispute over terms
May 1901	Swinton	Non-payment of bonuses
February 1902	Oldham (four Welsh players)	Wanted extra pay for mid-week game
March 1902	Rochdale	Non-payment of wages
April 1902	Castleford	Wanted increased wages for cup-tie
November 1902	Runcorn	Wanted higher pay
February 1904	Cleckheaton	Non-payment of wages
October 1904	Pontefract (forwards only)	Reduction in terms
September 1905	Wakefield Trinity (3 players)	Reduction in terms

Sources: *Athletic News*, *Warrington Guardian*, *The Yorkshireman*, *Yorkshire Post*, *St Helens Lantern*, *Barrow News*, *Oldham Evening Chronicle*, *Salford Reporter*, NU General Committee minutes. I have defined a strike as being a refusal to play by three or more players for reasons other than on-pitch activities.

TABLE A.7
OCCUPATIONS OF NORTHERN UNION GENERAL COMMITTEE MEMBERS 1895–1910*

Licensee/Hotel keeper	6	Oil importer	1
Textile manufacture	3	Paper tube manufacturer	1
Foreman	2	Pawnbroker	1
Salesman	2	Private resident	1
Schoolmaster	2	Railway booking clerk	1
Builder	1	Solicitor	1
Builders' merchant	1	Surveyor/Music hall proprietor	1
Clerk	1	Travelling draper	1
Coal merchant	1	Wholesale jeweller	1
Furniture shop owner	1	Wood engraver	1
Hosier and hat shop owner	1	Works manager	1
Jeweller	1		

* Extant Northern Union *Official Guides* list 47 members of the General Committee, the Union's ruling body, during this period, of which I have been able to trace the occupations of 33.

TABLE A.8
OCCUPATIONAL ANALYSIS OF NORTHERN UNION CLUB SHAREHOLDERS
AND DIRECTORS 1895–1910

Leeds (1889)
£25,000 × £1

Holbeck (1897)
£2,500 × £1

	Shareholders No.	%	Shareholdings No.	%	Shareholders No.	%	Shareholdings No.	%
A	7	2.5	555	5.3	5	6.0	215	14.1
B	49	17.6	4,247	40.9	2	2.4	85	5.6
C	6	2.2	96	0.9	3	3.6	40	2.6
D	10	3.6	925	8.9	10	12.0	176	11.6
E	68	24.4	2,176	20.9	26	31.3	761	50.0
F	28	10.0	720	6.9	4	4.8	45	3.0
G	52	18.6	452	4.3	2	2.4	20	1.3
H	1	0.4	5	–	3	3.6	33	2.2
I	47	16.8	1,102	10.6	21	25.3	121	8.0
J	9	3.2	96	0.9	6	7.2	25	1.6
K	2	0.7	35	0.3	1	1.2	1	–
Total traced	279	100	10,419	100	83	100	1,522	100
L	49	–	3,324	–	–	–	–	–

Castleford (1899)
£1,500 × 10s

Salford (1901)
£2,500 × £1

	Shareholders No.	%	Shareholdings No.	%	Shareholders No.	%	Shareholdings No.	%
A	1	2.1	60	5.3	6	1.3	119	8.6
B	3	6.4	130	11.4	6	1.3	16	1.2
C	3	6.4	50	4.4	36	7.9	138	10.0
D	17	36.2	465	40.8	21	4.6	165	12.0
E	14	29.8	245	21.5	81	17.8	291	21.1
F	2	4.3	60	5.3	15	3.3	37	2.1
G	2	4.3	30	2.6	85	18.7	260	18.9
H	2	4.3	25	2.2	13	2.9	44	3.2
I	3	6.4	75	6.6	131	28.7	216	15.7
J	–	–	–	–	47	10.3	68	4.9
K	–	–	–	–	15	3.3	25	1.8
Total traced	47	100	1,140	100	456	100	1,379	100
L	–	–	–	–	146	–	305	–

(Table A.8 continued)

Rochdale (1906)
£1,000 × 10s

Ebbw Vale (1907)
£250 × 10s

	Shareholders No.	%	Shareholdings No.	%	Shareholders No.	%	Shareholdings No.	%
A	1	0.7	10	0.9	–	–	–	–
B	10	6.8	131	11.4	1	1.0	5	1.4
C	7	4.8	60	5.2	3	3.1	10	2.7
D	9	6.2	117	10.2	10	10.2	67	18.3
E	49	33.6	499	43.5	21	21.4	67	18.3
F	12	8.2	74	6.5	6	6.1	28	7.7
G	12	8.2	98	8.5	4	4.1	24	6.6
H	1	0.7	10	0.9	7	7.1	20	5.5
I	43	29.9	139	12.1	18	18.4	35	9.6
J	1	0.7	5	0.4	28	28.8	75	20.5
K	1	0.7	4	0.3	–	–	–	–
Total traced	146	100	1,147	100	98	100	366	100
L	–	–	–	–	–	–	–	–

Aberdare (1908)
£500 × £1

Barry (1908)
£250 × 10s

	Shareholders No.	%	Shareholdings No.	%	Shareholders No.	%	Shareholdings No.	%
A	–	–	–	–	–	–	–	–
B	–	–	–	–	–	–	–	–
C	–	–	–	–	2	8.7	11	7.5
D	9	25.7	40	25.5	–	–	–	–
E	16	45.7	75	47.8	8	34.6	58	39.5
F	2	5.7	8	5.1	1	4.3	10	6.8
G	1	1.9	5	3.2	2	8.7	6	4.1
H	–	–	–	–	1	4.3	10	6.8
I	2	5.7	8	5.1	7	30.4	40	27.2
J	4	11.3	12	7.6	2	8.7	12	8.2
K	1	2.9	9	5.7	–	–	–	–
Total traced	35	100	157	100	23	100	147	100
L	–	–	–	–	–	–	5	–

(Table A.8 continued)

| | Coventry (1909) £2,000 × £1 | | | | Broughton Rangers (1910) £2,000 × 10s | | | |
	Shareholders No.	%	Shareholders No.	%	Shareholders No.	%	Shareholders No.	%
A	2	2.2	20	1.4	–	–	–	–
B	2	2.2	60	4.3	2	2.5	14	2.3
C	15	18.3	102	7.4	6	7.6	39	6.5
D	11	13.4	201	14.5	5	6.4	67	11.2
E	30	36.6	647	46.8	21	26.9	255	42.8
F	9	11.0	287	20.8	10	12.8	61	10.2
G	5	6.1	31	2.2	8	10.2	44	7.3
H	1	0.1	5	0.4	3	3.8	41	6.9
I	5	6.1	23	1.7	16	20.5	46	7.7
J	2	2.2	6	0.4	6	7.6	27	4.5
K	–	–	–	–	1	1.2	1	0.1
Total traced	82	100	1,382	100	78	100	595	100
L	1	–	1	–	2	–	3	–

DIRECTORS OF NU CLUBS – BREAKDOWN OF 124 DIRECTORS OF SEVEN CLUBS BY
OCCUPATIONAL CATEGORY – PERCENTAGES ONLY

Category	%
A	3.2
B	4.0
C	8.9
D	14.5
E	37.1
F	4.0
G	7.3
H	4.0
I	12.9
J	4.0
K	–

Sources: Wray Vamplew, *Pay Up and Play the Game*, Cambridge, 1988. Paul Greenhalgh, *The History of the Northern Rugby Football Union 1895–1915*, unpublished Ph.D. thesis, University of Lancaster, 1992 – see p. 198 for breakdown of directors' occupations. PRO BT 31 32073/111081. PRO BT 31 7363/52183. PRO BT 31 9364/69546. PRO BT 12142/95202.

Key: Year in brackets is date of incorporation. Figures below indicate authorised share capital and cost of a single share. A: Aristocracy and gentry. B: Upper professional. C: Lower professional. D: Proprietors and employers associated with the drink trade. E: Other proprietors and employers. F: Managers and higher administrators. G: Clerical. H: Foremen, supervisors and inspectors. I: Skilled manual workers. J: Semi-skilled manual workers. K: Unskilled manual workers. L: Occupations untraced.

TABLE A.9

NORTHERN UNION AND SOCCER CROWDS – A COMPARISON

Season	Hull FC	Hull City	Leeds NU	Leeds City	Bradford	Bradford City	Bradford Park Avenue
1902–3	5,181	–	5,774	–	7,026	–	–
1903–4	5,025	–	7,593	–	8,333	9,941	–
1904–5	5,628	–	9,022	–	n/a	10,700	–
1905–6	4,041	6,500	5,632	9,978	n/a	9,531	–
1906–7	3,000	7,833	4,735	10,131	4,166	10,789	–
1907–8	4,904	8,305	5,476	11,210	–	16,317	9,342
1908–9	4,809	7,368	6,334	11,315	–	22,684	11,157
1909–10	5,119	9,342	7,071	7,026	–	21,052	10, 778

n/a = not available

Sources: Hull FC annual reports and accounts. Leeds Cricket, Football and Athletic Club annual reports and accounts. J. Goldthorpe, *Twenty Years' Records of Leeds FC*, Leeds, 1910. *Yorkshire Post*, *Athletic News*, *Bradford Observer*. Chris Elton, *Hull City – A Complete Record*, Derby, 1989. Martin Jarred and Malcolm Macdonald, *Leeds United – A Complete Record*, Derby, 1986. Terry Frost, *Bradford City – A Complete Record*, Derby, 1988. Malcolm Hartley and Tim Clapham, *The Avenue*, Nottingham, 1987.

TABLE A.10

A COMPARISON OF SHAREHOLDERS IN RIVAL NORTHERN UNION AND SOCCER CLUBS

	Holbeck (66 × £1)	Leeds City (61 × £1)		Holbeck (66 × £1)	Leeds City (61 × £1)
Gentleman/Scholar	3	1	Foreman	1	1
Surgeon/Physician	2	–	Mechanic	9	–
Manufacturer	1	6	Engineer	7	1
Company director	–	2	Joiner	6	1
Manager	1	4	Slater	3	–
Woollen merchant	1	–	Contractor	3	2
Timber merchant	1	–	Printer	1	1
			Decorator	1	–
Auctioneer	–	1	Coach builder	1	–
Schoolmaster	–	7	Brick maker	1	–
Tax officer	–	2	Mill hand	1	–
Manufacturing			Warehouseman	1	–
Chemist	–	1	Wheelwright	–	1
General agent	–	1	Blacksmith	–	1
Commission agent	–	1	Gardener	–	1
			Boat attendant	–	1
Publican	10	5	Steel worker	–	1
Shopkeepers	5	8			
Tailors/Drapers	3	4	Married woman	–	1
Salesman	3	3			
Landlady	–	1			
Clerk	–	2			
Cashier	1	–			

Sources: Shareholders' registers. PRO BT31 7363 52138 (Holbeck) and BT 31 17428 84163 (Leeds City).

TABLE A.11
CROWD DISTURBANCES AT NORTHERN UNION SENIOR MATCHES 1895–1910

Club	Date	Offence	Punishment
Rochdale	Feb. 1896	Referee attacked after match	Ground closed – six weeks
Wakefield	March 1896	Referee attacked after match	Ground closed – eight weeks
Rochdale	Nov. 1896	Opponents attacked after match	Ground closed – five weeks
Bradford	Jan. 1897	Referee snowballed after game	No action taken
Rochdale	Dec. 1897	'Rowdy conduct' by boys	200 notices put up in town/ boys' prices raised to 6d
Swinton	April 1898	'Rowdyism'	Ground closed – four weeks
Castlef'd	Oct. 1898	Stones thrown at opponents	Fined £5
Swinton	March 1899	Ref/opponents attacked after match	Ground closed
Salford	Nov. 1899	Opponents stoned after match	Notices put up
Castlef'd	Feb. 1900	'Rowdyism'	Fined £25
Batley	March 1900	Referee 'mobbed' after match	Fined £25
Leeds PC	Oct. 1900	Opponents stoned after match	Fined £20
Hudd'f'ld	Jan 1902	Ref/opponents attacked after match	Not recorded
Hull KR	Jan. 1902	'Rowdyism'	Notices put up
Sowerby	March 1902	Stones thrown at referee and police	Fined £10
Rochdale	March 1902	Referee attacked after match	Ground closed – two weeks
Dewsbury	March 1902	Referee attacked after match	Ground closed – four weeks
Runcorn	Nov. 1902	Referee punched by spectator	Ground closed – three weeks
Hudd'f'ld	Feb. 1903	Referee attacked after match	Ground closed – two weeks
Keighley	Dec. 1903	Referee kicked by spectators	No action taken
Batley	Sept. 1904	Referee stoned after match	Ground closed – four weeks
Hull	March 1905	Opponents stoned after match	Ground closed – four weeks
Merthyr	March 1908	Mud thrown at referee after game	Ground closed – two weeks
Hunslet	March 1908	Referee kicked by spectator after game	Notices put up
Bramley	April 1908	Referee stoned after match	Ground closed – four weeks
Hull	April 1908	Opponents 'barracked' and attacked	Notices put up
Widnes	Sept. 1908	Referee 'shouted and hooted' at	Notices put up
Keighley	Feb. 1909	Opposing player punched after match	Notices put up
Keighley	Dec. 1909	Crowd kicked opponents after game	Club ordered to provide dressing rooms on ground
Merthyr	Jan. 1910	Referee stoned after match	Ground closed – four weeks

Sources: NU General Committee minutes, *Yorkshire Post* and *Athletic News*.

TABLE A.12
DEATHS IN THE NORTHERN UNION 1895–1910

Date	Name	Club	Cause of death
Nov. 1897	Robert Cuss	Ripon	Fractured spine
Aug. 1898	Joe Gerrard	St Helens (practice game)	Unknown
Oct. 1900	Harry Lovell	Half Acre Trinity	Unknown
Dec. 1900	Fred Croft	Brighouse Rangers	Unknown
Jan. 1902	Thomas Leather	Tyldesley Shamrocks	Unknown
Nov. 1902	John Richardson	Cumberland	Abdominal injuries
Nov. 1902	William Long	Barrow Primrose	Concussion
Dec. 1902	G. Harwood	North West Manchester	Unknown
April 1904	F. Green	Fairburn	Lockjaw
Feb. 1906	A. Hanson	Warmfield	Drowning
Dec. 1906	Harry Myers	Keighley	Damaged spinal cord
Oct. 1909	Albert Barraclough	Lane End United	Unknown

Sources: *Yorkshire Post*, *Athletic News*, Northern Union General Committee minutes.

Bibliography

MANUSCRIPT SOURCES AND OFFICIAL PUBLICATIONS

Batley and District Junior Football Vase Competition	Rules 1902–3
Bradford and District Junior Football League (NRU)	Bye-laws 1899–1900,1902–3, 1905–6
British Playing Fields Society	Committee Minutes 1909–10
Cheshire Junior Rugby Football League	Rules 1905–6
Cumberland Junior Rugby Football Union	Rules 1903–4
Cumberland Northern Football Union Shield Competition	Rules 1899–1900
East Riding Rugby League	Bye-laws 1907–8
Furness and District Junior Rugby Football League	Rules 1901–2
Halifax and District Junior Football League (NU)	Bye-laws 1900–1
Halifax Charity Cup	Rules 1899–1900
Heavy Woollen District Football League (NU)	Rules 1900–1, 1903–4
Hull Football Club	Committee Minutes 1883–84
	Report and Accounts 1881–1910
Hull Kingstone Rovers FC	Report and Accounts 1897–1910
Keighley and District Football Charity Cup (NU)	Rules 1902–3
Lancashire County Football Club (Lancashire RU)	Committee Minutes 1881–95
Leeds and District NRU Junior Football League	Rules 1899–1900
Leeds and District Rugby Football League Challenge Cup	Rules 1905–6
Leeds Athletic Club	Annual Report 1871
Leeds Cricket, Football and Athletic Club Ltd	Reports and Accounts 1890–1911

Leeds Grammar School	Admission Books 1820–1900
Leeds Schools Rugby Football Union (NU)	Minutes of General Committee 1903–14
Manchester and District Rugby Football League	Rules 1901–2, 1902–3
Northern Rugby Football Union	Minutes of General Committee 1899–1914
	Minutes of Professionalism Sub Committee 1899–1905
	Minutes of Cup Committee 1899–1914
	Official Guide 1898–99, 1899–1900, 1903–4, 1904–5, 1907–8, 1908–9, 1909–10, 1910–11
	Report and Balance Sheet 1899–1900, 1900–1, 1902–3, 1903–4, 1904–5, 1905–6, 1906–7, 1907–8, 1908–9, 1909–10
	Players' Register 1906–9
Northern Rugby League	Minutes of General Committee 1903–5
	Report and Balance Sheet 1903–4, 1905–6, 1907–8, 1908–9, 1910–11
North Lancashire District NU Football League	Rules 1900–1
North West Junior Rugby Football League	Rules 1899–1900
Rugby Football Union	Minutes 1871–95
St Helens and District Intermediate Rugby Football League	Rules 1908–9
Southcoates Football Club	MSS Notebook of W. Corlyon 1881–89
South West Lancashire and Border Towns Cup	Rules 1899–1900, 1900–1
Swinton Football Club Junior Challenge Cup	Rules 1899–1900
Wakefield and District Junior Football League	Bye-laws 1904–5, 1905–6
Welsh Rugby Football League	Bye-laws 1907–8
West Riding of Yorkshire Rifle Volunteer Corps	Scrapbooks 1859–1938
Wigan and District Junior Rugby Football League	Rules 1903–4, 1908–9

Yorkshire County (Northern) Football Union — Committee Minutes 1905–8

York Football Club — Correspondence and general documents 1881–83 – Papers (Munby and Scott, Solicitors)

Yorkshire Rugby Football Union — Commemoration Book 1914–1919 and Official Handbook 1919–20

CONTEMPORARY PUBLICATIONS (PRIOR TO 1921)

Newspapers and Periodicals

Almondburian, The
Athletic News
Barrow Herald and Dalton Advertiser
Barrow News
Barrow Times
Bradford Daily Argus
Bradford Daily Telegraph
Bradford Observer
Bramham College magazine
Bell's Life
Brighouse and Elland Echo
Burnley Express and Advertiser
Burnley Gazette
Clarion
Cleckheaton Advertiser
Dewsbury Reporter
Field, The
Football Field and Sports Telegram (Bolton)
Football Programme and Weekly Calendar (Manchester)
Green Final (Oldham)
Halifax Daily Courier
Halifax Guardian
Heckmondwike Herald
Huddersfield Daily Chronicle
Huddersfield Daily Examiner
Hull and East Riding Athlete
Hull Critic
Hull Daily Mail
Hull Times
Illustrated Weekly Telegraph (Bradford), The
Justice

Keighley News
Lancashire Evening Post
Lantern (St Helens), The
Llanelli and County Guardian
Leeds Daily News
Leeds Evening Express
Leeds Intelligencer
Leeds Loiners' Comic Olmenac, T'
Leeds Mercury
Leeds Parish Church Magazine
Leodiensian, The
Magazine of Sport, The
Magazine of Sports and Outdoor Life by C. B. Fry
Manchester Evening News
Manchester Examiner and Times
Manchester Guardian
Mascot, The
New Wortley Almanack
North West Daily Mail
Oldham Evening Chronicle
Oldham Standard
Pall Mall Gazette
Pastime
Pendleton Reporter
Pontefract and Castleford Express
Preston Herald
Rochdale Observer
Salford Chronicle
Salford Reporter
Saturday Review
Sheffield Telegraph
Sporting Chronicle
Sportsman, The
St Helens Newspaper
St Helens Standard
St James's Gazette
Times, The
Toby, the Yorkshire Tyke
To-Day
Ulverston Advertiser
Umpire, The (Manchester)
Wakefield Express
Wakefield Free Press
Wakefield and West Riding Herald

Warrington Examiner
Warrington Guardian
Weever's Awn Comic Olmenack, The
Widnes Weekly News
Wigan Examiner
Wigan Observer
Yorkshire Busy Bee
Yorkshire Chat
Yorkshire Evening Post
Yorkshire Factory Times
Yorkshire Football
Yorkshireman, The
Yorkshire Owl, The
Yorkshire Post
Yorkshire Weekly Post

Articles and contributions to books

Almond, H. H., 'Football as a Moral Agent', *The Nineteenth Century*, Vol. 34, 1893
Anonymous, 'Sport and Decadence', *The Quarterly Review*, Vol. 211, Oct. 1909
Creston, 'Football', *The Fortnightly Review*, Vol. 55, 1894
Edwardes, C., 'The New Football Mania', *The Nineteenth Century*, Vol. 32, 1892
Ensor, E., 'The Football Madness', *The Contemporary Review*, Vol. 74, Nov. 1898
Graves, H., 'A Philosophy of Sport', *The Contemporary Review*, Vol. 78, Dec. 1900
Jackson, N. L., 'Professionalism and Sport', *The Fortnightly Review*, Vol. 67, 1900
Sewell, E. H. D., 'Rugby Football and the Colonial Tours', *The Fortnightly Review*, Vol. 82, 1907
Sewell, E. H. D., 'Rugby Football', *The Fortnightly Review*, Vol. 85, 1909
Sturdee, R. J., 'The Ethics of Football', *The Westminster Review*, Vol. 159, Feb. 1903

Books

Alcock, C. W. (ed), *The Football Annual*, London, 1868–1900
Alcock, C. W. and R. Hill, *Famous Footballers, 1895–96*, London, 1895
Alken, H., *The National Sports of Great Britain*, London, 1903
Arnold, M., *Culture and Anarchy*, London, 1869
Athletic News Annuals, Manchester 1892–1901
Baines, T., *The Industrial North in the Last Decade of the Nineteenth Century*, Leeds, 1928
Barrow FC Yearbook, Barrow, 1895
Bedell, A. W., *An Account of Hornsea in Holderness*, Hull, 1848
Bradby, H. C., *Rugby*, London, 1900

Budd, A., C. B. Fry, B. F. Robinson and T. A. Cook, *Football*, London, 1897
Cassell's Complete Book of Sports and Pastimes, London, 1893
Clarkson, H., *Memories of Merry Wakefield*, Wakefield, 1889
Cooper, G. H., *Spen Valley Rugby Football Reminiscences*, Cleckheaton, 1920
Dickens, C., *Hard Times*, London, 1854
Gallaher, D. and W. J. Stead, *The Complete Rugby Footballer*, London, 1906
Gaskell, E., *North and South*, London, 1855
Goldthorpe, J., *Twenty Years' Records of Leeds FC*, Leeds, 1910
Goulburn, E. M., *The Book of Rugby School*, Rugby, 1856
Halifax FC, *History of Halifax Cricket and Football Club*, Halifax, 1900
Hardy, H. H., *Public School Life – Rugby*, London, 1911
Higson, J., *History of Salford Football Club*, Salford, 1892
Hughes, T., *Tom Brown's Schooldays*, London, 1857
Hull Football Almanack, Hull, 1888
Kay's Illustrated Yorkshire Football Guide 1894–95, Bradford, 1894
Lawson, J., *Letters to the Young on Progress in Pudsey during the Last Sixty Years*,
    Stanningley, 1887
Lennox, Lord W., *Merrie England, Its Sports and Pastimes*, London, 1858
Marshall, Revd F. (ed), *Football – The Rugby Union Game*, London, 1892
Masterman, C. F. G., *The Condition of England*, 1909
Masterman, C. F. G., *The Heart of Empire*, London, 1901
Old Rugbeian Society, *The Origin of Rugby Football*, Rugby, 1897
Pike, W. T. (ed), *The West Riding of Yorkshire at the Opening of the 20th Century*,
    Brighton, 1902
Price, A. C., *A History of the Leeds Grammar School from its Foundation until the
    End of 1918*, Leeds, 1919
Rahilly, Jerome J., *Rugby Football*, London, 1904
Referee, The, *History of Barrow Football Club*, Barrow, 1914
Robinson, B. Fletcher, *Rugby Football*, London, 1896
Rochdale Hornets FC, *Grand Bazaar Official Guide and Handbook*, Rochdale, 1901
Rouse, W. H. D., *A History of Rugby School*, London, 1898
Rugby Union Football Handbook, The, London, 1889–96
Russell, C. E. B., *Manchester Boys*, Manchester, 1905
Selfe, Lt Col S., *Chapters from the History of Rugby School*, Rugby, 1910
Shaw, C. F., *The Gallant Youths*, Batley, 1899
Shearman, M., *Athletics and Football*, London, 1887
Smith, H., *Festivals, Games and Amusements*, London, 1831
Smith, W. (ed), *Old Yorkshire*, London, 1882
Sportsman, The *British Sports and Sportsmen Past and Present*, London, 1908
Strutt, J., *The Sports and Pastimes of the People of England*, London, 1801
Terrett, J. J., *H. H. Asquith and the Featherstone Massacre*, London, 1906
Tosswill, L. R. and Revd F. Marshall (eds), *Football – The Rugby Union Game*,
    London, 1925
Vassall, H., *Rugby Football*, London, 1889

Watson, A. E. T. (ed), *The Year's Sport: A Review of British Sports and Pastimes for the Year 1885*, London, 1886

Whadcoat, J. H., *An Account of the West Yorkshire Educational and Benevolent Institution*, Bradford, 1906

Whellan, W., *The History and Topography of the Counties of Cumberland and Westmoreland*, Pontefract, 1860

Yorkshire Football Handbook, Leeds, 1881–82 and 1885–86

Yorkshire Lives – Social and Political, London, 1899

Yorkshire Men of Mark, Exeter, 1898

Yorkshire Owl Cricket Annual 1896, Leeds, 1896

Yorkshire Sporting Almanack for 1862, Leeds, 1862

Yorkshire Who's Who, London, 1912

Local Directories

Directory of Barrow in Furness, C. J. Roberts, Barrow, 1886,

Barrow and District Yearbook, E. Foster, Barrow, 1906

Kelly's West Riding Directory, 1889

Slater's Directory of Leeds and District 1892–93, 1893

Slater's Directory of Warrington, 1887 and 1891

Slater's Directory of the West Riding, 1887 and 1891

White's Clothing District Directory, 1881

White's General and Commercial Directory of Leeds and the West Riding, 1870

PUBLICATIONS SINCE 1920

Articles, papers and contributions to books

Adair, D., 'Competing or Complementary Forces? The "Civilising" Process and the Commitment to Winning in Nineteenth Century English Rugby and Association Football', *Canadian Journal of the History of Sport*, Vol. 24, No. 2, Dec. 1993

Arnold, A. J., 'Shall it be Bradford or Leeds? The Origins of Professional Football in the West Riding Textile District', *Publications of the Thoresby Society – Miscellany*, Vol. 19, 1990

Arscott, C. and J. Wolff, 'Cultivated Capital', *History Today*, Vol. 37, 1987

Baker, W. J., 'The Making of a Working-Class Football Culture in Victorian England', *Journal of Social History*, Vol. 13, No. 2, 1979

Baker, W. J., 'William Webb Ellis and the Origins of Rugby Football The Life and Death of a Victorian Myth', *Albion*, Vol. 13, 1981

Barlow, S., 'The Diffusion of "Rugby" Football in the Industrialised Context of Rochdale, 1868–90', *International Journal of the History of Sport*, Vol. 10, No. 1, April 1993

Birley, D., 'Sportsmen and the Deadly Game', *British Journal of Sports History*, Vol. 3, Dec. 1986

Briggs, A., 'The View from Badminton' in A. Briggs (ed), *Essays in the History of Publishing: Longman 1724–1974*, London, 1974

Cunningham, H., 'Leisure and Culture', *The Cambridge Social History of Britain 1750–1950*, Vol. 2, Cambridge, 1990

Cunningham, H., 'Leisure', *The Working Class in England 1875–1914*, John Benson (ed), London, 1985

Davies, B., 'Bifurcation in Sport: Some Preliminary Thoughts on the Case of Rugby League', *The Journal of Regional and Local Studies*, Vol. 8, No. 1, spring 1988

Delaney, T., 'A Brief History of Brighouse Rangers 1878–1906', *Code 13*, No. 9, Dec. 1988

Delaney, T., 'The Great Betrayal at Park Avenue Bradford', *Code 13*, No. 7, June 1988

Dellheim, C., 'Imagining England: Victorian Views of the North', *Northern History*, Vol. 22, 1986

Dunning, E. and K. Sheard, 'The Bifurcation of Rugby Union and Rugby League: A Case Study Of Organisational Conflict and Change', *International Review of Sports Sociology*, II, 1976

Elias, N. and Dunning, E., 'Folk Football in Medieval and Early Modern Britain', E. Dunning (ed), *The Sociology of Sport*, London, 1971

Elton, A., 'Becoming a City: Leeds, 1893', *Publications of the Thoresby Society – Miscellany*, Second Series, Vol. 3, 1993

Farr, E., 'A History of Morley Northern', *Code 13*, No. 13, Dec. 1989

Gould, S. J., 'Creation Myths of Cooperstown' in *Bully for Brontosaurus*, London, 1991

Greenhalgh, P., '"The Work and Play Principle": The Professional Regulations of the NRFU, 1898–1905', *International Journal of the History of Sport*, Vol. 9, No. 3, Dec. 1992

Halladay, E. 'Of Pride and Prejudice: The Amateur Question in English Nineteenth Century Rowing', *The International Journal of the History of Sport*, Vol. 4, No. 1, May 1987

Harrison, B., 'Religion and Recreation in Nineteenth Century England', *Past and Present*, No. 38, Dec. 1967

Hendrick, H., 'The Leeds Gas Strike', *Publications of the Thoresby Society – Miscellany*, Vol. 16, Pt. 2, 1993

Hill, C., 'The Norman Yoke', *Puritanism and Revolution*, London, 1958

Hobsbawm, E. J., 'Labour in the Great City', *New Left Review*, 166, Nov.–Dec. 1987

Holt, R., 'Contrasting Nationalisms', *International Journal of the History of Sport*, Vol. 12, No. 2, Aug. 1995.

James, D., 'The First Ever Northern Union International', *Code 13*, Sept. 1989

Jowitt, T., *Late Victorian and Edwardian Bradford*, Bradford Centre Occasional Papers, Vol. 2, Leeds, 1980

Kirby, H. T., 'Some Notes on the Bloxam Family of Rugby', *Essays in Honour of Philip B. Chatwin*, Oxford, 1962

Maguire, J., 'Images of Manliness and Competing Ways of Living in Late Victorian and Edwardian Britain', *British Journal of Sports History*, Vol. 3, Dec. 1986

Mandle, W. F., 'Games People Played: Cricket and Football in England and Victoria in the Late Nineteenth Century', *Historical Studies*, April 1972

Mandle, W. F, 'W. G. Grace as a Victorian Hero', *Historical Studies*, April 1980

Mangan, J. A., 'Duty unto Death: English Masculinity and Militarism in the Age of the New Imperialism', *International Journal of the History of Sport*, Vol. 12, No. 2, Aug. 1995

Mann, L., and D. Pearce, 'Social Psychology of Sports Spectators', in D. Glencross (ed), *Psychology and Sport*, Sydney, 1979

Mather, T., 'A History of Fleetwood NUFC', *The Greatest Game*, No. 11, Sept. 1992; 12, Nov. 1992; and 13, Feb. 1993

Metcalfe, A., 'Football in the Mining Communities of East Northumberland', *International Journal of the History of Sport*, Vol. 5, No. 3, Dec. 1988

Metcalfe, A., 'Organised Sport in the Mining Communities of South Northumberland', *Victorian Studies*, No. 25, summer 1982

Morris, R. J., 'Middle Class Culture 1700–1914' in Derek Fraser (ed), *A History of Modern Leeds*, Manchester, 1980

Nairn, T., 'The English Working Class', in Robin Blackburn (ed), *Ideology in Social Science*, London, 1972

Nauright, J., 'Sport, Manhood and Empire', *The International Journal of the History of Sport*, Vol. 8, No. 2, Sept. 1991

Oddy, D. J., 'Working Class Diets', *Economic History Review*, Vol. 23, 1970

Reid, D. A., 'Folk Football, the Aristocracy and Cultural Change: A Critique of Dunning and Sheard', *The International Journal of the History of Sport*, Vol. 5, No. 2, Sept. 1988

Reid, D. A., 'The Decline of Saint Monday', *Past & Present*, No. 71, May 1976

Rhind, N,. 'Blackheath Football Club 1862–1870', *Transactions of the Greenwich and Lewisham Antiquarian Society*, Vol. 10, No. 1, 1985

Roberts, E., 'Working Class Standards of Living in Barrow and Lancaster 1890–1914', *Economic History Review*, Vol. 30, 1977

Russell, D., '"Sporadic and Curious": The Emergence of Rugby and Soccer Zones in Yorkshire and Lancashire c.1860–1914', *The International Journal of the History of Sport*, Vol. 5, No. 2, Sept. 1988

Stedman-Jones, G., 'Class Expression Versus Social Control? A Critique of Recent Trends in the Social History of "Leisure"', *History Workshop Journal*, No. 4, autumn 1977

Stedman-Jones, G., 'Working-Class Politics and Working-Class Culture in London 1870–1900', *Journal of Social History*, Vol. 7, summer 1974

Storch, R. D., 'The Policeman as "Domestic Missionary": Urban Discipline and Popular Culture in Northern England 1850–1880', *Journal of Social History*, Vol. 9, 1976

Thompson, F. M. L., 'Social Control in Victorian Britain', *Economic History Review*, Vol. 34, No. 2, 1981

Tranter, N. L., 'The Cappielow Riot and the Composition and Behaviour of Soccer Crowds in Late Victorian Scotland', *The International Journal of the History of Sport*, Vol. 12, No. 3, Dec. 1995

Vamplew, W., 'Paying for Play: The Earnings of Professional Sportsmen in England 1870–1914', in R. Cashman and M. McKernan (eds), *Sport, Money, Morality and the Media*, New South Wales, 1982

Vamplew, W., 'Profit or Utility Maximisation? An Analysis of English County Cricket Before 1914' in W. Vamplew (ed), *The Economic History of Leisure*, Adelaide, 1983

Vamplew, W., 'The Economics of a Sports Industry: Scottish Gate Money Football 1890–1914', *Economic History Review*, Vol. 35, Nov. 1982

Vamplew, W., 'Ungentlemanly Conduct: The Control of Soccer Crowd Behaviour 1888–1914', in T. C. Smout (ed), *The Search for Wealth and Stability*, London, 1979

Vamplew, W., 'Sports Crowd Disorder in Britain 1870–1914', *Journal of Sport History*, Vol. 7, No. 1, 1980

Veitch, C., '"Play Up! Play Up! and Win the War!" Football, the Nation and the First World War', *Journal of Contemporary History*, Vol. 20, July 1985

Walton, J., 'Professor Musgrove's North of England: A Critique', *Journal of Regional and Local Studies*, Vol. 12, No. 2, 1992

Walton, J., 'Residential Amenity, Respectable Morality and the Rise of the Entertainment Industry: The Case of Blackpool 1860–1914', *Literature and History*, Vol. 1, 1975

Williams, Graham, 'If at first you can't decide: A History of South Shields', *Code 13*, No. 15, June 1990

Williams, Graham, 'Initiating the Liverpudlians – A History of the First Liverpool City', *Code 13*, No. 13, Dec. 1989

Books

Adams, T., *The Hit Men*, Sydney, 1994

Arlott, J. (ed), *The Oxford Companion to Sports and Games*, Oxford, 1976

Arnold, A. J., *A Game that would pay, A Business History of Professional Football in Bradford*, London, 1988

Auty, T. W., *Centenary History of Headingley Football Club*, Leeds, 1978

Bailey, P., *Leisure and Class in Victorian England*, Second Edition, London, 1987

Balaam, L., *Manchester Football Club 1860–1985*, Manchester, 1985

Bale, J., *Sport and Place*, London, 1982

Barak, M., *A Century of Rugby at Sale*, Sale, 1962

Benson, J., *The Penny Capitalists: A Study of Working Class Entrepreneurs*, Dublin, 1983

Bergin, T. E., *The Game: The Harvard–Yale Football Rivalry 1875–1983*, Yale, 1984

Best, G., *Mid-Victorian Britain 1851–75*, London, 1979

Birley, D., *Land of Sport and Glory: Sport and British Society 1887–1910*, Manchester, 1995

Birley, D., *Sport and the Making of Britain*, Manchester, 1993

Birley, D., *The Willow Wand*, London, 1979

Briggs, A., and J. Saville (eds), *Essays in Labour History*, London, 1960

Briggs, A., *Victorian Cities*, London, 1963

Briggs, A., *Victorian People*, London, 1965

Calder, A., *The Myth of the Blitz*, London, 1991

Cartwright, B. F., *A Ton Full of Memories*, Batley, 1987

Cashman, R., and M. McKernan (eds), *Sport in History*, Queensland, 1979

Chadwick, S., *Claret and Gold*, Huddersfield, 1945

Chadwick, S., *Northern Union*, Huddersfield, 1946

Clarke, J., and C. Critcher, *The Devil Makes Work: Leisure in Capitalist Britain*, London, 1985

Coffey, J., *Canterbury XIII*, Christchurch, 1987

Cox, R. W., *History of Sport: A Guide to the Literature and Sources of Information*, Cheshire, 1994

Croxford, W. B., *Rugby Union in Lancashire and Cheshire*, Liverpool, 1950

Cunningham, H., *Leisure in the Industrial Revolution*, London, 1980

Cunningham, H., *The Volunteer Force*, London, 1975

Dalby, K., *The Headingley Story 1890–1955*, Leeds, 1955

Dalglish, J. R. A., *Red, Black & Blue: The First 125 Years of Liverpool Football Club*, Swinton, 1983

Davies, A., and S. Fielding (eds), *Workers' Worlds: Cultures and Communities in Manchester and Salford 1880–1939*, Manchester, 1992

Delaney, T., *Rugby Disunion*, Keighley, 1993

Delaney, T., *The Grounds of Rugby League*, Keighley, 1991

Delaney, T., *The Roots of Rugby League*, Keighley, 1984

Dobbs, B., *Edwardians at Play*, London, 1973

Dunning, E., and K. Sheard, *Barbarians, Gentlemen and Players*, New York, 1979

Dyos, H. J., and M. Wolff (eds), *The Victorian City: Images and Realities*, London, 1973

Elias, N., *The Civilising Process*, Oxford, 1978

Elton, C., *Hull City – A Complete Record*, Derby, 1989

Ensor, R. C. K., *England 1870–1914*, London, 1936

Firth, D., *My Dear Victorious Stod*, London, 1977

Firth, G., *Victorian Yorkshire at Play*, Nelson, 1989

Frost, T., *Bradford City – A Complete Record*, Derby, 1988

Gate, R., *Gone North* (two vols.), Sowerby Bridge, 1986

Gate, R., *Rugby League, An Illustrated History*, London, 1989

Gate, R., *The Struggle for the Ashes*, Ripponden, 1986

Genovese, E., *Roll, Jordan, Roll: The World the Slaves Made*, London, 1974

Gill, E., *Skipton RUFC Centenary*, Skipton, 1974

Gillett, E., and K. A. MacMahon, *A History of Hull*, Hull, 1980

Golby, J. (ed), *Culture and Society in Britain 1850–90*, London, 1986

Golby, J. M., and A. W. Purdue, *The Civilisation of the Crowd*, London, 1984

Green, B. (ed), *The Wisden Book of Cricketer's Lives*, London, 1986

Green, M., and L. Hoole, *The Parksiders, A Brief History of Hunslet RLFC*, Leeds, n.d.

Green, M., *The Villagers, A Brief History of Bramley RLFC*, Leeds, n.d.

Greenland, W. J., *The History of the Amateur Football Alliance*, London, 1965

Guttmann, A., *From Ritual to Record: The Nature of Modern Sports*, New York, 1978

Guttmann, A., *Sports Spectators*, New York, 1986

Haight, G. (ed), *A Victorian Reader*, New York, 1972

Haley, B., *The Healthy Body in Victorian Culture*, Cambridge, MA, 1978

Hardcastle, A., *The Thrum Hall Story*, Halifax, 1986

Harding, J., *Billy Meredith*, Derby, 1985

Harding, J., *For the Good of the Game*, London, 1991

Hargreaves, Jennifer (ed), *Sport, Culture and Ideology*, London, 1982

Hargreaves, John, *Sport Power and Culture: A Social and Historical Analysis of Popular Sports in Britain*, Cambridge, 1986

Harris, H. A., *Sport and Britain*, London, 1975

Harrison, J. F. C., *Late Victorian Britain 1875–1901*, London, 1990

Hartley, M. and T. Clapham, *The Avenue*, Nottingham, 1987

Heads, I., *The Kangaroos*, Sydney, 1990

Heads, I., *True Blue*, Sydney, 1992

Hinchliffe, G., *A History of King James's Grammar School in Almondbury*, Huddersfield, 1963

History of the Lancashire Football Association, Blackburn, 1928

Hobsbawm, E. J., and T. Ranger (eds), *The Invention of Tradition*, London, 1983

Hobsbawm, E. J., *Worlds of Labour*, London, 1984

Hoggart, R., *The Uses of Literacy*, London, 1957

Holt, R. (ed), *Sport and the Working Class in Modern Britain*, Manchester, 1990

Holt, R., *Sport and the British*, Oxford, 1989

Hope-Simpson, J. B., *Rugby since Arnold*, London, 1967

Houghton, W. E., *The Victorian Frame of Mind*, London, 1957

Hughes, G., *One Hundred Years of Scarlet*, Llanelli, 1983

Humphries, S., *Hooligans or Rebels? An Oral History of Working-Class Childhood and Youth, 1889–1939*, Oxford, 1981

Hynes, S., *The Edwardian Turn of Mind*, Princeton, 1968

Inglis, K., *The Churches and the Working Classes in Victorian England*, London, 1963

Inglis, S., *League Football and the Men who Made it*, London, 1988

Inglis, S., *The Football Grounds of Great Britain*, London, 1987

Jackson, H., *The Eighteen Nineties*, London, 1913

James, C. L. R., *Beyond a Boundary*, London, 1963

Jarred, M., and M. Macdonald, *Leeds United – A Complete Record*, Derby, 1986

Jewell, H. M., *The North–South Divide: The Origins of Northern Consciousness in England*, Manchester, 1994

Joyce, P., *Visions of the People*, Cambridge, 1991

Joyce, P., *Work, Society and Politics*, Brighton, 1980

Kidd, A. J., and K. W. Roberts (eds), *City, Class and Culture: Studies of Cultural Production and Social Policy in Victorian Manchester*, Manchester, 1985

Korr, C., *West Ham United*, London, 1986

Latham, M, and T. Mather, *The Rugby League Myth*, Adlington, 1993

Latham, M., *Buff Berry and the Mighty Bongers*, Adlington, 1995

Lindley, J. C., *A Hundred Years of Rugby*, Wakefield, 1973

Lorimar, D. A., *Colour, Class and the Victorians*, Leicester, 1978

Lovesey, P., *The Official Centenary of the Amateur Athletics Association*, London, 1979

Lowerson, J., and J. Myerscough, *Time to Spare in Victorian England*, Sussex, 1977

Lowerson, J., *Sport and the English Middle Classes*, Manchester, 1993

Mackenzie, J. M., *Imperialism and Popular Culture*, Manchester, 1986

Macrory, J., *Running with the Ball, The Birth of Rugby Football*, London, 1991

Malcolmson, R. W., *Popular Recreations in English Society 1770–1850*, London, 1975

Mangan, J. A., and R. J. Park (eds), *From 'Fair Sex' to Feminism: Sport and the Socialisation of Women in the Industrial and Post-Industrial Eras*, London, 1987

Mangan, J. A. (ed), *Pleasure, Profit, Proselytism*, London, 1988

Mangan, J. A., and J. Walvin (eds), *Manliness and Morality: Middle Class Masculinity in Britain and America, 1800–1940*, Manchester, 1987

Mangan, J. A., *Athleticism in the Victorian and Edwardian Public School*, Cambridge, 1981

Mangan, J. A., *The Games Ethic and Imperialism*, London, 1986

Marples, M., *A History of Football*, London, 1954

Marsden, A., *Preston Grasshoppers' Centenary Brochure*, Preston, 1969

Marx, K., and F. Engels, *On Britain*, Moscow, 1971

Mason, T. (ed), *Sport in Britain: A Social History*, Cambridge, 1989

Mason, T., *Association Football and English Society 1863–1915*, Brighton, 1980

McIntosh, P. C., *Physical Education in England since 1800*, London, 1968

McIntosh, P. C., *Sport in Society*, London, 1963

McKibbin, R., *The Ideologies of Class*, Oxford, 1990

Meacham, S., *A Life Apart: The English Working Class 1890–1914*, London, 1977

Meller, H., *Leisure and the Changing City, 1870–1914*, London, 1976

Melling, P., *Man of Amman*, Llandysul, Dyfed, 1993

Messenger, D. M., *The Master*, Sydney, 1982

Mitchell, W. R., *By Gum, Life were Sparse!*, London, 1981

Montefiore, D., *Cricket in the Doldrums*, Campbelltown (Australia), 1992

Moorhouse, G., *A People's Game*, London, 1995

Morris, R. J., and R. Rodger (eds), *The Victorian City: A Reader in British Urban History*, Harlow, Essex, 1993

Musgrove, F., *The North of England. A History from Roman Times to the Present*, Oxford, 1990

Nauright, J., and T. Chandler (eds), *Making Men*, London, 1996

Oriard, M., *Reading Football: How the Popular Press Created an American Spectacle*, Chapel Hill, 1993

Owen, O. L., *The History of the Rugby Football Union*, London, 1955

Pearce, C., *The Manningham Mills Strike*, Hull, 1975

Pearson, G., *Hooligan: A History of Respectable Fears*, London, 1983

Phillips, C. B., and J. H. Smith, *Lancashire and Cheshire from AD1540*, London, 1994

Phillips, J., *A Man's Country: The Image of the Pakeha Male: A History*, Auckland, 1987

Pullin, A. W., *Alfred Shaw, Cricketer: His Career and Reminiscences*, London, 1902

Read, D., *The Age of Urban Democracy*, London, 1979

Read, D., *The English Provinces*, London, 1964

Roberts, R., *The Classic Slum*, Manchester, 1971

Robertson, J., *Uppies and Doonies*, Aberdeen, 1967

Rubinstein, W. D., *Capitalism, Culture and Decline in Britain 1750–1990*, London, 1993

Ryan, G., *Forerunners of the All Blacks*, Canterbury, NZ, 1993

Sandiford, K., *Cricket and the Victorians*, Aldershot, 1994

Service, A., *Saints in their Glory*, St Helens, 1985

Sissons, R., *The Professionals: A Social History of the Professional Cricketer*, London, 1988

Smith, D., and G. Williams, *Fields of Praise: The Official History of the Welsh Rugby Union, 1881–1981*, Cardiff, 1980

Souvenir History of Swinton, Swinton, 1929

Storch, R. D. (ed), *Popular Culture and Custom in Nineteenth Century England*, London, 1982

Thompson, E. P., *Customs in Common*, London, 1991

Thompson, F. M. L. (ed), *The Cambridge Social History of Britain 1750–1950*, Cambridge, 1990

Thompson, F. M. L. *The Rise of Respectable Society*, London, 1988

Thompson, P., *The Edwardians*, London, 1975

Thorburn, S., *The History of Scottish Rugby*, London, 1970

Thornton, A. P., *The Habit of Authority*, London, 1966

Tischler, S., *Footballers and Businessmen*, New York, 1981

Titley, U. A., and R. McWhirter, *A Centenary History of the Rugby Football Union*, London, 1970

Trescatheric, B., *Sport and Leisure in Victorian Barrow*, Barrow, 1983.

Vamplew, W., *Pay Up and Play the Game*, Cambridge, 1988

Waites, B., *Popular Culture in Late Nineteenth and Early Twentieth Century Lancashire*, Open University Course U203, Unit 6, n.d.

Waller, P. J., *Town, City and Nation: England 1850–1914*, Oxford, 1983

Walton, J., and J. Walvin (eds), *Leisure in Britain, 1780–1939*, Manchester, 1983

Walton, J., *Lancashire: A Social History 1558–1939*, Manchester, 1987

Walvin, J., *Leisure and Society, 1830–1950*, London, 1978

Walvin, J., *The People's Game*, London, 1975

Waters, C., *British Socialists and the Politics of Popular Culture*, Manchester, 1990

Wiener, M., *English Culture and the Decline of the Industrial Spirit 1850–1980*, Cambridge, 1981

Williams, Gareth, *1905 and All That*, Llandysul, Dyfed, 1991

Williams, Graham, *The Code War*, Harefield, 1994

Williams, R., *Culture and Society 1780–1950*, London, 1958

Williams, R., *The Long Revolution*, London, 1961

Wright, A. R., *British Calendar Customs*, London, 1936

Wynne-Thomas, P., *Give Me Arthur*, London, 1985

Yeo, E. and S. (eds), *Popular Culture and Class Conflict 1590–1914*, Brighton, 1981

Young, P., *A History of British Football*, London, 1968

Young, P., *Football in Sheffield*, London, 1964

Young, P., *Manchester United*, London, 1960

Video, CD-Rom and Electronic Media

Rugby League Tours, Micron Video, Wigan, 1988

Oxford English Dictionary, Second Edition on CD-Rom, Oxford, 1993

Theses

Arnold, J., *The Influence of Pilkington Brothers (Glass Manufacturers) on the Growth of Sport and Community Recreation in St Helens*, MEd thesis, University of Liverpool, 1977

Blackledge, P., *William Cail, Amateurism and the Rugby Football Union*, MA thesis, University of Northumbria, 1994

Bradley, S., *Leisure and Society in Huddersfield 1868–95*, BA thesis, University of Bristol, 1989

Greenhalgh, P., *The History of the Northern Rugby Football Union 1895–1915*, PhD thesis, University of Lancaster, 1992

Lewis, R. W., *The Development of Professional Football in Lancashire, 1870–1914*, PhD thesis, University of Lancaster, 1993

Martens, J. W., *Rugby Union Football and English Society 1871–1914*, PhD thesis, University of Manitoba, 1988

Index

Titles of Related Interest

THE RUGBY WORLD
Race, Gender, Commerce and Rugby Union
Timothy J L Chandler, Kent State University and
John Nauright, University of Queensland (Eds)

This book explores the expansion of rugby from its imperial and amateur upper-class white male core into other contexts throughout the late nineteenth and twentieth centuries. The development of rugby in the racially divided communities of the setter empire and how this was viewed are explored initially. Then the editors turn to four case studies of rugby's expansion beyond the bounds of the British Empire (France, Italy, Japan and the USA). The role of women in rugby is examined and the subsequent development of women's rugby as one of the fastest growing sports for women in Europe, North America and Australasia in the 1980s and 1990s. The final section analyses the impact of commercialisation, professionalisation and media on rugby and the impact on the historic rugby culture linked to an ethos of amateurism.

256 pages   1999
0 7146 4853 1 cloth   0 7146 4411 0 paper
Sport in the Global Society No. 10

MAKING MEN
Rugby and Masculine Identity
John Nauright, University of Queensland, and
Timothy J L Chandler, Kent State University, Ohio (Eds)

This collection of essays charts the development of rugby football from its origins in the English public schools and ancient universities to its acceptance in the farthest reaches of the empire. As the authors show, central to an understanding of the place of rugby in all these settings is evidence demonstrating that the game was a form of both hegemonic masculinity and homosocial behaviour, as well as a means of promoting nationalism and social control. A major aim of the editors has been to highlight the changes and continuities which the game of rugby and its traditions of manliness and masculinity have undergone due to the effects of both time and place. The book concludes with a discussion on the current state and future of rugby, particularly of the impact of the World Cup, professionalism and commercialism on this still 'gendered' sport.

256 pages illus.   1996   repr. 1998
0 7146 4637 7 cloth   0 7146 4156 1 paper

THE GAMES ETHIC AND IMPERIALISM
Aspects of the Diffusion of an Ideal
J A Mangan, University of Strathclyde
New Preface and Foreword

Comments on the first edition

> '... *not only injects fresh vigour into the old, old story but emphasises the very peculiar nature, both of those institutions where character was elevated above intellect by the encouragement of team games, and of the formidable headmasters who held sway over them.*'
> **The Daily Telegraph**

> '... *as much a study of British ethnocentrism as of sport in the empire...others need to look at how the study of sport can contribute to knowledge of local society. With this stimulating work of Mangan, new directions for future research have been pointed out.*'
> **The American Historical Review**

This book is more than a description of the imperial spread of public school games: it is a consideration of hegemony and patronage, ideals and idealism, educational values and aspirations, cultural assimilation and adaptation, and perhaps most fascinating of all, the dissemination throughout the empire of the hugely influential moralistic ideology athleticism. The author's purpose is to capture some of the more fascinating aspects of this extraordinary and sometimes whimsical story of the spread of a moral imperative; to recall for modern sceptics the period certainties of propagandist, proselytizer and publicist; to observe 'manliness' viewed as a valuable political expedient ensuring the retention of the most precious jewel in the Imperial Crown; and lastly, to follow with more than a little admiration in the footsteps of English upper-class missionaries, reliving their energetic and well-meaning efforts to win souls for Christ on far-flung and wide-spread imperial playing-fields.

240 pages 1985; 2nd revised edition 1998
0 7146 4399 8 paper
Sport in the Global Society No. 2

THE RACE GAME
Sport and Politics in South Africa
Douglas Booth, University of Otago, New Zealand

In this book Douglas Booth takes a fresh look at the role of sport in the fostering of a new national identity in South Africa. It looks at the thirty-year course and the changes in the objectives of the sports boycott of South Africa. Black South Africans initially proposed the boycott as a strategy to integrate sport, and Western governments and international sporting federations such as the International Olympic Committee later applied the boycott with similar intentions. At first, South Africa's ruling National Party dismissed all demands either to integrate sport or to extend political rights to blacks, but prolonged international isolation forced it to make concessions, and by the mid-1980s the government had accepted integrated sport. The international sporting community readmitted South Africa to competition in the early 1980s in acknowledgement of state president F W de Klerk's political initiatives and commitment to a universal franchise. Sport remains an integral element of post-apartheid politics. State president Nelson Mandela and his government believe that sport can unite black and white South Africans and contribute to social and political change. Indeed there have been moments, such as South Africa's victory in the 1995 World Rugby Cup, when unity through sport seemed possible. But through careful analysis Booth argues that sport will never unite South Africans except in the most fleeting and superficial manner.

272 pages   1998
0 7146 4799 3 cloth   0 7146 4354 8 paper
Sport in the Global Society No. 4

EUROPEAN HEROES
Myth, Identity, Sport
J A Mangan, University of Strathclyde, **Richard Holt**, University of Leuven, Belgium and **Pierre Lanfranchi**, De Montfort University (Eds)

Historians of popular culture have recently been addressing the role of myth, and now it is time that social historians of sport also examined it. The contributors to this collection of essays explore the symbolic meanings that have been attached to sport in Europe by considering some of the mythic heroes who have dominated the sporting landscapes of their own countries. The ambition is to understand what these icons stood for in the eyes of those who watched or read about these vessels into which poured all manner of gender, class and patriotic expectations.

184 pages   1996
0 7146 4578 8 cloth   0 7146 4125 1 paper
A special issue of The International Journal of the History of Sport

FRANCE AND THE 1998 WORLD CUP
The National Impact of a World Sporting Event
Hugh Dauncey and **Geoff Hare**, both at the University of Newcastle (Eds)

This book examines France's hosting of the soccer World Cup, held in ten cities in summer 1998. It covers the major socio-economic, political, cultural and sporting dimensions of this global sports event, including bidding for and organizing the Finals, the improvement of sporting and transport infra-structures, marketing, merchandizing and media coverage, policing and security during the month-long competition and building a national team. The analysis of France '98 is set within the sporting context of the recent history and organization of French football (the links between football, money and politics; the sporting public) and more broadly within the French tradition of using major cultural and sporting events to focus world attention of France as a leader in the international community. The book concludes with an evocation of the day-to-day impact of four weeks of sporting festivities, and the lessons to be drawn concerning sport and national identity in an era of increasing economic, political, cultural and sporting globalization.

212 pages   1998
0 7146 4887 6 cloth   0 7146 4438 2 paper
Sport in the Global Society No. 7
A special issue of the journal Culture, Sport, Society

SPORTING NATIONALISMS
Identity, Ethnicity, Immigration and Assimilation
David Mayall and **Michael Cronin** both at Sheffield Hallam University (Eds)

This volume examines the ways in which sport shapes the experiences of various immigrant and minority groups and, in particular, looks at the relationship between sport, ethnic identity and ethnic relations. The articles in this volume are concerned primarily with British, American and Australian sporting traditions and the themes covered include the consolidation of ethnic identity in host societies through participation immigrant sports and exclusive sporting organizations, assimilation into 'host' societies through participation in indigenous, national sports, and the construction by outsiders of separate ethnic identities according to sporting criteria.

160 pages   1998
07146 44896 5 cloth   07146 4449 8 paper
A special issue of the journal Immigrants and Minorities
Sport in the Global Society No. 6

ARTHUR WHARTON 1865–1930

The Forgotten History of the First Black Professional Footballer

Phil Vasili

With a Foreword by **Irvine Welsh** and an Introduction by **Tony Whelan**, Manchester United FC

Arthur Wharton was the world's first black professional footballer. He was also the first 100 yards world record holder and twice amateur sprint champion of Britain. He came from a wealthy Gold Coast/Ghanaian family, enjoyed national celebrity in England as an all-round athlete, but died a pauper in a South Yorkshire pit village.

Recounted within the social, cultural and political context of Victorian England, Wharton's story not only remembers the turbulent personal and professional life of an eminent sportsman but offers fresh insight into the onset of professionalism in British sport, the class divide and the beginnings of institutionalized racism.

240 pages 25 photographs 1998
0 7146 4903 1 cloth   0 7146 4459 5 paper

TRIBAL IDENTITIES

Nationalism, Europe, Sport

J A Mangan, University of Strathclyde (Ed)

'This volume represents an important and welcome contribution to the literature on creation and reproduction of national identity and nationalism. The book can be read with interest by specialists and nonspecialists, including upper level undergraduates and graduate students.'

Antonio V. Menendez-Alarcon, Butler University,
Nationalism & Ethnic Politics

'A fascinating insight into the links between sport and nationalism in Europe and beyond. An important and valuable text.'

Contemporary British History

'Each author has something perceptive to say.'

The International History Review

256 pages   1996
0 7146 4666 0 cloth   0 7146 4201 0 paper
A special issue of The International Journal of the History of Sport

CRICKET AND ENGLAND

A Cultural and Social History of Cricket in England between the Wars

Jack Williams, John Moores University, Liverpool

A study of how cricket in England between the Wars reflected the social relations and cultural values of the time. The author explores English social and cultural history through the sport by analysing the relationships between classes, Church and society, as well as gender roles. He points out cricket's role as part of the national image and the influence it had on evaluating the 'English character'. Williams carefully outlines how the sport demonstrates the tendencies and morals of the time; for example, in the game of cricket social and economic differences were made obvious. The game was intertwined with the convictions of whether a person's moral fitness for political and social leadership was shown by prowess in the sport. Examining cricket playing among women and their support for the sport provides an unusual perspective on gender roles. Beliefs that cricket sportmanship expressed Christian teachings and the Church's presence in recreational cricket established the role of Christianity in English social life and ethical values. The images of cricket and how far the world of cricket conformed to these ideas are essential for understanding English culture and society between the Wars.

256 pages illus.   1999
0 7146 4861 2 cloth   0 7146 4418 8 paper
Sport in the Global Society No. 8

THE GLOBAL SPORTS ARENA

Athletic Talent Migration in an Interdependent World

John Bale, Keele University and
Joseph Maguire, Loughborough University (Eds)

Athletes are on the move. In some sports this involves labour, movement from one country to another within or between continents. In other sports, athletes assume an almost nomadic migratory lifestyle, constantly on the move from one sport festival to another. In addition, it appears that sport migration is gaining momentum and that it is closely interwoven with the broader process of global sport development taking place in the late twentieth century.

304 pages   1994
0 7146 3489 1 cloth   0 7146 4116 2 paper

THE NORDIC WORLD
Sport in Society
Henrik Meinander, University of Helsinki and
J A Mangan, University of Strathclyde (Eds)

In the Nordic countries (Denmark, Norway, Sweden, Finland and Iceland), as elsewhere, sport has been an assertion of individual and group identity, a demonstration of modernity, a source of personal, local and regional self-esteem, a symbol of confrontation and a preparation for war.
This volume is the first major work in the English language to bring together the research and reflections of scholars who have chosen to concentrate on the cultural impact of sport – the modern opium of the masses – in a Scandinavian setting. It explores the political, social and aesthetic impact of modern sport on Northern Europe, and the relationship between the Nordic nations and Nordic cultures, attitudes to the body and the evolution of specific Nordic visions of sport. *The Nordic World* shows why sport has played such an important part in both twentieth-century Nordic society and contemporary European culture.

224 pages   1998
0 7146 4825 6 cloth   0 7146 4391 2 paper
A special issue of The International Journal of the History of Sport
Sport in the Global Society No. 3

THE CULTURAL BOND
Sport, Empire, Society
J A Mangan, University of Strathclyde (Ed)

For Britain's empire-builders, sport was much more than merely an agreeable recreation. It became elevated to the status of a moral discipline, a symbol of imperial solidarity and superiority, even a salve for conscience. The contributors to this volume examine the aspects of the cultural associations, symbolic interpretations and emotional significance of the idea of empire and, to some extent, with the post-imperial consequences. Collectively and cumulatively, their view is that sport was an important instrument of imperial cultural association and subsequent cultural change, promoting at various times and in various places imperial unity, national identity, social reform, recreational development and post-imperial goodwill.

228 pages illus.   1993
0 7146 3398 4 cloth   0 7146 4075 1 paper

THE EVOLUTION OF ENGLISH SPORT

Neil Wigglesworth, Lancaster University

Until recently sporting history was written by middle-class amateurs, many of whom were Oxbridge graduates. Much of the resulting history of English sport therefore suffers from a narrowness of cultural perspective. The growth of many and varied sporting clubs and the development of sport throughout the country is a vast topic which has largely escaped the attention of those historians who have tended to concentrate on the activities of a metropolitan élite. *The Evolution of English Sport* uses original material from clubs and sporting organizations to illuminate the evolution of sporting activity nationwide. It relates these documents to themes such as commercialism, professionalism, amateurism, recreationalism and club fortunes. It concludes by discussing the outlook for English sport in the next decade.

192 pages 1996
0 7146 4685 7 cloth   0 7146 4219 3 paper

KENYAN RUNNING

John Bale and Joe Sang, both at Keele University

Winner of the British Sports History Prize for Best Book, 1997

> *'An excellent monograph on the phenomenal success of Kenyan middle distance running which will be of interest to a wide readership including everyone with a serious interest in athletics from all over the world, scholars with a specialist interest in socio-cultural studies of sport and specialists in African Studies. Provides an exemplar for future scholarly work in comparative studies of sport and studies of the sports globalisation process.'*
> **African Affairs**

The record-breaking achievements of Kenyan athletes have caught the imagination of the world of sport. How significant really is Kenya in the world of sports? This book, the first to look in detail at the evolution and significance of a single sport in an African country, seeks to answer these and many other questions. *Kenyan Running* blends history, geography, sociology and anthropology in its quest to describe the emergence of Kenyan athletics from its pre-colonial traditions to its position in the modern world of globalized sport. The authors show the qualities of stamina and long distance running were recognized by early twentieth century travellers in east Africa and how modern running was imposed by colonial administrators and school teachers as a means of social control to replace the indigenous fold traditions.

228 pages illus. 1996
0 7146 4684 9 cloth   0 7146 4218 5 paper

FOOTBINDING, FEMINISM AND FREEDOM

The Liberation of Women's Bodies in Modern China

Fan Hong, De Montfort University

This original book brings Chinese women to the centre of the Chinese cultural stage by examining the role which exercise and, subsequently, sport played in their liberation. Physical emancipation, particularly in the custom of footbinding, which continued to be practised to some extent in China until 1949, was the prerequisite for wider emancipation. Through the medium of women's bodies, Fan Hong explores the significance of religious beliefs, cultural codes and political dogmas for gender relations, gender concepts and the human body in an Asian setting.

Until now no academic work has discussed women, emancipation and exercise within the social, cultural and political setting of China from the mid-nineteenth century to the mid-twentieth centuries. Inquiry into the evolving relationship between women's emancipation and exercise over this period is necessary and overdue if there is to be a full understanding of China in an era of gender role reconstruction. Moreover the dramatic and brutal patriarchal tradition of physical repression of the female body in Chinese history, particularly the inhuman institution of footbinding, makes the physical emancipation of Chinese women an issue of special significance in the history of liberation of the modern female body.

352 pages   1997
0 7146 4633 4 cloth   0 7146 4334 3 paper
Sport in the Global Society No. 1

SCORING FOR BRITAIN
International Football and
International Politics, 1900–1939

P J Beck, Kingston University

Despite traditional images regarding the separation of politics and sport in Britain, the history of British international football illuminates the emerging use of sport as an instrument of British foreign policy, most notably, in terms of complementing the government s cultural propaganda programme.

This study considers the nature and development of linkages between international football and politics in Britain between 1900 and 1939. It provides also a history of international football in Britain. Beck examines how the growing politicization of sport in other countries, encouraged British governments to interpret sport as offering an instrument of policy supportive of British interests in the wider world. He points out that association football, Britain's major sport, came to be seen as a means of projecting favourable images of Britain as a 'great nation' to a large and often responsive overseas audience. The British government's intervention in international football is examined. Throughout this study football is viewed alongside other types of international sport, including the Olympics. Other themes highlighted include the official attitudes towards professional sport and the ongoing debate about international sport as a potential cause of international co-operation or conflict. It is based on British government records, private papers, the press as well as the archives of FIFA and the four British football associations.

272 pages 1999
0 7146 4899 X cloth   0 7146 4454 4 paper
Sport in the Global Society No. 9